EGYPT'S GOLDEN COUPLE

Also by John Coleman Darnell and Colleen Darnell

The Ancient Egyptian Netherworld Books

Tutankhamun's Armies

Also by John Coleman Darnell

Egypt and the Desert

Theban Desert Road Survey II

The Inscription of Queen Katimala at Semna

The Enigmatic Netherworld Books of the Solar-Osirian Unity

Also by Colleen Darnell

Imagining the Past

The Late Egyptian Underworld

EGYPT'S GOLDEN COUPLE

WHEN AKHENATEN AND
NEFERTITI
WERE GODS ON EARTH

JOHN COLEMAN DARNELL
COLLEEN DARNELL

ST. MARTIN'S PRESS
NEW YORK

First published in the United States by St. Martin's Press, an imprint of
St. Martin's Publishing Group

EGYPT'S GOLDEN COUPLE. Copyright © 2022 by John Coleman Darnell
and Colleen Darnell. All rights reserved. Printed in the United States
of America. For information, address St. Martin's Publishing Group,
120 Broadway, New York, NY 10271.

www.stmartins.com

Design by Meryl Sussman Levavi

Library of Congress Cataloging-in-Publication Data

Names: Darnell, John Coleman, author. | Darnell, Colleen Manassa,
   author.
Title: Egypt's golden couple : when Akhenaten and Nefertiti were
   Gods on Earth / John Coleman Darnell, Colleen Darnell.
Description: First edition. | New York : St. Martin's Press, 2022. |
   Includes bibliographical references and index. |
Identifiers: LCCN 2022023810 | ISBN 9781250272874 (hardcover) |
   ISBN 9781250272881 (ebook)
Subjects: LCSH: Akhenaton, King of Egypt. | Nefertiti, Queen of
   Egypt, active 14th century B.C. | Egypt—Kings and rulers—
   Biography. | Egypt—History—Eighteenth dynasty, ca. 1570–1320 B.C.
Classification: LCC DT87.4 .D37 2022 | DDC 932/.014—dc23/
   eng/20220629
LC record available at https://lccn.loc.gov/2022023810

Our books may be purchased in bulk for promotional, educational,
or business use. Please contact your local bookseller or the
Macmillan Corporate and Premium Sales Department at
1-800-221-7945, extension 5442, or by email at
MacmillanSpecialMarkets@macmillan.com.

First Edition: 2022

1   3   5   7   9   10   8   6   4   2

Give to him the love of your heart like the innumerable grains of sand on the shore, the scales of fish in the river, and the strands of hair of cattle! Allow him to remain here until the swan becomes black, until the black bird becomes white, until the mountains arise and depart, until the flood flows south.

—Hymn beseeching the god Aten
to bestow love and life on Akhenaten[1]

Contents

IV. GODS ON EARTH: THE TRINITY

V. TWILIGHT OF THE GOD: DEATH AND TRANSFIGURATION

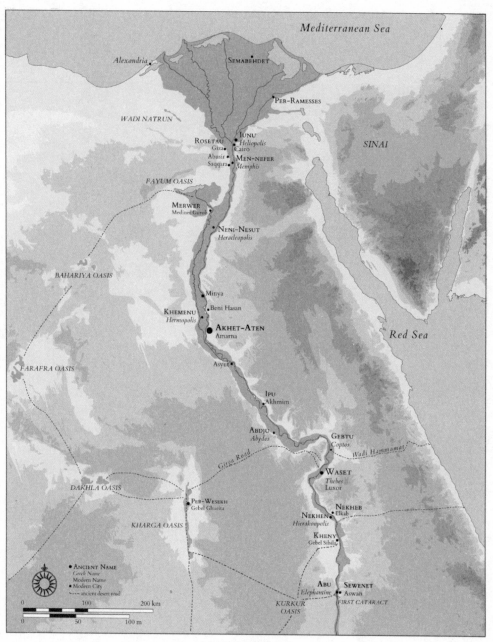

Mediterranean Sea

Alexandria

SEMABEHDET

PER-RAMESSES

WADI NATRUN

SINAI

ROSETAU
Giza
IUNU
Heliopolis
Cairo
Abusir
Saqqara
MEN-NEFER
Memphis

FAYUM OASIS

MERWER
Medinet Gurob

NENI-NESUT
Heracleopolis

BAHARIYA OASIS

Minya

Beni Hasan

KHEMENU
Hermopolis

AKHET-ATEN
Amarna

Red Sea

FARAFRA OASIS

Asyut

IPU
Akhmim

ABDJU
Abydos

GEBTU
Coptos

Wadi Hammamat

Girga Road

WASET
Thebes
Luxor

DAKHLA OASIS

PER-WESEKH
Gebel Ghueita

NEKHEB
Elkab

KHARGA OASIS

NEKHEN
Hierakonpolis

KHENY
Gebel Silsila

● ANCIENT NAME
   Greek Name
   Modern Name
■ Modern City
--- *ancient desert road*

ABU
Elephantine

SEWENET
Aswan
FIRST CATARACT

KURKUR OASIS

0   100   200 km
0   50   100 m

MAP OF EGYPT

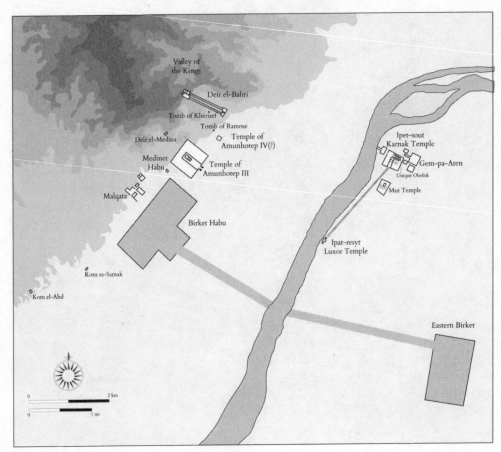

Valley of
the Kings

Deir el-Bahri

Tomb of Kheruef

Tomb of Ramose

Deir el-Medina

Temple of
Amunhotep IV(?)

Medinet
Habu

Temple of
Amunhotep III

Malqata

Birket Habu

Kom es-Samak

Kom el-Abd

Ipet-sout
Karnak Temple

Gem-pa-Aten

Unique Obelisk

Mut Temple

Ipat-resyt
Luxor Temple

Eastern Birket

0   2 km

0   1 mi

MAP OF WASET

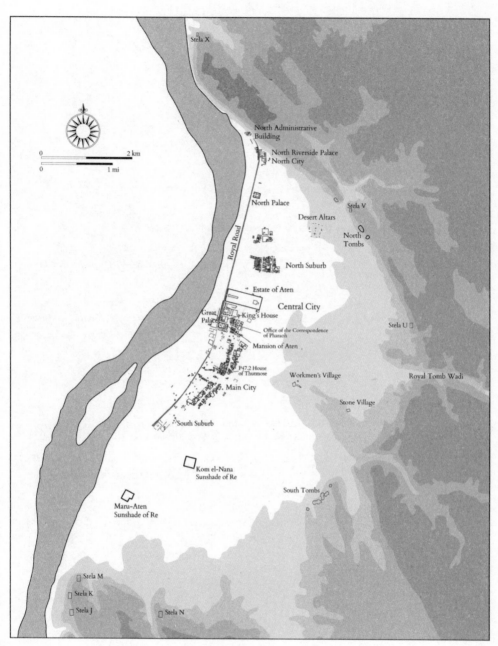

Stela X

North Administrative
Building

North Riverside Palace
North City

North Palace

Stela V

Desert Altars

North
Tombs

Royal Road

North Suburb

Estate of Aten

Central City

Great
Palace

King's House

Stela U

Office of the Correspondence
of Pharaoh

Mansion of Aten

P47.2 House
of Thutmose

Main City

Workmen's Village

Stone Village

Royal Tomb Wadi

South Suburb

Kom el-Nana
Sunshade of Re

South Tombs

Maru-Aten
Sunshade of Re

Stela M

Stela K

Stela J

Stela N

0   2 km
0   1 mi

MAP OF AKHET-ATEN

FAMILY TREE OF THE LATE EIGHTEENTH DYNASTY

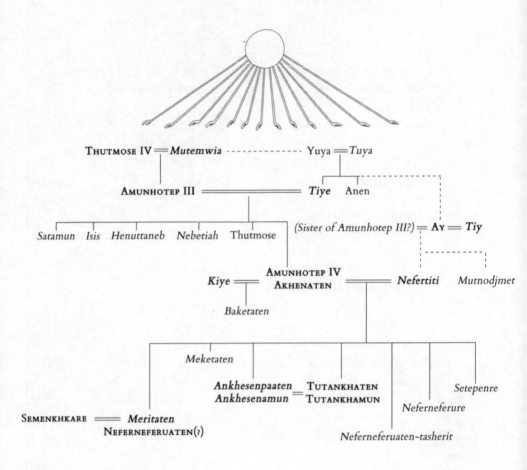

Cast of Characters

Akhenaten (coronation name Neferkheperure) begins his reign as Amunhotep IV, ruling for a total of seventeen years, for most of them alongside his great royal wife Nefertiti.

Amun, king of the gods, whose name means "Hidden One," is a creator deity and divine imperial protector of Egypt who is often syncretized with the sun god, Re.

Amunhotep III (coronation name Nebmaatre) rules for thirty-eight years and celebrates three jubilee festivals with his great royal wife Tiye.

Ankhesenamun (born Ankhesenpaaten) is the third daughter of Akhenaten and Nefertiti and becomes the wife of her brother Tutankhamun.

Aten, the divine solar disk, is given two cartouches during the reign of Akhenaten that identify the god as "Re-Horakhty, who rejoices in the horizon in his name of light who is in the sun disk," which is later changed to "Living one, Re, ruler of the two horizons, who rejoices in the horizon in his name of Re, the father, who has returned as the sun disk."

Ay, god's father during the reign of Akhenaten, is a member of an important family from Ipu (modern Akhmim). He may be Nefertiti's father, and, after the death of Tutankhamun, Ay becomes king of Egypt.

Kiye is the "greatly beloved wife" of Akhenaten and likely the mother of the princess Baketaten; her family is unknown, and she falls out of favor late in the reign of her husband.

Meritaten is the eldest daughter of Akhenaten and Nefertiti, great royal wife of Semenkhkare, and possibly rules as King Neferneferuaten.

Neferneferuaten (coronation name Ankhetkheperure) is a female king, likely the princess Meritaten, but possibly Queen Nefertiti.

Nefertiti is the great royal wife of Akhenaten, and her cartouche often includes the epithet Neferneferuaten. She bears her husband six daughters and a son.

Semenkhkare (coronation name Ankhkheperure) is of unknown origin and likely rules for less than a year as co-regent of Akhenaten; his chief royal wife is Meritaten.

Tiye is a member of an important family from Ipu, the great royal wife of Amunhotep III, and mother of Akhenaten.

Tutankhamun (born Tutankhaten) is a son of Akhenaten and Nefertiti who marries his sister Ankhesenpaaten (later Ankhesenamun). He is king of Egypt for nine years.

Prologue

A PALE AND SICKLY YOUNG MAN ASCENDS THE THRONE OF EGYPT. Sheltered by his keen-witted and powerful mother, he uses his new-found authority to study an ancient religion—the cult of the sun god. His scholarly explorations in temple libraries lead him to revolt against Amun-Re, king of the gods, and the deity's corrupt priesthood. The young king is as mentally robust as he is physically awkward and strangely proportioned. His strong and unyielding will is at odds with the brittle weakness of his spindly limbs. The young ruler quickly perceives how the priesthood, glutted with booty from the military campaigns of his pugnacious predecessors, now feeds like a bloated parasite off the body of the Egyptian people.

Only in his beautiful young wife does the king find consolation and support. Together they create a revolutionary cult of a loving and universal god, who cannot be contained within the often animal-headed and stiffly posed idols of the old religion. The royal couple devote themselves and all of Egypt's resources to the worship of a single god who is everywhere, and yet without physical form, except for the blazing orb of the sun. The young ruler rejoices in the love that his universal solar deity bestows upon humanity, reserving his ire for the ancient gods, whose statues and reliefs the king's devoted adherents zealously attack.

The king shows his devotion to his one true father in ostentatious expressions of love for his own family, especially his daughters, doting on his ever-increasing offspring and his serenely gorgeous consort.

In a few short years, the new pharaoh presides over a kingdom ruled by peace and a higher calling, a new religion that lifts Egypt out of the animal-worshipping superstitions of yore. Where once priests stalked through temples to offer on darkened altars, now the royal family presents tables of food in vast, open courts to the solar father whose light suffuses the white-washed and roofless temples of the king's new city. At the center of this royal court of love, basking in the light of the benevolent solar deity—whose hands literally caress the bodies of the royal family—is the world's first individual. He is a ruler of such moral strength as to dare to challenge the conventions of an already ancient civilization, and a man of profound learning and flights of spiritual ecstasy who composes beautiful poetry in honor of his god.

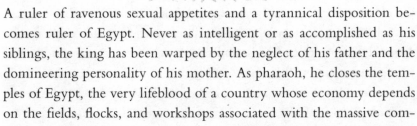

A ruler of ravenous sexual appetites and a tyrannical disposition becomes ruler of Egypt. Never as intelligent or as accomplished as his siblings, the king has been warped by the neglect of his father and the domineering personality of his mother. As pharaoh, he closes the temples of Egypt, the very lifeblood of a country whose economy depends on the fields, flocks, and workshops associated with the massive complexes. Following the luxurious reign of his father, and with an obsessive focus on his own divinity, the new ruler plunges Egypt into nearly two decades of darkness and tumult.

The officials in his bureaucracy are loyal to him alone. In their abject groveling, they manipulate the misshapen heretic who controls Egypt with an iron fist. The king and his court revel in the delights of the flesh, gorging themselves on daily banquets, reclining languidly in painted chambers, their sense of time all but erased by the unending cycle of slothful indulgence. The incestuous desire of the king begets two daughters who are simultaneously his granddaughters. One daughter-wife dies in childbirth—herself barely beyond childhood, brought low by her father's twisted impulses. The population of Egypt—outside of the small group of obsequious courtiers—have never witnessed a time so full of misery.

Histories of ancient Egypt often begin with the establishment of a single government over the Nile Valley and end three millennia later with Roman subjugation. Between King Narmer's unification of Upper and Lower Egypt around 3100 BCE and the death of Cleopatra VII in 30 BCE, not all who ruled in the valley of the Nile were pious monarchs, nor did all give full rein to personal whim and desire. The two sketches of rule appearing above could well illuminate the extreme points to which the pendulum of Egyptian kingship might have swung. Among the portraits of Egypt's rulers, in the great gallery of three thousand years of history, most would probably fit somewhere between the two described above. Peering into the faces of ancient Egypt's rulers, we seek evidence for how people, power, and tradition interact. One might even attempt a psychology of the individual rulers themselves.

In November 1912, Sigmund Freud, founder of modern psychoanalysis, met in Munich with five of his colleagues to discuss the possibility of establishing a new journal for their growing field of study. During a luncheon, they turned their attention to an Egyptian ruler whose reign had just been the topic of an important study by Karl Abraham, a re-spected member of Freud's circle. Though Freud disagreed with Abra-ham's assessment of this ancient ruler as a neurotic, he was excited by the application of his new field of study to the problems of Egyptian history. Freud and Abraham agreed that the ancient ruler's animosity toward his royal father had influenced the erasure and destruction of many inscrip-tions, including those of the ruler's own progenitor.

Carl Jung, a young colleague with whom Freud felt he had a close relationship, strongly objected to Freud's and Abraham's understanding of the ancient monarch. Jung observed that the name of a god in the fa-ther's name, not the father's name as such, was the object of the younger ruler's iconoclasm. The Egyptian king bore no animosity toward his father. But so pleased was Freud that psychoanalysis had helped—in his opinion—to interpret a puzzle from ancient history, and so intense was his father-son bond with Jung, that the argument was literally too much to bear. Freud slid to the floor in a faint.

The Egyptian ruler at the root of Jung's disagreement with Freud is one and the same man as the subject of *both* reconstructions above: Akhenaten, who, with Queen Nefertiti, ruled Egypt for the seventeen years from 1352 to 1336 BCE. Akhenaten has achieved fame as the world's first individual, as the world's first monotheist, and as the father of Tutankhamun, whose golden treasure has become synonymous with ancient Egypt. Radically different accounts have been written of the lives of Akhenaten and Nefertiti. The queen's face is perhaps more famous than nearly any other from the ancient world. But what can we really say about two people who lived 3,350 years ago?

The ancient Egyptians wrote neither personal diaries nor biographies, in the modern sense, so we cannot read the private thoughts of Akhenaten and Nefertiti. No ancient narrative of their rule has come down to us, and the ancient Egyptians do not appear to have written historical texts that covered a broad sweep of time. We can, however, experience the objects and places that were part of the royal couple's lives and read speeches that Akhenaten made, hymns the king and queen recited, and records of historical events over which they presided. We can study the art and inscriptions of their reign, visit the tombs of their highest officials, and even walk through their palaces and the homes of artists, workmen, and soldiers who served them.

Who were Akhenaten and Nefertiti? Why did they change the religion of ancient Egypt? How did they go about this grand project? By investigating the monuments and texts of the royal couple and their immediate predecessors and successors, and through a search for parallels to the statements and actions of Akhenaten, we provide some answers to these questions in these pages.

Akhenaten's life has been used and abused in the modern world. In often mutually contradictory books spanning a century, and all titled *Akhenaten*—in various spellings and with a variety of subtitles—we see extreme interpretations: the king's teachings of peace and love are as close to those of Jesus as any pagan belief could be, *or* the king's actions are expressions of the ultimate physical and mental corruption; Akhenaten is either the perfect father or an incestuous pedophile, either a messianic prophet of monotheism or a totalitarian ruler who cast off all controlling checks to his power. For Freud, Akhenaten was a chance to prove the validity of the Oedipal complex, and in the psychoanalyst's final book, even Moses became an Egyptian follower of Akhenaten's creed. On one point all agree: Akhenaten and Nefertiti are uniquely important figures of Egypt's ancient and enduringly popular civilization.

Akhenaten and Nefertiti lived during the Eighteenth Dynasty, the first of the three dynasties of the New Kingdom (1550–1069 BCE). Two thousand years of Egyptian history preceded them, and many glorious monuments were yet to come. Egypt became an international power under the leadership of early Eighteenth Dynasty kings, and the immediate predecessors of Akhenaten and Nefertiti inherited a stable and expansive empire. To the northeast, Egypt's authority reached the banks of the Euphrates, while to the south, Egyptian control extended far into Nubia. Splendid new temples graced cities throughout Egypt, and in the Valley of the Kings, royal artisans hewed large, elaborately decorated tombs for their sovereigns.

Coming to the throne around 1390 BCE, Akhenaten's father, Amunhotep III, presided over a golden age, with Egypt's power unrivaled abroad and its wealth bountiful at home. Amunhotep III's chief wife, Tiye, was a remarkable queen, and together the royal couple took pageantry to new heights. Observing these events was a prince, named Amunhotep like his father. After thirty-eight years on the throne, Amunhotep III joined with the sun god in heaven, and the prince became pharaoh. From the first year of his reign, Amunhotep IV forged a new path, ultimately replacing the worship of Egypt's many gods with devotion to a unique solar deity, Aten. Amunhotep later abandoned his birth name, rechristening himself Akhenaten, "He who is effective for Aten." Ruling alongside her husband was Nefertiti, a queen whose prominence overshadows nearly all other pharaohs' wives.

This is the story of Akhenaten and Nefertiti, their religious beliefs, their historical achievements, and their vision for Egypt—how, together, the king and queen ruled as gods on earth. Amunhotep III and Tiye provide the starting point for our narrative, as their actions presaged many of the most seemingly unusual events during the reign of their successors. Without the deification of his parents, Akhenaten would not have achieved his own divine status so quickly, nor would he have been able to elevate Nefertiti to the level of a goddess.

These two couples—Amunhotep III and Tiye, Akhenaten and Nefertiti—transformed ancient Egypt. Over three millennia later, what survives of their remarkable reigns spans the continuum from colossal statues to sadly broken inscriptions. We might have a wonderfully pre-served temple to illuminate one part of this history, but for another, an ink scrawl on a shard of pottery. Only by casting our net beyond the half century of the two couples at the heart of our narrative can we truly bring the past to life.

Each of the following chapters opens with a scene from the lives and times of our historical characters. These are not wholly imagined events but a tapestry woven from multiple sources: objects of daily life; elaborate paintings, reliefs, and statuary; hieroglyphic texts and hieratic papyri. Much of the dialogue in these scenes directly quotes from an-cient texts or includes statements in keeping with the known sources. Each setting—be it a temple, palace, or private home—is based on an archaeological site, and each object within the scenes is based on a real artifact or something depicted in a work of art or described textually. Most of the people in the reconstructions are historically attested indi-viduals, and for minor characters, like artists' assistants or scribes, we have at times provided common New Kingdom names to bring them to life. For events that occurred on a recorded ancient date, a modern approximation is also provided.

Our bibliographic essays collect the sources that we have used for the reconstructions—look there if you want to know where to find the ceiling painting with pigeons, a scene of a drunken partygoer vomiting, images of Akhenaten's chariot horses and bodyguard, the remains of the house that may have belonged to the sculptor Thutmose, or the letter where the Assyrian king laments of envoys dying in the sun. Missing from this great diversity of sources is any certain hint of Akhenaten and Nefertiti's personalities, so here and there we have taken the small liberty of providing the royal couple with personal quirks. The bibliographic essays also provide basic references and background readings for each historical event, religious concept, work of art, and ancient site that we discuss. Endnotes provide citations to the hieroglyphic or hieratic texts that we quote, and all translations of ancient Egyptian texts are our own.

Occasionally, we enter the narrative as Egyptologists to reveal how the ancient sites and museums can be experienced now by visitors and how we acquire the information that enables us to write this history. We take you along as we puzzle out the translation of a key verb in a damaged inscription and collect passages from texts that explain what it was like to live under the rule of sovereigns who styled themselves as divine beings. These vignettes of our research and travels take place over the course of a typical year, which is divided between teaching responsibilities at home in Connecticut and fieldwork in Egypt.

Akhenaten has been called a heretic, a false prophet, and an incestuous tyrant by some, and a loving, compassionate, peaceful precursor to Moses and Jesus by others. Nefertiti remains even more mysterious, her historical reality eternally obscured by the beauty and fame of her painted bust now in Berlin. Perhaps Akhenaten really was a megalomaniac; perhaps Nefertiti really was the most beautiful woman in the world. But without proof for these assumptions, they only take us further away from the real—and immensely richer and more fascinating—lives of Akhenaten and Nefertiti. We have sought to write their biographies in such a way that the king and queen would recognize themselves in these pages.

Trying to understand Akhenaten and Nefertiti must entail placing them within their own history and culture—we do not have to sympathize with Akhenaten and Nefertiti to be sympathetic toward them. The ancient Egyptians believed that to be remembered was to attain immortality. When Akhenaten and Nefertiti lived, the pyramids of Giza were already over a thousand years old, and they had every reason to expect that their own monuments would be standing millennia after their death. Despite later pharaohs' attempts to erase Akhenaten and Nefertiti from history, the royal couple's desire for immortality has in the end been fulfilled. We hope that you find their stories as compelling as we do, for the ancient Egyptians understood that we all have a part to play in preserving the memories of those who have come before.

I
THE
PARENTS

AMUNHOTEP III
AND TIYE

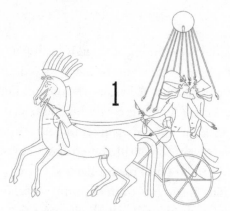

A Divine Conception

HIS EYES ROAM OVER THE CONTENTS OF THE BEDCHAMBER, ILLU-minated by moonlight through a window high in one wall. In a corner of the room, an inlaid wooden box on tall legs holds the wig of closely plaited human hair that the royal woman wore earlier in the day; it rests beside other, equally elaborate coiffures. In another corner, wooden stands support large jars, their whitewashed surfaces highlighting blue painted garlands of lotus buds encircling the vessels. Through a curtain of gauzy linen draped over a gilded canopy near the middle of the room, he glimpses Mutemwia, a sheer linen sheet barely concealing the queen's form nestled on an ebony bed, its four supports shaped like the legs and paws of a lion.

Mutemwia stirs, lifting her head from the gilded wooden support positioned next to the mattress. A sliver of light illuminates a flock of pigeons flying above her, the painter having captured the moment their pale blue outstretched wings overlapped. Pulling back the curtain, Mutemwia sees her husband, Prince Thutmose. An all-pervasive aroma of myrrh and incense, the odors of the land of the gods, overpowers her senses. Now fully awake, Mutemwia realizes that the figure standing before her is not her husband or any man. This is Amun-Re, king of the gods.

Shedding his outward form of Prince Thutmose, the god moves toward the queen, gold skin shining as though casting its own light. What the queen sees is a figure that seems to have walked off the walls of the temples she frequents. Amun-Re wears a white, pleated kilt, its straight hem falling to his knees. A cuirass covers his chest, its overlapping pieces of turquoise, lapis lazuli, and carnelian set in gold frames shaped like the feathers of a divine falcon. The brilliant red and blues of the god's armor match the jeweled bands of his broad collar and bracelets on his wrists. A deep blue lapis lazuli beard juts from his chin, its prominence balanced by a crown topped with two tall ostrich plumes.

Mutemwia rejoices in the perfection of the gold-skinned god, love courses through her limbs, and the god's aroma inundates the entire palace. Suddenly, the walls of the chamber no longer exist as two goddesses lift Mutemwia and Amun-Re above the earthly realm and set them upon the firmament of heaven. Amun-Re raises an *ankh*, the symbol of life, up to the queen's nose and reveals to her the purpose of his nocturnal visit: "Amunhotep, ruler of Waset, is the name of this child that I have placed in your womb. He shall rule as a mighty king over this entire land! My power be to him! My strength be to him!"[1] The third Egyptian king to bear the name Amunhotep, "Amun is content," had just been conceived.

LUXOR, EGYPT

Through the Airbus A220's small windows we see the rays of the setting sun transform the Nile into a ribbon of light. Our EgyptAir flight is making its descent into Luxor International Airport, after a three-hundred-mile flight south from Cairo. Soon the aircraft, bearing the sleek falcon-headed logo of the god Horus on its stabilizer, will taxi along the runway at the desert edge. The bustling modern city of Luxor is the latest in a line of urban incarnations that have existed in roughly this same location for over four and a half millennia. Called Waset by the ancient Egyptians and Thebes by the Greeks, this was one of the greatest cities of the ancient world, a status appropriate to the meaning of its Egyptian name: She Who Holds Dominion.

The Nile divided Waset into eastern and western halves, and seen from above, some of the city's ancient monuments are still easily recognizable. The houses and palaces of ancient Waset, built predominantly of mud brick, are, for the most part, buried beneath modern buildings, streets, and fields, thousands of years of history resting unseen below the feet of Luxor's inhabitants. But the great stone temples still stand, many battered, some nearly as complete as when they were first erected, gloriously defying the omnivorous fangs of time.

Within one of those temples, today given the name Luxor, like its eponymous city, King Amunhotep III recorded how his mother, Queen Mutemwia, was impregnated by the god Amun-Re. The conception of Amunhotep III, Akhenaten's father, is an appropriate starting point for the lives of both Akhenaten and Nefertiti. The mythical presentation of this event says much about the divinity of the king, the role of royal women, and Amun-Re's position at the pinnacle of the pantheon.

The city's modern airport lies northeast of the ancient settlement, near dry, desert canyons through which caravans once passed. We exit the arrival hall and meet Abdu Abdullah Hassan, one of our oldest friends, whose expertise in the logistics of archaeological expeditions has been essential to our work for decades. This is the start of the winter portion of our field season, a roughly monthlong period in which we and our colleagues will record ancient rock art and inscriptions, some nearly six thousand years old, excavate desert settlements constructed a comparatively recent fifteen hundred years ago, and record ancient caravan routes.

We load our baggage into one of our old Series III Land Rovers, and soon we are driving along a road heading roughly west, toward the Nile, as the afterglow recedes and true night begins. Just before reaching the river, we turn south and pass several long and broad excavations exposing considerable remains of an ancient processional route, paved with large stone blocks and lined on each side by seemingly endless rows of sphinxes that linked Karnak Temple to the north with Luxor Temple in the south.

The monumental entrance of Luxor Temple is a prominent element of the skyline. The two towers of the pylon gateway rise nearly eighty feet, providing a stony backdrop to colossal statues, themselves forty feet from sole to crown. At night, a spotlight illuminates a single obelisk in front of the eastern tower of the pylon, a monolith eighty-two feet tall.

The hieroglyphs are so crisply carved into the granite that in the artificial light they look as if they were cut by laser rather than bronze chisels. Since 1831, this obelisk has been a widow, its mate now the centerpiece of the Place de la Concorde in Paris, proclaiming—like many of its fellows, from Istanbul to New York—the glories of ancient Egypt to lands far beyond the knowledge of the pharaohs.

A walk through Luxor Temple is a journey back in time in more ways than one. To the temple's ancient founders, this sacred building was Ipat-resyt, "the Southern Private Quarters," which was also the companion of a northern Ipat in Iunu, the city of the sun god Re (now part of modern-day Cairo). The sphinxes of the processional avenue connecting Karnak Temple (ancient Ipet-sout, "Choice of Places") with Luxor Temple are a bit younger than 400 BCE. The pylon façade of Ipat-resyt and the temple's first open court were erected approximately nine centuries earlier than those long lines of sphinxes. We walk across the court toward the south end of the column and statue-edged space, where two additional seated colossi of the long-lived pharaoh Ramesses II rear up on either side of the damaged, once soaring, and still imposing portal to a long hall.

Amunhotep III began construction on this, the Colonnade Hall, near the end of his reign but did not live to see its walls fully decorated, a task mostly completed by his grandson Tutankhamun. Carved along the walls are priests carrying on their shoulders the gilded and bejeweled boats of the gods; lines of soldiers hauling on great ropes, singing hymns in praise of the king as they tow the great riverine barges of the gods; women performing acrobatic dances, butchers rushing to and fro with their offerings, and priestly assistants pouring libations of wine, the makings for endless divine repasts. In the relative silence of the temple on this cool winter night, the sounds of the raucous celebrations seem almost audible, the ancient hymns just at the edge of one's hearing.

The Colonnade Hall leads south to another open court lined with dozens of elegant columns, in the form of papyrus bundles, which enhance the court's spacious proportions. The name of one king is now visible everywhere: Amunhotep III. The grandeur of the Colonnade Hall and the wide court then give way to the smaller courts and rooms that form the inner portion of the temple. What was once a door leading to the rear portion of the temple was closed by a curved niche when the

Romans incorporated the temple into a fortress, transforming the room into an imperial shrine. Roman emperors were now kings of Egypt, but Luxor Temple remained, as it had for over fifteen centuries, the place where rituals confirmed a pharaoh's status as son of Amun.

We pass through a narrow opening cut relatively recently into the niche that once held the standards of the legions. In front of us is the central bark shrine of Amun, the place where the statue of the god in its ceremonial boat would rest and the focus of constant offerings of giant bouquets, wine and water, vegetables of every variety, and the choicest cuts of meat. Instead of continuing through the bark shrine, we walk through a doorway to the left, take another left turn, and enter the goal of our visit to the temple, the room in which Amunhotep III recorded his own divine conception.

Originally, the shallow raised-relief decoration was painted in brilliant blues and bright yellows, deep reds and greens, all set against a light bluish gray background. Those colors have all but disappeared, but the reliefs still reveal a scene-by-scene exposition of Amunhotep's divine heritage. In the middle of the wall, at nearly eye level, is the pivotal moment when Amun impregnates the queen, as the hieroglyphs say: "The majesty of this god did everything which he pleased with her."[2]

Between the hieroglyphic captions is a large carving of Amun and Mutemwia on the night of the conception. Held aloft by two goddesses, the god and queen face one another, sitting upon a thin rectangle. This is not a piece of furniture or indeed any physical object, but a hieroglyph that writes the word "heaven," a simple shape that catapults the encounter into a celestial sphere.

The only overt expression of intimacy between the god and the queen is that they hold hands, Amun's fingers just touching Mutemwia's upturned palm. But an ancient Egyptian would have noted the erotic overtones of Amun's legs overlapping those of Mutemwia, how she cups the god's elbow with her free hand, and how he holds to her nose the hieroglyph for "life," the *ankh* sign. In combination with the explicit description in the hieroglyphic text, the sexual nature of the scene is obvious.

The caption states that the bedchamber in which we are to imagine the king's divine conception taking place is located inside the palace, although where in Egypt that might be is left unsaid. Pharaohs possessed

The conception of Amunhotep III:
Mutemwia and Amun are lifted into heaven by two goddesses.
(Drawing of a scene in the divine birth chamber, Luxor Temple)

multiple palaces, their stays dictated by the demands of state and religion. The night upon which Prince Thutmose, later to become the fourth king of that name, conceived his heir was only documented after Amunhotep III became king. We can merely guess, then, about the timing of the night in question or the location of the royal bedchamber. If Mutemwia traveled with her husband on his hunting and sporting trips in the north, they could have spent their nights at a small palace nestled near the pyramids of Giza (ancient Rosetau), or in the larger palace at Mennefer (Greek Memphis) ten miles distant. Three hundred miles to the south, Waset boasted several palaces, royal residences occupied during the annual festivals of Amun's journeys between the city's temples.

Thutmose IV and Mutemwia might instead have conceived the future Amunhotep III in another palace located sixty miles south of modern-day Cairo, in a fertile basin known as the Fayum, where a branch of the Nile feeds a large lake. The Fayum was a favorite royal hunting ground, and a palace graced the idyllic countryside. Merwer, named for the "great canal" near which it lay, was specifically a residence for female members of the royal family. Women and palaces immediately conjure the harem, the forbidden area of the Ottoman palace where wives and consorts were strictly se- cluded, eunuchs their intermediaries to the outside world. Unfortunately, despite abundant evidence that Egypt had no such institution—including the absence of eunuchs as a court rank or professional group—the term is often applied to ancient Egypt, distorting our understanding of what it meant to be a pharaoh or a queen.

Rather than a place for the sexual control of royal women, the palace at Merwer was indicative of those women's economic power. The queen owned vast estates and oversaw an administration, land holdings, and numerous employees. During the lifetime of Thutmose IV, Mutemwia was not the chief queen, in ancient Egyptian "the king's great wife," and that title would be bestowed upon her only retrospectively by her son, Amunhotep III.

Standing within the chamber of the divine birth at Luxor Temple, we see Mutemwia, swept up into the company of gods and goddesses. After Amun-Re impregnates her, he consults with the ram-headed god Khnum, who carries out the physical act of creation. Khnum fashions the newly conceived Amunhotep III with the aid of the potter's wheel, a lump of clay becoming the future king, more perfect even than all the gods.

As Khnum sits at his wheel, we see the results of his labor: two iden- tical boys, their youth marked by their nudity and their hairstyle—each has a single braided lock of hair. One is the physical body of the child who will become Amunhotep III, while the other is the future king's ka-spirit. The ka-spirit is one of several components of an individual that transcended the corporeal world. Ka is written in hieroglyphs with a pair of arms opened as if about to embrace, and the spiritual force of the ka was believed to be transmitted from father to child. The king possessed a special *ka*-spirit, a soul that was the essence of kingship, be-stowed by the god Amun himself.

Khnum intones over the images of the young king and his *ka*-spirit the majestic fate of the future Amunhotep III: "You will be the king of the Black Land, ruler of the Red Land!"[3] The Black Land, *kemet,* was an ancient name for Nilotic Egypt, the strip of rich black soil depos-ited on the banks of the Nile during the annual flood. The Red Land, *desheret,* encompassed the high desert plateau east and west of the river, through which the Nile Valley was cut. The desolate stretches of sand and rock were to some extent natural barriers protecting the Nile Val-ley. Just as importantly, they were the sources of Egypt's vast mineral wealth and regions of busy trade routes. The Black Land made Egypt abound in food, but the Red Land made it rich in gold, stones, ostrich feathers, leopard skins, incense, and a myriad of other goods. Khnum's pronouncement predicts Amunhotep's reign over a land well fed and replete with splendid monuments, a land at peace in its verdant heaven on earth, and in control of its desert territories.

Then it is time for Thoth, the ibis-headed god of writing, to an-nounce Amun's satisfaction with Queen Mutemwia, whose womb now holds the future king of Egypt. The temple reliefs show the queen's changed body: Mutemwia's belly swells, ever so slightly, with child. This is one of only a handful of depictions of normal human pregnancy from three thousand years of ancient Egyptian art. For the birth itself, Mutemwia sits enthroned, surrounded by more than two dozen deities. Goddesses grasp her outstretched arms, a clue that Mutemwia is not simply sitting but giving birth. In actuality, the queen, like most ancient Egyptian women, probably would have squatted atop four decorated bricks as she delivered her son.

After the successful birth, the prince is presented to Amun, who reaches out to embrace his son. The arms of Amun mimic the arms of the hi-eroglyph *ka,* and indeed, just behind the infant Amunhotep is his own *ka*-spirit, his twin, held in the arms of falcon-headed Horus, the di-vine template for the pharaoh on earth. Each boy sucks his index finger (rather than his thumb), a habit apparently so common among Egyptian youngsters that it early became a defining aspect of the hieroglyph for "child."

The twin children are here a visual conceit, signaling Amunhotep's possession of the royal *ka*-spirit. At this moment the child and his *ka* have already become one, destined to rule over Egypt, as Amun proclaims:

> *My son of my body, my beloved, Nebmaatre, whom I made as one flesh*
> *with me in the palace! I have given to you all life and dominion, with*
> *the result that you have (already) appeared in glory as king of Upper*
> *and Lower Egypt upon the throne of Horus. May your heart be joyous,*
> *together with (that of) your* ka-*spirit, like Re!*[4]

The text makes clear that the king, here called by his coronation name Nebmaatre, is *one flesh* with the god, literally Amun's earthly incarnation. The sacred and sexual union of Amun and the queen has implanted in her womb both that physical form of Egypt's next ruler and the very spirit of kingship, his *ka*. The texts tell us that Amunhotep, possessed of the royal *ka*, "will rule all that the sun disk encircles," a common phrase in royal texts that describes the king as master of everything within the circuit of the sun.[5] Here, the ancient Egyptians employed the customary word for sun disk: *aten*. By the time the royal *ka* passed from Amunhotep III to his own son, Amunhotep IV, *aten* became more than just the disk of the sun, but Aten, the unique god, father and mother of all creation. Soon after that passing on of the royal *ka*, Aten would eclipse all the other gods of Egypt.

Standing in the divine birth room in Luxor Temple, we see laid out before us the theological underpinning of kingship in Egypt. As the physical mediator between this world and the divine realm, the king possessed a status unique among all people. He was the son of the god Amun, destined to rule Egypt and—at least in theory—every land touched by the rays of the sun. The record of Amunhotep III's conception and birth was not unique to him, far from it. Image by image, word for word—replacing only the names—Amunhotep III copied the divine birth treatise from Hatshepsut, a queen who ruled as pharaoh. While these scenes and texts were preserved for the first time during Hatshepsut's reign, the concepts behind them likely were not of her invention either but extended back at least six centuries.

After thirty years on the throne, Amunhotep III built upon his divine ancestry to begin a personal transformation from the son of the sun god to the embodiment of the sun god on earth. The king was not alone in this journey: at his side was the king's great wife, Tiye, a woman who was central to all aspects of her husband's reign. She was the mother of the next king, Amunhotep IV, and before her husband's death, she became a reigning goddess.

An Angry Goddess

A GROUP OF A DOZEN MARINES RUN FROM A LOW MUD-BRICK building toward the Nile, an officer racing ahead and urging tumbling acrobats and lute-tuning musicians out of the way. Behind them, staggering forward, another group of soldiers half carry and half drag an enormous length of rope, nearly half a cubit in thickness. The officer in charge, palm rib baton raised, shouts that one of the ropes of the god's barge, "Amun Mighty of Prow," has broken, and a replacement is urgently required. Upsetting a few wine amphorae—spilling the contents of one onto an altar piled high with all manner of food—the soldiers rush on.

A trumpeter sounds several short and long blasts, transferring the orders of the nearby officer to long lines of soldiers and sailors hauling on massive ropes connected to the gold-plated and jewel-encrusted barges of the gods Amun, Mut, and Khonsu. Tugboats assist the boats as they sail against the current. That morning, a complex choreography had taken Amun's barge out of Amunhotep III's newly decorated pylon at Ipet-sout, then south to meet the bark of Khonsu, on to the complex of Mut to welcome her to the procession, and then off to the south. Along the way, the divine boats pass riverbanks thronged with the citizens of Waset attired in their finest clothes and jewelry.

At Ipat-resyt, they dock, and priests begin the nerve-racking and time-consuming process of taking from their decks miniature versions of those very barges. Then the trumpeter advances to meet the line of priests carrying on their shoulders the portable boats of Amun, Mut, Khonsu, and indeed the king himself. The musician sounds the notes of the royal entry—the king of the gods is coming. The procession passes the acrobats, women leaping backward onto handstands before vaulting back onto their feet, while lute-playing musicians accompany a singing group of clapping priests and sistrum-jingling priestesses.

The crowd grows silent after another signal from the king's trumpeter, the procession pauses, and all attend to the words of the temple chorus. The first song rings out, an ancient hymn, parts of which were first sung a millennium earlier: "O Amun, Lord of the Thrones of the Two Lands, may you live forever! A drinking place is hewn out, the sky is folded back to the south; a drinking place is hewn out, the sky is folded back to the north."[1] A cheer erupts, drowning out the final line of the song. This is the sign for the multitude of worshippers to begin imbibing wine and beer, until they become so intoxicated that their drinking places resemble heaven itself.

After another sounding of the trumpet, the procession nears the mud-brick outer court of the unfinished temple of Ipat-resyt. This time the chorus turns directly toward the bark of Amun, moving in close, and singing the final words of the song: "It is Horus, strong of arm, who conveys the god with her, the good lady of the god. For the king has Hathor already done the best of good things."[2]

At that last line, not a few couples evoke that amorous conclusion to the song, leading up to their own best things with prolonged kisses. Amunhotep, in the role of the powerful Horus, will achieve his own perfection with Hathor, embodied in his great royal wife Tiye. And as the god Amun unites with his divine consort Mut, their human worshippers will eat, drink, and make love during the nights of the festival. When it is all over, Egypt and the entire world is reborn.

Such were the sights and sounds of the annual festival called Opet, the same word as Ipat in the ancient name of Luxor Temple. The walls of the Colonnade Hall of Ipat-resyt record the events of the multiday celebrations. This was one of several festivals that punctuated the year for the citizens of Waset. Most work stopped; even the royal tomb builders laid down their tools, and farmers were treated to the luxuries of wine and beef.

Amunhotep III and Tiye were certain to be in Waset during the festival days, taking up residence in a palace adjacent to Karnak Temple (Ipet-sout). If Tiye did the best of things for Amunhotep III on one of those nights, then Amun would have had a short commute on his way to transmit the royal *ka*. For the duration of the festival of Opet, Tiye was not only the queen of queens but also the goddess Hathor on earth. Sex with her husband became a sacred act, a mirroring of the marriage of Amun and Mut. Through the co-opting of myth and ritual, Tiye achieved in her lifetime a divinity that only a few queens attained.

Tiye transmitted to Nefertiti a more exalted queenship, although neither woman was born a member of the direct royal line. The two queens may have been members of the same extended family, a powerful clan from Ipu (modern Akhmim), in Middle Egypt. Tiye's father, Yuya, was a chariotry commander and priest of Min, a god associated with fertility, made manifest in the deity's large, erect phallus. Yuya was also a "god's father," a title reserved for the closest royal advisors and tutors, the god in question being the living king. Tiye's mother, Tuya, served Min, leading the god's musical troupe and directing temple rituals.

Normally, we know nothing about the origins of queens born outside of the royal family. But Tiye's role as the king's great wife was so significant that a series of large scarabs was carved with the royal names of Amunhotep III, the cartouche of Tiye, and two sentences identifying her parents. Yuya and Tuya were also given the rare honor of a tomb within the Valley of the Kings, posthumously reposing among the royal family their daughter had joined. There they rested, almost undisturbed, until the spectacular discovery of their tomb in 1905. We can now look upon the faces of Tiye's parents, but the written sources are mute about how the daughter of a prominent family from Middle Egypt became the king's great wife.

DNA testing of royal mummies provides a clue: Mutemwia, Amunhotep III's mother, may have been the sister of Tiye's father, Yuya. Tiye was probably educated by her father, Yuya, who also served as tutor to her future husband, Amunhotep III. Nefertiti's family connections rest on more circumstantial evidence, but that same DNA analysis implies

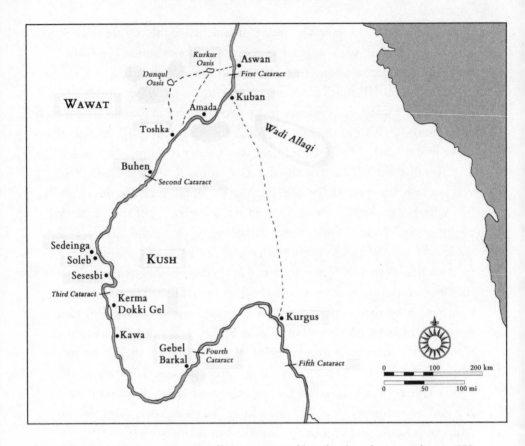

that she could have been a first cousin of her husband, Amunhotep IV, on both his maternal and paternal sides. This would mean that Eighteenth Dynasty pharaohs of three generations, from Thutmose IV to Amunhotep IV, married into the same family from Ipu. Tiye and Nefertiti's queenship may have had less to do with their presumed physical beauty and more to do with their intellect and schooling.

Both Tiye and Nefertiti were catapulted from queen to goddess; they were worshipped as divinities alongside their husbands, even during their lifetimes. For Tiye and Amunhotep III, nowhere is this more evident than in Nubia, the land south of Egypt. During the Eighteenth Dynasty, Nubia was an Egyptian province overseen by Egyptian administrators and local princes. The southern land was not only Egypt's chief source of gold but also a lynchpin of trade routes, as well as the origin of many military recruits (not always volunteering for service). By the reign of Amunhotep III, Egypt and Nubia had already engaged in over two

Soleb Temple, by Francis Frith. (1862)

millennia of economic and cultural exchange, frequently punctuated by military conflict.

Egyptian gods accompanied the Egyptian traders, settlers, and troops in Nubia, a presence made permanent through the construction of Egyptian temples. In time, some of the deities within these temples became at home in Nubia, no longer foreign imports but essentially native Nubian cults. A pharaoh could also insert himself among the gods in Nubia, although queens prior to Tiye do not appear to have had that honor. Amunhotep III not only deified himself at a temple now called Soleb, about three hundred miles south of Aswan, but he also made Tiye a goddess at the nearby temple of Sedeinga.

A handful of standing columns and fragmentary walls only vaguely evoke Soleb's former magnificence. In the temple's reliefs Amunhotep III performs ritual offerings for two different gods. The first is Amun, who can also manifest as Amun-Re or Amun-Min, the latter with his distinctive erect phallus. The second deity of Soleb Temple is called Nebmaatre, who appears nowhere else in the Egyptian pantheon for a simple reason: Nebmaatre is Amunhotep III *as a god*. Nebmaatre, "The lord of *maat* is Re," is the king's coronation name, normally written in a cartouche preceded by the title "King of Upper and Lower Egypt." The term *maat* does not correspond to any single English term, as it encompasses morality, justice, and universal equilibrium. Personified, this principle of cosmic order is the goddess Maat, daughter of Re, and the king was the guarantor of *maat* on earth.

No hieroglyphic text explains why Amunhotep III chose to elevate himself to a god in Nubia. Other Egyptian kings who had divine manifestations in foreign countries became avatars of Horus, whom foreigners could worship along with their own gods. Perhaps ruling an empire at peace and unable to showcase his military prowess, Amunhotep III desired to outdo all other pharaohs in his divine status.

On the walls of Soleb Temple, Amunhotep III as king can present offerings to his own deified self, and in such scenes the two kings face one another. In one scene, to the right is the living ruler Amunhotep III, facing to the left and burning incense. The recipient of Amunhotep III's ritual action is Nebmaatre, who faces to the right and wears a *nemes,* a striped royal headcloth, just like the king in front of him. The divine Nebmaatre is crowned with a lunar disk resting within a lunar crescent. As we imagine the smoke from the incense wafting over him, Nebmaatre in recompense grants his earthly self all life, stability, dominion, and health.

The lunar crown is a significant clue to the role of the god Nebmaatre at Soleb. Thoth was one of the most important Egyptian deities related to the moon, responsible for the regulation of the hours, days, months, and years, as calculated through the lunar cycle. He was the "lord of hieroglyphs" and was predictably a divine patron of scribes. He could take the form of an ibis or a baboon, or a man with the head of either creature. As a god of both ritual books and the calendars that determined their proper use, Thoth played a role in a foundational Egyptian myth about the goddess Hathor. To understand why Amunhotep's divine image wears a lunar disk, we must examine this myth as well as the ancient Egyptian calendar.

The Egyptians believed that not long after the creation of the world, gods and humans dwelt together on earth. Re is king of all, a resplendent deity with flesh of gold, bones of silver, and hair of true lapis lazuli, but he learns that mankind is plotting against him. Hastily, the sun god assembles

King Amunhotep III offers to his divine self, Nebmaatre.
(Drawing of a scene in Soleb Temple)

his council, addressing the deities he had created. Together, they decide
that mankind must be punished, and Re's eye, the goddess Hathor, should
be unleashed to slaughter the people that rebelled against their creator.

Even so, Re hesitates. He prefers to have power over people as king,
not to annihilate them. Unfortunately, the sun god's doubts come only
after his eye, Hathor, had departed on her mission in her form of the
lioness Sakhmet, literally the "Powerful One." Unable to stop the goddess directly, Re needs to devise a plan that would save humans from
the goddess's murderous rampage. The aging solar deity calls for great

quantities of red ocher to be brought from the south, while female servants brew enough beer to fill seven thousand jars. The ground ocher and intoxicating brew are mixed and poured out, flooding the fields.

When Hathor arrives early the next morning, she finds a sea of what she thinks is human blood and soon becomes so drunk that she is unable to recognize the humans she had come to slaughter. The next day she awakens, pacified, but with an enormous headache. Re has saved mankind from destruction, but wearied from his toil, he retires to the heavens. Forever after, humans would dwell on earth, separated from the gods yet illumined each day by Re's journey through the sky.

That story about the red-tinted beer was the origin of the riotous celebrations at the time of the New Year, when everyone played their part in the cosmic drama, drinking like the goddess so that humankind would be spared destruction. Two events coincided to mark the beginning of the year: the start of the annual Nile flood, which deposited a rich, black silt reliably every summer, and the appearance of the star Sirius, one of the brightest stars in the Egyptian sky, after being invisible for seventy days.

For the ancient Egyptians, Sirius was the goddess Sepdet, who, like Hathor, could be identified as the eye of the sun. Her reappearance was an observable astronomical event, although a quirk of the Egyptian calendar meant that it did not always happen on the literal first day of the year: day one of month one of Akhet (Inundation) season. The civil calendar of ancient Egypt was a solar calendar divided into three seasons—Akhet (Inundation), Peret (Growing), and Shomu (Harvest)—each of four thirty-day months. At the end of their 360-day year, the Egyptians added five extra days, which they called *heriu renpet,* "those in addition to the year." The priests who kept such precise records, which were essential for the proper celebration of festivals, were certainly aware of the missing one quarter day, yet they never adjusted the calendar accordingly.

Without a leap day, after four years, the civil calendar lagged by roughly a day, and after seven centuries, the first day of the first month fell in January, the coldest season. As the reappearance of Sirius cycled through the civil calendar, it took 1,460 years to completely reset, where the first day of the first month was actually the date that the star's rising was observed. A few hieratic papyri record the civil calendar date on which Sirius reappeared. Those dates then become the anchoring points where the wandering civil calendar can be tied to a known and predictable astronomical event. Literally for lack of a leap day, we can calibrate the chronology of ancient Egypt to an extraordinary degree.

The reappearance of the divine star also signaled the rising of the floodwaters. Just as the drunken celebrations of the New Year had their origins in Re's attempted destruction of mankind, so too was the goddess's return part of a larger set of myths. No ancient title has survived for this sacred story, so Egyptologists call it "The Wandering of the Eye of the Sun," and it may not have been codified as a continuous tale until a thousand years after the reign of Amunhotep III. The narrative begins with the eye of the sun—normally called Hathor or Sakhmet— becoming angry with her father, Re. She flees far to the south, into Nubia, transforming into a raging lioness. The departure of the goddess causes suffering in Egypt and for the sun god personally, who has lost his eye, so Re sends a god to entice her back home. Most often, Thoth is the one given this unenviable but eminently necessary task.

In Nubia, Amunhotep III and Tiye concretized the myth of the Eye of the Sun in stone, with themselves as the protagonists. The lunar-crowned Nebmaatre embodies Thoth, while the goddess he brings back to Egypt is Tiye, worshipped at the temple of Sedeinga, nine miles north of Soleb. Sedeinga is only fragmentarily preserved, but enough survives to show that Tiye and the fearsome goddess Hathor became one within the sacred space.

The single standing column at Sedeinga, once part of a columned hall, has the shape of the tinkling sistrum, an instrument closely associated with goddesses like Hathor. Elsewhere at Sedeinga, Tiye's image appears prominently above a false door in a wall carving that imitated a paneled portal, a focus for ritual since the doorway was permeable to the psychic forces of living and dead, humans and divinities.

The carving shows symbols of Hathor and her violent avatar Sakhmet surrounding cartouches of Tiye and Amunhotep III. Among the images are two rearing cobras, which are so ubiquitous in Egyptian imagery that we identify them with a specific name, *uraeus* (plural, *uraei*), a Greek-derived version of the ancient Egyptian *iareret* (the *t*-ending of the Egyptian noun marks it as feminine). The Egyptians equated the venom of the cobra with the blasting power of the sun's rays. Thus, the uraeus on the brow of a king or queen symbolized both blinding light and the fiery striking power

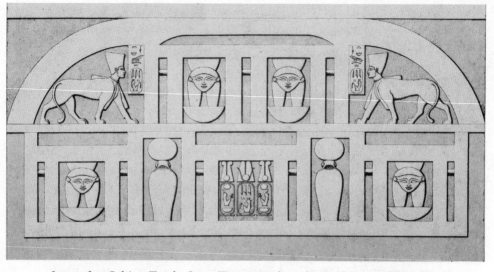

Lunette from Sedeinga Temple. Queen Tiye as a striding sphinx with images of the goddess Hathor; in the lower register, Tiye's cartouche is flanked by those of her husband, Amunhotep III. (Drawing by Émile Prisse d'Avennes, 1878)

of the sun. Hathor herself was believed to sit atop the forehead of her father Re as a uraeus, protecting him from all evil and aggression.

In the uppermost portion of the carving stride images of female sphinxes, the human-headed, lion-bodied creatures that symbolized the fearsome power of Sakhmet. But here at Sedeinga the composite creatures are not the goddess but rather, as the hieroglyphic labels state, "the king's great wife Tiye." Another hieroglyphic text at Sedeinga Temple bestows upon Tiye the title "lady of all lands" in conjunction with an otherwise unique epithet for a queen: "great of fearsomeness."[3] The queen holds symbolic dominion over foreign territories that are in awe of her power.

Soleb and Sedeinga were architectural machines that transformed Amunhotep III and Tiye into the divine protagonists of the myth of the Eye of the Sun. If the king, as Thoth, successfully returned Tiye, the angry goddess, to Egypt, the annual floodwaters would rise, and the new year would not spell catastrophe. The god and goddess, reconciled in the far south, now returned to Egypt to consummate their union and renew the cosmos. Whether Amunhotep III and Tiye ever visited Nubia is unknown, but a month and a half after the rising of Sirius, they were in Waset for the celebration of the festival of Opet. As a royal trumpeter

Tiye seated on a throne that
shows the queen as a female
sphinx trampling enemies,
with images of two bound
foreign women below.
(Drawing of a relief from
the tomb of Kheruef, after
Epigraphic Survey, The Tomb
of Kheruef, Theban Tomb
192 [Chicago: Oriental Institute
of the University of Chicago,
1980], pl. 49)

sounded the calls to coordinate the docking of the divine ships, Amunhotep III and Tiye were inside Luxor Temple, prepared to greet the gods
and take upon themselves the mantle of divinity. The rituals that the
royal couple performed would ensure the divine union needed to guar-
antee the world's continued existence, just as their own "best of good
things" guaranteed that their dynasty would continue to rule Egypt.

3

Ancient Rites

Tɪʏᴇ STANDS BEFORE HER HUSBAND, ADMIRING HIS SPECIAL JUBI-
lee garb. Amunhotep has been king for thirty years, and according to
royal tradition, now is the time to renew his reign. He has swapped his
usual pleated linen kilt and bare chest for the archaic white jubilee robe,
a tight-fitting garment with long sleeves, its hem ending just above his
knees. Atop his head is the crown of Upper Egypt, a conical white shape
with a bulbous top. Usually, a single cobra rears protectively from his
brow, but today, a ribbon fastens a small falcon to the front of the crown,
the snake improbably emerging from the head of the royal bird. Truly,
Amunhotep is Horus on earth! How else could he have sprouted the tail
feathers that she sees protruding from the front of his cloak?

At that thought, Tiye reaches up to her own forehead, adjusting the
uraeus attached to her head cloth and feeling the tiny cow horns and sun
disk that crowned the snake. She, the daughter of a chariot commander
and a priestess, is not just the queen of queens but Hathor in human form.

The royal couple are about to emerge from the great double doors
of their palace, the House of Rejoicing, on the west bank of the river.

In front of Tiye strides her trusted steward Kheruef, one of the men responsible for planning the multiday festivities; alongside them, priests carry the royal and divine standards. Beautiful girls, the daughters of kings near and far, hold shining gold vessels, pouring out pure water four times in succession as they recite, "O sovereign, living, prosperous, and healthy—may you exist continually!"[1]

Suddenly, a calf leaps forward, a duck flies up, and a monkey scampers toward them. Upon the release of the animals, a troupe of female performers begins an elaborate dance. As some take up a tune on their flutes and others play drums and clap, dancers start to move to the beat. Wearing kilts reaching just below their knees and their chests bound with bands crossing between their bared breasts, the young women toss their hair forward, dangling their arms to the ground, then whip around to face the sky.

As Tiye advances at her husband's side, she recognizes the song they are singing, one as ancient as those she hears each year at the festival of Opet: "Come, be exalted! Come that I might perform for you jubilation at dusk and music at twilight! O Hathor, you are exalted in the hair of Re, the hair of Re! To you has been given the sky, the deep of the night and the stars. Great is her Majesty by means of her becoming pacified."[2] Now, Tiye focuses her full energies in calling upon the goddess to protect her husband, give him life, and grant him many more years on the throne. In the queen, the golden goddess has found a willing receptacle.

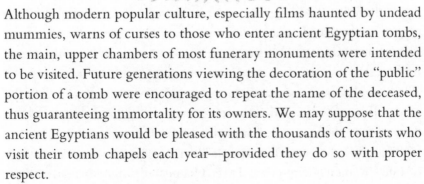

Although modern popular culture, especially films haunted by undead mummies, warns of curses to those who enter ancient Egyptian tombs, the main, upper chambers of most funerary monuments were intended to be visited. Future generations viewing the decoration of the "public" portion of a tomb were encouraged to repeat the name of the deceased, thus guaranteeing immortality for its owners. We may suppose that the ancient Egyptians would be pleased with the thousands of tourists who visit their tomb chapels each year—provided they do so with proper respect.

One of the most impressive nonroyal tombs constructed at Waset during the New Kingdom was that of Kheruef. Among his titles, Kheruef was the "steward," literally overseer of the household, of Tiye, and she likely interacted with him daily. He also planned the elaborate ceremonies of the first jubilee, during the cusp of the second and third months of Shomu of Amunhotep III's thirtieth year on the throne. Vignettes from these rituals and explanatory hieroglyphic texts fill the wall south of the doorway of the west portico in the tomb of Kheruef.

The events of the jubilee open with a scene of Amunhotep III enthroned with the goddess Hathor and Queen Tiye standing behind them. A block of eleven lines of hieroglyphic text in front of the threesome describes the events of Regnal Year 30, second month of Shomu, day 27, the first day of the first jubilee. The most important sentence appears in line 9: "It was his Majesty who did this in accordance with ancient writings. Past generations of people since the time of the ancestors had never celebrated such rites of the jubilee."[3]

Egyptian texts, especially hieroglyphic inscriptions displayed prominently in tombs and temples, can be prone to bombast. A favorite expression is "never has the like been done!" Kings delight in boldly going—at least in description—where no one has gone before in military conquest or temple construction. So we approach with caution Amunhotep III's claim to the antiquity and unparalleled nature of his jubilee rituals. But a thorough vetting of the statement reveals a surprising amount of evidence for its veracity.

Amunhotep III was not the first pharaoh to claim to be a scholar. Kings were expected to be literate and learned, although we know only the barest outlines of the education that princes received, or even the curriculum for the average bureaucrat. Yet we have a wealth of hieroglyphic texts that describe *what* a pharaoh was expected to know. A king's knowledge was not simply the product of book learning, memorizing religious treatises stored in a temple library. He needed to be able to apply that information to the proper performance of ritual, the manipulation of objects, the reciting of magically powerful hymns, even the choice of the materials and plans for temple construction.

The scrolls that once filled temple libraries, called the *per-ankh*, Houses of Life, in ancient Egyptian, have disappeared; instead, many of the papyri housed in museum collections today were discovered in tombs:

reading material for the afterlife. One extraordinary survival is a king's list compiled during the reign of Ramesses II, about 1220 BCE, which records the name of every king and the number of years, months, and sometimes even days of their reign (the Twelfth Dynasty female king Sobeknoferu was included, so "his" would not be an accurate pronoun here).

The papyrus, now in the Egyptian Museum of Turin, is frustratingly filled with lacunae, but the list begins with gods who ruled Egypt, followed by demigods, compiling data for a total of 13,200 years before it begins to enumerate kings that we would accept as part of the historical record. Kings are grouped by dynasty, the system we still follow, and the years of individual reigns within a dynasty are conveniently added for reference. Any scribe during the reign of Amunhotep III could have had access to a similar record to quickly calculate the number of years from the present to any king's reign in the past. Not only did Egyptian scholars consult ancient documents, as claimed in Kheruef's inscription, but they would have known how ancient those documents were.

A remarkable object, a decorated palette, may be direct evidence that archival research during the reign of Amunhotep III extended to records predating the invention of the hieroglyphic script. On one side of the palette, a flat stone used for grinding eye makeup, an artist—probably in the ancient city of Abdju (modern Abydos) around 3200 BCE—carved images of a royal festival before Egypt was the united "Two Lands." Amunhotep III celebrated his first jubilee according to the established timeline of thirty years, but he is the only king to say that he did so "in accordance with ancient writings." Almost two thousand years after an artist carved images related to an early jubilee on this decorated palette, another artist, attached to the sumptuous court of Amunhotep III, decorated the other side of the object. Scholars researching at the behest of Amunhotep III in preparation for his jubilee celebrations likely found the palette and then added the royal couple to the fortuitously blank side. The steward Kheruef may not be exaggerating when he says, "As for generations of people since ancestral times—they have not celebrated (such) rituals of the *heb sed*. But it is Khaemmaat (Amunhotep III) for whom it was decreed, the son of Amun who receives the bequest [of his father], he is given life like Re forever!"[4]

Around 3250 BCE, Upper Egypt seems to have coalesced into a single political entity ruled by one line of kings that we call "Dynasty 0," because their existence was only discovered well after the numbering of the dynasties. At around the same time, the Egyptians first employed hieroglyphs to write their language. Though they could not know it, those who carved one side of the palette were living at the end of the Predynastic Period, so called because it predates Narmer, the first king of the First Dynasty. Early rituals of royal power became the jubilee festival, called the *heb sed* in ancient Egyptian; *heb* is the word for "festival," while the etymology of the term *sed* remains disputed but may relate to the bull's tail, also called a *sed,* that the king wore attached to his kilt. Among these early festivals were naval processions, depicted in Predynastic tombs, ceramics, and rock art.

As we learn from Kheruef's tomb, Amunhotep III resurrected these nautical events, which, based on surviving records, had not been used for any jubilee since around 3000 BCE. In the upper left portion of the Kheruef reliefs of the first jubilee is a large boat carrying the king, Tiye, and five officials. This is not the usual royal craft but the "Night Bark," and elsewhere Kheruef informs us, "They (the assembled courtiers) took up the tow ropes of the Night Bark and the prow rope of the Day Bark."[5] The Night Bark and the Day Bark are the two vessels in which Re navigates the sky and the Underworld. The sun god sails in the Day Bark between sunrise and sunset, transferring to the Night Bark until the next dawn.

Reduced to its simplest and most essential features, Egyptian religion was a solar religion. All life depended on the sun, as did all life after death. The Egyptians believed that at sunset, Re descended into the Underworld and traversed the twelve hours of the night, which were units of both time and space. Sailing in the Night Bark protected by a divine crew, Re must unite with Osiris, his corpse. By analogy with Osiris, mummies were also receptacles for the visitation of the soul, a soul whose eternal existence was guaranteed by that unending, daily journey of Re.

Life and death, sunrise and sunset, order and chaos—those dichotomies defined Egyptian religion and the patterns by which the ancient dwellers on the Nile structured their lives. Upsetting the solar cycle meant not only the end of life in this world but also the annihilation of

King Amunhotep III and Queen Tiye sailing in the Night Bark during the king's first heb sed in Regnal Year 30. (Drawing of a scene from the tomb of Kheruef, after Epigraphic Survey, The Tomb of Kheruef, Theban Tomb 192 *[Chicago: Oriental Institute of the University of Chicago, 1980], pl. 46)*

the triad of created space: heaven, earth, and the Underworld. When the tomb of Kheruef claims that Amunhotep III sailed in the sun's bark, the king himself becomes the lynchpin of the universe. The king was expected to merge with Re after his death, but Amunhotep III did something unprecedented: he sailed in the Day Bark and the Night Bark *while still alive.*

Not only did Amunhotep III send forth his scribes to libraries throughout Egypt to research ancient documents, he also commissioned his artisans and engineers to construct an entire city in which to celebrate the carefully reconstructed rites of the primordial jubilee. The site of that city is now called Malqata, from *al malqat,* "the place where things are picked up," a name that will forever ring true since thousands of broken clay jars still litter the ground.

What Amunhotep III did at Malqata, and the name that he called himself within his new city—Dazzling Sun Disk—explains much about his son's late radical relocation of Egypt's capital city. Amunhotep III and Amunhotep IV were both unusual in expanding royal palaces into an entire urban landscape—the father integrated Malqata into the sacred landscape of ancient Waset, while the son decamped to an entirely new location in Middle Egypt. As with so many of the seemingly innovative, unusual, or revolutionary actions of Amunhotep IV, his father's reign provided a precedent.

If residents of Amunhotep III's Waset were to identify the most important features of their city, they might well list four temples of Amun corresponding to the city's "corners": Karnak Temple (northeast), Deir el-Bahri (northwest), Luxor Temple (southeast), and Medinet Habu (southwest). Each temple was also a node in the annual festival cycle, a religious celebration and holiday for the local population. Amunhotep III constructed his jubilee city, modern Malqata, on the west bank of Waset, just south of the Estate of Amun, as the Egyptians called the rectangular area bounded by the four temples.

Malqata contained a large royal palace (55 × 137 yards), and some of its bricks were stamped with the name "House of Rejoicing."[6] The palace gateway that Amunhotep III and Tiye leave to begin the jubilee, as depicted in the tomb of Kheruef, has the same name, granting certainty to Malqata's identification as the jubilee city. Smaller royal buildings may have been assigned to Tiye or held other functions during rituals, such as when the king or queen changed their wardrobe and crowns. Villas for high-ranking officials, villages for support staff, and storage magazines provided the human infrastructure for the elaborate ceremonies.

East of the complex of palaces are large, evenly spaced mounds of earth. These are some of the spoil heaps created when a great volume of sand, earth, and gravel was removed during the excavation of the lake, which we call by its modern designation the "Birket Habu" (*birket* is Arabic for "lake," while Habu is a personal name). In its final form, which it probably achieved some time after the first jubilee, the lake was a mile and a half long along its north-south axis and two-thirds of

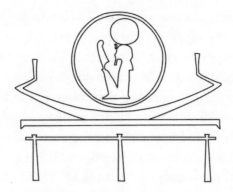

Seal impression from Malqata with hieroglyphs that state
"Amunhotep III is the Dazzling Sun Disk."

a mile along its east-west axis—a significant outlay of resources. The lake's eastern side narrows to a canal that would have connected to the Nile, whose waters filled the artificial basin. It was only a short distance from the House of Rejoicing to the western edge of the man-made lake, where Amunhotep III, Tiye, and some of their high officials mounted the Night Bark. The corresponding ritual with the Day Bark occurred on the east bank of the Nile; although the site has never been excavated, it is visible even in satellite imagery. Amunhotep III sailed on two lakes, just as he used two models of solar boats.

The Birket Habu and its east bank counterpart are not the first large-scale lakes excavated during the reign of Amunhotep III. In Regnal Year 11, as commemorated in a text carved on a series of large scarabs, Amunhotep commanded that a lake be dug for Tiye at "her town, Djarukha," not far from Ipu, her family's hometown. The small hieroglyphs on the scarab give the dimensions of the lake—3,700 cubits by 700 cubits (equivalent to one mile by a quarter mile)—and describe the opening festivities: "His Majesty was rowed upon it (the lake) in the royal barge Dazzling Sun Disk."[7]

The word for "sun disk" in the name of the royal boat is *aten,* the term for the physical, light-producing orb that traveled through the sky each day and, in Egyptian belief, descended into the Underworld every evening. Already in his eleventh regnal year, the king sailed in a vessel identifying himself with Re. At the same time as the Regnal Year 30 jubilee, a new phrase appeared on wine jar sealings from Malqata:

"Nebmaatre is the Dazzling Sun Disk." The words are spelled out in hieroglyphs, but the signs are also juxtaposed in such a way that the images of the hieroglyphs create a scene that illustrates how Amunhotep III became the shining orb. The sealing consists of seven signs.

The central image is a sun disk that contains a seated king, distinguished by his headdress and the uraeus at his brow; the king wears a sun disk on his head and holds in his hand an ostrich feather. Each of these images has a corresponding hieroglyphic value: the seated king writes *neb,* "lord," the ostrich feather he holds, "Maat," and the sun disk on his head, "Re." Nebmaatre, the coronation name of Amunhotep III, was normally enclosed within a cartouche, but here the solar disk encircles the name. The disk holding the royal name sits in the center of a solar boat, sailing on a hieroglyph that writes "sky"—Amunhotep III sails across heaven as the Dazzling Sun Disk. The adjective "dazzling" is provided by the hieroglyph immediately below the sky sign: the sign of a pectoral made of faience beads. These jar sealings are eloquent testimony to how the Egyptians seamlessly intertwine art and writing, the inventive arrangement of the hieroglyphs adding meaning to the phonetically read text.

Amunhotep III also expressed his divine status through clothing. As he and Tiye departed from their palace, the House of Rejoicing, on the first day of the jubilee, feathers peeked out from his white cloak. In the tomb of Kheruef, this unusual, but not unparalleled, item of royal regalia appears as five to eight rectangular elements with rounded ends emerging from Amunhotep's robe at the middle of his thighs. These unusual features are the tail feathers of a falcon; the king has become one with the god Horus, sprouting the plumage of the cosmic, solar bird. In the Night Bark, Tiye stands behind her husband: she was the daughter Maat to his Re, the consort Hathor to his Horus.

Beyond the depictions in the tomb of Kheruef, the transformation of Amunhotep III and Tiye during the first jubilee appeared in statuary distributed throughout Egypt, part of the tremendous artistic production of this golden age. Two- and three-dimensional representations of kings and queens, like all Egyptian works of art, were idealized, but they could possess individualized features. We can recognize the stoic faces of the pyramid builders Khufu and Khafre, the weary features of

King Amunhotep III enthroned with Hathor, with Queen Tiye standing behind,
presiding over the ceremonies of the king's first heb sed *in Regnal Year 30.*
(Drawing of a scene from the tomb of Kheruef, after Epigraphic Survey,
The Tomb of Kheruef, Theban Tomb 192 *[Chicago: Oriental Institute*
of the University of Chicago, 1980], pl. 26)

the Middle Kingdom ruler Senwosret III, and the distinctive noses of
Hatshepsut and Thutmose III. In the first phase of Amunhotep III's art,
he maintained the style of his father, Thutmose IV, which itself was a
continuation of earlier Eighteenth Dynasty royal portraits.

A second style altered Amunhotep III's facial features: almond-
shaped eyes, a short nose, and full lips characterized the portraits of the
king. A thin raised line rims the lips, and the king's mouth has an unusual asymmetry: the bow of his upper lip, which is always fuller than

his lower lip, is slightly off center. The king's neck is also thicker than that of his royal predecessors. Then, in some statuary of Amunhotep III and Tiye commissioned after the first jubilee festival, the royal couple seem to have drunk from the fountain of youth: their full and rounded faces, large eyes, button noses, and large yet delicate mouths are all the hallmarks of the faces of children.

It is notoriously difficult to estimate the age of pharaohs at death, even when their mummies are extant, relatively intact, and available for study. If Amunhotep III ascended to the throne at an early age, he would have been at least in his forties when he celebrated his first jubilee. Tiye may have been younger, for she died two decades after the celebrations at Malqata. The oft-repeated estimate for ancient Egypt that life expectancy at birth was thirty to thirty-five is misleading, as infant mortality significantly skews the numbers. If an ancient Egyptian survived childhood, he or she could enjoy a lifetime of five, six, or even seven decades, although none probably reached the 110 years that some ancient sources indicated was an ideal lifespan.

The childlike portraits of Amunhotep III and Tiye do not represent physical reality but rather serve a theological objective. After Re travels through the twelve hours of the night in the Underworld and unites with the god Osiris, he emerges triumphantly from the eastern horizon. The newborn sun can appear as a naked boy, his index finger raised to his mouth. After the first jubilee, Amunhotep III *and* Tiye could similarly appear as solar children, reborn to a new day.

Nearly a thousand statues from Amunhotep III's thirty-eight-year reign have survived, a staggering number. Many of these statues appear to come from a single location: a massive temple of Amunhotep III, located immediately north of Malqata. This temple, which served his mortuary cult, featured statues of a hugely diverse array of gods and goddesses. Inscriptions on many of the statues mention the jubilee, so the sculptures were likely included in the celebrations of the king's *heb sed,* allowing him to be literally among the gods.

By the conclusion of the first jubilee, Amunhotep III and Tiye were counted among those gods, represented in youthful, rejuvenated forms. In Regnal Years 34 and 37 of his reign, Amunhotep III celebrated his second and third jubilees. No pictorial evidence survives for the second jubilee, but the tomb of Kheruef provides uniquely detailed evidence for the third and final celebration. The key event of the Regnal Year 37 ceremonies was the raising of the *djed*-pillar, a symbol of the god Osiris, the king of the Underworld.

A year later, Amunhotep III's soul departed from his body, and the king physically joined Re and Osiris in the afterlife. At the end of the seventy days of the mummification process, the ceremony of the Opening of the Mouth was performed, giving Amunhotep III's soul the ability to eat, drink, and engage in sexual activity in the afterlife. The priest who performed this ritual was none other than the king's heir, a prince also named Amunhotep.

II

WASET

A NEW HORIZON

A Mysterious Prince

THE YOUNG TUTOR LOOKS WITH ENVY ON THE LONG TENT FILLED with revelers. The little boy straining to escape the hold of his hand is, by his very presence, preventing the tutor from joining the party. The young prince Amunhotep needs a quiet and long sleep more than a night of running around. The little boy has been fascinated all day by the boats waiting in the great artificial lake nearby. His mother told him that they would carry his father to join the sun and then bring him back. Nothing will induce the boy to go to sleep before he has stepped onto the deck of at least one of the bejeweled vessels, and the harried nurse has decided the evening stroll would be the tutor's task.

Their trip from bedroom to harbor takes them past the partygoers seated beneath awnings on the lakeshore. Low folding chairs line both long sides of the hall. On one side are men in linen kilts, most worn over diaphanous shirts; on the other side sit women in equally sheer dresses. Some of the men are bareheaded, others wear wigs, and all of the women have donned the largest of their wigs, garlanded with wreaths of flowers.

Suddenly taking advantage of his tutor's lack of attention, the child breaks free. Five-year-old Amunhotep runs, weaving his way among the tables of food and stands of wine jars, small sandals slapping as he

darts in and out of the festival furniture. Down comes one of the particularly elongated jars from the southern oasis as the child steadies
himself. As he reaches the line of drinking women, young Amunhotep
decides he should imitate his father. He has seen the old king inspect
lines of the palace guard, and now the child paces slowly in front of the
line of women, head turned to the right in order to see his subjects in
festal array.

One particularly disheveled girl, perhaps the youngest of the group,
attempts to straighten the top of her incense-covered dress, and the child
pauses as she smiles. Suddenly she frowns, her cheeks puff out slightly,
and jerking her head to the side she vomits forth the last goblet of wine
onto the sandals of the woman behind her. An attendant races forward
with a bowl and manages to catch a second eruption, while young
Amunhotep looks down to see if anything had splattered on his kilt.

Hearing his tutor's voice, the escaped royal child darts behind his new
but queasy friend and begins to run through the line of seated women.
Suddenly two girls, each about twice his age, both wearing only jeweled
belts and other decorative baubles, hastily set down their serving jars
and gently catch the running child. Both bow, make their apologies,
and hold Amunhotep until the arrival of his tutor, who agrees to the
girls' request that they might wait upon the young prince. And soon the
future king of Egypt sits on a miniature chair, laughing with delight
at his escapade, drinking liberally watered wine served by his young
attendants. They will all see the boats and harbor of his father's coming
apotheosis soon enough.

NEW YORK, NEW YORK

After completing a successful field season, we return from Egypt in January in time to begin teaching our spring-semester classes. Weekends
offer a prime opportunity to continue research in the extensive ancient
Egyptian collections of museums in the United States. Approximately
two hours from our home in Connecticut is one of our favorite institutions, the Metropolitan Museum of Art on the Upper East Side of

Manhattan. Usually when we enter the cavernous atrium the din of the crowd remains distracting until we turn right, pass the checkpoint for tickets, and enter the Egyptian section.

After several twists and turns, we reach the galleries that showcase the art of the New Kingdom before finally arriving in a high-ceilinged room dedicated to the reign of Amunhotep III. Among the pieces hanging on the walls are portions of painted plaster from the palace of Malqata, including the scene of a flock of pigeons in flight that we had in mind when we recreated the night on which Mutemwia conceived her son. At one end of the same room is a narrow study gallery, its entrance easily missed on your right as you pass between the glorious reign of Amunhotep and the room displaying art from the reign of his son, with the Temple of Dendur beckoning just beyond.

A casual visitor peeking into Gallery 120 might not be immediately rewarded for their interest: most of the clearly visible objects are broken pieces of pottery. To those who know what they are and whence they come, however, the seemingly uninteresting collection of sherds brings to the ears the sounds of talk and laughter, the singing of musicians, the playing of harps, the rhythmic sound of naked feet dancing on a cool plaster floor, the plucking of lutes, and the pouring and spilling of wine. Pause a bit longer and you might smell the aroma of sweat, scented oils, and incense mingled with those of freely flowing beer and wine.

In Gallery 120 is a small sampling of the remains of thousands upon thousands of ceramic jars that once filled the storerooms of Malqata, containers for preserved meats, beer, wine, fruit, honey, animal fat, and incense. The contents were consumed long ago, but ink labels on the jars' shoulders allow us to read not only the former contents of the vessels but also often the date and place of their bottling. The vintages drunk at Amunhotep III's jubilees were sourced from a variety of vineyards, some from such exotic locales as Kharga Oasis, 150 miles west of Luxor. Were it not for the pottery sherds mentioning a *heb sed* in Regnal Year 34, we might not even know that Amunhotep III celebrated his second iteration of the jubilee festival in that year.

Among the finds from the Malqata palace complex is a clay stopper that once sealed a jar and which bears a hieroglyphic text recording the origin of the vessel's contents as the "domain of the king's true

Seal impression from Malqata mentioning the
"domain of the king's true son Amunhotep."

son Amunhotep."[1] This stamped text is the only surviving reference to Prince Amunhotep, who would become the fourth and final king of that name in the Eighteenth Dynasty. This absence of any other reference to the young prince Amunhotep is not entirely unexpected; princes are often invisible in the monumental record prior to their ascension to the throne.

The same cannot be said for prince Amunhotep's sisters, who frequently appear as small figures on colossal statues of their parents. Two sixty-foot-high, seated, monolithic statues of Amunhotep III still mark the eastern entrance to the king's temple on the west bank of Waset. Twelve-foot-high statues of his mother Mutemwia and his consort Tiye flank the king's legs; between the legs of each of the two colossi are the remnants of a smaller female figure. While only the feet remain, we can identify them as princesses, with Isis and Satamun being the likeliest candidates. Both women were ultimately elevated to the position of "royal wife" alongside their own mother. Satamun even held the same title as Tiye: "king's great wife."

The colossi of Amunhotep III depict the enthroned king with three generations of royal women. In their company, the king is an embodiment of Re, whose mother, spouse, and daughter can each represent

Hathor, the cosmic goddess who aids the sun in his unending cycle of aging and rejuvenation. The theological resonance of a father-daughter marriage was powerful, but, as far as we know, a princess could inhabit the ritual role without necessarily being physically intimate with her own father.

In royal artworks, no similar mythological template appears to have required the presence of a prince. As "king's true son," the future Amunhotep IV was probably assigned official duties, although no surviving text specifies what those might have been. At the death of the old sovereign the son was called upon to assume a ritually powerful role, playing the part of Horus burying his father Osiris.

We know slightly more about the early life of Prince Amunhotep's only attested brother, Thutmose, who would have become the fifth king of that name. Thutmose was the "king's eldest son," the crown prince and the high priest of the creator god Ptah in Men-nefer. An unparalleled monument commissioned by Prince Thutmose seems to give us a glimpse into one aspect of his personality: he was a cat lover, and he provided his pet, Tamiut, with a stone sarcophagus in which to spend eternity.

Miu is the ancient Egyptian word "cat," an onomatopoetic term for the familiar "meow," and an apt translation of "Tamiut" would be "The Kitty." It does not seem like a great leap to assume that this cat—a pet, not a specifically sacred animal—was as pampered in life as she certainly was in death. Perhaps an infant Amunhotep's puppy once chased Thutmose's cat through the palace as Satamun's pet goose ran circles around both, squawking all the time—if only we could know the details of childhood in the court of Amunhotep III!

Since Prince Thutmose appears nowhere in the thousands of jar labels and stoppers thus far recovered from Malqata, he probably died before the thirtieth year of his father's reign. The mantle of heir then passed to Prince Amunhotep. As a prince, the future Amunhotep IV was likely present at all three of the jubilee ceremonies that transfigured his father into the Dazzling Sun Disk and his mother into Hathor. We cannot be certain what role, if any, he had in the rituals, as he does not appear in any of the surviving visual representations.

No sources allow us to accurately calculate Amunhotep IV's age at his accession to the throne. Even the king's mummy—identified with some confidence as the body buried in a small tomb (King's Valley 55) not far from the much more famous tomb of his son Tutankhamun—does not help matters much. Osteological analyses have underestimated ages at death of royal mummies, sometimes contradicting records that prove a longer reign. Such discrepancies are mostly due to the rather limited and primarily modern populations from which the comparative data derives. So we proceed from the assumption that Amunhotep was around thirteen or fourteen when he became king, although possibly as young as nine or ten. In either scenario, Tiye wielded influence in the official position of "king's mother," but the king was likely old enough to begin to make his personal preferences known.

On the second day of the first month of the Peret (Growing) season, which corresponds to approximately November 25, 1352 BCE, Amunhotep IV was crowned king and his five-fold royal titulary proclaimed. These five names, each preceded by a label and symbolically written on the leaves of the sacred tree called the *ished*, in the temple of Re at Iunu (Heliopolis), were borne in essentially the same order by all true rulers of Egypt by around 2000 BCE. Amunhotep IV became:

> *Horus: Victorious Bull, High of Plumes*
> *He of the Two Ladies: Great of Kingship in* Ipet-sout
> *Horus of Gold: Exalted of Crowns in Southern Iunu*
> *King of Upper and Lower Egypt: Neferkheperure-Waenre*
> *Son of Re: Amunhotep*

These names identify the king with Horus, the divine template of kingship, and place him under the protection of the "Two Ladies," Nekhbet, vulture goddess of Upper Egypt, and Wadjet, cobra goddess of Lower Egypt. Two of Amunhotep IV's names associate him with Waset: Amunhotep's regalia is glorified in Ipet-sout, "Choicest of Places," the ancient name of the temple of Karnak; in his Horus of Gold name, Waset is referenced as "Southern Iunu," linking the religious center in Upper Egypt with the main center of solar worship in the north. His coronation name, preceded by the title King of Upper and Lower Egypt, is *Nefer-kheperu-re Wa-en-re,* "Perfect (*nefer*) are the Manifestations (*kheperu*) of Re, Unique One of (*wa-en*) Re," emphasizing the king's relationship with the sun god Re, which follows a royal tradition over a millennium old. The king's birth name became his Son of Re name, Amunhotep, "Amun is content (*hotep*)."

But Amun was not the deity to whom the young king directed his great energy, and he retained his birth name for only the first five years of his rule. In Regnal Year 5, he took the unusual and dramatic step of changing his name from "Amun is content" to Akhenaten, "He who is effective for Aten." Amunhotep IV achieved his goals in tandem with a remarkable woman, his great royal wife Nefertiti. Early in his reign Amunhotep IV at times appeared alone, but as Akhenaten, he and Nefertiti were an all but inseparable pair, possibly shaped by their experiences living at the court of Amunhotep III and Tiye.

From the day of his coronation, Amunhotep IV embarked on a massive series of construction projects, commissioning monuments, thousands of square feet of reliefs, and colossal statues, all to proclaim his unique relationship with his divine father Aten. At first, Amunhotep IV did not attack Amun's temple at Karnak, but he shifted focus away from it, creating a new solar cult. Aten became the only possible manifestation of solar power. Only Amunhotep IV, the "Unique One of Re," could make Aten known to a previously benighted humanity. In Regnal Year 5, when the king changed his name to Akhenaten, he made an even more momentous decision, founding a new capital in Middle Egypt: Akhet-Aten. With that new name and in that new city, his new religion found its full expression.

Many major developments of the reign of Akhenaten were foreshadowed, if not enacted, during the five years he ruled from Waset. Amunhotep IV may seem like Akhenaten to us even from his birth, as we know what will come, and indeed the king altered many of his own inscriptions in order to update his cartouches. But to call him Akhenaten from the beginning is to assume that Amunhotep IV's change in identity was inevitable. In describing monuments in Waset, from Karnak Temple to private tomb reliefs, Amunhotep IV will be Amunhotep—the name that appeared alongside the early images of the king. Only when he replaced his name with Akhenaten will we follow the royal lead and speak exclusively of him thus.

During the seventeen years of his reign, Akhenaten greatly, one might say at times almost catastrophically, altered the religious infrastructure of Egypt, the position of the monarchy, and the economy of the country. Such was the strangeness, even violence, of some of Akhenaten's breaks with tradition that later Egyptians believed the revolutionary ruler had offended *maat,* the cosmic order that all pharaohs swore to defend. He would become, within a few decades, a man to whom one did not refer by name, but merely as the "rebel of Akhet-Aten."

It is easy to judge the first five years of Amunhotep IV's reign, his years in Waset, with the hindsight of the rest of his rule. More rewarding, and ultimately more historically sound, is to examine the beginning of Amunhotep IV's reign as if his later decisions were not fated, and to explore how many parallels exist between the last decade of Amunhotep III's reign and his son's first five years on the throne. By the time those years were over, Amunhotep was not ruling alone but with a single queen at his side. Together, Akhenaten and Nefertiti changed the course of Egyptian history.

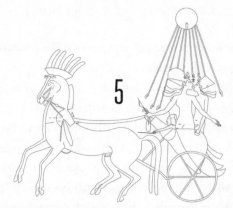

5

The Beautiful One Has Come

Pᴿᴵɴᴄᴇ Aᴍᴜɴʜᴏᴛᴇᴘ ᴡᴀʟᴋꜱ ꜱʟᴏᴡʟʏ ɪɴᴛᴏ ᴛʜᴇ ꜱᴍᴀʟʟ ᴄʜᴀᴍʙᴇʀ that served as classroom for him and his closest compatriots at the court. In her favorite corner, a girl about the same age as Amunhotep perches on a low stool, holding a scribal tablet appropriate to her small size, dipping her diminutive reed pen in an equally tiny pot of water, and writing on a little piece of papyrus.

Amunhotep knows the girl's father well—the great horseman Ay, who has given him many a lesson in driving a chariot, holding on to the young prince with one arm and grasping the side of the chariot body with the other. They often practice close to a police outpost on a mud-brick platform far to the south of the festival city, or on a portion of a great cleared track in the desert, where the larger surface stones have been removed.

Ay sometimes brings his little girl, the same one who habitually sits in the corner of the classroom. She has a remarkably long neck, a pronounced chin, and a somewhat prominent nose. The girl resembles Amunhotep, at least from her forehead to her nose. She is always appropriately deferential, but Amunhotep thinks she looks slightly haughty, as though she were already a queen instead of his cousin. Amunhotep does not bother to use her name anymore—like everyone else he calls her Neferet, simply, "the beauty."

Amunhotep and Neferet are copying an old text today about a dead king giving advice to his son about how to be a ruler. One passage asks, "Had women marshaled troops?" Amunhotep thinks Neferet just might do that one day. She likes driving her chariot all too well, and she often practices the old smiting pose of the pharaoh on other children. For some reason he enjoys seeing her pantomime the violent gesture, but at the same time he prefers that she leave that royal prerogative to him, even on the playground.

By the fourth year of Amunhotep IV's reign, the woman who became one of the most visually prominent royal wives in Egyptian history burst onto the scene: Queen Nefertiti. In the earliest representations of Amunhotep IV, the king appeared alongside his mother Tiye, and perhaps he was not married at the time of his accession. Tiye played an important part at court, participating in international negotiations and continuing her sacred function within the royal family. She and Nefertiti may have shared more than just an official capacity as king's great wife—they may have been members of the same family.

Nowhere are Nefertiti's parents identified, but some evidence allows us to propose a likely family tree for her. The crux of Nefertiti's identity lies in the decoration of the tomb of the official Ay at Akhet-Aten. Among his titles are "god's father," whose duties included royal tutoring, and "master of the horse," two titles that Yuya, Queen Tiye's father, held. In the tomb, Ay's wife, a woman named Tiy, appears prominently and bears a unique title, "chief nurse of the king's great wife" Nefertiti and "nurse who raised the goddess," another reference to the queen. We also know from the tombs at Akhet-Aten that Nefertiti had a sister named Mutnodjmet who was part of the royal court.

Ay and Tiy, scions of the court at Akhet-Aten, achieved yet greater status a decade after the death of Akhenaten, at the time of the early demise of his son Tutankhamun. Ay became pharaoh, and Tiy stepped into the role of queen. As king, Ay commissioned a shrine at Ipu, the hometown of Yuya, Tuya, and Tiye. Taken together, the titles of Ay and his connections with Ipu indicate that Ay was a son of Yuya and Tuya, a brother of Queen Tiye. That Ay's wife Tiy was nurse to Nefertiti suggests another possible connection between Ay and Nefertiti. Might Ay have been Nefertiti's father? Could Nefertiti's mother have died in childbirth, with Tiy becoming stepmother to the future queen? This hypothetical relationship to the royal family may have been a factor in Ay's eventual assumption of the pharaonic office.

DNA analysis of the royal mummies of the Eighteenth Dynasty provides some evidence to support this scenario. During the early first millennium BCE, just after the end of the New Kingdom, the need for gold led the pharaohs to an extreme measure: official plundering of the precious materials buried in the Valley of the Kings. In the process, most of the mummies of the rulers of the New Kingdom were reinterred in collective burials, so we rely to some extent on labels and notations made by those who rewrapped the royal bodies, sometimes several centuries after the deaths of the rulers. Nevertheless, the test results from the mummies' DNA are consistent with the accuracy of those ancient identifications and appear to be free of modern contamination, making the results worthy of consideration.

The parents of Akhenaten were Amunhotep III and Tiye. His paternal grandparents were Thutmose IV and Mutemwia, while on his mother's side his grandparents were Yuya and Tuya. DNA evidence suggests that one of Nefertiti's parents was a sibling of Amunhotep III, the other a sibling of Tiye—thus a child of Yuya and Tuya—making Nefertiti a first cousin of Akhenaten from both sides of her family. In Nefertiti, who likely had an education on par with a prince, Amunhotep IV may have found an intellectual peer, if not perhaps even a superior. Nefertiti may be an enigma to us, but she was probably a childhood acquaintance of Akhenaten.

Whatever Nefertiti's origins, we know that after her marriage to Amunhotep IV she appeared at the king's side during every major event of his reign, and nearly every depiction of him included her in the role of king's great wife. Nefertiti's titulary invariably followed the king's; as queen she was:

The noblewoman, majestic one in the palace, of beautiful visage, resplendent in the two plumes, mistress of joy at the hearing of whose voice one delights, possessor of graciousness, great of love, with whose character the Lord of the Two Lands is pleased, great one of the [palace] of Aten, she who pacifies him at his rising from the horizon. All that she says—it is done for her! The king's great wife, his beloved, mistress of the Two Lands, Nefertiti, may she be given life forever![1]

The first part of her name, *neferet,* relates to a root indicating the ultimate, the perfect, the beautiful, while the second part, *iti,* is a verbal phrase meaning "has come" or "arrived." We can thus translate Nefertiti as "The Beautiful One Has Come," which can be read as a description of the goddess Hathor, a divine beauty having arrived back in Egypt following her annual sojourn to the south. The name Nefertiti, so perfectly evocative of the goddess consort of the sun god, was given to the woman who was the consort to the sun's embodiment on earth. This may be more than a coincidence: Nefertiti may not have been the new queen's birth name but rather one adopted at the time of her marriage. If this is the case, then from the first moment we meet Nefertiti, she had already clothed herself with the mythology of queenship.

6

Transformation

A GROUP OF WORKMEN ARE CARRYING AWAY THE LAST PIECES OF the wooden scaffolding and rolling up the various bits of rope with which they have tied it together. The team of artists laboring in the tomb of the vizier Ramose have just stepped back to take in the entire relief. The scene shows Amunhotep, the goddess Maat seated behind him, enthroned within a pavilion. Final cleaning of the surface is about to begin, and then the painters will commence their work.

To the right of the doorway, an outline artist has laid out a grid and the basic sketch of another scene. The apprentices start to elaborate the initial design but pause when they hear raised voices and exclamations of surprise outside in the courtyard; then, the chief artist enters the tomb, along with a stranger. By his appearance, starched white garments covered in red and black—traces of the drawing and correcting already done that day—he is an artist from the royal court. After a brief conference, the apprentices go back to the grid lines, now to erase them. They will wash down the entire wall and apply an adjusted grid.

As the light through the entrance corridor begins to wane and the afternoon progresses, the scene rapidly takes shape, much of the work being done by the court artist himself. The other artists watch with interest and some with bewilderment. They will need to learn a new style and acquaint themselves with new imagery.

The focus of the revised scene is King Amunhotep and Queen Nefertiti. The royal couple is not static, as kings and queens usually are, but caught in a moment of interaction with members of the court. From a cushioned balcony, Amunhotep leans forward and gestures to his vizier Ramose, while Nefertiti stands behind the sovereign observing the scene. The balcony on which the royal couple stand is an opening in a palace wall. This is not merely new to the artists and their apprentices; it is new to the architects of the palace at Ipet-sout who have recently constructed such a place of royal display—someone suggested terming them "Windows of Glorious Appearances," but the designation has not yet gained popularity.

The apprentices are truly shocked at the appearance of the royal couple. They see the king and queen from the hips up, their legs hidden by the low wall of the balcony. At first glance, it is difficult to identify the ruler at all or even determine his gender. The swell of Amunhotep's abdomen, his prominent breasts, and the diaphanous pleated robe he wears all read as feminine in the context of the art they know. Not only does Nefertiti share these features with her husband but their profiles are also strikingly similar: elongated faces and drooping chins set on thin necks.

Most surprising of all, however, is that strange multirayed depiction of the sun that hovers over the scene—the new supreme god of the king. The literate draftsmen explain that the orb can be called simply Aten, "the Disk." The royal artist puts off other questions regarding the solar god, promising to explain the developing concept of Aten before he leaves. Eventually the apprentices and the other artists join in transferring the last details of the official papyrus sketch to the wall; they never notice the royal artist as he quietly backs out of the tomb's entrance. It is too late on a busy day to review his own somewhat sketchy understanding of the king's developing religious thoughts.

Nefertiti first appeared in official monuments in Waset at the time of a profound shift in her husband's reign. In the tomb of the vizier Ramose,

Amunhotep IV enthroned with Maat from the tomb of Ramose.
(After Norman de Garis Davies, The Tomb of Vizier Ramose *[London, 1941], plate 29)*

Amunhotep and Nefertiti became the icons of a revolutionary change in Egyptian art. Like his colleague Kheruef, Ramose had a lengthy career serving Amunhotep III and was rewarded with an elaborate tomb. The most imposing portion of Ramose's tomb chapel is a large room carved out of solid rock, in which the expert stonecutters left elements of the stone matrix in place to form thick papyrus columns, squat versions of those that line the solar courts of Amunhotep III's temples. The roof of Ramose's tomb collapsed in antiquity, an architectural disaster that inadvertently contributed to the remarkable preservation of the wall decoration.

And what decoration it is! We find it impossible to exaggerate the sheer beauty of the subtly carved raised relief of the men and women whose seated images fill the eastern wall, forever frozen in attendance at a funerary banquet. Each lock of hair on the large wigs donned by both men and women is carefully carved, and it is difficult to comprehend the skill required to align the wavy lines of the tight braids. The tomb is a masterpiece of the stonemason's art, perhaps even more so because its wall art was unfinished, its limestone carvings never painted.

The incomplete nature of the tomb's decorations becomes even more apparent if we stand in the middle of the columned chamber, facing to the west. Here, on a wall partially carved and partially painted in simple black outlines, we can see history unfold. To the left of the central doorway, leading to the inner portion of the tomb chapel, is a scene of Amunhotep IV and the goddess Maat enthroned, a visual expression of the king's common epithet "one who lives on *maat*," his very sustenance being cosmic order.

In front of the couple, the vizier Ramose offers a standard with the ram head of Amun. The speech that Ramose delivers to Amunhotep IV emphasizes the favor and love, as well as the dominion over Egypt's enemies, that Amun grants to the new sovereign. The vizier appears a second time in the same scene, delivering another speech, describing the benefices of another divine father of the king: Re-Horus of the Horizon. This entire image, and its divinities, would have been at home in the reign of Amunhotep III. But if we shift our gaze to the right side of the west wall of the tomb of Ramose, we are met with a very different conception of both king and god.

Here, the king and queen lean out from the balcony of a palace window, bestowing favor on Ramose. Hovering above the royal couple is the disk of the sun, with long rays extending downward and outward from the lower limb of the orb. Each of the rays ends in a human hand, the whole array of solar arms embracing Amunhotep IV and Nefertiti

Amunhotep IV and Nefertiti at the Window of Appearances from the tomb of Ramose.
(After Norman de Garis Davies, The Tomb of Vizier Ramose
[London, 1941], plate 33)

and holding signs of life, the *ankh* hieroglyph, to their nostrils. Never before had Egyptian art represented the sun in this manner at such a large scale.

Also innovative is how the god's names appear during the reign of Amunhotep IV: two sets of cartouches flank the sun disk and give Aten's full name, "Re-Horus of the Horizon who rejoices in the horizon in his name of light who is in the sun disk." The sun disk at the end of the name is *aten,* the same word used in the epithet "Dazzling Sun Disk" that Amunhotep III adopted during his first jubilee. A simplified name for the multi-armed sun disk with the two cartouches is Aten; he is the divine force contained within the orb that produces light and heat, the god who ruled heaven and earth and whose form no craftsman knew. A profound visual shift has occurred, one that signals a corresponding ideological transformation.

But despite the differences in the two main scenes on the interior west wall in the tomb chapel of Ramose, both segments of decoration adhere to a fundamental principle of two-dimensional representations: the human form incorporates different perspectives into a single, unified whole. Thus, a face is rendered in profile while the eye is viewed frontally; shoulders are viewed straight on, while torso, buttocks, and legs are seen in profile. The overlaying of clothing onto a body viewed simultaneously from multiple vantage points can lead to unusual results. A woman's breast is seen in profile, peeking out from the strap of her dress (as in the image of the goddess Maat), even though statuary shows that the straps of a wrap dress normally covered the breasts.

Egyptian art appears remarkably consistent over time because the teams of artists who collaborated on a monument often used a grid, created by snapping ocher-coated strings across the wall. Then, an outline artist would, again in red, draw the main elements in a scene. While many exceptions occur, a human figure typically occupies a prescribed number of squares, and each part of the body could be further subdivided into predictable units. A standing male is eighteen squares from the bottom of his feet to his hairline; the width of his shoulder was six squares; his entire head three squares. Seated figures have their own proportions, and hieroglyphs in turn were arranged to fit into imaginary squares.

Trained artists transferred smaller gridded images from papyrus onto a larger grid on a wall. A master artist provided further quality control when he made the final outline in black ink. Only then would a stone-cutter take chisel and mallet to the wall, the grid and fluid line work disappearing beneath the completed carving. An unfinished tomb like Ramose's offers a snapshot of the artistic process. When the artists and sculptors set aside their brushes and chisels and departed the tomb of

Ramose, probably in the year 1347 BCE, they left the subtle beauty of their graceful and confident line drawings on the northern half of the wall.

Ramose's relief of Amunhotep IV seated with the goddess Maat incorporates standard, earlier Eighteenth Dynasty proportions, essentially the same as those that prevailed during the second and third decades of the reign of Amunhotep III. In the image of the royal balcony, however, a grid of twenty squares replaced the standard eighteen, which attenuated the body of the king and queen, as the extra squares were added to the torso and the head and neck, allowing space for the elongated faces. These changes in the vertical proportions were accompanied by others: the width of the shoulders was narrowed, as was the waist, becoming almost waspish, a feature further emphasizing the width of the buttocks and thighs.

Modern authors have offered an impressive array of theories for the unusual features of Akhenaten's images. One Egyptologist has gone so far as to speculate: "It may well be that he was intentionally kept in the background because of a congenital ailment which made him hideous to behold."[1] Some nineteenth-century authors thought his unusual appearance marked him as a eunuch. By the twentieth century many resorted to medical diagnoses: Did Amunhotep IV have Fröhlich's syndrome? Or Marfan syndrome? Each proposed condition comes with a host of symptoms and physical effects that conflict with the existing evidence: eunuchs did not exist as a type of court functionary in New Kingdom Egypt; Fröhlich's syndrome causes infertility, while Akhenaten fathered six daughters and a son (also an insurmountable problem for the earlier eunuch suggestion); the king's skeleton, an identification made likely through historical and genetic evidence, shows no trace of Marfan syndrome, nor does it provide evidence of any particularly unusual physiognomy.

The most reasonable conclusion is that Akhenaten's art was a form of religious and political expression. Excellent ancient Egyptian prototypes exist for the theologically oriented "portraiture" of Akhenaten's reign. The closest is the post-jubilee art of Amunhotep III, in which the rejuvenated royal couple take on childlike features as they are reborn as manifestations of the sun god's own youthfulness at dawn. Another parallel is the artistic gender transformation of the female king Hatshepsut. Following the death of her husband Thutmose II, Hatshepsut ruled on behalf of her young nephew Thutmose III. In a highly unusual turn of events, after seven years, she declared herself co-ruler. If the phrase "female king" sounds odd in translation, it was equally odd in antiquity: Hatshepsut adopted the titles, monumental building prerogatives, and later the physical form of a male pharaoh.

Hatshepsut's earliest statuary showed her fully female, wearing a dress, even though she dons the *nemes,* the royal striped headdress. As her art developed, images of Hatshepsut assumed an androgynous form, the ruler often wearing only a kilt and exposing her torso, which now has less prominent breasts. In relief sculpture, even when she wears a dress, Hatshepsut had the wide stride of a male pharaoh. Some of Hatshepsut's images from this style of her royal representation also show the adoption of a hybrid skin tone, a pink that bridges the traditional yellow of female skin and the reddish brown of male representations.

By the end of her reign, Hatshepsut appeared in her statuary as a male king, her features and body nearly indistinguishable from those of her co-ruler Thutmose III, who by then was a teenager. We have no reason to assume that Hatshepsut changed her gender presentation in her day-to-day life. She may have worn traditionally male pharaonic clothing only, or she may have worn it over a dress. For the latter scenario, she had a precedent: a statue of Sobeknoferu, a late Twelfth Dynasty queen who ruled as king around 1775 BCE, shows the female king of the late Middle Kingdom wearing the belt and kilt of a male ruler over a form-fitting sheath dress.

The artistic transformations of Hatshepsut and Amunhotep III are indisputable evidence that Akhenaten's and Nefertiti's physical metamorphoses were not the result of pathology. The elongated faces, spindly limbs, ample thighs and buttocks, and rounded bellies, and the mirroring of that physiognomy in images of high officials, were expressions of ideological changes. Those developments were tied to the identity of Aten, the sole deity whom they worshipped. He was the creator deity, and Akhenaten and Nefertiti were his first offspring. The royal couple were so close to the moment of the world's birth that they retained the androgyny of Aten, the primordial deity.

The Unique God

ODAY IS A HOLIDAY IN THE VILLAGE, THE FIRST OF THE FOUR DAYS celebrating the great king Amunhotep, the first to bear the name, who lived two hundred years ago. On the western bank of Waset, many gods are worshipped, but this king is special for the people of the village, including a man named Seta. He and his colleagues—scribes, draftsmen, and workmen—are charged with the important task of excavating and decorating the pharaoh's tomb in the Place of Truth. Their village is located southeast of that large valley, and they must hike over the cliffs each week, returning home for days of rest or to celebrate holidays, like today's festival.

Seta, who like many of the artisans in the village has the imposing title "one who hears the summons in the Place of Truth," is using this holiday to further his son's education. Hori attends the local school most days, never leaving behind his scribal kit—reed pens in their wooden holder with its cakes of black and red ink, and a small water jar—and his gessoed writing board. Father and son are enjoying the cool breeze from the roof of their home in the village, sitting in the shade of a wooden canopy that makes this one of the best "rooms" of all. Seta sits in the standard cross-legged pose of a scribe, his kilt drawn taught against his thighs, creating a flat surface perfect for writing. Hori mimics his father's pose and hands over his latest school exercise.

Hori is an exceptional student, and Seta admires the well-formed and large cursive signs on the writing board. How fondly he remembers the lines that he learned decades ago! "May your voice be true before the powerful spirits of Iunu, before all the gods! May they grant you life and make all beautiful things for you every day!"[1] Seta praises Hori and then presents him with a surprise—a new writing board.

Seta hands over to Hori a larger, brightly gessoed board that already has a grid with a carefully drawn scene. "Your cursive script, Hori, is very good, and I think it is time to continue your study of the more elaborate words of god. You have before you a sketch of a scene that I saw today in the tomb of the vizier Ramose—see if you can decipher the hieroglyphs."

"To read a hieroglyphic text, first find where the inscription begins," says the child, consciously quoting his father. "Hieroglyphs can be oriented either right to left or left to right. The signs can also be arranged in vertical columns or horizontal lines, creating four basic patterns that have no distinction in meaning."

"Why do that?" Seta quizzes his son.

"Changing directions lets the signs decorate a monument. They can frame scenes and direct the viewer's eye to something on the wall. So here, each set of hieroglyphs faces toward the sun disk."

Seta has to suppress a chuckle—his son is repeating one of his earlier lessons verbatim.

"And how," asks Seta, "do we know the direction in which to read?"

"Read toward the faces, the fronts of the signs," says the boy, with confidence.

Seta then points to a group of four signs written to either side of the shining disk drawn out on the board in his lap. His son excitedly responds, "But father, this is not a challenge! The first, tall sign is the flowering reed, an *i*; the half-circle is a bread loaf writing *t*; and the zig-zag line is the water sign for *n*. This is *i-t-n*!"

Seta claps his son approvingly on the shoulder. "And now, for the final question. What is the circle doing at the end of the word?"

The aspiring scribe explains, "That is a disk, and it means that the word *i-t-n* relates to light or time, or in this case," he pauses for dramatic effect, "the shining orb of the sun!" Seta explains that his son has just read the name of the shining disk that spreads its many hands down above the image of the royal family. Then it is Hori's turn to ask a question. "But why have you drawn just the shining disk, Father? That's a very odd shape for a god!"

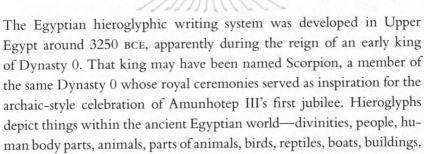

The Egyptian hieroglyphic writing system was developed in Upper Egypt around 3250 BCE, apparently during the reign of an early king of Dynasty 0. That king may have been named Scorpion, a member of the same Dynasty 0 whose royal ceremonies served as inspiration for the archaic-style celebration of Amunhotep III's first jubilee. Hieroglyphs depict things within the ancient Egyptian world—divinities, people, human body parts, animals, parts of animals, birds, reptiles, boats, buildings, weapons, tools, and much besides. Most signs, and especially hieroglyphs that depict animate beings, have a front and a back. Phonetic writing seems to appear quite suddenly, but we can trace a thousand-year-long development of the protohistory of writing in the animal and nautical imagery of rock art and painted pottery of the Predynastic Period.

The ancient Egyptian scripts—hieroglyphs, and the derived cursive hieratic and demotic scripts—are one of the longest-lived writing systems ever created, remaining in use for over three and a half millennia. Some hieroglyphic signs retained the same shape over millennia, but new signs could be introduced to describe new technology. The hieroglyph of the horse-drawn chariot was added to the script when the complex machine became part of the Egyptian military arsenal around 1550 BCE.

The grammar of the spoken ancient Egyptian language evolved over time. Older registers of the language did not necessarily die out but could be retained in texts. After the king changed his name to Akhenaten, he introduced some spoken forms into royal monuments, language unexpected in such formal inscriptions and a signal of how he bent kingship to his personal desires.

The common noun *aten,* "sun disk," and the divine name Aten are usually written in an identical fashion, employing four hieroglyphs. As Seta's son explained in our dramatic reconstruction, each hieroglyph writes a single consonant, and we call them uniliteral signs. Other hieroglyphic words can have biliteral and triliteral signs with two or three consonants,

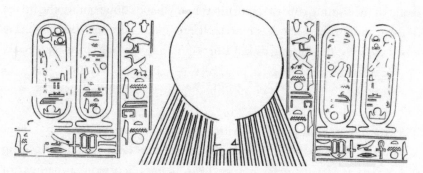

Hieroglyphs labeling Aten from the tomb of Ramose.
(After Norman de Garis Davies, The Tomb of Vizier Ramose *[London, 1941], plate 33)*

as their names suggest. In the absence of written vowels, the consonantal skeleton *itn* (*i* written by the flowering reed is technically a semivocalic consonant) has a number of potential pronunciations; for convenience, we use *aten,* adding a short *e* vowel between consonants.

The last sign in Aten's name is a sun disk, which functions as a determinative or signifier, a classifying sign that has no phonetic value in the word but provides a clue to the word's meaning. The sun disk can appear elsewhere as a logogram, a sign that conveys both the phonetics of a word and means what the sign depicts. A sun disk with a single vertical stroke next to or beneath the disk is read *re,* "sun," the stroke often being used to signal a logogram. If the disk and stroke are written with an added determinative of a seated god, then *re* becomes Re, the solar divinity.

The first known attestation of the noun *aten,* "sun disk," dates to the later Old Kingdom, specifically the Fifth Dynasty, circa 2350 BCE, in a temple inventory. The word *aten* there described an element of decoration on a cult object that would have been part of rituals at a temple to the sun god, not far from the king's pyramid. By the Middle Kingdom, around 1800 BCE, the noun *aten* appeared in the religious compositions that we call the Coffin Texts, as they are known primarily from copies on wooden coffins, most often belonging to local elites. The Coffin Texts can describe the sun god Re entering his *aten,* traveling within the disk in a manner similar to his journey within the Day Bark and the Night Bark.

Middle Kingdom rulers already claimed to rule "all which the sun disk encircles," an expression of universal domination that remained popular through the New Kingdom. During the reign of Akhenaten, the word for disk became the name of the solar deity, which we signal through the capitalization of "Aten." Amunhotep IV's royal predecessors in the Eighteenth Dynasty manifested as the sun disk, brightening the two lands. Hatshepsut was the "female Re, who shines like the sun disk."[2] And she described herself as "the sun disk (*aten*), who creates manifestations!"[3] Amunhotep III expanded upon that identification by becoming the "Dazzling *Aten*."

While Amunhotep IV's representation of the sun god as a shining disk may seem an obvious choice to us, it was not an expected form for a god to take in ancient Egypt. On the walls of temples and tombs, in statuary, and on privately owned objects, deities generally assume three possible forms: fully anthropomorphic; human-bodied with animal heads; or fully zoomorphic. The hybrid animal-human representation is the one that the non-Egyptian world has viewed as the most characteristically—even caricature-ishly—"Egyptian" since the days of ancient Rome. Artists avoided a monstrous marriage of human and animal through the addition of a large wig, which smoothed the transition between species. Re manifested in a great many forms, including the scarab beetle, Khepri, whose very name means "manifesting one" or "he who transforms." The most common form of Re was as a man or falcon-headed man crowned by a disk. Yet this standard representation was only one among many within the richness of Egyptian religious iconography.

Appearing on magical implements of the Middle Kingdom—ivory wands shaped like knives that were believed to cut through disease, danger, and evil—is a solar disk walking on legs. In the Underworld treatises of the post-Akhenaten New Kingdom, even on the second gilded shrine surrounding the sarcophagus of Tutankhamun, some compositions emphasize the solar disk, without rays, floating like a great bouncing ball through the chambers, caverns, and hours of the night. Those disembodied disks may well be the descendants of Akhenaten's Aten.

The greatest variety of visual manifestations of the sun god appear in a text known as *The Book of Adoring Re in the West*. This composition adorns columns and a shroud from the tomb of Thutmose III in the Valley of the Kings and the walls of many royal tombs after the reign of Akhenaten. The text names seventy-five different forms of Re in the Underworld, and a portion of the book depicts those forms juxtaposed with a short hymn of praise to each. One of the seventy-five manifestations of the sun god is indeed a disk, praised as *atenyt,* "He of the Disk."

Most of the other forms of Re, however, combine a mummy's body with a different head, some male, some female, and others of animals: among them a scarab, ram, falcon, cat, pig, and bull. Some combinations of attributes, such as a loaf of bread or two ropes in place of a head, can be bizarre, and were probably intended to be such. *The Book of Adoring Re in the West* also includes a form that Amunhotep IV's brother, the deceased prince Thutmose, would have appreciated: a large, seated tomcat, the *miu a-a,* "Great Cat."

If one asked an artistically inclined Egyptian to draw the sun god, a falcon-headed man or a large cat might have sprung to mind just as easily as a disk. Gods, like Re, could wear the sun disk as a crown, but the disk in that case functioned like a hieroglyph labeling the god as solar in nature. In the hieroglyphic script, the sun disk is used as a determinative after words like "hour," "day," "to rise," or "cyclical eternity." During the reign of Amunhotep IV, the sun disk hieroglyph served as a classifier for both the common noun *aten,* "sun disk," as well as for the divine name Aten. We see a variation of the sun disk hieroglyph already in the Pyramid Texts, religious texts carved in the chambers of the pyramid tombs of kings and queens beginning circa 2350 BCE. A sun disk with three rays (although without hands) could serve as a determinative for verbs like "to shine," or function as an ideogram for a noun for "luminosity," usages that continued for the rest of Egyptian history.

The root meaning "luminosity," so closely associated with the shining sun disk, is *akh* in ancient Egyptian, that phonetic value written with the hieroglyph of the bald ibis. Amunhotep IV employed variations on this root *akh* when he changed his name to *Akh*enaten and founded a new capital, *Akhet*-Aten. In essence one might translate Akhenaten as "the one who is luminous for Aten," just as Akhet-Aten is "the place of luminosity of Aten." The names Akhenaten and Akhet-Aten reinforced a unity of sovereign and city. In Egyptian beliefs, *akh* is also a force and can be translated as "effectiveness": the king's *akh*-spells effectively ward off evil, and within the *akhet*-horizon the sun god grows powerful enough to make another journey through the sky.

From the first few years of Amunhotep IV's reign, Aten also had a more complex name, "Re–Horus of the Horizon who rejoices in the horizon in his name of light who is in the sun disk." For the sake of brevity, we will henceforth refer to this lengthy name as the didactic name of Aten. From Regnal Year 4 onward, the didactic name was enclosed within two cartouches, the first time in ancient Egyptian history that a god's name was placed within what was otherwise a signifier of royal status. Queens can have a single cartouche, but the king alone writes two of his names in cartouches. Aten's name, a single continuous statement, is divided between two cartouches, a surprising choice. In the writing of his god's name, Akhenaten introduces to Egypt a theocracy of a sort no previous ruler appears to have imagined.

While each divine element within the name was well attested in Egyptian religion for over a millennium, the precise combination of words within Aten's name was believed to be unparalleled before the reign of Amunhotep IV. This changed in 2007, when, in the course of building work at an antiquities office on the west bank of the Nile at Luxor, a round-topped granite stela was discovered beneath the courtyard. At the top of the stela, Amunhotep III makes an offering to two gods, one of whom is a falcon-headed deity crowned with a sun disk and labeled as Re–Horus of the Horizon (*akhty*).

Following the name, which we will henceforth translate as Re–Horakhty, is the phrase "in his name of light who is in the sun disk." The word for "light," *shu,* has a sun disk determinative. For an ancient Egyptian, the word for light also recalled the god Shu, the embodiment of luminous space. The only difference between the didactic name of Aten and the name of Re–Horakhty on the stela of Amunhotep III is Amunhotep IV's addition of the phrase "who rejoices in the horizon."

Amunhotep IV witnessed his father become Re on earth and inherited from his father a new conception of the falcon-headed solar god. Amunhotep III accomplished his solar resurrection in the Night Bark on a great lake before his palace called "House of Rejoicing." Together, Amunhotep IV and Nefertiti took the worship of Aten to a new level, and they needed a new sacred space to enact rituals and confirm their status as gods on earth. Our next stop is the sacred site that would be the first focus of the king's innovative architectural program.

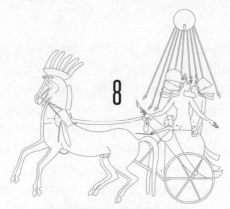

A Royal Warrior

THE DEATH OF THE OLD KING, DURING HIS THIRTY-EIGHTH REG-
nal year, is not a great surprise. In his final years, Egypt's pharaoh still
traveled frequently to visit this office and that temple, but he did more of
this seated in a palanquin, borne on the shoulders of courtiers, or cruis-
ing opulently on a great royal barge than on his own two feet. His teeth
pained him greatly, but he still managed to enjoy his meals and eat on a
heroic scale up until the time of his death.

The ruler met often with Prince Amunhotep and his tutor Ay during
his final years at the House of Rejoicing. As he grew rounder and older,
he spent most of his days languidly reclining on the cool and shaded
divans of the palace, mentally involved as ever in the functioning of
the state but leaving youth and activity and visible solar kingship to his
baby-faced statues and reliefs. Nevertheless, mornings often found him
walking haltingly out to the stables, his one hand on the younger and
much more agile Tiye's shoulder, the other grasping one of numerous
staves he kept propped up at strategic points around the palace.

Often the old king would find Prince Amunhotep in the middle of a
circular enclosure, exercising horses on long reins, while their younger
paddock-mates, not yet broken to the bit, frolicked and ran about. Ultimately, Prince Amunhotep would train the horses at all stages, accus-

toming them to the bit and teaching them how to run as swift as the wind as they pulled the future king's chariot.

From the time he was quite small, Prince Amunhotep had also trained in other martial pursuits. He began with a bow; first a small self bow made to his exact and still diminutive height. Then he progressed to using the more powerful composite bow, which required more strength to pull. At first he shot at leather targets in the shape of ox skins before working his way up, in terms of distance and accuracy, to shooting at thin copper ingots, still in the shape of ox hides.

Today he was to have his first lesson in shooting from the cab of a moving chariot, with Ay there as always to encourage him and ensure that he did not tumble from the hurtling piece of military equipment. Perhaps one day Amunhotep would race around his target at great speed, leaning over to counterbalance the cab as the chariot rounded a turn, the streamers of his crown floating out behind him, reins tied about his waist, firing arrow after arrow into a copper ingot, just like his illustrious great-grandfather.

Egyptian religion incorporated dozens of major gods and goddesses—some were deities at home in particular regions, while others might have a main temple in one city but still be national gods. Amun-Re was worshipped throughout Egypt, and he was *the* god of Waset, alongside his divine consort Mut and their son Khonsu. Amun's name means "the hidden one," and his purview was expansive: he was a creator god, divine champion of Egypt's empire, and as the syncretized Amun-Re, also a solar god.

Ipet-sout (modern Karnak) was the greatest temple of Amun-Re, a site of continuous building activity for over two millennia, beginning as a seemingly modest shrine by the reign of Antef II, around 2100 BCE, and remaining an active cult center when Roman emperors ruled as pharaohs in the first centuries of our era. The most visually stunning feature of the temple of Amun-Re is the Hypostyle Hall, twelve central columns nearly seventy feet high set within a forest of 122 additional columns, each fifty feet high. But those numbers entirely fail to capture the grandeur of the space.

When Amunhotep IV became king and initiated plans for his own additions to the ancient Karnak complex, those columns in the Hypostyle Hall were still seventy years in the future. Yet Amun-Re's temple was already a massive site, with three pylons along the east-west axis and two along its north-south axis. During the great annual festivals, the sacred barges of Amun-Re, at times accompanied by those of Mut and Khonsu, would sail in and out of a T-shaped basin, allowing the smaller, portable barks of the gods to be smoothly transferred onto the shoulders of priests. Bark shrines served as waystations, rest stops for the priests along the lengthy processional routes and places for popular devotion.

The Third Pylon, facing the river, moved the temple's entrance farther east, a shift from the general westward trajectory of the complex's sprawl. To construct the new, grand entrance, Amunhotep III's architects and masons needed to take apart some earlier structures, including bark shrines and a court of Thutmose II. The blocks from those older monuments were stacked as fill within what became the Third Pylon. What once was sacred retained an aura of holiness—hence old temples could be reused as fill in the cores of later monuments, and an overabundance of statues might be buried in a courtyard. Thanks to this Egyptian practice of recycling blocks, we know many of the details of Amunhotep IV's construction projects at Karnak.

When Amunhotep III died and Amunhotep IV ascended the throne, the new king fulfilled his filial duties by completing at least some of his predecessor's monuments. At the temple of Soleb in Nubia, Amunhotep IV began finalizing construction and decoration of the entrance pylon to his father's temple. At the temple of Amun-Re at Karnak, Amunhotep IV added a stone vestibule to the front (east side) of his father's Third Pylon. In a damaged relief from this vestibule, Amunhotep IV appears at a monumental scale smiting dozens of cowering enemies, a typically pharaonic scene of domination for a new ruler who would be anything but a typical pharaoh. During the reign of Seti I, the walls of Amunhotep IV's vestibule were incorporated into the engineering marvel that became the Hypostyle Hall of Karnak Temple. Seti I succeeded in obscuring Amunhotep's decoration for three millennia, until restoration work by the Egyptian Antiquities Service in late 1950s and early 1960s revealed the scene of the king killing his enemies.

This iconic scene of a pharaoh poised to smash the skulls of his foreign foes is standard iconography for New Kingdom temple pylons. By smiting human representatives of chaos, the king guaranteed the triumph of *maat* and ensured that cosmic balance permeated the sacred space within the temple enclosure. A representation of a king's foreign victories, whether they happened in real life or not, guarded the temple from *isfet,* "chaos," preventing disturbances to the world-preserving rituals that occurred daily within the inner sanctuary. At the same time, images of struggle with foreign enemies reinforced the symbolism of the temple as a model of the world, with the outer wall of the temple mirroring the borders of Egypt.

In the scene of eternal victory in front of the Third Pylon, Amunhotep IV enacts the imagery of ritual violence that originated two thousand years earlier and was still in use fifteen hundred years later, when Roman emperors presented themselves as pharaohs of Egypt. In Arthur Weigall's early and influential biography of Amunhotep IV, *The Life and Times of Akhnaton, Pharaoh of Egypt,* first published in 1910, the king is a nature-loving pacifist whose very rejection of warfare inspired scorn: "How they laughed at the young Pharaoh who had set aside the sword for the psalter, who hoped to rule his restless dominions by love alone!"[1]

Many later authors have seen the king's obsession with the sun disk as incompatible with a pharaoh who maintained his empire. Thus Weigall's claim—for which we now have abundant evidence to the contrary—that "Akhnaton definitely refused to do battle, believing that a resort to arms was an offence to God."[2] Otherwise more sedate scholars have also been oddly comfortable with linking assumed physical characteristics, Aten worship, and Amunhotep IV's presumed ineffectiveness as a pharaoh: "Physically weak and unprepossessing, with a frail, effeminate body and an emaciated, lantern-jawed face, the new king had in him nothing of either the soldier or the statesman."[3]

Not only should we dismiss the idea that the king's "lantern-jawed face" is a reflection of his actual appearance, we should also look critically at the king's supposed lack of skill in dealing with foreign powers, be they well-disposed or inimical to Egypt. Amunhotep IV's earliest

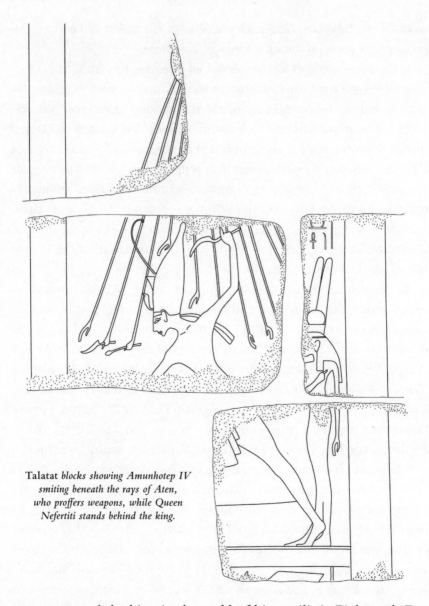

Talatat *blocks showing Amunhotep IV*
smiting beneath the rays of Aten,
who proffers weapons, while Queen
Nefertiti stands behind the king.

years presented the king in the mold of his pugilistic Eighteenth Dynasty forefathers, and his later Aten-centered images did not eschew violence. In one noteworthy relief from Karnak, Aten's arms offer a choice of weapons—a *khepesh*-sword and a mace—to the king, who is in the act of smiting an enemy. Even Nefertiti's ships of state can depict the queen dispatching female enemies or trampling them as a sphinx, following in the paw prints of the sphinx manifestation of her predecessor Tiye. The real-life foreign policy of Amunhotep IV was far from pacifistic, although the king's armies would apparently fight few pitched battles during his seventeen years on the throne.

The vestibule of Amunhotep IV is but a modest addition to his father's constructions at Ipet-sout, a prequel to a grand scheme to come. The new king had a vision for a transformed Karnak, one dedicated to Re-Horakhty as Aten, with Amunhotep and Nefertiti as his earthly vicars. To accomplish this goal in record time, royal artisans needed to innovate in construction techniques as well as in their representations of the royal family and Akhenaten's unique solar god.

9

A Bustling Quarry

As the men managing the topping lifts continue to lower the yardarms, other crew members begin rolling up the still gently bellying sail. At a command from the pilot, the steersman throws the tiller hard to starboard, bringing the prow—pointed south till now—quickly around to port. Having relinquished the power of the wind, the vessel is pushed north by the current, while a handful of oarsmen commence to row. As they enter the narrow channel cut into the high sandstone cliff bordering the Nile, the influence of wind from the north and the current from the south cease, and the small cargo vessel glides into the T-shaped harbor.

In few places could one sail so completely and dramatically into the living rock and take on stones directly from quarry to deck in minutes. They are in the northern end of the east side of the quarries of Kheny, an area where the Nile cuts through the sandstone with no real cultivation intervening. The captain has visited these quarries for over a decade now. His is not one of the enormous cargo vessels able to transport an obelisk, but it can sail during more of the year. Even when the Nile level is well in decline he can carry a half dozen decent-sized stones. He suspects his cargo today might be just as heavy but represent a much larger number of blocks. He passed another cargo boat a few *iteru* to the north, and it seemed to be carrying a load of stones that were larger than bricks but much smaller than the typical bright sandstone blocks from Kheny.

Most of the crew has heard rumors of a new type of building block, the brainchild of the king himself, or so the story goes. The sight that meets their eyes now leaves no doubt as to what their cargo will be. Ahead of them is one of the new quarries, just above the eastern back of the harbor; others stretch off to the south. Docking and tying up to the edge of the harbor, the captain and most of the crew decide to investigate the quarry.

Instead of seeing many stonecutters moving across the face of a few large blocks, some cutting grooves below, others on wooden scaffolding enlarging the vertical grooves separating the stones, the crew see gently terraced stone. Masons move along the terraces, cutting a grid of separation lines, the whole surface looking like a field near the Nile, with narrow runnels creating a rectangular pattern. The stones on the outer edge of the quarry are awaiting only the bottom cut, looking like a row of bricks set out to dry in the sun.

The captain strikes up a conversation with the foreman, who explains that the new "stone bricks" involve a much faster quarrying process that does not need to await the architect's calculations for different stone sizes and shapes. Anyone who has mastered the use of bricks in their homes and storehouses can now help raise stone temples alongside the trained stonemasons of the last generation. Gone, for the most part, are the ubiquitous oxen and sleds. Where once long lines of men hauled on the multiple ropes attached to enormous blocks, lowering them by ramps to the loading area at the harbor, now stonemasons, farmers, and soldiers pressed into duty pick up a roughly shaped stone as it is freed from the quarry and do not put it down until they cross the gangplank and deposit it on the deck of a waiting vessel. Some colossi are still being erected, and no doubt more massive objects will continue to move from quarry to final position in the old-fashioned manner that was first perfected when Snofru of happy memory reared his pyramids far to the north. But a new era is upon them all!

The temples within the great Karnak enclosure primarily originated in quarries known today as Gebel Silsila, ancient Kheny. The site is essentially a great sandstone cataract, through which the Nile long ago cut its channel, and the quarries exploited stone deposits that extend far to the east and west. Not only is the stone of an ideal quality for temple construction but the proximity of the quarries to the Nile also facilitated transportation. Located about one hundred miles south of Luxor, the modern toponym Gebel Silsila means "mountain of the chain," deriving from a myth about a metal chain that could block Nile traffic.

The western quarries of Gebel Silsila, particularly the area directly overlooking the Nile, are known for their decorated chapels, some as elaborate as small rock-cut temples. Whether during low Nile or high Nile, the landscape of Gebel Silsila is always one in which the opposites of desert and Nile meet. Eternally in flood, eternally in festival, the Gebel Silsila quarries were also sacred places because they were one of the origins of stones that would become the walls and statues of Egypt's temples.

In the Gebel Silsila quarry east of the Nile, Amunhotep IV had a large stela carved directly into the sandstone. The lunette, the curved upper portion of the stela, shows the king and Amun-Re, king of the gods, facing one another. The hieroglyphic text begins with a wish for the king to live, followed by his five royal names and a unique title, "chief priest of Horakhty in the horizon in his name of light who is in the sun disk." Aten's name is not written in cartouches, a signal that the Silsila stela dates early in the young ruler's reign.

In the next passage, Amunhotep IV is beloved of Amun-Re, the lord of heaven and ruler of eternity. Although Amun's name is damaged— destruction at the command of Amunhotep IV after he had become Akhenaten—the damage itself makes the restoration all but certain. The text then gets down to business:

> *The first occasion of his Majesty giving the order to [the royal scribe(?)] and general Amun[emheb(?)] to pursue all work projects from Abu to Semabehdet; (and to) the commanders of the army to carry out the great compulsory labor project of quarrying sandstone in order to make the Great Benben of Re-Horakhty in his name of light who is in the sun*

disk in Ipet-sout, at the same time the officials, companions, and chief
standard-bearers being chief(s) of his assessments for transporting stone.[1]

The king mentions building projects up and down the Nile Valley, from Abu (Elephantine) to the city of Semabehdet in the Delta. But the most significant endeavor, the one for which the expeditionary leaders used compulsory labor, is the building called the "Great Benben" for Re-Horakhty in Ipet-sout, Karnak Temple.

We know from later New Kingdom texts that a "chief of assessment" was often attached to a temple and oversaw the accounting of grain stores, cereals being one of the most important commodities in the Nile Valley. In Amunhotep IV's stela, the "chiefs of assessments" oversee stone transport, this involving necessarily the requisitioning of boats. The task was set under the authority of one man, a general, whose power stretched from the First Cataract to the Delta.

In the midst of Karnak Temple, whose chief god was Amunhotep IV's own namesake, the king embarked on a new monument for Aten. On the Gebel Silsila stela, Amunhotep IV unusually refers to himself as the chief priest of Horakhty, almost as though, in arranging the work at Karnak Temple, he is assuming the authority of the high priest. A man named May held the title "high priest of Amun" during the early reign of Amunhotep IV, and we know that he dutifully went into the Eastern Desert at the behest of the king in the latter's Regnal Year 4 in order to fetch stone from the Wadi Hammamat for a statue of the king. If only the high priest had left there, among the numerous inscriptions attesting to the activities of quarrying expeditions over several centuries, a text that described his reaction to the new Aten cult!

While May probably would have found Amunhotep's singular focus on Aten, to the exclusion of Amun, unsettling at best, he would have recognized the Great Benben as the continuation of solar worship that began over a thousand years before. The Benben was not an innovation of the young Amunhotep IV but an object that had inspired the kings of the Old Kingdom to build the pyramids. Here, the new king was reaching back to hoary antiquity to mold a new kingship.

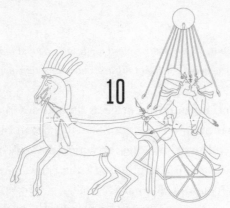

10

City of the Sun

PRINCE AMUNHOTEP IS PAYING A BRIEF VISIT TO THE REGION OF
Men-nefer and Iunu, following his tutor Ay as he carries out research
for the second jubilee of the prince's father. Despite his youth, Amunhotep has expressed a desire to see the sites of the old solar religion. His
tutor has drawn a basic plan of the great temple of the sun at Iunu, and
they consulted what treatises they could in the libraries of Waset. Ay
forewarned him that so much construction has occurred at the great
temple that he would have difficulty grasping some aspects of the earlier
architecture and the forms of worship it accommodated.

After visiting Iunu, they decide to linger a bit longer in the north and
devote several days to the ancient pyramids on the west bank. They begin with the great enclosure of King Djoser, which imparts something
of the character of the prehistoric solar worship. The outer stone walls
resemble even older mud-brick enclosures still standing at Nekhen and
Abdju. An open court to the south is where Djoser's spirit could run,
forever enacting his jubilee ceremonies, while his mummy rested safely
far underground. In the northern court is an enormous altar, flat and
broad, a vast offering table on which one might hold a feast. Indeed, it
was for a feast, so Ay assures him: the feast of the sun. Amunhotep's favorite part of the tour is the stepped pyramid itself, a colossal version of

the stepped platform where his father had sat enthroned during his first two jubilees, and which he will soon again occupy.

They descend the escarpment on donkeys and board a small skiff at a canal that brings them north to another pyramid field. The outline of Djoser's stepped pyramid stands out strongly to the south, while the largest pyramids in Egypt, those at Rosetau, are clearly visible to the north despite their great distance. Ay turns to his pupil and quizzes him about the modest pyramids they are approaching: "Which kings are buried in these pyramids that stretch out along the desert to the west of Men-nefer?" Prince Amunhotep at first avoids the question, remarking on how Khufu's pyramid at Rosetau is so much more impressive. But then the boy remembers that among them are the pyramids of the three kings in a story he loved, and exclaims, "The priest's wife Rudjedet gave birth to them, the sons of the sun god!"

Satisfied with the additional details that the prince recites, Ay leads Amunhotep up the remains of a long causeway that connects a ruined valley temple with the top of the escarpment. Here they find several dilapidated enclosures—but they only have time for one. Ruined as the structure is, they can see that an open court is the most important element of the edifice, just like the broad spaces of King Djoser's complex. Behind a large altar at the western end of the enclosure, atop a truncated pyramidal base, are the tumbledown remains of an enormous but stumpy obelisk, the Benben in monumental form. Along the northern side of the enclosure are nine large alabaster basins, set below a limestone floor in which channels have been carved.

Immediately thinking of the great sacrifices of cattle that coincided with religious festivals at Waset, the young prince decides that the channels must be for catching the blood spurting from the necks of hundreds of beasts. Surely, the basins once overflowed with the life-giving blood, red drink for the blood red sun disk itself.

Ay apologetically disagrees with his young charge. Gesturing to make his point, he asks, "Do you see any tethering stones for the cattle?" No such stone rings are visible, though they are a necessary piece of equipment for the butchers to lower the heads of the cattle before neatly slitting their throats with flint knives. Perhaps, the tutor offers, the channels might symbolically have contained the blood of the meat offerings to the sun, but what actually ran through that myriad of run-nels was wine and water poured out for the sun god.

After rowing a short way on the skiff eastward along the canal lead-ing from the valley, they see a large vessel, a sparkling golden crescent on the river. As Prince Amunhotep and Ay board the royal barge on their way to the old palace in the shadow of Snofru's first pyramid, they agree on one thing: the ancient solar cult loved open spaces, large altars, and massive offerings. This religion did not demand dark sanctuaries containing small statues that needed to be purified and clothed. Here, the ever-present and fiery father sun gloried in oblations and sacrifices. Of course, the young prince insists one last time that Re loved to drink the blood of whole herds, just like Hathor in another of his favorite tales. The tutor does not reply, and Amunhotep drifts off to sleep at the rhyth-mic splash of the oars, with visions of great offering courts and Benben monuments to color his dreams.

When Amunhotep III conducted research in ancient records to discover the proper template for his jubilee ceremonies, he and his scholars likely came across references to the sun god from Egypt's first dynasties. Some of that research took place at Iunu, today most often called after the Greek name Heliopolis, the oldest and most important cult center for the solar gods Re and Atum, sometimes imagined as the polarities of day and night, respectively. Almost a thousand years after the reign of Amunhotep III, the Greek historian Herodotus reported that the people of Heliopolis were the "most learned of Egyptians."[1]

Today, only a portion of the massive ancient city is accessible, most of it lying beneath the Cairo suburbs adjacent to the garden city founded in 1905 named Heliopolis after its ancient ancestor, and about five miles west of Cairo International Airport. All that remains standing of the Hut-aat, literally the "Great Temple," is a single sixty-eight-foot-high obelisk, erected by Senwosret I around 1950 BCE. Other obelisks that once stood in the same temple complex now grace the cities of London, Rome, and New York.

The sacred object at the core of the Great Temple was the Benben.

According to the Heliopolitan account of creation, at the beginning of time, the god Atum, whose name the Egyptians could interpret as both "Complete One" and "One Who Is Not (Yet Existing)," was alone within the undifferentiated waters of Nun. From this oneness, Atum generated dry earth, the primeval mound—the Benben was that mound, symbolizing the first land. Amunhotep IV described his monument for Aten as a Great Benben, signaling that the new work had a direct connection to Iunu and the Great Temple of Re and Atum.

Almost nothing survives of the Great Temple at Iunu, so how are we to envisage Amunhotep IV's Great Benben for Aten at Karnak? Pyramids like the famous Fourth Dynasty monuments at Giza (ancient Rosetau) were models of the upper portion of the Benben, the pyramidion. The first kings of the Fifth Dynasty (who were described in a fictional tale as the offspring of Rudjedet, the wife of a priest of Re) built their pyramids at Abu Sir. Nearby, they constructed solar temples, complete with monumental versions of the Benben, intermingling the worship of the sun with their own mortuary cults.

Whatever the form of the original Benben, the Egyptians could stylize it as an obelisk, a rectangular pillar with sloping sides, topped by a pyramidion. Egyptian obelisks are monolithic, and often a pair of them are placed before the grand pylon entranceways of a temple. In the eastern portion of the Karnak complex, where Amunhotep IV ordered construction of the Great Benben, an obelisk already stood alone as a monument to the solar aspect of Amun-Re, king of the gods. Thutmose III had decreed that the single obelisk be quarried, a project finally completed during the reign of his grandson Thutmose IV (the grandfather of Amunhotep IV). At 105 feet high, that lone obelisk was one of the tallest ever erected in Egypt. In the Gebel Silsila stela, when Amunhotep IV stated that he was building a Great Benben for Aten, the hieroglyph of an obelisk determined the word "Benben," indicating that the king was augmenting the sole obelisk of Thutmose IV.

It is easy as an Egyptologist to witness Amunhotep IV and Nefertiti worshipping the shining sun disk of Aten to the exclusion of all other deities and exclaim in shock at how they transgress millennia-old norms. It is especially easy to do so, because within a few years after the death of the royal pair, their own son Tutankhamun accused them of causing the gods to abandon Egypt. But if we were to imagine ourselves among the priests and priestesses standing at the base of the unique obelisk in east Karnak four years into the reign of Amunhotep IV and looking around at the newly completed temples to Aten, we might see as much continuity as innovation.

Those freshly erected Aten temples were versions of the Great Temple at Iunu, and all were dedicated to the sun god, Re-Horakhty. But Ipet-sout, the temple of Amun-Re at Karnak, had been identified with the Hut-aat of Iunu since its founding over fifteen hundred years earlier. Amun-Re was frequently equated with Re-Horakhty, both of them powerful solar gods who conferred to the pharaoh his rule of the cosmos. Waset and Iunu—Greek Thebes and Heliopolis, respectively— were so closely related in Egypt's sacred geography that a century before Amunhotep IV a text called the two cities "Iunu of Upper Egypt and Lower Egypt."[2]

Today, we see only the base of the unique obelisk: the mighty monolith vanished, a spoil taken by a Christian emperor of Rome. The giant blocks of the obelisk base are a monument in their own right. On the seams between the massive stones are rectangular holes that curve in a bit on their long sides, once filled with metal clamps that prevented shifting of the base beneath its mammoth burden. If we walk a dozen yards south, looking that direction, we see more pylons, Karnak's north-south axis, and a dissonant note rings from the temple's ancient skyline: a massive crane. That piece of modern machinery is a striking reminder of the history that has emerged from within the pylons themselves. This is especially true for Amunhotep IV—entire temples, recycled as filler, have been hauled out from where they were encased in later constructions. Nothing of Amunhotep IV's constructions still stand.

From within the Ninth and Tenth Pylons and scattered other locations, Amunhotep IV's bold new plan for the sacred site can be reconstructed. Tens of thousands of decorated blocks have been cataloged, and the addition of undecorated cut stones pushes the number over one hundred thousand. Unlike monumental stones—some weighing multiple tons, common in earlier and later temple architecture—the stone blocks from the constructions of Amunhotep IV are small. Commonly called *talatat,* a modern term that probably references the fact that they

Man carrying a talatat *block, from a* talatat *belonging to one of
Amunhotep IV's constructions at Karnak Temple.
(Drawing of Brooklyn Museum, Charles Edwin Wilbour Fund, 61.195.1)*

are three hand lengths (*talata* is Arabic for three), the blocks are a standard size: 20.5 inches wide, 9.8 inches high, and 8.6 inches deep; or to
an ancient Egyptian, one cubit long and a half cubit in height, and a half
cubit minus two fingers in depth. A *talatat* is light enough for a single
man to carry, which facilitated rapid construction and allowed for a
large workforce of nonskilled laborers.

Recognizing the unusual size and uniformity of *talatat* blocks, the
ancient Egyptians called them "bricks of stone," and they were assembled in the same patterns of headers and stretchers used for brick walls.
The small size of the *talatat* increased the speed of a building's construction, from quarry extraction and transportation by boat to their final
placement. But their portability also hastened the demolition of Akhenaten's monuments after his death. Ironically, later rulers preserved the
pieces of the very temples they razed by incorporating the small *talatat*
of Akhenaten in the fill of their own monuments.

A handful of early, larger blocks, the plethora of *talatat,* and a unique
set of statues—but a fraction of an original phalanx of colossi—are what
survive of Amunhotep IV's building program at Karnak. From these
remains we can trace the origins of the king's promotion of Aten to the
pinnacle of the Egyptian pantheon; we can read Amunhotep IV's own
words about his solar deity and the statues of other divinities; we can

Talatat *showing bowing courtiers behind Queen Nefertiti. (From a temple at Akhet-Aten)*

trace how Nefertiti already played a uniquely powerful role as king's great wife.

Dated inscriptions do not appear on the surviving blocks from the Karnak constructions of Amunhotep IV. If we compare the reliefs on the larger blocks with those on the smaller *talatat,* we see the same artistic transformation as that at work in the tomb of Ramose. The style of representation on the larger blocks of Amunhotep IV resembles that of Amunhotep III prior to the first jubilee. During this initial phase, Re-Horakhty appears as a falcon-headed man, and his lengthy name is not enclosed within cartouches.

With the true *talatat* blocks of Amunhotep IV, we see the shining sun disk of Aten and the extreme elongation and androgyny of the "Amarna" style, so named for the modern designation of the ancient city of Akhet-Aten. The placement of Aten's didactic name within two cartouches can be dated to the end of the king's fourth regnal year, a precision supplied by two objects found within the tomb of Amunhotep IV's son Tutankhamun. These are old textiles with ink annotations; the one dated to Regnal Year 3 of Amunhotep IV writes the name of Re-Horakhty without a cartouche, while another linen dated to Regnal Year 4, specifically the second month of Shomu, bears the same divine name written within cartouches.

For a brief transitional period, the falcon-headed god, shown with spindly limbs and a pronounced paunch, could appear with the didactic name written in two cartouches. The manifestation of the new solar god in the form of a disk with rays ending in hands then replaced the anthropomorphic image of Re-Horakhty by the end of Regnal Year 4.

Among the *talatat,* the repetition of certain images—such as the king and queen worshipping Aten—means that even small fragments of relief can be reconstructed with confidence. A part of a face can be identified as the king or queen; the curve of a disk or a slanting ray as Aten; the leg of a roasted goose as an offering table laden with food. Similarly, cartouches of the royal couple or their god can also be restored from even one or two hieroglyphs, especially if a part of the curving name ring is also present. Such is not the case, however, with fragmentary parts of lengthier texts. If a hieroglyphic text is innovative or unusual, as many from Amunhotep IV's reign are, we cannot simply fill in the gaps. Instead, we must translate every word carefully or risk quite literally putting words in the king's mouth.

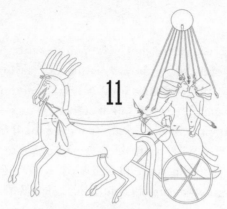

11

An Erudite King

Amunhotep has no idea how he comes to be running through the desert, bow and arrows in his hands, or how he could possibly be gaining on the ostriches running ahead of him. Strange that no tall and lean desert scout, no winded and wheezing courtier is in sight—only a pack of hunting hounds racing alongside him, matching his superhuman speed. How peculiar that his heart pounds with excitement, even as his feet barely feel the ground. Wonder gives way to anxiety when a great griffin, dappled wings held close to its body, bounds up on his right, leonine paws slapping against the desert surface, great falcon beak open in a cry of attack. A dream, Amunhotep now realizes, but one too exhilarating to leave.

With a leap the griffin spreads its wings, screeching in fear; the ostriches abruptly begin to run in circles, wings outspread. The king and the dogs stop as the ground begins to shake violently. The sky darkens in spite of the yet brilliant solar orb, and five-pointed stars appear, growing larger and taking on the shapes of tumbling humans, legs and arms outspread, falling earthward as a great voice fills all of the sky and rumbles through the cracking earth. A divine manifestation, of the sort the old religious texts of his pyramid-building forebears described, has found the prince and penetrated even his dream.

The god is Re-Horakhty, ancient falcon lord of the eastern horizon. His message fills Amunhotep's mind in an instant: Only the power of the solar god rules the cosmos and manifests divinity. The statues of the gods have ceased to work. Whether they are of gold, granite, limestone or clay, they cannot receive the spirits of the gods any more than they can move or speak. The only divine image is Re-Horakhty's son, Amunhotep.

Suddenly awake, drenched in sweat in his bed, the king determines to share with his subjects what the sole deity has revealed. Today he is to oversee a discussion of the divine statues he should commission as a newly crowned king. He listens to their confused attempts to make sense of the question at hand: How should the gods and goddesses of Egypt appear? The king then announces the answer—the artfully crafted statues of Egypt's gods do not function. Amunhotep requests an inventory of the temples, a catalog of the plethora of dead images and the fabulous wealth of their costly manufacture, uselessly enshrined throughout Egypt. Only the solar deity exists, so perhaps he will find some other use for the gold and jewels that encrust those defunct images.

> Or perhaps, this is how it happened. . . .

For several days Amunhotep had arisen early each morning and called for a group of scribes to accompany him. Slung about with their palettes of reed pens and cakes of red and black ink, water pots sealed but inevitably leaking onto their freshly starched garments, they answered occasional questions from the king concerning the location of this or that scroll.

Again today, the king is on his way to the House of Life, a vast mud-brick structure with numerous storage rooms situated around a central scriptorium. There, beneath the gaze of a large statue of the baboon form of the god Thoth, patron of writing and learning, sit row upon row of scribes, busily copying out texts. On one side of the room, three men transcribe notes and letters from military administrators, while other scribes copy lengthy literary texts, tasks that require several weeks.

The king is not interested in administration or literature as such but in religion. He has already dispatched messengers to a variety of temples, from the massive, ancient piles of the pyramid fields to smaller and no less frequently visited shrines in ancient Nekhen. Amunhotep is on a quest to understand the nature of statues, temples, even Waset as a holy city.

Eventually he hits upon what he seeks. He knows how the statues of the deities ought to look. They should be based not simply on the shapes of older statues but on how those statues related to their temples and how those temples and their cities related to each other. This means that even statues just completed at the end of his own father's reign may need to be replaced. The king has become increasingly obsessed with the sun of the eastern horizon, the god Re-Horakhty, as the ultimate expression of cosmic power. The statues, the temples, should not simply reflect their individual natures but also show how they all are but aspects of that great solar oneness.

Today the young king sits enthroned within the palace, listening to his officials. They are full of information, yet for the most part they seem perplexed when it comes to offering a solution to the apparent problem—how properly to renew the statues of Egypt's deities, as all kings must do. The king, confident in the unassailable accuracy of his divinely inspired wisdom, requests a great inventory of the statues and other holdings of all the temples of Egypt. The task is to decide what the gods desire and how to fashion the statues out of the mineral wealth of Egypt. Each king must give artistic birth to the one who bore him, and a survey of the state of the cults of Egypt will certainly help with that.

As a conclusion to this meeting, the king presents a paean to the efficacy of the god Re-Horakhty. He does not tell his audience—perhaps he only half acknowledges the thoughts himself—but his mind returns again and again to a meditation on the power, the primacy, the uniqueness of the solar deity. What might Re-Horakhty want him to do with all that wealth if he can but devise a plan grander than any of those of his illustrious forebears?

Royal meetings with officials were normal occurrences, but objective records of the proceedings have not survived. The accounts of such conferences that have come down to us portray the pharaoh as the source of ultimate wisdom. The king begins by listening to his advisors, who are then often presented as befuddled or at a loss for answers. Ultimately, only the king can offer a timely and effective solution to a crisis. Kings frequently needed to repair temples and their statues, to renovate earlier structures as well as build new ones. This was an important duty in honor of the gods, and Amunhotep IV apparently confronted just such a crisis about divine statues.

Most biographers claim that Akhenaten had a revelation, a sudden flash of divine inspiration to revolutionize Egyptian religion. In the first reconstruction, we have imagined how Re-Horakhty could have visited the king in a dream using imagery that was well known to an Eighteenth Dynasty king: ostrich hunting, griffins, and the momentous signs of a divine epiphany. The acquisition of insight through a dream is well attested for ancient Egyptian kings.

Thutmose IV, Akhenaten's grandfather, while yet a prince, claimed to encounter Re-Horakhty in a dream as he slept in the shadow of the head of the Sphinx, the massive statue on the Giza Plateau that embodied the solar god. At that point, the Sphinx was already a thousand years old and covered up to his neck in sand; Re-Horakhty promises the prince that if the young man will remove the sand, then he will become king. As pharaoh, Thutmose erects a stela between the Sphinx's paws that records his dream and fulfillment of Re-Horakhty's request.

In the second reconstruction above, Amunhotep IV acquires his knowledge through less dramatic means. One ideal of kingship was a sovereign as scholar who could perform research in the House of Life. Both the dream revelation and royal scholarship are plausible reconstructions of a single, relatively short, and sadly broken inscription from the reign of Amunhotep IV, once part of his temple constructions at Karnak. The two readings are rather consistent in all but one thing— either the gods desire something, presumably new or refurbished statuary, or they, in the forms of their statues, have simply ceased to function. Ultimately this point rests on a single word in the damaged inscription.

What event might have triggered Amunhotep IV's transition to Akhenaten, and all of the momentous changes that entailed, has fascinated all who have encountered this remarkable ruler. Some believe that Tiye influenced the young king or that he absorbed insights from sages at his father's court. Some modern authors have surmised that the promotion of Aten at the expense of Amun might be a reaction to the power of an overweening and even corrupt priesthood at Karnak. Many have seen in Amunhotep IV a monotheistic prophet, grafting onto the king terminology, feelings, and perceptions not always warranted by the surviving ancient sources. These various Akhenatens have even merged into a messianic prophet over a millennium ahead of his time, one who fought an ancient priesthood sunk into moral turpitude, economic corruption, and theological tyranny. None of these interpretations, however, reflect what we can confidently see in the surviving archaeological and textual remains.

One of the only truly concrete pieces of evidence for how Amunhotep embarked on his new religious project is the fragmentary text from Karnak. The inscription in question is spread across two blocks that were part of the fill of the Tenth Pylon and first brought to scholarly attention by the Akhenaten Temple Project, which spent decades studying the remains of Amunhotep IV's constructions at Karnak. One block has a depiction of a deity, almost certainly Re-Horakhty, to the left, followed by an introductory text giving the full titulary of Amunhotep IV and referencing "Re-Horakhty who rejoices in the horizon in his name of light [who is in the disk]." The second block, the main part of the surviving text, has parts of fourteen columns of hieroglyphs. Even in their broken state, these passages can be divided into three major sections: a description of the sad state of affairs that the king has discovered; a proclamation of the royal solution to that awful situation; and a hymn to the solar deity.

The first publication of the blocks, cited subsequently and uncritically by numerous later publications, reached the sweeping conclusion that they expressed Amunhotep IV's "manifesto" that the statues of all other gods had ceased being powerful and that Aten was the only god who existed. But does the hieroglyphic text actually say this, as many Egyptologists continue to believe? As we seek to answer this question, we examine the text word by word, dive into hieroglyphic dictionaries, pull book upon book from our shelves to check parallels, and then settle down to determine the grammar and put it all together. As frustratingly fragmentary as this text might be, it is the single most important record of the king's thoughts early in his reign.

A brief note about the scholarly apparatus used here: superscript numbers reference the columns of the hieroglyphs (x+1 means the first column after an unknown number of earlier lines); brackets indicate words that have been restored in missing or damaged areas; question marks indicate uncertainty; words in parentheses provide additional clarification, including information present within determinative signs.

The text begins with an obscure quotation by people called knowledgeable ones:

> $^{x+1}$[. . .] Horus(?) [. . .] $^{x+2}$[. . . temples(?) fallen into] ruin, without any (divine) beings [. . .] $^{x+3}$[. . . royal(?)] august ones(?)," so say the knowledgeable ones [. . .]

Although only the word "ruin" survives at the beginning of line x+2, parallels show that the word commonly appears in the expression "fallen into ruin." In other royal inscriptions, that phrase describes the state of derelict structures, and we may reasonably suggest that the text here likewise described damaged sacred buildings. As the rest of the inscription is concerned with the gods of Egypt, this reading is as close to certain as we can be.

This phrase "fallen into ruin" is well associated with historical retrospectives in which a ruler compares the glory and power of his or her own construction works with the shamefully neglected, decaying, even desecrated condition of earlier buildings. A parallel of sorts appears in Hatshepsut's description of abandoned temples, recorded in a text carved onto the façade of the rock-cut shrine of the lioness goddess Pakhet, near Beni Hasan in Middle Egypt. Hatshepsut describes architecture so dilapidated that it was as if the earth had swallowed the temple sanctuary. The female pharaoh bemoans the absence of knowledgeable people, even referring to priests as "empty-headed." Hatshepsut casts herself as one supremely knowledgeable regarding the cults of Egypt, the only one capable of saving the temple.

Like Hatshepsut, Amunhotep IV likely mentioned "knowledgeable ones" only to criticize them. The two groups appearing earlier in the damaged Karnak block, beings, possibly divine, and august ones, possibly royal, are obscure in the extreme. Fortunately, a search for similar passages again offers insight into the situation, and a hunt through dictionaries leads us back to Hatshepsut.

A potentially illuminating occurrence of the designation "august ones" appears in a red-and-black granite chapel that she constructed at Karnak, which was dismantled by her nephew but is now gloriously re-erected in the Open Air Museum just north of the temple of Amun-Re. Looking for a hieroglyphic inscription, particularly one that might be high on the wall, would be challenging, so instead we pull from our shelf the 1977 edition of Hatshepsut's chapel, Pierre Lacau and Henri Chevrier's *Une chapelle d'Hatshepsout à Karnak* (a copy we purchased in Cairo years ago), and check the index.

The first two entries are not helpful, but on page 98 we come across a remarkable passage: "The entire land grows silent. 'One does not understand,' so say the royal august ones. The officials of the palace lower (their) face(s); his (the god's) followers say 'Why?'" It is then up to Hatshepsut to answer the "why?" and she goes on to enlighten her officials about the oracle of Amun. The disjointed text of lines x+1 to x+3 on Amunhotep IV's block now comes into sharper focus. Even the wise men of the court, the "august ones" and "knowledgeable ones," are at a loss to understand what needs to be done about a temple that has fallen into ruin.

This is how one must approach an Egyptian text—always assume you might find a parallel, in whole or in part, perhaps not with identical words but with an evocative pattern. Following Hatshepsut's lead, we can expect that the next passage in Amunhotep IV's block will describe the ruler as a hero who comes to the rescue with his unique insight. Indeed, in line x+4 Amunhotep IV intervenes, and for the first time in the king's reign we can read a record of his own words:

> *x+4Behold, I am speaking that I might cause [you] to know [. . .] x+5[. . .] manifestations of the gods, so that I might understand the temples [. . .] x+6[. . .] writings of the inventory of their majesties, the antiquity [. . .] x+7[. . .] which they desire, one after another, out of all precious stones [. . .]*

Other royal inscriptions that begin with the king saying "pay attention" or "I cause you to know" are followed by a solution to the problem. For Amunhotep IV, his response to a derelict temple involves images of the gods, their "manifestations." A concern for the statues and their proper appearance also occupied Horemhab, final king of the Eighteenth Dynasty, who claims that "He raised up their shrines and fashioned their statues in each of their exact forms, from every precious stone."[1] Horemhab's action toward statues recalls the "one after another, out of all precious stones" of Amunhotep IV's text.

The mention of "understanding" and an "inventory" finds interesting parallels with a stela of the late Middle Kingdom ruler Neferhotep I, who lived about four centuries before Amunhotep IV. In this text from Abydos, Neferhotep I desires to see a "great inventory" at the time of his refashioning of a statue of the god Osiris. Neferhotep I, in the company of "true hieroglyphic scribes" and "masters of mysteries," conducts research in the sacred library, seeking clues to the proper appearance of the statue; the king then decrees the solution that begins with "My heart has desired to see the writings of the first antiquity of Atum. Open up for me the great inventory!" and concludes, "so that I might come to know the god in his visible form, and fashion him like his former condition."[2]

The proper ruler must discover the theoretical underpinnings of an image and even identify the specific mines from which the raw materials will come. According to such texts of heroic royal scholarship, the pharaoh's knowledge enables valuable natural resources to be transformed into even more valuable and magically potent divine images.

The Karnak block we are translating follows the word "inventory" with "of their majesties," again a reference to divine statues. The king requires the inventory to know what the gods want, and what they may well want is new statuary. On the basis of this text, Amunhotep IV seems intent on accommodating the cults of Egypt, even as he emphasized the worship of Aten. We need not just take Amunhotep's word that he performed this inventory, because we have a record of economic results from his accounting of temples and their offerings.

A series of 173 *talatat* blocks discovered within the fill of the Ninth Pylon allow for the reconstruction of a portion of a wall of approximately

33 feet long by 7 feet high. The specific temple of Amunhotep IV at Karnak to which the wall belonged remains uncertain, and the text was recarved during the short time of the king's constructions at the complex. The initial decoration of the wall depicted the king and Nefertiti standing before a series of offering tables; opposite the royal pair was a single image of Aten as a disk with multiple arm-rays. Later, a sun disk was added above each of the offering tables, and a list of fixed and variable taxes paid to the temple of Aten was carved on the wall.

Each temple, from the Delta to Upper Egypt, was required to supply the following: one *deben* of silver; one *men*-measurement of incense; two *men*-measurements of wine; and two bolts of ordinary cloth. These quantities are so small—a *deben* of silver is only three ounces—as to be virtually symbolic. In some places the tax lists were squeezed into the available space, encroaching upon some of the elements of the offering tables. As late as Regnal Year 5, third month of Peret (Growing Season), day 19, a man named Ipy, who served as steward in the city of Men-nefer, sent a letter to Amunhotep IV reassuring the king that all offerings for the gods and goddesses of the city, including Ptah, were in good order, with nothing lacking. Less than a month later, the king changed his name to Akhenaten and established his new capital at Akhet-Aten.

Rather than being a starry-eyed mystic obsessed with the solar disk and disdaining the physical manifestations of the gods, Amunhotep IV was interested in an economic accounting of the infrastructures of the divine cults of Egypt. On the Karnak block, following Amunhotep IV's description of a royal solution to the ruinous situation that he inherited, the king continues with a soliloquy to the solar creator god. Here, at last, theology takes precedence over fiscal concerns:

> $^{x+8}$[. . . who bore] himself, [whose] secrets cannot be known [. . .]
> $^{x+9}$[. . .] he [coming(?)] to the place he has desired. They will not know his going [. . .] $^{x+10}$[. . .] night; but I approach(?) [. . .] $^{x+11}$[. . .] which he made, how exalted are they [. . .] $^{x+12}$[. . .] their [. . .]s as stars. Hail to you in your rays [. . .] $^{x+13}$[. . .] What is he like, another like you? You are [. . .] $^{x+14}$[. . .] they [. . .] in that your name [. . .]

Line x+8 appears to begin a section describing the sun as a god who gave birth to himself, the only god to exist at the beginning of time. From other monuments dating to the early reign of Amunhotep IV, and the adjoining block to the one we are translating, we know this deity to be Aten. This god's secrets and movements are unknowable. We have the tantalizing rhetorical question: "What is he like, another like you?" From the grammar, we know that Amunhotep IV surely intended his audience to answer: There is none besides Aten, Re-Horakhty who rejoices in the horizon in his name of light who is in the sun disk!

Knowing that Amunhotep IV concludes his speech with praise of the sun god, we now return to the passage that we have translated: "[. . .] which they desire, one after another, out of all precious stones [. . .]." Other translations of this block render the verb at the beginning of line x+7 as "to cease." Since the statues of gods within temples are often said to be made out of costly materials, that translation leads to the conclusion that the cult images of the gods, "one after another, out of all precious stones," have stopped functioning. It is difficult to overstate the significance of the translation: many discussions of the motivations and philosophy of Amunhotep IV assume that the king baldly stated that cult statues "ceased." This in turn becomes the basis for understanding the king's other actions.

The interpretation of what the text says hinges on how we read a single word in line x+7, a verb that the original editor of the block initially took to mean "cease," translating the fragmentary passage as: "[. . .] they have ceased, one after the other, whether of precious stones, [. . .]." We translate the verb instead as "desire," and we must turn to the hieroglyphs themselves to make our case.

The verb 𓄑 is written with three phonetic signs. The first sign is a chisel functioning as a biliteral sign, which we can approximately pronounce as "ab" (like the beginning of the word "ab-solute"). As Egyptologists, we use a system called "transliteration" to represent each consonant of ancient Egyptian, including those that do not exist in Western alphabets—so we transliterate 𓄑 as *3b*. The first letter is not a cursive number "3" but rather represents an *aleph*, a glottal stop. The chisel hieroglyph is followed by a human leg that is the uniliteral *b*, here a phonetic complement, meaning that it repeats the second consonant of *ab,* without adding any new sounds. The second leg gives us the repetition of the *b*-sound, so we can sound out the entire word as "abeb" (the transliteration is *3bb*). As written on the Karnak block, *abeb* does not have a determinative, a classifier sign. Had the Karnak block included a determinative for *abeb,* that would have greatly decreased the ambiguity of the writing and likely obviated this discussion over three thousand years later.

The first stop in the oft-repeated looking up of a word is the massive Egyptian–German dictionary, *Wörterbuch der ägyptischen Sprache,* a project begun in 1897, its five volumes of entries eventually published between 1926 and 1931. The archive of note slips that were used to compile this dictionary—still a standard reference for hieroglyphic texts—has now been digitized. By inputting the page number and word entry from the published *Wörterbuch,* we can scroll through scans of paper slips containing handwritten copies of snippets of ancient Egyptian texts containing a particular word.

Uncertainty as to the proper reading of the word *abeb* on the Karnak block is possible because, as the ancient Egyptian scripts did not write vowels, two words might have a similar consonantal skeleton. We take down the first volume of the *Wörterbuch der ägyptischen Sprache.* On pages 6–7 we indeed see several words with the basic spelling of *ab* (listed in the dictionary under the transliteration *3b*). We note that *abeb* might well be a writing of the word "*abey*" (transliteration *3bi*), "to desire, to wish." We also see another verb *ab,* "to cease."

Does the writing of the verb on the Karnak block favor either reading? The verb *ab* (*3b*), "to cease," appears usually to take walking legs ⋀ as a determinative. The verb we chose, *abey* (*3bi*), "to desire, to wish," normally has a tied-up papyrus scroll ⸺ as a determinative. Of the two verbs, according to the dictionaries, "to desire, to wish" is the one more likely to appear without a determinative.

What of the reduplication of the *b*? We have *abeb* instead of *ab.* Now the verb *abey,* "to desire, to wish," normally shows a reduplication of the *b* in several verb forms. The verb *ab,* "to cease," does not normally show this feature. On the basis of both the lack of determinative and the presence of a reduplication of the *b,* we may favor a translation "to desire, to wish," but we cannot rule out a slight aberrant writing of the verb "to cease."

How then does one decide? We cannot ask an ancient Egyptian directly how to say this, that, or the other thing. A myriad of turns of phrase, words, and nuances of expression are as yet lost to us. Only by gathering examples of obscure Egyptian words and looking at them in context can we reconstruct their meanings.

If gods or statues of gods were the subjects of the verb *ab*, "to cease," what would that likely mean? Would such a use of "to cease" actually describe deities or their statues as "ceasing (to do something)," with that something not mentioned? If we look for ancient texts that use this verb, including a letter from the reign of Akhenaten, we see that *ab* can refer to "remaining" in a place. Most often, a text using the verb says that the gods will not cease (*3b*) an activity—the turn of phrase actually reinforces the ongoing action of the deity.

We do have another inscription, however, in which the verb *ab*, "cease," occurs in the context of a failed cult. An inscription from the reign of Ramesses II describes an unfinished temple as being in disarray, and "cessation (*3bw*) had occurred in the offerings."[3] What ceases are not statues but the offerings to them.

If we turn to the verb *abey*, "to desire," we find that gods do, in fact, frequently desire things. The number of texts where gods desire greatly outstrips sentences where anything to do with gods or temples ceases. Most significantly, the verb "to desire" occurs in several texts from the reign of Akhenaten; Aten can *abey*, "desire," actions that Akhenaten should perform, and, crucially, the verb can occur without a determinative. On the Karnak blocks, Akhenaten apparently discusses what the old deities desire, whereas later he is only concerned with what Aten desires.

What might the gods on the Karnak block desire that would involve precious stones? The answer is statuary. By examining parallels in other royal inscriptions, we can recognize the text we have been translating as a variation on a standard genre about a crisis that the wisest priests and royal advisors cannot solve until the pharaoh reveals his effective plan. Just as the Gebel Silsila stela records Amunhotep IV directing his new construction activity for Re-Horakhty, the Karnak block emphasizes the unique and unknowable nature of Aten. Inscrutable, that is, to all but the king.

The tomb of a man named Parennefer, who oversaw the king's constructions in the Domain of Aten, provides more evidence that Amunhotep IV placed Aten above all the gods but did not at first neglect the rest of the pantheon. Within the tomb, Amunhotep IV instructs his chief of works: "Direct your attention to the divine offerings for Aten!" Parennefer replies: "The taxes for each god are measured with grain scoops, but one measures for Aten with overflowing heaps!"[4] No one can doubt that Amunhotep IV directed his energies to Aten, whom he viewed as a god above all other gods. But our new translation of the Karnak block reveals that during his initial years as pharaoh of Egypt, Amunhotep IV neither entirely ignored the cults of other gods nor believed that they have simply ceased to be effective. He does appear, however, to have been interested in inventorying the cults of Egypt and ultimately taxing them—even small, nominal sums—on behalf of his new cult of Aten.

12

A Temple of Her Own

Eyes straight ahead when not glancing back at Meritaten, Nefertiti strides slowly up the avenue of sphinxes. With a dance-like gait she advances three paces, stops for a moment, and then advances again, leading now with the right foot, now with the left, so that Meritaten can keep up. The portal is still some distance to the east. They pass by 128 sphinxes, alternating pairs with the heads of Nefertiti herself and her husband, arranged so that a sphinx of Nefertiti gazes across the processional way into the serene and stony eyes of a sphinx of the king.

Light glinting from the electrum pyramidions atop the obelisks of her husband's immediate royal ancestors showily reveals the great bulk of the temple of Amun-Re to the south. With its massive pylon gates, Ipet-sout is impressive, but a bit cramped in places. It has a reasonably imposing entrance, but nothing so impressive as the sphinx-lined avenue along which she and her daughter are making their way. One would be forgiven for thinking this is the main access to the main temple, though it actually leads to the sprawling and airy Gem-pa-Aten temple that her husband has added just east and north of the back portion of Amun-Re's temple.

Nefertiti's goal is not the inner portion of Gem-pa-Aten; she exits the avenue near its eastern end—of course, Meritaten has other ideas and must be reminded, after a brief run around a couple of the sphinxes, that she must accompany her mother on a short walk to the south. They quickly reach the Great Benben. Akhenaten is absent from today's proceedings, driving home the point that she, Queen Nefertiti, is the high priestess of the new cult.

The queen and her daughter enter a temple decorated with soaring pillars depicting them offering to Aten. They begin to do in real life what appears on pillar after pillar—holding out their sistra and shaking them before altars piled with food, while Aten reaches out to accept their offerings and gives the breath of life to their nostrils. From the time she became queen, Nefertiti was included by Akhenaten in his offering ceremonies. As the king and queen merge into an inseparable royal pair, Nefertiti has become the embodiment of female divinity, supreme in worshipping the solar god.

Of course, Akhenaten hopes everyone will eventually understand that his absence as a human is because he is one with his solar father. Nefertiti often tells Akhenaten she is afraid that his general avoidance of explanatory texts might be a source of some confusion in the future. Akhenaten contends that the necessary treatises already exist in the temple libraries, many since time immemorial! For Akhenaten, no new texts are needed, only a new teaching, a summary of all that he has learned, all that he now understands. He needs not to write, or even to talk, but for he and Nefertiti to act.

No source from the reign of Akhenaten and Nefertiti records words that the queen spoke. So we turn to relief carvings and statuary to understand the role she played as her husband focused increasingly on the cult of Aten. One temple, called the Mansion of the Benben, speaks especially loudly on her behalf.

The sacred spaces of Egyptian temple complexes were not simply the domains of male priests in their many ranks and functions. Priestesses served important cultic functions for both gods and goddesses, prominently but not exclusively as songstresses and members of musical troupes that created the sacred soundscapes in which deities could be properly worshipped. In the temple of Karnak, no priestess wielded more power or influence than the God's Wife of Amun. In Amunhotep IV's fifth regnal year, a priestess walking into the newly constructed Mansion of the Benben would have been surprised by the absence of the king and any god other than the shining sun disk. But she would have understood Nefertiti's prominence as a reflection of a long-standing office of high priestess at Karnak.

From the beginning of the Eighteenth Dynasty, the God's Wife of Amun led priestesses and priests in ritual celebrations at Karnak. A queen often held the office, which placed her among the highest ranks of the Amun priesthood and granted her access to the innermost sanctuary. In a remarkable stela, the first king of the Eighteenth Dynasty, Ahmose, granted to his great royal wife Ahmose-Nefertari the revenue from the position of Second Priest of Amun. Ahmose-Nefertari already had the title God's Wife of Amun, but the stela takes pains to describe the queen as impoverished in that role. Ahmose not only transferred the position of Second Priest of Amun to Ahmose-Nefertari, but he also endowed her with a substantial amount of additional property in gold, silver, copper, clothing, wigs, ointments, male and female servants, grain, and tracts of land. She, and the God's Wives who followed her, wielded economic as well as religious power.

Two generations later, Hatshepsut, the daughter of a king (Thutmose I) and wife of a king (her half-brother Thutmose II), inherited the office of God's Wife of Amun. After the early demise of Thutmose II, an official named Ineny plainly stated the political reality in Egypt upon the coronation of Thutmose III, a mere child: "The God's Wife, Hatshepsut, controlled the affairs of the land, the Two Lands being under her authority."[1] Seven years later, Hatshepsut adopted pharaonic titles, ruling as coregent with Thutmose III. The property and power Hatshepsut wielded as God's Wife likely made her ascent to kingship possible.

For Tiye, who does not bear the title God's Wife of Amun in any of the surviving records, the lack of that priestly office certainly did not diminish the prominence of her role, either practically or sacerdotally. Tiye's extraordinary deification at Sedeinga and during the jubilee rites suggests that her economic and religious power rivaled that of

Ahmose-Nefertari and Hatshepsut. Similarly, Nefertiti did not hold the God's Wife office, which would have been at odds with the religious changes and theological emphasis of her husband, but that did not lessen her authority.

The office of God's Wife overlapped with two other titles: Adorer of the God and Hand of the God. The identification of a woman with Amun's hand alludes to the manner in which the god Atum of Iunu created the first male-female divine pair, Shu and Tefnut. At the beginning of the world, he existed alone in the primordial waters, so his initial act of creation was autoerotic.

Because all nouns in ancient Egyptian had grammatical gender and the word for hand, *djeret,* is feminine, Atum's solo act is still a union of male and female elements. When the God's Wife of Amun was called the Hand of the God, she was that element of the creator god, the means of arousal and sexual gratification. Even if a queen did not hold the title Hand of the God, her association with Hathor functioned in much the same way. The sexual union of Re and Hathor guaranteed on the cosmic scale the continued existence of the world and, at the earthly level, the birth of an heir to maintain the royal lineage. Nefertiti's name might be an allusion to Hathor, the beautiful one who comes back to Egypt, and the queen's regalia and her ritual role in the Aten temples of Karnak show how she embodied that goddess.

One of the temples constructed at Karnak during the first five years of Amunhotep IV's reign was called the "Mansion of the Benben." The ancient Egyptian word "mansion" was often used in the names of temples, and the most commonly used term for "temple" was literally "mansion of the god." The Benben of the temple's name is the same as the Great Benben, and they both referenced the unique obelisk at Karnak as a representation of the most sacred solar object.

What we know of the Mansion of the Benben and Nefertiti's uniquely important role within the cult of Aten comes from *talatat* blocks extracted from the Second and Ninth Pylons at Karnak. Careful examination of the *talatat* has allowed the reconstruction of reliefs on a pylon gateway and a series of large rectangular pillars (each of the pillars was about 33 feet high). The shining Aten disk, labeled with his two cartouches, appears at the top of each scene, the divine imagery thus

Talatat of Queen Nefertiti making offerings beneath the rays of Aten, probably from the Mansion of the Benben at Karnak Temple.

dating the construction of the Mansion of the Benben to sometime between the middle of Regnal Year 4 and the end of Regnal Year 5.

In every scene, Nefertiti performs the rituals, and to her alone does Aten offer signs of life. Amunhotep IV appears nowhere in the temple. On the pylon of the Mansion of the Benben, and elsewhere at Karnak, Nefertiti wears a crown that consists of a short platform (often called a modius) serving as a base for cow horns that frame a sun disk. The horns and disk are attributes of Hathor, representing her bovine form as a celestial deity and her solar identity. Nefertiti's crown also has two tall ostrich feathers, which were worn by earlier Eighteenth Dynasty queens as counterparts of Amun's tall plumes. Tiye was the first queen to combine the horns and disk with the ostrich feathers, and Nefertiti's crown signals that she too is both queen and goddess.

Beginning at the time of the Mansion of the Benben's construction, Nefertiti's cartouche enclosed a longer name: Neferneferuaten ("Beautiful is the Perfection of Aten") Nefertiti ("The Beautiful One Has Come"). The principle of honorific transposition, in which words like "god," "king," or names of the gods are written first in a phrase, even if read later, dictates that the divine name Aten is placed at the beginning of the cartouche. Within the cartouche, Aten is written in the opposite orientation as the rest of the hieroglyphs, as if the god is confronting the name Nefertiti. Such a reversal of a god's name occurs frequently in cartouches in which two divine names appear, further confirmation that the name Nefertiti is at once the designation of an earthly woman and a heavenly goddess.

In the Mansion of the Benben, Nefertiti holds in each hand a large, elaborate sistrum. In its most basic form, a sistrum is a percussion instrument with a handle supporting a curved metal frame for rods on which disks could slide back and forth, making a tinkling sound when shaken. Nefertiti's sistrum replaces the simple metal frame with a shrine-shaped box, while behind her a diminutive Meritaten grasps a small sistrum with the head of Hathor at the top of the handle. For the remainder of Akhenaten's reign, Nefertiti, Meritaten, and later additional princesses accompany the king in nearly every depiction of rituals or offerings. This is itself highly unusual—throughout most of Egyptian history, queens were not shown actively participating in divine cults. We know that queens performed such ritual activities, but their actions were not depicted on temple walls. The same is true for most ceremonies that took place within a temple: priests carried out the day-to-day operations, but the standard versions of the ritual scenes on the walls of a temple represent the king alone before the gods.

The sole exception to this rule is the woman whose depictions we have found so illuminating for the reigns of Akhenaten and Nefertiti: Hatshepsut. As queen, before taking royal titles, Hatshepsut offers to the gods without a male ruler being present. The God's Wife of Amun had no need for a royal intermediary; she was literate, able to read and recite the proper hymns, and properly inducted into the temple rituals.

One of the most important rituals a God's Wife, and subsequently Nefertiti, performed was the shaking of the sistrum. When Hathor shakes the sistrum, she is pleasing her father, Re, delighting him with her beauty as well as the sound of the metal disks. The tintinnabulation of the sistrum evoked the soundscape of the New Year, when Hathor, the goddess of the eye of the sun, returned from her annual winter sojourn to Nubia. As her once leonine and bloodthirsty (but now pacified and bovine) incarnation emerged from the desert and entered the marshes that lined the Nile, Hathor's body rustled the papyrus plants through which she moved. Two separate rituals—the rustling of papyrus stalks or the shaking of a sistrum in a temple—reenacted the goddess's return. The God's Wife playing the sistrum at once pacified the goddess and placed the priestess in the role of the daughter who appeases and entertains her solar father.

In the Mansion of the Benben, Nefertiti shakes the sistrum as she consecrates offerings before Aten and becomes "one who unites with her beauty, she who satisfies Aten, her hands beautiful as they bear the sistrum."[2] Nefertiti did not physically join with Aten as God's Wife, but *talatat* from Karnak are surprisingly explicit about the sexual union of Nefertiti and her husband. In one scene, Nefertiti takes Amunhotep IV by the hand, her other hand seductively cupping his elbow (as Mutemwia did to the god Amun in the divine birth scenes), leading the sovereign to an empty bed. Just as the God's Wife sexually stimulated the god (although the mechanics of the ritual were likely more symbolic than physical), this *talatat* depicts the moment before the king and queen ideally conceive another heir, embodying the bounty of Aten's life-giving force.

Nefertiti was unique among queens in one more way: she could appear in the guise of the bellicose ruler, executing female prisoners. But her imagery finds strong parallels in Tiye's depictions, including the decoration on Tiye's throne in the tomb of Kheruef, where the queen appears as a rampaging sphinx trampling foreign women. When Egypt was still in the throes of war with the foreign Hyksos in the north, around the year 1575 BCE, a queen named Ahhotep may even have led an army into battle. This would explain why Ahhotep was buried with a necklace of three large golden flies, the mark of valorous military service. Ahhotep was the mother of Queen Ahmose-Nefertari and thus set the stage for the powerful queens of the Eighteenth Dynasty, even if they no longer needed to participate in actual military combat.

Benefiting from the militaristic activities and bellicose imagery of her exceptional predecessors, Nefertiti could appear both as a sphinx, crushing an enemy, or as a human, in a smiting pose. On a *talatat* block reused in Luxor Temple, four kiosks on the decks of vessels show alternating images of Nefertiti as a sphinx and Nefertiti smiting. The queen performs each set of actions against two of Egypt's traditional enemies, the Syrians to the north and the Nubians to the south. Two *talatat* from Akhet-Aten, once part of an Aten temple, also depict Nefertiti's ship of state. Its stern has a kiosk with Nefertiti grasping a foreign woman's hair in one hand, about to deliver a sword blow. Aten spreads his rays protectively over the queen, sanctioning her action with divine approval.

Both Tiye and Nefertiti share an unusual prominence in the art of their husbands' reigns, but we cannot be certain if those images reflected the reality of the queens' positions in the governance of Egypt. Whether or not the women had roles in foreign policy, we know that they participated to an extraordinary degree in the jubilee celebrations of their husbands. At Karnak, the Mansion of the Benben was part of a larger temple complex decorated with depictions of Amunhotep IV's jubilee, which he celebrated with Nefertiti beneath the rays of Aten. Unlike his father, who waited the expected thirty years, Amunhotep IV celebrated his jubilee after only a few years on the throne. At the completion of the ceremonies, both king and queen were newly transformed into children of Aten.

13

A Precocious Jubilee

THE PLATOON PREPARES ITS CAMP FOR THE EVENING. RE WILL
soon descend into the western cliffs, and now that his rays are no longer
upon it, the desert grows steadily cooler. While his fellow soldiers set
up tents and start a small fire over which they will cook their evening
meal, Dedi wanders downslope to where two faces of the cliffs meet.
Each time his platoon camps here, Dedi makes time to add a small
carving to the rock. He fondly remembers visiting this place on a previous patrol and helping his Nubian comrade Ruiu carve an image of
himself.

Dedi has been practicing his technique—creating precise cuts with
the tip of a sharp flint is more difficult than it looks! In honor of the momentous events that await him tomorrow, Dedi has mentally sketched
out his most ambitious carving yet: an image of the king making an
offering beneath the rays of the new god, Aten. The artistically inclined
soldier warms up by drawing his platoon's standard, a ship with a round
cabin placed on the end of a tall pole.

Pleased with how the rock feels beneath his flint tool, Dedi decides
to tackle the most difficult part of his composition. Keeping in his mind
some of the artworks that his friend Seta, an artisan who works in the
royal tomb, has shown him, Dedi starts his portrait of the king. He

draws a small cobra, then the most important line—the stroke that will represent the king's face. His flint hits an unusually soft spot in the rock, and suddenly the nose is already too large. By Thoth, Dedi exclaims, at least he can make the king's chin appropriately long, too. When Dedi has finished his image, adding the last few hands of Aten, the actual flaming disk has nearly disappeared from the sky. Taking a step back from the rock, the soldier admires his creation—the detailing on the broad collar and the pleats of the king's kilt are really quite nice.

At first light the next morning, Dedi and his platoon start down the mountain along a track that gradually widens as they head southeast through the desert toward the northern edge of Waset. Then it is time to board their ship for the short sail across the river to the great temple of Ipet-sout. Today will be a day like no other—Dedi's platoon has been chosen to don their finest military uniforms, tie their hair with pristine white linen, and carry the poles of the king's throne.

He cannot believe that this is the first day of the *heb sed* of the King of Upper and Lower Egypt Neferkheperure, the son of Re Amunhotep. It was only a few years ago that Dedi was part of the celebrations of the king's father, may he be true of voice! As Dedi and his comrades walk through the sacred precincts of Ipet-sout, they marvel at the size of the king's new temple complex. The priest guiding the soldiers to their proper stations informs them that the temple's name is Gem-pa-Aten, the place where the king discovered the perfect site for the worship of his god, the disk in heaven. The massive open courts create a grand stage, but Dedi barely has time to appreciate the host of people assembled around him. He must focus on his own task: elevating his divine sovereign above the crowd of celebrants. At the appointed time, Dedi and his comrades kneel, shouldering the long poles, ready to lift as one.

If they fail, and the throne tips just a bit too far in one direction, will the king's tall white crown stay upright? The sovereign's hands each hold a scepter—what would he even do if the crown started to slide? Dedi pushes those thoughts away, stares straight ahead, and awaits the command. Arise! Just as they have practiced, the soldiers move on cue, smoothly hoisting their king aloft. The jubilee of Amunhotep and Nefertiti—and their god Aten—has commenced.

Some rituals that Amunhotep IV performed during his jubilee had been part of *heb sed* celebrations for over a thousand years, such as the washing of the king's feet and the royal run around signs that represented the borders of the world. Often, a single *talatat* with just a portion of an image allows a traditional jubilee rite to be identified. Some *talatat* show events copied from the jubilees of Amunhotep III, ceremonies thus far unattested for any other ruler.

The jubilee celebrations of Amunhotep IV and Nefertiti also included rituals unique to their reign: presenting offerings to Aten in open-roofed kiosks; partaking of massive feasts while musicians played enormous harps; driving chariots; and sitting in elaborately decorated carrying chairs atop the shoulders of soldiers. The jubilee was not purged of depictions of other gods: hymns were sung to Hathor, the ancient standard of a jackal was held by a priest, and the stepped platform that the king ascends and descends was decorated with a host of deities. But the *talatat* leave no doubt that the chief deity of the jubilee was Aten, and his presence distinguishes the jubilee of Amunhotep IV from the *heb sed* ceremonies of all other kings.

Amunhotep IV's early jubilee may have been considered a continuation of events from the reign of Amunhotep III. The three jubilees of Amunhotep III occurred in Regnal Years 30, 34, and 37, and the king died in the following year, which then also became the Regnal Year 1 of Amunhotep IV. If Amunhotep IV believed himself to be maintaining the solar kingship of his father, then a jubilee in the early years of his own reign, perhaps around Regnal Year 4, fits perfectly as a continuation of Amunhotep III's festival timetable.

The jubilee of Amunhotep IV was also a jubilee for Aten, and from this point onward the two cartouches of the sun disk were almost invariably followed by the epithet "one who is in jubilee." Aten, Amunhotep IV, and Nefertiti became a new trinity and were soon the only objects of worship that the king acknowledged in his monuments. The recently crowned Amunhotep IV did not need the *heb sed* to rejuvenate his kingship; instead, it transformed him into the unique son of Aten, in perpetual, reign-renewing festival, like his heavenly father.

On the jubilee blocks of Amunhotep IV, a man follows the king, holding the ruler's sandals. Royal sandal-bearers performed their task in a tradition nearly as old as royal ceremonies themselves, extending back to the First Dynasty. What made Amunhotep IV's sandal-bearer unusual was the man's title, First Priest of Neferkheperure. The word "priest" here translates literally as "servant of the god." The god that this man serves was not an unseen divine power but Neferkheperure, which was the coronation name of the king.

The unnamed First Priest of Neferkheperure adopts an unusually deep bowing posture as he follows behind the king. People around Amunhotep IV and Nefertiti—be it a running soldier, a censing priest, or a message-relaying vizier—declined their upper body forward, sometimes even approaching a ninety-degree angle with their legs. A slight bow before the pharaoh was common in ancient Egyptian imagery, as it surely was in reality, and the prostrations of foreigners before the pharaoh could be extreme (including rolling on one's back). Yet the degree of the bowed back in the reign of Amunhotep IV and its ubiquity is astonishing, another sign of the king and queen's elevation to godlike status.

Within the record of Amunhotep IV's jubilee, a chorus of thirty-two celebrants was collectively labeled "royal children." Although their carved depiction is incomplete, the group appears originally to have been evenly divided between male and female participants. This group cannot be true children of Akhenaten, and perhaps only a few rulers, such as Ramesses II—prolific in all that he did—could have filled its ranks with biological offspring. These participants are a group of ritualists enacting the role of royal children.

In keeping with the emphasis on the king himself, these "royal children" sing in the jubilee a song apparently of the king's own composing. Though the text is sorely fragmentary, enough survives to give some sense of the performance:

> *[Words spoken by] the [royal] child[ren]: "[Hail to you] Re, every day! Hail to you, falcon, every day! Hail to you, our father, [every] day! Hail*

to you [. . .]! Hail to you King Neferkheperure, unique one of Re, lord
[. . .] his [. . .], alone, who accumulates magic. Your [jubilee] writings
are [. . .] himself, like his writings, the lifetime of [. . .], who uncovers
himself according to the transformations therein. The jubilee song: [. . .]
in the jubilee rituals like Re [. . .] the foremost of the gods [. . .]"][1]

The song of the "royal children," sadly incomplete as it is, references
the king's "jubilee writings." The royal children call out with four addresses, the sorts of exclamations, even shouts, that might well accompany transformation rituals. Amunhotep IV was hailed as a "falcon," the
same bird whose plumage protruded from the jubilee robe of Amunhotep III. Four is the number of the cardinal directions, and a recitation
repeated four times took on cosmic importance. We can imagine the
men and women playing the role of royal children facing a different direction for each of their four exclamations. By the time they completed
their four statements, Amunhotep IV had truly become a falcon, one
who "accumulates magic."

To see exactly how far Amunhotep IV took his own transfiguration
into a divine entity while still resident in Waset, we must turn to colossal statues erected in the same temple on whose walls the jubilee festival
scenes were carved.

14

Strange Colossi

THE GREAT COLOSSUS IS ONE OF A PAIR, BUT THE MORE SPECIAL one. Intended as the southern member of the two, the great and as yet unfinished statue has its own name and had already received worship in its own right before it left the quarry. The cutting of the block, roughing out the shape, and transporting it to the closest Nile harbor were minor epics. Quarried at the Red Mountain, northeast of Men-nefer, the monstrous creation had required a great barge the size of the transport vessel that Hatshepsut had earlier employed to transport two enormous obelisks. The barge itself weighed about the same as the colossus it carried.

The journey of the obelisks generations earlier had been shorter—Sewenet to Waset—and the crews had the benefit of traveling with the current. The chief of royal works, Men, and his son Bak, had just overseen an equally gargantuan barge, but for a distance almost three times as far and against the Nile current all the way. Whereas the obelisks required a fleet of tow boats with 864 oarsmen, the colossus required yet more tow boats, all with sails set. Every oarsman (far outnumbering Hatshepsut's old crew) prayed to Amun for a good north wind even as he perpetually strained at the oars.

In addition, long lines of haulers pulled on massive ropes from shore, slowly moving the colossi up the Nile—they and the oarsmen together numbered approximately two thousand. In the great bend of the Nile north of Waset, the river flows to the southwest, and the sails often fell limp as the flotilla struggled against both the current and the wind.

They finally reach Waset and gratefully pull into the canal leading to the lake in front of the king's festival city. The chief of works knows the draft of the loaded vessel is rather deep—a carrier for a single large obelisk drew about five cubits and a couple of palms. But he trusts the vessel's commander, who is confident the harbor in its present state is nowhere less than six cubits in depth, and where they will dock the depth is closer to ten cubits.

At the still unfinished harbor, numerous mooring posts are pounded home, hawsers securely lashed, and the great stone—already strapped securely to a large wooden sledge—begins its journey to the king's temple. The barge heels dramatically as the great stone slowly slides over the side onto the ramp constructed to receive it. As its burden leaves it, the broad and shallow vessel rises so high that it seems almost to float above the lake.

Long ropes stretch ahead of the colossus, some attached to the sled, others to the lower portion of the stone. If the oarsmen and those towing from shore were many, those hauling the statue the short distance overland are at least double their number. They need to cover only about 1,600 cubits, but it is a grueling task. Planks used to strengthen the causeway along which the statue moves—raised ground is imperative during the time of the receding waters—are mostly taken from old ships that have been broken up. Workmen remove the wood after the colossus has passed and run ahead to re-lay the planks.

Limestone powder is poured on the wood-paved track; moistened, it forms a slippery gypsum film along which the colossus slides. Bak decides to take up a position on the front of the sledge, supervising. All the while the hauling soldiers and sailors chant the songs they usually sing at such occasions, as when they hauled on the tow ropes of the divine barges in the festivals of Waset. The one they seem to prefer today begins with "How flourishing is the perfect ruler!" and ends with "Victory be to the ruler!" Groups of priests and priestesses, with sistra and lutes, walk next to the statue as it slowly slides forward, singing hymns to the morning sun, whom the enormous statue would soon face for all time.

Now and then one of the scorpion specialists, the physicians of Sakhmet, jogs ahead and inspects the ground over which the men will soon haul on their tow lines. The floodwater being high, and the causeway having remained dry, there is indeed some danger of scorpions. In any event, the unit has just returned from Sinai, and their medical crews are anxious to appear useful and engaged. Bak initially worried about how properly to position and finish the sculpture—soon to be one of a pair, as the other colossus is en route—within the forecourt of the temple. He has to admit his father was correct—these logistics make the work within the temple seem like an easy afterthought.

One hundred and twenty-five miles south of Waset, on a granite boulder in what is now Aswan (ancient Sewenet), a man named Men, the chief sculptor responsible for Amunhotep III's colossi, carved his own inscription. Standing in front of the boulder with the sunlight raking from above, we can see that Men holds two braziers aloft before a table teetering beneath a massive pile of offerings; the object of his adoration is a colossal statue of Amunhotep III—one of the pair on the west bank of Waset. Men's inscription labels the statue whose carving he directed as the "son of Re, Nebmaatre, ruler of rulers"; the superlative epithet is also carved on the back of the southern colossus at Waset, which must be the object of Men's devotion in his rock inscription.

Men's inscription at Aswan also includes his son and protégé, Bak, who stands back-to-back with his father. Father and son shared the title "overseer of works in the Red Mountain," the quartzite quarries now engulfed by modern-day Cairo that were the source of much royal statuary, including the seated colossi of Amunhotep III. In the hieroglyphic columns above, Bak calls himself "one whom his Majesty himself instructed, chief of sculptors in the great and large monuments of the king in the Estate of Aten, in Akhet-Aten." Bak bows slightly before a now defaced image of Akhenaten burning incense beneath the rays of Aten.

Men and Bak faithfully served their kings, overseeing monumental sculpture that transformed a pharaoh into a divine image. In describing his artistry, Bak made the unusual claim that Akhenaten personally instructed him. A pharaoh was expected to have a decision-making role in his royal imagery. Hieroglyphic texts record how pharaohs Seti I and Ramesses II personally visited quarries in order to identify the blocks of stone from which their colossal statuary would emerge.

The type of image that Amunhotep IV devised for his own statuary emerged from the encumbering debris of time in July 1925. Colossal statues of the king were inadvertently uncovered that month during the digging of a drainage area to the east of the temple of Amun-Re at Karnak, a project attempting to combat the rising water table that was threatening the monuments of the entire complex. The results of excavations that followed were impressive: bases of two dozen square pillars (5 feet 10 inches × 6 feet 6 inches) lined the walls of an expansive court, and in front of each pillar were the remains of a colossus of Amunhotep IV; together, these shattered images are some of the most unusual and controversial statuary from ancient Egypt.

Fifty years after the French mission first uncovered the colossi, the Akhenaten Temple Project reinvestigated the area, hoping to trace additional walls and better understand the temple's form. Among the finds of the excavations during the 1970s were *talatat* that included jubilee scenes; even more importantly, an inscription on one of the blocks mentions the name of the temple, Gem-pa-Aten. The ancient name, which means "The Aten (*pa-aten*) is found (*gem*)," indicates that this was a place in which Aten revealed himself and that Amunhotep IV himself discovered. We encountered the name Gem-pa-Aten already in the tomb of Ramose, where Amunhotep IV and Nefertiti dispensed rewards from the Window of Appearances. Thanks to the excavations in the area of the Gem-pa-Aten and the painstaking reconstruction of *talatat* scenes, we can imagine the original appearance of the temple. What is now a series of mounds, patches of camel thorn, and a drainage ditch was once a massive stone complex that proclaimed the might of Amunhotep IV and his heavenly father, Aten.

The desolation of the site today is a fitting starting point for our reconstruction of the temple, for the land that would become the Gem-pa-Aten was essentially a patch of terra firma where once flowed the waters of the Nile. To begin his construction, Amunhotep IV might have needed to fill in marshland and even the remnants of an arm of the

Nile that once flowed to the east of Karnak Temple. From images on the *talatat,* we know that the king himself wielded a hoe to begin the digging of the temple's foundations, and stacked the first blocks, while Nefertiti looked on. The symbolic cornerstones laid, armies of work-men unloaded the continuous flow of small blocks shipped from the quarries at Gebel Silsila, stacking stone upon stone, arranged just like mud bricks in rows of headers and stretchers. The joints between the *ta-latat* were smoothed with plaster, and then teams of artisans laid out the wall decoration. They had a massive task: each wall of the central open courtyard measured 715 feet in length.

Later work crews, dispatched by pharaohs who wanted to rid Karnak of the taint of the king who called himself Akhenaten, dismantled those same walls, so we cannot reconstruct the entire decorative program of the temple. We can, however, confidently assign the carved scenes of Amunhotep IV's jubilee celebration to the wall that stood behind the piers that supported the colossal statues. Outside of the central court-yard, the architecture of the complex is more difficult to trace. Both the Mansion of the Benben and another building called the Kiosk of Aten were said to be "within Gem-pa-Aten," making it a massive complex with multiple structures.

Substantial portions and smaller fragments of nearly sixty colossi, each originally about thirteen feet high, have been recorded during ar-chaeological work in the Gem-pa-Aten. All are of sandstone, probably from Gebel Silsila, like the *talatat*; like the wall reliefs, the statues were originally brightly painted. All were intentionally broken in antiquity, although not obliterated, even if some of the faces were disfigured; in some instances, the statues were broken at the knees and then their upper portions pushed over. While individual elements may differ, one colossus shall serve to introduce the group: a statue in the Egyptian Mu-seum, bearing the number JE 48529 (objects that entered the museum were recorded in large logbooks, the *Journal d'Entrée,* abbreviated as JE).

JE 48529 is a representation of Amunhotep IV wearing a kilt and a double crown. The crown sits atop a headdress called the *khat,* which resembles a cloth covering a wig that extends to the king's shoulders. The statue is broken at the knees, making its current height just over seven and a half feet. As the eye travels up from half-preserved knee-

Colossal statues of Amunhotep IV from the Gem-pa-Aten *(left, JE 48529; right, JE 55938).*

caps, the first feature that strikes the viewer is the width of the king's thighs and hips; the kilt is pleated, the widening of the pleats around the king's thighs and their narrowing near the knees further emphasizing the rounded silhouette of the king's lower body. The thick thighs and wide hips contrast strongly with the normally trim and muscled forms of other pharaohs. Like the statuary of Amunhotep III after his first jubilee, the front of Amunhotep IV's kilt has a decorated sporran, a term borrowed from the pouch that hangs from a Scottish kilt.

The sporrans of Amunhotep III and IV emphasize solar imagery, with disk-crowned uraeus serpents rearing up to either side. The thick waist and pronounced paunch of the final phase of Amunhotep III's art, including two statues that show the king with his belly resembling that of a pregnant woman, became, in the representations of his son, a narrow, high waist and a long, sagging belly. As in two-dimensional images of Amunhotep IV, the belt of the king's kilt slopes from back to front at an extreme angle, emphasizing the belly amply threatening to tumble over it. From the side, the belt appears between two protuberances: the king's abdomen above and his fleshy thighs below.

The cartouches of Amunhotep IV are written on his belt; seven raised plaques placed in the middle of the king's torso, on his clavicles, upper arms, and wrists are carved with the two cartouches of Aten. Like the king's unusual body, these raised rectangular shapes are unique to Amunhotep IV. Later statues of Akhenaten and Nefertiti have Aten's names carved onto the body rather than on raised surfaces; the bodies of nonroyal statues sometimes display a royal cartouche, often at the shoulder. One of the few times a name carved into skin reflected reality was the practice of branding foreign war captives with the name of the king who conquered them. The divine name of Aten on the king's body, particularly as an object rather than just an incision, recalls the use of written magical charms tied on the body, whereby a person might place themselves under the protection of a deity. The plaques may signify that the king is stamped with the name of his god, eternally guarded by Aten. By having the name of his solar father festooned over his body, the king presents himself to us literally clothed in the life-giving light of Aten.

On the colossus JE 48529, as on all the statues known from the Gem-pa-Aten, the king's arms are crossed at his chest. In his right hand he holds a flail, and in his left hand a crook, symbols of kingship. The crook can even be read as the hieroglyph that writes the noun "ruler" or the verb "to rule." Just as the royal crook would have been fashioned from gold and lapis lazuli, the king's flail was no simple whip but a gilded affair with semiprecious stones making up the thongs.

A long rectangular beard with a blunt end extends from the king's chin to the point where the crook and flail cross. The beard was not the king's facial hair but rather a part of his ceremonial attire that would be tied on, and royal statues occasionally show the straps that were used to attach the beard. Above Amunhotep IV's beard, we come at last to his face, the feature that has elicited the strongest reactions from modern viewers. Seen almost at eye level, the features of Amunhotep IV are exaggerated, especially in their narrowness: an attenuated face; long, thin nose; and a pinched mouth, the lower lip broader than the upper lip.

The best way to characterize the king's face is that the artist took two profiles but omitted a bit of the face in the middle when those halves were combined. Amunhotep IV's elongated, almond-shaped eyes—echoing the rather otherworldly appearance of the eyes of the baby-like visages of Amunhotep III after his first jubilee—slant down toward the nose; his eyelids are carved slightly lowered, giving his eyes a hooded appearance. The king's facial features would have appeared less extreme from the perspective of an ancient viewer standing at ground level. Even so, Akhenaten's body would have been shocking to a priest traveling the short distance from the Temple of Amun-Re to the Gem-pa-Aten. That same ancient priest would have understood, however, that artistic expression was a prerogative of kingship.

Aten had shed any vestige of human form, except for the hands at the ends of his rays, but even he had a sacred monument on earth: the Benben. The Gem-pa-Aten was located just east of the unique obelisk, which became the Great Benben for Amunhotep IV, a model of the first dry land to emerge from the primordial waters. In that creation myth we find not only the template for Amunhotep IV's constructions in the eastern part of Karnak but also clues to the changes he made to his royal images.

The Egyptians could describe creation through intellectual means—thought and speech—or physical actions, like the masturbation of a creator deity. In all ancient Egyptian creation accounts, the unifying theme is how order and multiplicity emerge from an undifferentiated oneness. The creator god contained within himself the possibility of all beings. In artistic representations the default image of a creator deity is an adult male, but other options did exist. The sun god Re can take the form of a scarab, literally the "transforming one," or a baby, reborn each day.

Amunhotep IV chose a different artistic path, emphasizing the androgyny of a creator god. Once Aten became a shining disk, gender was irrelevant, but the king by necessity retained his human form, and so in his art he reflected within himself both male and female elements. The first clue is the shape of the king's body: he adopts iconographic features that are more typical of women than men in Egyptian art. This is why in both two- and three-dimensional representations of Nefertiti those parts of her body are nearly identical to the king's own.

In reliefs, Nefertiti is normally shown with more prominent breasts, but Amunhotep IV's chest is still often closer in shape to Nefertiti's than to those of male kings. On the colossi that once lined the great open court of the Gem-pa-Aten, Amunhotep IV has a bare chest with nipples carved in relief, a bit more prominently than usual, but still as we would expect in a male statue. Yet the shape of his breasts is neither that of a male king nor that of a woman according to the traditional artistic styles of ancient Egypt. Again, Hatshepsut offers a useful parallel: Amunhotep IV's chest resembles the middle phase of Hatshepsut's art, when her body assumes a more androgynous form.

If we look further at Amunhotep IV's torso, we find another surprising choice: the king's navel has a fan shape. So much ancient Egyptian royal statuary survives that one can make comparisons of royal belly buttons over two thousand years and confidently state that Akhenaten was the only king to depart from the expected round or oval shape. The explanation for the odd navel can be found in the most unusual of the king's colossi from the Gem-pa-Aten, a statue without a kilt.

If JE 48529, the colossus of Amunhotep IV we have just examined, is an unusual royal image, then the other colossus displayed alongside it in the Egyptian Museum, officially JE 55938, is downright bizarre. The statues share the same elongated face, arms crossed at the torso, crook and flail, name plaques of Aten, and overall proportions. The most obvious difference is the lack of clothing: JE 55938 is apparently nude, the legs clearly carved up to the pubic area, but with no male genitalia visible.

Debate rages: is this really an image of Amunhotep IV? Should we not instead identify this as a statue of Nefertiti? Queens, including Nefertiti, did have monumental statuary, and from the waist down JE 55938 appears to be an image of a woman. In statuary of Nefertiti from Akhet-Aten, her finely pleated gown can hug her body's curves so closely that the sculptor even carved the queen's fan-shaped navel and the fold of her belly just above her pubic triangle. Were it not for the pleats of the fabric, one would think that Nefertiti was depicted nude in this statue. So, in isolation, the legs of JE 55938 could be reasonably interpreted as a clothed image of Nefertiti.

From the waist up, it is a different matter entirely: the bottom half of the statue would be an unparalleled representation of a male king, but the top half would be an equally unparalleled representation of a queen. Even Hatshepsut only wore the false beard or held the crook and flail when her body was represented as that of a man. If JE 55938 is Nefertiti, then she has masculine features, including a beard, attested nowhere else among images of her as queen.

Why would Amunhotep IV have instructed his sculptors to carve him, in at least this one case, unclothed and lacking genitalia? One proposed answer is that the statue originally was clothed, its kilt attached separately; however, statues of other kings made of multiple stone elements had a smooth slot for the kilt, not finished carving for the upper thighs. The androgynous appearance of the colossal image JE 55938 appears to be an intentional combination of masculine and feminine features in order to signal that Amunhotep IV embodies a creator god, specifically Re-Atum, who fashioned the twins Shu and Tefnut.

In other colossi from the Gem-pa-Aten, Amunhotep IV takes the form of Shu, the god of luminous space. Three statue heads of Amunhotep IV from the Gem-pa-Aten wear four ostrich feathers atop the striped *nemes*-headdress. A single ostrich feather is sufficient to write the name Shu, but the four feathers link the king to a specific aspect of Shu as Iny-heret, Greek "Onuris," a name that means "He who brings back she who is distant." This is Shu who retrieves Tefnut, one of the goddesses of the eye of the sun, from distant Nubia.

In the Gem-pa-Aten, Amunhotep IV embodied a god who is essential to the annual cycle of the return of the goddess. The king was simultaneously the creator god and his firstborn son. Nefertiti's name, "The Beautiful One Has Come," means that the goddess has returned to Egypt in the form of the queen. Playing the parts of gods, the royal couple ensured the continued existence of the world that they had created.

The androgynous, nude image of Amunhotep IV may identify the king with another aspect of the annual cycle so essential to life on the Nile: the inundation. Here, the fan-shaped navel is a prominent clue. Prior to the reign of Amunhotep IV, the fan-shaped navel appears almost exclusively in images of Hapi, the divine personification of the Nile flood. A male god, Hapi nonetheless has pendulous breasts, a rounded stomach, and a fan-shaped navel. Images of heavier-set individuals, including officials who chose to show their physical enjoyment of wealth in added weight at their midsection, have deeper, round navels. The fan shape signals something different, a claim to fertility: that same belly button shape can be the result of pregnancy and birth, as the skin is stretched and then does not fully regain its former elasticity. When Amunhotep IV commanded that some of the navels on his colossi be recarved, bringing them in line with the nude colossus, he emphasized his own life-giving role as king. After the move to Akhet-Aten, hymns in praise of the king describe him as Hapi who brings fertility to the Black Land.

Amunhotep IV, avatar of the creator god, with Nefertiti, the feminine principle of creation, were now ready for the next act of their drama: a new city, a new horizon.

III

AKHET-ATEN

THE FINAL HORIZON

15

"This Is It!"

REGNAL YEAR 5, FOURTH MONTH OF PERET, DAY 13
(FEBRUARY 22, 1347 BCE)

Akhenaten awakes suddenly, and for a moment he is not sure where he is. The space is dark, but canvas ripples above him, and he realizes that his left leg is draped over the side of a folding camp bed— gold and ivory embellished as befits the son of the sun. He lies still for a moment, reviewing the day's schedule, the very list that had lulled him to sleep last night.

The king lifts his head from the wooden headrest, throws back the blanket that kept him warm during the chill desert night, and bounds out of bed. Small puffs of the underlying desert sand and dust come up through the loosely woven floor mat as he walks to the entrance. Anxious to confirm that the morning glow is not yet visible, he throws back the tent flap and surveys the still darkened desert—no brightening of the land yet. He motions to a guard, and a hushed and brief discussion ensues about star positions and the constantly watched water clock. No one must be late for today's events.

A quick summons to his retainers in the neighboring tents produces a line of slightly sleepy men laden with palm rib trays bending beneath piles of bread and vegetables, baskets filled to the brim with vessels of beer and wine. Having washed his face and hands in a golden bowl with water poured from a matching golden ewer, Akhenaten snatches up a folding stool—an ivory-inlaid ebony masterpiece—so that he can enjoy the morning repast. Nefertiti, now awake as well, joins him beneath the conical roof of the large tent.

After breakfast, two royal attendants enter to dress the king and queen. Akhenaten stands as a pleated kilt of white linen is wrapped around his waist. Over the kilt, the male attendant fastens a jeweled belt from the back of which hangs a long, beaded bull's tail. Truly, the king is the victorious bull, beloved of Aten! A gold broad collar with alternating bands of lapis lazuli, turquoise, and carnelian beads is laid upon the king's chest. Carefully, the attendant affixes the crown: the curved and flaring sides of its brilliant blue surface adorned with dozens of small, gilded circles. A female attendant dresses Nefertiti in a diaphanous pleated gown, revealing the sinuous curves of the queen's body. The attendant places an elaborately bejeweled gold collar over the queen's chest and the cylindrical blue crown on her head.

Akhenaten and Nefertiti emerge from the tent, courtiers greeting them, attendants holding out cloaks to warm them against the early morning chill. Meritaten, attired in a smaller version of her mother's pleated dress, runs up to hug her parents. Armed men form a perimeter around the royal family. Unlike the courtiers, dressed uniformly in white, pleated linen garments, the soldiers' clothes are a riot of styles, reflecting their equally diverse origins.

A vast desert plain stretches beyond the encampment. In the morning twilight, the tall cliffs that ring the broad bay are but darker shapes set against the slowly brightening sky. The only noise that chilly morning is the snorting of the stallions harnessed to the royal chariots, their electrum-plated cabs flashing in the light of the campfires. The king mounts his chariot, taking the reins from the groom in one hand and lifting his whip in the other.

In that moment, as Akhenaten appears within the gleaming chariot, he is quite literally the son of the sun, the god on earth, most beloved of Aten. Just as Aten will soon rise in the horizon, so Akhenaten will ride out into the desert of that very horizon in his own solar vehicle. The stallions need little prompting before galloping off. The royal retinue makes its way to a great stretch of flat and undistinguished low desert ground that is about to be declared the holiest place in Egypt.

Akhenaten points his chariot toward a mud-brick platform that has been carefully prepared for the day's ceremonies. He dismounts and stands in the rapidly brightening darkness, facing east, bringing his fringed cloak close around him to ward off the cool northern breeze. He fixes his gaze at the single spot to the east, the wadi that will one day be his final resting place. Today, the king will lay out his vision for the earthly demesne of his god.

First, Akhenaten needs to complete the proper rites. On the platform is arrayed a massive feast for Aten: loaves of bread stacked next to jars full of beer and wine; slaughtered oxen, their choice cuts—head and hind legs—set neatly aside; plucked geese and ducks, laid out upon row after row of fruit; and around all this, fresh green plants. Among this great pile of food are large cones of myrrh and frankincense, smoldering within small metal cups. Akhenaten lifts a bronze vessel, its body shaped like the hieroglyph for life, the king's names delicately etched into the metal, and pours out its contents, inundating the cuts of meat and fresh vegetables with the cool water of the Nile.

At that moment, the first rays burst forth from that cleft in the eastern mountains. "Behold Aten!" exclaims the king. "Behold Aten!" chant Nefertiti and Meritaten in unison, as the burning, life-giving orb bathes the royal family in his holy radiance. The king lifts his arms heavenward and swears an oath:

> It is in this very place that I shall make Horizon of Aten for Aten, my father! I shall not make Horizon of Aten for him south of it, north of it, west of it, or east of it. I shall not go beyond the southern stela of Horizon of Aten toward the south, nor shall I go beyond the northern stela of Horizon of Aten toward the north, to make Horizon of Aten for him there. Nor shall I make it for him on the western side of Horizon of Aten. It is on the eastern side of Horizon of Aten that I shall make Horizon of Aten for Aten, my father—the place he made—that it might be encompassed for him by the mountain itself. Just as he shall attain happiness in it, so shall I offer to him in it. This is it![1]

Three thousand, three hundred and seventy years is a remarkably long time for knowledge of the events of a single day to survive. On the day in question, February 22, 1347 BCE (give or take a week or two), there were only a few places in the world where such knowledge even had a chance of surviving. Of course, Egypt had hieroglyphs—the "word of god" as the Egyptians termed it. The ancient Near East employed the cuneiform script, first developed for Sumerian in the southern portion of Mesopotamia (roughly the modern countries between the eastern Mediterranean coast and the Tigris River), then adapted for Akkadian and later for Hittite (and other languages). Early Greek was written in the syllabic Linear B script of the Mycenaean world, while in Shang Dynasty China, written characters were in use as aspects of divinatory practices. As far as we know, no other culture possessed a writing system at this time.

Trained in a temple school, the House of Life, a scribe became a rare person within the ancient world: one who was fully literate. The ability to read and write might catapult anyone into the upper echelons of a bureaucratic society, into the class of officials and artisans; most priestly offices similarly required literacy. Students were trained initially in the cursive system, hieratic, the script particularly well adapted to rapid writing with an ink-dipped reed on papyrus, the script anyone would need to know, if to do nothing but sign their name.

When we imagine Akhenaten and Nefertiti's daily routine as sovereigns, we need to insert at least a few royal scribes seated on the floor, pens tucked behind their ears, palettes of pigment cakes and jars of water slung over their shoulders, fresh papyrus scrolls at the ready, starched kilts stretched tight over their crossed legs to form portable writing surfaces. The resulting diaries of royal activity have not survived, and only the tiniest fraction of ancient papyri have escaped unscathed through the millennia (those that made their ways into tombs had the greatest chance of survival). In one spectacular case, however, excerpts from a daily royal log were "published": Thutmose III, Akhenaten's great-great-grandfather, commemorated his military victories in ancient Syria by having some of his military journals carved in hieroglyphs on the walls of Karnak Temple.

On that February day when Akhenaten founded his new city, scribes would have taken notes on the events and pronouncements, later to be copied afresh onto a papyrus scroll. That papyrus and the numerous duplicates that may have been made to be distributed to various libraries and offices have not survived. We know the words that Akhenaten spoke—at least as he wanted them known—the people who accompanied him, even some specifics of the royal tent and chariot, because the king chose to record them on massive stone stelae, some as tall as twenty-five feet. The earliest stelae were dated to the day on which the events above (and speeches to come) occurred: Regnal Year 5, fourth month of Peret (Growing Season), day 13.

The other details that we have used to reconstruct that day are all illustrated in once vibrantly painted reliefs in the tombs of the royal couple's courtiers. Combined with the setting of Akhet-Aten itself, this unique conjunction of ancient evidence allows our reconstructions of Akhenaten's and Nefertiti's lives to become suddenly richer.

And so we begin with the first day that Akhenaten and Nefertiti spent at what would become their new residence, as described in hieroglyphic texts on the stelae carved into the cliffs at the corners of Akhenaten's new city. Those are the stelae mentioned in Akhenaten's oath. At the very beginning of the hieroglyphic inscriptions we read the first momentous change that the king made upon coming to this site: he was no longer Amunhotep, the name he received from his parents at birth, but Akhenaten. With his new city, the king fulfilled the promise of his new name, to be truly effective for Aten.

After making that enormous offering to Aten, Akhenaten commanded that his court be assembled: the king's attendants, the great ones of the palace, the army commanders, the overseers of works, the officials, indeed, the court in its entirety. Ushered into the royal presence and under the gaze of their zealous and renamed pharaoh, they lay upon the ground, "kissing the earth" before his majesty. Akhenaten then addressed his prostrated courtiers, and the hieroglyphic texts of the boundary stelae seem to record the actual words that the king spoke that day.

During the Eighteenth Dynasty, official royal proclamations carved into stone did not employ the grammar and vocabulary of spoken Egyptian. Rather, they were composed in what we call Middle Egyptian, which was written and spoken in the few centuries following 2000 BCE, at least in more educated circles. Boundaries between such stages of an ancient language are of necessity fuzzy, especially since the Egyptian writing system did not express the vowels that would have marked many of the changes from one stage to another. Middle Egyptian was the language of the classics of Egyptian literature, and it retained cachet as a formal means of speech for Eighteenth Dynasty kings and other pharaohs who would rule for the next thousand years and more.

Akhenaten made a radically different choice. The grammar of the boundary stelae is distinctly closer to the spoken language of his day, which we call Late Egyptian, than to Middle Egyptian. To his assembled officials who are stretched out, facedown on the ground, Akhenaten said,

> *Behold Aten! Aten desires to make [it] for himself as a monument in an eternal and everlasting name. Now it is Aten, my father, who advised me about it: Horizon of Aten.*[2]

In the vastness of the desert plain, Akhenaten had proclaimed a *place*. By bestowing a name upon it, nowhere became somewhere: Akhet-Aten, Horizon of Aten.

In his speech, Akhenaten was quick to give sole credit to his divine father for the entire project of Akhet-Aten (the grammar employs clearly Late Egyptian forms—and a bit of the king's personality shines through after three millennia):

> *No official advised me about it nor did any other person in the entire land advise me about it, telling me [a plan] for making Akhet-Aten in this place except for Aten, my father.*[3]

Repetitive passages within the boundary stelae relate to the wording of legal documents—the king professes a list of things he will not do, thereby binding himself legally to the plan. It is amusing to imagine the potential arguments that could have erupted between the king and queen when Akhenaten spoke the following:

> *The Great Royal Wife (Nefertiti) will not say to me: "Look, there is a good place for Akhet-Aten in another place"—I will not listen to her! No official in my presence, whether a favored official or a more distant official or a chamberlain or any person who is in this entire land, will say to me: "Look, there is a good place for Akhet-Aten in another place"—I will not listen to them (whether it be downstream, whether it be to the south, whether it be to the west, or whether it be to the region of the rising sun)!*[4]

AMARNA, EGYPT

Before beginning our summer field season, we take a few days to visit the place that fulfilled Aten's—and thereby Akhenaten's—vision of heaven on earth. We have driven nearly 220 miles north from Luxor, ancient Waset, on a desert highway to see the place that Aten chose. As we come out of the desert, the Nile and its lush vegetation are visible directly in front of us. At the north side of the road, we see a massive cemetery—row after row of modern graves, continuing a five-millennia-old tradition of using this desert for burials.

At the very spot at which the tan desert becomes green cultivation—the same stark line between ancient Egyptian *desheret,* the Red Land, and *kemet,* the Black Land—we turn left. Five miles to the south we reach our destination, known inaccurately but ubiquitously as Tell el-Amarna. Many villages in Egypt, indeed in the entire Near East, are prefixed with *tell,* Arabic for "mound," elevated areas that are formed by the accumulated remains of human habitation that over centuries have elevated the site above surrounding fields and plains. In the case of Tell el-Amarna, the name is a misnomer, a nineteenth-century confusion between the common use of Arabic *tell* and the name of a nearby village called el-Till. The village of el-Amarna is one of several that surround ancient Akhet-Aten, and that name, often shortened just to Amarna, provides one of the most frequent designations for Akhenaten's reign.

Looking east, across the remains of the Mansion of Aten.
The altar where one of the authors stands is coordinates 27°38'43.58" N, 30°53'44.30" E.

In 1932, British archaeologists employed aerial photography to get a bird's-eye view of the city they were excavating. Now, using Google Earth, we can explore the remains of Akhet-Aten, if somewhat fuzzily, from the comfort of our homes. If you enter the coordinates 27°38'43.58" N, 30°53'44.30" E, Google Earth will fly you across the globe and land you as close as one may estimate to the exact location where Akhenaten stood on that February day in 1347 BCE. The thin lines that enclose that spot are the walls of the first court of the smaller of Akhet-Aten's two temples, the Mansion of Aten.

Zoom out a bit and you can see the almost seven-mile-wide bay of cliffs that encloses the desert and a thin strip of cultivation next to the Nile. A little over two and a half miles to the east of the spot where Akhenaten stood, along the axis of the mud-brick altar that was later incorporated into the first court of the temple Mansion of Aten, is a break in the cliffs, the entrance to a wadi. When the sun rose on that momentous morning, Akhenaten exclaimed, "Behold Aten," as the disk appeared to rise from that gap in the cliffs, or at the least from very nearby.

For Akhenaten, as for any literate Egyptian, two eminences flanking a depression from which the sun rises represented more than an aesthetically balanced vista; it was a hieroglyph. Phonetically, this hieroglyph writes the word *akhet,* designating a place of brilliance and light, a space

Hieroglyphs writing Akhet-Aten.

between heaven and earth, which we translate as "horizon." Standing where Akhenaten stood, the sun rising from a gap in the cliffs to the east formed a hieroglyph in three dimensions.

What would Akhenaten have seen when he stood at the point we now call part of Amarna? Aside from the desert and the cliffs, the short answer is nothing at all. As Akhenaten elaborated, "Behold, it is the Pharaoh, may he live, prosper and be healthy, that found it, not belonging to a god; nor to a goddess; nor to a male ruler; nor to a female ruler; nor belonging to any person so that they might do something with it."[5]

In the popular conception of pharaoh as autocrat, Akhenaten's statements might seem exaggerated or even unnecessary. Could the pharaoh not simply seize any territory he desired for his royal purposes? Perhaps in some circumstances, but the ancient Egyptians, pharaohs included, took pains to adhere to the rule of law, or at least to seem as if they did. When Akhenaten claimed that the land did not belong to any other divine, royal, or private entity, he was also emphasizing his legal rights. Modern archaeological work has not discovered evidence of any considerable earlier settlement at the site, confirming Akhenaten's contention.

So begins our own tour of what remains of the city of Akhenaten and Nefertiti. We drive past modern settlements and cemeteries and then turn onto a dirt road that takes us east toward the cliffs. To the north and the south stretches a cratered landscape, its terrain masked by the monotony of the rock and sand of the desert surface. As we approach the bluff, on average rising about three hundred feet from the desert plain, we see a sharply rectangular shape carved into the rough limestone. A sandy slope becomes tan cliffs, stark against the brilliant blue sky. Weeks can pass in Egypt with barely a cloud being visible, and February 22, 1347 BCE, was likely a cloudless day.

We reach the base of a staircase, its steps blending in with the surrounding sand, a necessary addition to the ancient landscape to accommodate modern visitors. As we climb the stairs, we begin to see the sunken relief carvings on the rectangular surface of the stela. Closer still, we can make out the statues of Akhenaten and Nefertiti that emerge to either side of the stela's base. The steps stop about ten feet below the bottom of the stela, and we crane our necks to see the top of the monument, twenty-five feet above its base.

Horizon of Aten

Mahu, THE CHIEF OF POLICE OF AKHET-ATEN, HAS BEEN UP SINCE
well before dawn, preparing for one of his most important tasks: escort-
ing the royal family on their chariot ride into the city. The road requires
daily inspection; the chief scours the reports gathered from the watch-
men who surveil the desert plain and dispatches scouts to investigate
any suspicious activity.

An urgent message arrived late last night, requiring Mahu's presence at the far northern edge of Akhet-Aten. Mahu had driven his
chariot horses at a gallop, speeding along the city's main thoroughfare.
Dismounting near the palace where the royal family spend their nights,
he heads eastward on foot up the cliffs. His destination is a small light
about four hundred cubits above him. He soon reaches a metal brazier
full of coals, which give off a pleasant warmth in the chill night. Six of
Mahu's policemen, their simple kilts signaling their lower rank, greet
their commander, bending slightly at the waist and touching the left
shoulder with the right fist.

Two of the patrolmen explain that they caught a group of men
climbing the cliffs near the northern palace. A series of niches have
recently been cut into the cliff in the area—Mahu is uncertain of why,
although he favors the notion that Akhenaten intends to insert faience

plaques, so the substance called "scintillating" would indeed scintillate in the setting sun as the royal family drives north at the end of the day. One of the patrolmen suggests that perhaps the intruders were looking for treasure near the niches.

The following day, after a hectic morning, Mahu arrives at the vizier's office and greets him formally: "As Aten endures, so endures the ruler!"[1] The vizier nods in assent, and Mahu gestures toward three manacled men standing behind him. Two bow obsequiously, but the third man still stands upright—Mahu has a feeling the baton in his colleague's hand will soon rectify that stubbornness.

Mahu explains the gravity of the situation: Yesterday morning his scouts had apprehended the three men ascending the cliffs opposite the northern riverside palace. Concluding his report, Mahu makes a straightforward and formal request: "Investigate, o officials, the people who climb the mountain!"[2]

Heading due east from the vizier's office, Mahu makes his way to his headquarters in the police barracks. He pulls a well-worn papyrus scroll off a shelf, not even needing to consult the small tag that labels its contents. Settling into his favorite chair, he unrolls the papyrus, a schematic plan of Akhet-Aten. The great bay of cliffs are painted a reddish brown, with small round-topped rectangles, painted white, marking each of the boundary stelae. The desert surface is a mottled pink color, while the palaces, temples, and residential districts are set off in white, small hieratic labels giving their names. A straight line, edged in black and painted light brown, represents the impressive north-south highway that connects the palaces, temples, and main portions of the city.

Mahu consults this map daily, his scribal assistants keeping a separate log for commissariat reports, lists of criminal activity, and notes about personnel. Within the rapidly expanding city and on its bustling streets, there are always thefts from royal storehouses or violent crimes to be investigated. Mahu instructs his secretary to send in the officers to report on their assigned sectors. First, Mahu summarizes the events of the previous night and orders that an extra platoon be dispatched to increase patrols in the cliffs east of the riverside palace. Apy, a royal scribe and steward who often assists Mahu, suggests that another platoon also be sent even further north, to the point where nearly sheer cliffs rise from the riverbank. Here, an administrative building lies terraced along the small access point between the Nile and the desert.

Mahu agrees, and then traces his finger down the papyrus map to the North Suburb, a residential district, where many high-ranking officials have constructed their villas. One of these grandees, the Overseer of Royal Works Hatiay, came in earlier that day to report a theft. Hatiay was distraught—a well-hidden clay jar containing no less than thirty-seven *deben* of gold and twelve *deben* of silver was gone! A tragedy!

Mahu turns to the officer in charge of that suburb, who claims to have seen nothing suspicious; no, he has not received any reports of other thefts in the area. Mahu hopes Hatiay's misfortune is not the start of a trend—a thief targeting the villas of the wealthy would be a headache for the police chief.

The Central City is next on Mahu's list, a little over an *iteru* south of the North Suburb. The abundance of large squares on Mahu's map marks this as the true heart of Akhet-Aten, the location of its main temples and palaces. Units of police continually patrol the four most important buildings in this area, including the two main Aten temples and the largest palaces. Occasionally Mahu accompanies these patrols, and he is always awed by the bridge that spans the large road, its massive mud-brick piers supporting a passageway that allows the king and his retinue to travel between the two palaces without leaving their protected confines. That certainly makes Mahu's job easier!

The police in charge of patrolling and maintaining order in the three residential areas south of the Central City always have much to report. Along the riverfront next to the houses are large buildings that serve as storerooms, administrative centers, and manufacturing sites, whose material stockpiles occasionally attract thieves. Among the local residents, disputes sometimes arise over property lines, or an apprentice alleges abusive treatment by a master artisan. Occasionally an enterprising official moves a stone that marks the planned extent of his villa compound under construction. Will anyone even notice? Mahu is relieved that today nothing requires his specific attention.

Next, the police chief calls for reports from outlying regions. Any unusual activity around the Sunshade of Re, the Maru-Aten? Mahu's deputy answers in the negative and then asks his superior if he might

Akhet-Aten Chief of Police Mahu presenting captured men to the vizier and other high officials. (Drawing from the tomb of Mahu, after N. de G. Davies, The Rock Tombs of El Amarna, *vol. 4,* The Tombs of Penthu, Mahu, and Others *[London: Egypt Exploration Fund, 1906], plate 26)*

continue to participate in patrols in that area, just in case. The deputy admits that when he checks the storerooms inside the temple, he enjoys walking through the cool gardens and admiring the painted plaster floors surrounding picturesque pools. Mahu chuckles and says that he can have south sector duty through the end of the year.

The last reports of the day come from the police whose roving patrols protect the tombs in the eastern cliffs. The greatest concentrations of patrolmen are stationed at the royal tomb, deep in the wadi opposite the Mansion of Aten. Tracks cleared of rocks allow the men, often accompanied by hunting dogs, to monitor both the north and south cluster of tombs of Akhet-Aten's highest officials. Since few of the tombs are yet completed, there is little to fear from robbers, so these patrols also check in on the royal workmen who live in their own settlement east of the main city.

As Mahu steps outside for a moment, he sees how the shadows have lengthened. Time to return home, get some rest, and prepare for another busy day ensuring his sovereign's safety and the smooth functioning of the city of the sun.

There are two Akhet-Atens: the city that a man like Mahu helped to protect, a city of approximately thirty thousand inhabitants that needed

food, water, and shelter; and the city of Aten's command and Akhenaten's vision, a city of rituals and offerings, a holy place. For twelve
years, these two cities shared the same desert plain. As the royal family
transformed their daily life into a series of sacred activities, the rest of
the population hauled water, harvested crops, slaughtered cattle, quarried stones, carved monuments, smelted glass, patrolled roads, and performed hundreds of other tasks that made Akhet-Aten hum.

Akhet-Aten's human and physical infrastructures were still in their
infancy when Akhenaten celebrated the one-year anniversary of the
city's founding. Akhenaten had initially commanded the carving of the
first two boundary stelae to set the city's northern and southern limits,
and for the anniversary he commissioned a dozen more rock-cut monuments (given letter designations at the end of the nineteenth century).
Three of the new stelae were carved on the west bank of the river,
meaning that Akhet-Aten now officially straddled the Nile and included
within its boundaries a wide swath of cultivable land. The cliff-edged
bay that surrounds the city on the east is nearly devoid of arable land.

As we stand in the middle of the desert before Stela U, the most impressive of the surviving rock-cut boundary-marking monuments, we
can make out the date of the anniversary: Regnal Year 6, fourth month
of Peret, day 13. A relief at the top of the stela shows the royal family presenting offerings before the shining Aten disk, and they appear
in three dimensions as statues flanking the hieroglyphic monument:
Akhenaten, Nefertiti, Meritaten, and Princess Meketaten (born in the
first year of Akhet-Aten's existence).

As the stelae recount, on the anniversary day the king awakened
in a tent and set forth in his chariot to the southeastern corner of the
city limits. There, as Aten's rays spread life and dominion, rejuvenating
Akhenaten's body, the king swore an oath to his god. He reaffirmed the
geographical boundaries of Akhet-Aten, and grammatical details signal
that we are again reading the king's actual words:

> As for the southern stela that is on the eastern mountain of Akhet-Aten,
> it indeed is the stela of Akhet-Aten. This is the one at the place where I
> shall stop. I shall not go past it forever and ever. Carve the southwestern
> stela opposite it on the western side of Akhet-Aten, exactly![3]

Akhenaten obsessively repeated this same formula for the other stelae, giving measurements, down to the cubit (20.5 inches, the same
length as the ubiquitous *talatat* blocks), of the distance between them.
Akhenaten concluded his oath to Aten on the Year 6 stelae thus:

> *As for what is inside the four stelae, beginning with the eastern mountain*
> *of Akhet-Aten and ending with the western mountain of Akhet-Aten—*
> *this is Akhet-Aten in its entirety! It belongs to my father Re-Horakhty*
> *who rejoices in the horizon in his name of light who is in the sun disk,*
> *given life forever and ever!*[4]

The king then listed the city's geographical features, from its hills
and mountains to its fields and marshes to its people, cattle, and trees.
All of this belonged to Aten, which was appropriate, since he was the
one who gives life to all creation. Akhenaten swore never to neglect the
oath, and just as a seal might be affixed to a royal document, the stelae
sealed Akhenaten's words on the sacred landscape.

The final lines of the stelae betray the typical Egyptian obsession
with permanence. "It (the stela) will not be destroyed; it will not be
washed away; it will not be plastered over! It will not disappear! But if it
fades away or if the stela on which it is (carved) falls down, then I shall
renew it!"[5] The Egyptians planned and built for eternity.

More than a century's worth of archaeological work at the site of
Akhet-Aten has confirmed that Akhenaten upheld his oath, construct-
ing no buildings beyond the territory marked by the boundary stelae.
In the initial proclamation on the two stelae dated to Regnal Year 5,
Akhenaten listed the names of the temples and other structures that
he would later build, repeating each time that these foundations are in
Akhet-Aten:

> *I shall make the Estate of Aten for Aten, my father, in Akhet-Aten, in*
> *this (very) place. I shall make the Mansion of Aten for Aten, my father,*
> *in Akhet-Aten, in this (very) place. I shall make the Sunshade of Re for*
> *the [great] royal wife [Neferneferuaten Nefertiti] for Aten, my father, in*
> *Akhet-Aten, in this (very) place.*[6]

These are the city's three main temples. While each had a unique architectural form, they were all entirely open to the sky, bathed in sunlight. There were no cult statues. Instead, Akhenaten and Nefertiti were Aten's images on earth, living embodiments of the solar disk.

The Estate of Aten and Mansion of Aten are situated close to one another in the Central City (a modern designation of the urban landscape), about a half mile east of the Nile and due west of the wadi that led to the royal tomb. The Estate of Aten is a massive complex, its exterior mud-brick wall bounding a rectangular area 328 yards by 875 yards. Within the enclosure are the remains of two stone temples and thousands of mud-brick offering platforms, which have survived only to the level of their foundations. Images of the Estate of Aten carved on the walls of the tombs of two high priests enable us to reconstruct the temple's architecture and many activities that occurred inside of it.

The site of what would become the smaller of the two temples, the Mansion of Aten, began as the location of the altar upon which Akhenaten offered on the founding day of the city. The temple's name is stamped on bricks within its now crumbled walls. The third temple, the Sunshade of Re for Queen Nefertiti, is located about two and a half miles south of the Central City. Nefertiti's Sunshade, like those built for other royal women at Akhet-Aten, is a solar temple filled with lakes and gardens. Stone fragments with the name of the temple enable its identification, and the king's great wife is the most prominent person depicted on the sadly sparse remains.

On the boundary stelae, the king provided further details of his vision for the city:

> I shall make a House of Rejoicing for Aten, my father, in the "island" of Aten, distinguished of jubilees, in Akhet-Aten in this (very) place. I shall make all taxes that are [in the entire land] be at the disposal of the Aten, my father in Akhet-Aten, in this (very) place. I shall make overflowing offerings for the Aten, my father, in Akhet-Aten, in this (very) place. I shall make for myself the apartments of Pharaoh, may he live, prosper, and be healthy; and I shall make the apartments of the king's great wife in Akhet-Aten in this (very) place.[7]

While we know the precise location of the temples of Aten, the identity of the building, or ensemble of structures, named the "House of Rejoicing" remains uncertain. Yet the name Akhenaten chose for this structure tells us something important: he was drawing a direct connection between his new city at Akhet-Aten and his father's jubilee city at Malqata, whose main palace area was also called the "House of Rejoicing." In the boundary stelae, the location of the "island of the Aten, called 'distinguished of jubilees'" is equally difficult to pinpoint. But the close association between the House of Rejoicing and jubilees again recalls Amunhotep III's jubilee city.

The "island of Aten" probably did not refer to an actual island within the Nile River. With the exception of the island of Elephantine, a rocky outcrop far to the south at modern-day Aswan, no islands in Upper Egypt seem to have allowed for year-round settlement. The "island" in the boundary stela was probably a district of the city, a poetic reference to the isolation of the buildings within the vast bay in the desert. If so, then we should seek the "House of Rejoicing" in the Central City, Akhet-Aten's downtown.

Between the Estate of Aten and the Mansion of Aten is a small palace that is given the modern designation "King's House." Across from the two temples and the King's House is a massive palace, known as the Great Palace in modern descriptions, with large courtyards, extensive stone elements, and elaborately painted plaster floors. These buildings were probably part of the "island of Aten," and the House of Rejoicing may be the ancient name for the Great Palace.

The king then addressed something without which no city could survive: income. As Akhenaten had already done for Aten at Waset, the king funneled the tax revenue of Egypt to his preferred deity, who was rapidly becoming unique, peerless, and omnipotent. The king promised that offerings will literally overflow, just like the flooding Nile.

Most likely, the "apartments of Pharaoh" that Akhenaten names in the stelae are not in the Central City but further north, and they are probably identical with a complex now called the North Riverside Palace. This palace is near the northern corner of the great bay of cliffs that enclose Akhet-Aten, a site both remote (two miles from the Central City) and

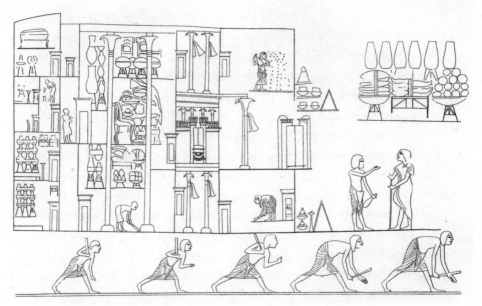

The palace where Akhenaten and Nefertiti spent their evenings, likely the North Riverside Palace. (Drawing of a relief in the tomb of the high priest Meryre, after N. de G. Davies, The Rock Tombs of El Amarna, *vol. 1,* The Tomb of Meryra *[London: Egypt Exploration Fund, 1903], plate 18)*

easily controlled, being overlooked by the steep cliffs to the west and north and having direct access to the river.

The residential portion of the North Riverside Palace has never been excavated, since modern cultivation covered it when British archaeologists began working at the site in the early 1930s. Excavations of surviving portions of outer areas of the palace revealed a massive double mud-brick wall, a portion of which still stands, and structures located just within the fortification wall, likely for guards and support staff. The location and architecture of the North Riverside Palace made it perhaps the most defensible structure in Akhet-Aten and the best candidate for the "apartments" of the king and queen.

Carved images of a palace in the tombs of Akhet-Aten's elite give us clues about the now-vanished structure. These reliefs show the ground plan of a palace, combined with doorways, columns, and furniture seen in elevation. This is not an architect's plan but rather a schematic rendering of the royal residence, an elaborately detailed hieroglyph for "palace." In the rear of a two-story structure we see the royal bedroom, its bed freshly made. The roofline of the bedroom slopes up to the right, which indicates an angled opening in the ceiling, known by its modern Arabic name *malqaf*. Such ventilation systems, oriented to the north, caught the prevailing wind and brought fresh air into mud-brick rooms with few windows. Perhaps these reliefs reflect the reality of Akhenaten and Nefertiti sleeping in the same bed, cooled on warm nights by the "sweet wind of the north," as the Egyptians called it.

The tomb reliefs depicting the palace frequently show the prosaic tasks needed to maintain the royal residence. An attendant sweeps the floor, another servant sprinkles water to keep down dust, storerooms are filled with amphorae and food, and a feast is set before two thrones. The door to the palace is closed, as are the doors on the balcony of the window where the sovereigns could appear to their subjects. A soldier and an official, their identities indicated by their clothes, converse before the palace gates.

A half mile south of the North Riverside Palace is the fourth major palace complex of Akhet-Aten, the so-called North Palace. It has a rectangular footprint, with a diversity of spaces inside, including a solar altar, a throne room, a large garden, animal pens, and brightly painted rooms. Inscriptions from the palace suggest that it belonged to Princess Meritaten, but we do not know if it was her primary residence. As a young child she may well have spent her nights behind the fortified walls of the North Riverside Palace, but the North Palace would have been available for ceremonial purposes. As Meritaten grew older, she may have overseen her own court at the North Palace.

The boundary stelae present Akhenaten's ideal vision for his city, and the text concludes with Akhenaten's provisions for his own tomb, those of Nefertiti and Meritaten, as well as the burials of the priests of Aten. The villas of officials, the houses of workmen and peasants, the vast workshops, dockyards, bakeries, police barracks—all these go unmentioned, because their existence would have been taken for granted in any Egyptian city. Neither did Akhenaten refer to one feature of his city that was essential to both its practical functioning as well as its religious symbolism: a great north-south road that connected the palaces and temples of Akhet-Aten.

Now called the Royal Road, it is a nearly straight line through the landscape, beginning with the North Riverside Palace and ending with the Sunshade of Re for Nefertiti. This was the axis on which the city was initially constructed, and only later was the southern part of the road moved west, more closely paralleling the course of the Nile. The Royal Road counts as one of the city's monuments in its own right: the smoothed surface of the ancient highway exceeds one hundred feet in width along some stretches and runs for over five miles. It was a place for royal pageantry, part thoroughfare and part promenading route, an element of Akhet-Aten's urban landscape akin to Fifth Avenue in New York City, the Champs-Élysées in Paris, and Unter den Linden in Berlin.

The Nile is Egypt's most obvious mode of transportation and conduit for trade. The river still connects most towns and cities in the Nile Valley, from Aswan to the Mediterranean coast of the Delta. Prior to the widespread construction of railroads in the nineteenth century of our era, boats could move the greatest amount of material using the fewest resources. In antiquity, massive, specially built ships were the only way to transport monumental statues and monolithic obelisks over long distances. Large institutions, like temples and palaces, had quays that enabled cargo to be unloaded from riverine vessels directly into storerooms.

Roads in the low desert, beyond the edge of the cultivated fields, whose trajectory paralleled the river, proved especially useful when the Nile was at its lowest point or during the heights of the inundation. At those two times, much river traffic was constricted; during the low Nile, large vessels could run aground, but during the high Nile, they were exposed to the risk of sandbars hidden by the floodwaters. The most significant land-based roads in ancient Egypt were desert highways. These required no engineering like ancient Roman roads in more temperate regions but were well-worn paths in the already solid and rocky desert surface, grooves formed by the millennial tramping of human feet and donkey hooves kicking aside stones and compacting the ground. Stone cairns marked the roads where geographic features might be few or none; police patrolled the heavily trafficked areas; and administrators maintained food and water depots, all of which allowed caravans of humans and donkeys to traverse hundreds of miles safely and efficiently.

The desert east of Akhet-Aten was crisscrossed by much smaller tracks, used by the workmen who constructed the tomb of the king and the tombs of the city's elite in the eastern cliffs. Police units used additional patrol tracks around the tombs and high on the cliffs to guard the tombs and to provide roving security for the large desert east of the city. Without spirited stallions pulling a gilded chariot, our own, modern progress along the Royal Road on foot seems prosaic, if perhaps somewhat safer. What was once the center of Akhet-Aten is now only the stumps of mud-brick walls, but the desert cliffs to the east remain unchanged.

Chariot of Solar Fire

AKHENATEN CLAPS HIS HANDS AND CALLS OUT TO HURRY HIS daughters along. Nefertiti is thinking about the roasted duck with honey glaze that awaits them. Tiye has joined the couple today, standing close by her son. While morning and evening meals might be rather informal and even quite light, Akhenaten insists that the midday meal for the vicars of Aten and their offspring should mirror Aten's own daily repast, and the tables are set accordingly.

Tall stands holding the ubiquitous, blue-painted wine jars are arranged next to two altar-like tables piled with food. On each are first arranged rows of breads, some stuffed with dates, topped by pomegranates, melons, cucumbers, all manner of vegetables, with platters of dates and bundles of onions near the top. Draped over all is a large bouquet of lotuses, just like those standing next to each altar of food in the great temple of Aten.

Usually Nefertiti sits opposite her husband, the pair together forming the edges of the world above which the solar disk shines. Today, Akhenaten and Nefertiti have devised a new mealtime tableau. At a signal from Akhenaten, his wife walks over to Tiye and leads her not to the place beside her son but to the chair opposite him. Today, the mother replaces the daughter-in-law. Tiye remarks on this new arrangement,

"Why would you do this? You are Tefnut, and my son is Shu; you are the divine pair, the children of Aten. I am certainly not that." Nefertiti smiles as two of her daughters run in, holding a tall golden crown, a solar disk between thin bovine horns, with two tall ostrich feathers rising up between them.

"Now what is this? What are we meant to be?" Tiye asks. "Well, as you two sit opposite one another, eating out in the open, you form the horizon, the two hills between which the solar disk rises. Now I correspond to Nefertiti, and a goddess." She pauses, and in concentrating takes on that pouting look that Amunhotep III loved so well, and that so many who did not know her had confused with a slightly hard disposition.

Tiye then laughs. Addressing her son, she reminds him, "You know how, in the first jubilee, I was the goddess Hathor herself." Akhenaten nods. "You are doing the same, but here you have two generations. I am Hathor the mother, the womb who births Re each day, and Nefertiti is Hathor as the daughter. We together become the perpetual motion of the sun." Akhenaten nods again, as his mother says, "It is a marvelous royal spectacle. Both your fathers would approve."

Their lavish repast consumed, the departure for the North Riverside Palace is at hand, their chariots waiting. The bright daylight is dazzling, but quickly dimmed by the dust rising from the soldiers who run to their appointed places. Egyptians with short, black wigs and white kilts reaching to their knees sling shields over their backs. Armed in one hand with a spear that rests against his shoulder, each carries an axe in the other hand, cutting edge pointed toward the back, as appropriate for a royal bodyguard. Long-bearded men from the lands to the northeast wear brightly patterned wool kilts with tasseled fringes and clutch short, curved swords. The men who hold bows offer a study in contrasts: Nubians in brightly dyed leather belts with long front aprons, and amply tattooed Libyans with long leather cloaks tied over one shoulder. This is an international guard for the ruler of rulers.

Grooms assist the family into their chariots; one vehicle for each, including the princesses. At a signal from the king, the trumpeter sounds a series of notes, and away they all rush to the north, along the great Royal Road. Ostrich plumes dance atop the horses' heads as they strain against the bit, and the red streamers attached to the king's blue crown flutter in the wind. The royal family's bodyguard runs beside the chariots, their upper bodies bowed, some still adjusting to the new, deferential pose.

After a while, the entourage reaches the North Palace. The signaler raises his trumpet—he is a bit winded. Finally, at the signal, the ranks re-form, the family dismounts, and Meritaten leads them into her palace.

In the red glow of the late afternoon sun, Nefertiti asks Meritaten to show them her favorite decorated room in the palace. Passing through the entrance gate and the inner gate, walking around the pool in the second court, Meritaten leads them to the far northeast corner of the enclosure, a rectangular interior garden surrounded by a series of rooms. Meritaten shows them what she calls the Green Room. "I know this is not an otherwise distinguished chamber, but it is my favorite."

Nefertiti admires the frescoes of birds in a lush marsh landscape: plants swaying in the breeze, others bending beneath the weight of pigeons and shrikes, while a kingfisher dives into the water. The effect of the paintings is fine, and the small size of the room, the green color dominating all, truly gives the feel of camping in the marshes, as one would have done in the old days, awaiting the return of the goddess of the eye of the sun.

One of the bodyguards is moved to agree today—he finds it a great masterpiece in this age of innovation. "Do you like to draw?" asks Meritaten. The officer replies that he has always loved to draw. "I have made some illustrations of an encounter some of our Libyan and Sherden auxiliaries had with a group of desert pirates last year. A copy is in the police archives in the Central City—shall I show it to you tomorrow?" he offers. Nefertiti whispers to Akhenaten, "We should bring this man with us to the artists' studio next week; perhaps his talents are wasted in the military."

Leaving Meritaten and her palace entourage in the second court, the royal family and their bodyguard are soon racing along the short distance to the North Riverside Palace. They pass below the thick eastern wall of the palace, the shadow already lengthening across the road, and pull up at the main entrance. The royal family disappears, and a new recruit asks the bodyguard closest to him, "What now?" "Just a minute," he's told. "There's a formal parting, then we all run home and start over again tomorrow morning." Above them, the royal couple and their daughters appear in the window on the second floor, overlooking the main gate. Formal goodbyes are quickly exchanged, and the sun of Akhet-Aten sets in his palace, as the sun of the world sets behind the western hills.

We veer off the Royal Road, following a modern route to a cluster of elite tombs. The North Tombs are carved at a height of about 150 feet from the desert plain, at the juncture of a sloping hill of loose rock and sand and a mostly vertical cliff face, a conjunction of geological features that Egyptian masons exploited as they carved large chambers into the cliff. Our tour of Akhet-Aten's sepulchers begins with the tomb of Meryre, the "Greatest of Seers of Aten" (a high priestly title) and "fan bearer on the right side of the king," meaning a high-ranking courtier and royal advisor.

As high priest of Aten, Meryre includes carvings of two detailed plans of the Estate of Aten in his tomb. But the biographical aspect of a tomb's decoration at Akhet-Aten is always subordinate to the depictions of Akhenaten, Nefertiti, and their children. Thanks to these reliefs in the tombs of Akhet-Aten, we can observe the royal family offering to Aten, consuming a feast, commuting into the Central City, visiting Aten's temple, rewarding loyal officials, and receiving tribute from every corner of the known world.

None of these images are accurate snapshots of royal life. They were always intended to be symbolic means of assisting the deceased in achieving eternal life after death. That deeper symbolism allows us a glimpse into the great sacred stage that was Akhet-Aten, one that the royal family used to signal their closeness to their god.

A pharaoh and his queen awakening in a royal palace, being greeted by their officials, and commencing their day with worship in a temple are all activities we might expect for any royal couple from Egypt's three-thousand-year history. Where Akhenaten and Nefertiti deviate from the norm is the distance between the palace in which they awoke and the temple in which they worshipped—and especially in how they

Akhenaten, Nefertiti, and the princesses dining with the king's mother, Tiye.
(Drawing of a relief in the tomb of Huya, after N. de G. Davies, The Rock Tombs of El
Amarna, *vol. 3,* The Tombs of Huya and Ahmes
[London: Egypt Exploration Fund, 1905], plate 4)

bridged that distance: a chariot ride. In the boundary stelae, Akhenaten equated his journey by chariot with Aten's journey through the sky: "His Majesty appeared in glory with his team of horses upon the great chariot of electrum like the Aten when he rises in the horizon, having filled the two lands with his love."[1] Driving her own chariot, or riding with Akhenaten in his chariot, Nefertiti is the only queen in Egyptian history to be depicted in a chariot on official monuments. The layout of Akhet-Aten elevated the royal family's daily commute into a divine epiphany.

The horse and chariot first appeared in the Egyptian historical record at the dawn of the New Kingdom, during the reign of Ahmose. The horse and its associated new technology, having swept out of the Central Asian steppes along with other military, political, and social changes, were rapidly incorporated into the Egyptian armed forces. The lightly built Egyptian chariots typically held two people, an archer and a shield bearer. The king in his chariot became an icon well suited to the militarism of

Akhenaten and Nefertiti driving their chariots along the Royal Road.
(Drawing of a relief in the tomb of Meryre, after N. de G. Davies,
The Rock Tombs of El Amarna, *vol. 1, The Tomb of Meryra*
[London: Egypt Exploration Fund, 1903], plate 17)

the Eighteenth Dynasty, and pharaohs like Thutmose III led armies into battle mounted on a chariot pulled by two stallions. When successful wars had rendered occasions for personal demonstration of bravery on the battlefield few and far between, kings like Amunhotep II (Akhenaten's great-grandfather) could show themselves as athletic heroes, shooting arrows at targets rather than at foreign enemies.

Amunhotep III's nearly four-decade-long reign was almost entirely free from conflict. But if a pharaoh's task was to strengthen *maat* and destroy chaos, he could be shown doing so, even if no battle took place. Akhenaten never personally led an army in war, as far as the records inform us, but he may have hunted desert game from his chariot, as many pharaohs and nobles did. All the royal family's chariots are shown with bow cases and quivers attached to the cab. The chariot ride at Akhet-Aten evoked solar supremacy over not just enemies and wild animals but the entire cosmos.

The pharaoh in his chariot, gilded corselet and bejeweled crown flashing in the sun as he drew back his bow, became a manifestation of a heavenly body, a brilliant light or a shooting star. Gilded wooden disks affixed to the yokes of royal chariots made it seem as if the horses were carrying the sun itself. As Akhenaten's son, Tutankhamun, would later be described, the king was one "appearing in glory upon the horse like Re rising, with everyone assembled in beholding him."[2]

But during no other period in Egyptian history does the chariot appear to be as essential to a pharaoh's daily life as it was during the reign of Akhenaten and Nefertiti. By chariot, a vehicle built to withstand speeds over twenty miles an hour, the two-mile commute between the North Riverside Palace and the Central City could be rapid. The royal couple probably kept a more sedate pace, but the width of the Royal Road would have made even a chariot race possible (oddly, we have no evidence that the ancient Egyptians engaged in either horse or chariot racing). The chariot was thus the perfect solution for the royal commute: prestigious, speedy, and with abundant opportunities for ornamentation on both the horses and the vehicle.

Prior to the reign of Akhenaten, large festivals punctuated the annual calendar. The ancient Egyptians did not imagine that the gods dwelt permanently in the temples but rather that their cult images were channels of communication with the world of the divine. For most of the year, those images remained within the temple sanctuary as the focus of offerings, hymns, and rituals. During festival processions, the divine statues were placed within small boats carried atop the shoulders of priests to be transported between temples. Though veiled within the shrine atop a portable bark, the deity was accessible to all—the city, and not just the temple, became the receptacle for the divine. Crowds thronged the processional routes, and soldiers joyfully sang hymns in honor of the king. Cattle from the temple stables were slaughtered and the meat given to worshippers; dancers and acrobats performed. Such was the human landscape of a festival, a pageant in which the city was the stage, its entire population the players.

Among the cities of Egypt, Waset was renowned for its festivals. When Akhenaten abandoned the worship of Amun and then removed the entire court from Waset, those festivals were apparently no more. At Akhet-Aten, when Akhenaten and Nefertiti mounted their chariots and drove along the Royal Road, they were usurping the journey of the divine statues. The king and queen became the earthly images of Aten, who cannot be represented as a cult image, for "Artistry does not know him!"[3] The soldiers who accompanied the royal family served dual purposes: one as a practical bodyguard and another as a signal that the chariot ride was a festival. Even as they ran alongside Akhenaten and Nefertiti's chariots, the soldiers hunched their bodies over in a bow, genuflecting to the king and queen as they would in the presence of gods.

In the tomb of Mahu, the chief of police, his men accompany the royal chariot, singing in praise of Akhenaten: "He brings up generations of recruits, [the good ruler who shines like] Aten: he is eternal! O good ruler, who makes monuments for his father—may he repeat that forever and ever, our good lord!"[4] These joyful refrains are similar to songs sung by soldiers during the festival of Opet in Waset.

A few hundred yards south of Mahu's tomb was the final resting place of another military leader, May, the General of the Lord of the Two Lands. May perhaps fell out of favor at court—not only was his tomb never completed but his image was hacked out. Within the unfinished chamber, the only surviving decoration is part of a scene sketched in ink in preparation for carving; it gives us some insight into another mode of transportation: a royal ship.

The details of the unfinished scene in the tomb of May are unique among the tombs of Akhet-Aten. Ships are docked at the waterfront of a large palace, almost certainly the Great Palace in the Central City, an indication that the river's course has changed little in three millennia. Along with the usual types of boats that plied the Nile during the Eighteenth Dynasty are representations of two royal ships; one is the state ship of Akhenaten, which we can easily recognize because the top of the steering oar is decorated with a carving of the king's head, while the head of Nefertiti on the steering oar of the smaller ship indicates the queen's ownership of that vessel.

No hieroglyphs are preserved with this scene, but on the left jamb of his tomb's entrance May calls himself one "who follows the king in the falcon-ship."[5] Other images from Akhet-Aten of Nefertiti's royal ship show her smiting foreign women, the queen acting the part of the bellicose sovereign who is often compared to the militaristic falcon-god Montu. The royal ships of Akhenaten and Nefertiti in the tomb of May are shown alongside smaller vessels, which may be the counterparts of tugboats used during riverine processions like the festival of Opet in Waset.

In so many cases we remain uncertain about Akhenaten's motivations, yet in the case of the royal commute the meaning is clear: When Akhenaten and Nefertiti traveled between the North Riverside Palace and the Central City by chariot or by royal ship, their movements were equated in every way with those of gods in processions. Akhenaten intentionally placed his residence far from the palaces and temples of the Central City so that the royal family needed to travel along the Royal Road or sail the Nile.

At the North Riverside Palace, the fortification walls and police patrols kept the royal family secure. Then, gleaming in the sunlight, Akhenaten and Nefertiti could mount their gilded solar chariots and hurtle into their city, the earthly counterparts of the flaming disk in the sky. Residents who caught sight of the magnificent procession were instantly transported into a state of festival. Before and after the reign of Akhenaten and Nefertiti, the king and queen accompanied images of the gods; at Akhet-Aten, Akhenaten and Nefertiti *were* the gods.

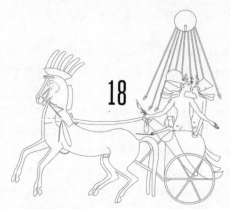

18

A Holy Place in the Sun

AKHENATEN GENTLY PULLS BACK ON THE REINS, BRINGING HIS stallions to a halt in front of the gleaming pylon, the outer gateway that pierces the wall surrounding the massive Estate of Aten. Bowing deeply, grooms take charge of the horses. As the royal family enters the temple, a chorus of women joyously shout and beat on drums. A girl dances among them, waving a palm branch. The blast of a trumpet welcomes the royal family, while kneeling soldiers hold ostrich-feather fans. Priests lead fatted bulls, the beasts so enormous, so accustomed to standing all day and eating in their stalls, that their hooves are malformed. These cattle are branded with the name of Aten or the king, destined to serve the sun god and his earthly vicar as cuts of sacrificial meat upon the myriad altars of Aten. Yet other priests hold bound fowl, stunned but not yet dead.

The royal family, with their priestly retinue, walk between the pylon towers that pierce the enclosure wall. The entrance is twelve cubits wide, and no door needs to be opened to admit the worshippers. The ground between the pylons is elevated, requiring everyone to walk up a gently sloped ramp and then descend another as they enter into the Estate of Aten. Here, they are on sacred ground.

Sixty cubits ahead is another massive pylon. As Akhenaten traverses that short distance, he looks to the right, taking pleasure in the abundance of offering tables. He cannot see all of them, but he knows that each of the nearly one thousand brick platforms is piled with bread, beef, and fowl, with a large floral bouquet for every offering table. His promises are being fulfilled: the taxes of all of Egypt are now at the disposal of his father, Aten. Although the immediate retinue has stopped in deference to the king, the procession of bulls is continuing, some already passing behind a wall into the slaughtering place, a courtyard where those fattened cattle are transformed into offerings.

And now Akhenaten and his attendants have come to the first pylon of the stone temple. Before each tower are five wooden poles, trunks of Lebanese cedar trees imported at great expense. The knots where each tree's branches were removed are still visible, and at the top of each pole are streamers snapping in the breeze and signaling the life-giving force of Aten. Once through the pylon, the royal family comes to the first court and their initial destination for the day. As Aten shines down upon them, they climb the steps to an altar overflowing with offerings.

Akhenaten and Nefertiti stand side by side, as if mirror images of each other, and raise their arms to heaven. They praise Aten, the creator of all life, he for whom the cattle prance and birds take flight. He whose rays allow the plants to grow and the flowers to bloom. A portion of the bounty of Aten's giving is on the altar, ready to be consecrated. As the ritual comes to a crescendo, the king overturns the golden tray of incense in his hand. The myrrh hits the flames of the burning braziers placed atop the offerings, rendering the earthly materials godlike; indeed, the word "incense" is *senetjer,* literally "to make divine." As the powerful aroma drifts up to Aten in heaven, Meritaten mimics her parents' actions, lifting up loaves of bread. Meketaten and their sister Ankhesenpaaten, still a toddler, shake sistra, the rattling sounds pacifying the god above. And now a chorus joins in with praising, singing, and joyous shouting.

When Akhenaten first trod the ground that would become his city, the desert surface, as today, was a mixture of sand and rocks. The first step in the construction of a temple was to clear the footprint of the entire complex; for the Estate of Aten at Akhet-Aten, that meant the twelve acres enclosed by the outer wall. A smoothed layer of gypsum plaster was then spread over the surface, becoming a full-scale drawing board. The king himself stretched the first cord that laid out the temple's axis. Architects then painted or scratched lines and notes onto the gypsum, indicating the positions of pylons, walls, columns, and other architectural features.

As the temple foundations were delineated, quarrymen were busily cutting out the *talatat*. The Gebel Silsila quarries continued to provide some sandstone *talatat* and larger elements of temple architecture, but locally available limestone was more commonly used in temple construction at Akhet-Aten. A particularly large quarry situated within a wadi adjacent to the city supplied thousands of *talatat* that were loaded on the backs of donkeys and transported to the construction sites. Granite blocks for statuary traveled downstream from Sewenet, while quartzite from near Iunu made a corresponding upstream journey.

As soon as masons had carefully stacked *talatat,* artisans could plaster over the joins in the stone and begin the process of carving the scenes that would decorate the temple. Then artists painted the reliefs, making the background a bright white, thereby highlighting each colorful figure. Many of the scenes in the temples were large-scale versions of the sort of decoration that appears in the tombs of Akhet-Aten. The *talatat* from Akhet-Aten's temples, like those Akhenaten built at Karnak, also depicted everyday actions of everyday people around the temple. The mundane had become sacred: the temple's walls could show the construction of the temple itself, even a guard who has fallen asleep on duty, butchers carrying out their bloody business, porters bowed under the weight of massive offering trays, all beneath the omnipresent rays of Aten.

When it was completed, the Estate of Aten (*Per-Aten*) was the most impressive structure in Akhet-Aten. Now often called the Great Aten Temple, it is indeed grand in scale, the long walls of the enclosure a half mile in length. This Per-Aten shares its name with the Per-Aten at Karnak; just as the Estate of Aten at Karnak contained separate temples, the eponymous domain in Akhet-Aten included two stone temples within its enclosure wall. In our reimagining of the royal family's visit to the

Estate of Aten, we left them in the first court of the temple in the western portion of the enclosure.

The modern name given to that building is the Long Temple, befitting its dimensions: 623 feet in length by 100 feet in width. The ancient name was likely Gem-pa-Aten, "The Aten is Found," the same name given to the structure at Karnak with the colossal royal statues and jubilee festival scenes. Akhenaten built a new city for Aten, Akhet-Aten, as a replacement for Waset. Akhenaten preferred to call Waset "Southern Iunu," the Upper Egyptian counterpart to the solar city in the north, but he could also call Waset Akhet-ni-Aten, "Horizon of Aten." Everything that Akhenaten did during the first five years of his reign in Waset was amplified with the move to Akhet-Aten in Middle Egypt, with an even bigger Estate of Aten and Gem-pa-Aten to replace their counterparts at Karnak.

Beyond the Gem-pa-Aten's first court (assuming that is the Long Temple's name) are an additional five open courts, each containing a plethora of offering tables, almost eight hundred in all. Pylon gateways divide the courts; a columned portico before the entrance of the fourth court was the only roofed portion of the temple. Colossal statues of Akhenaten and Nefertiti, carved from quartzite, granite, and a fine, white limestone, stood within some of the courts.

The Estate of Aten contains another stone temple situated just over a thousand feet to the east of the Long Temple. Often called the "Sanctuary," since its ancient name is uncertain, this temple is a rectangle 98 by 154 feet. In front of each pylon tower is a portico with columns interspersed with statues of the king wearing the red crown of Lower Egypt and the white crown of Upper Egypt. East of the pylon is an open court with a central altar and row upon row of offering tables.

The architecture of the Estate of Aten and the earlier Aten temples at Waset may be patterned after temples at Iunu, to the extent that we can characterize the nearly obliterated sacred structures in the solar cult center of the north. The ground plans of the temples in Iunu have not been excavated; however, a fragmentary carved plaque from Iunu has a drawing of a portion of a temple. The damaged image shows the temple as a series of open courts separated by pylons, just like the Estate of Aten and Mansion of Aten in Akhet-Aten.

Akhenaten, Nefertiti, and the princesses making an offering to Aten in the Estate of Aten.
(Drawing of relief from the tomb of Panehesy, after N. de G. Davies, The Rock Tombs of El
Amarna, *vol. 2,* The Tomb of Meryra II *[London: Egypt Exploration Fund, 1905], plate 18)*

Doorways within Aten temples, both at Waset and Akhet-Aten, did
not have lintels that stretched across the entire width of the portal. Instead, two short, stone elements, or "broken lintels," projected from the
sides of the doorway, at the height where the pivots of the wooden door
leaves could be socketed into the stone; the ancient Egyptians did not
employ hinges. Such a design was ideal for a temple of Aten, whose rays
should never be interrupted. Although Akhenaten is the first pharaoh
known to use the broken lintel throughout his temple architecture, this
is another design that may have been commonplace at Iunu.

The evidence of Akhenaten's building activity at Iunu is frustratingly incomplete. A quartzite slab, possibly from a parapet, depicts the
royal family worshipping Aten within a temple called Elevating Re in
Iunu. Some *talatat* have been discovered in the area adjacent to the obelisk of Senwosret I that was once part of the temple of Re. What seems
so unusual to a modern eye about Aten's temples—the multiple courts,

Talatat depicting Akhenaten wringing the neck of a duck beneath the rays of Aten; an additional duck in the lower right corner is being offered by Queen Kiye.

the broken lintels, and open-air sanctuaries—might not seem odd if we had the temples of Re and Atum at Iunu for comparison.

In a standard Egyptian temple, an open court, or a series of open courts, leads to an expansive columned hall, which then gives way to the increasingly smaller inner chambers. The floor rises as one goes back toward the sanctuary, while the ceiling becomes lower. The sanctuary, which contained a statue of the god (the same statues that Amunhotep IV inventoried in the first years of his rule), was a confined space, symbolizing the darkness of primordial times. As one walked out from the sanctuary, a hall with columns in the shape of massive marsh plants, papyri and lotuses, and one or more open courts represented the newly created world. The pylons that marked the temple's entrance were carved with smiting scenes to guard the sacred space from the chaos of the outside world. The temple became a model of the process of creation, a microcosm of the world, and rituals enacted each day within the sanctuary maintained *maat,* the proper balance of the created world.

The Aten temples, and other solar temples in Iunu, were instead open to the sky, the light-drenched spaces showing the god's immanence within the sacred enclosure. A relief within a suite of rooms for Meketaten in the royal tomb, deep in the wadi opposite the Mansion of Aten, provides a striking illustration of this concept. At the left of the scene, the sun disk rises from a tall mountain, the horizon-hieroglyph, bathing the Estate of Aten in light, its penetrating rays appearing as deeply cut lines intersecting the carving of the temple. On the boundary stelae, Akhenaten describes Akhet-Aten as Aten's "place of the primeval event," the moment of creation. Night is a time of death and stasis, while the light of day, Aten's rays, rejuvenate the world—each day, the cosmos is reborn.

The temples at Akhet-Aten designated as a Sunshade of Re were another way for the royal family—especially royal women—to worship Aten and celebrate the bounty of his creation. Two of these temples can be identified archaeologically. The first was the Sunshade of Re for Nefertiti, which was originally the southern terminus of the Royal Road, and consisted of an enclosure, 250 yards by 232 yards, divided into two rectangular courts, one larger than the other. Traces of stone buildings and sunken gardens hint at the colorful monuments and verdure that once filled it.

The better-preserved Sunshade temple came to light in the late nineteenth century, when impressive remains of painted plaster were uncovered nearly three miles south of the Central City. Fragmentary hieroglyphic inscriptions at the site provide the name of the complex: "The Sunshade of Re of the king's daughter Meritaten, in the Maru-Aten of Akhet-Aten." Meritaten's name was carved over the name of another royal woman, a mysterious queen named Kiye, whose existence remained unknown in modern times until 1959. Thus far, we have not had occasion to meet Akhenaten's second wife, as she is vanishingly rare in the textual and archaeological record. Akhenaten seems to have married only two women rather than the roughly half dozen queens attested for most kings of his dynasty, including his father. Kiye's identity is uncertain, and at some point, all of her representations were replaced, either with images of Meritaten, the eldest princess, or Ankhesenpaaten, the third daughter of Akhenaten and Nefertiti.

Kiye has a unique set of titles and epithets, including the "greatly beloved wife of the king."[1] In some texts she is also called the "beautiful child of living Aten," placing her among the offspring of the solar orb, alongside her husband and the king's great wife Nefertiti. Unfortunately, neither Kiye's unique titles nor her Sunshade temple fully illuminate her origins or role in Akhenaten's court. Perhaps she was the Mitannian

*Talatat of Queen Kiye undergoing a purification ritual;
the queen's image was later transformed into a representation of the princess Meritaten.*

princess Tadukhepa—her title "noble lady," uncommon for Egyptian queens, may support such a suggestion. Sources do not indicate when Kiye arrived at Akhet-Aten, only that a temple was constructed in her honor. A fragmentary label on a wine jar suggests that Kiye still possessed a vineyard as late as Year 16 of Akhenaten's reign, but we have no evidence as to the motivation for the erasure of Kiye's name and images.

The Sunshade of Re of Kiye, later assigned to Meritaten and known by its ancient name Maru-Aten, is archaeologically the best preserved of such complexes. The Maru-Aten was two rectangular enclosures of unequal size, with most of the space being open, landscaped with pools and gardens and adorned with small stone and brick shrines. In the southeast corner, a structure with columns shaded a series of interlocking T-shaped pools surrounded by painted plaster floors showing birds flying among marsh plants. Irrigating such a lush and bucolic environment was a logistical challenge, requiring water to be manually transported from deep wells, either in jars or using a *shaduf,* a bucket with counterweight mounted on a pole. The tremendous effort undoubtedly resulted in a visual delight for those who strolled through its beautiful grounds, collectively an homage to Aten's creation of the natural world.

A temple surrounded by a veritable paradise of trees and flowers was itself a form of solar worship. A poetical description of a temple from the reign of Merneptah, who ruled between 1213 and 1203 BCE, constructed in Queen Tiye's hometown of Ipu reveals that the temple gardens provided bouquets for the temple's deity, Thoth.

> *It is planted with all sorts of fruit trees, decorated with flowers.*
> *Its gardens yield lotuses, blooms, reeds, lotus buds, papyrus,*
> > *that they might be dedicated as daily garlands to the court of Thoth,*
> > *that they make green the foliage of the temple of Thoth afresh,*
> > > *with the result that the perfection of Amun of Merneptah rests*
> > > *within it,*
> > > > *he being like the sun upon rising.*[2]

Akhet-Aten contained a third Sunshade temple, but we know it only from reliefs in the tomb of Huya, overseer of the private royal apartments and treasurer and steward of Queen Tiye. Akhenaten's mother may have resided at Akhet-Aten part of the year, thus requiring Huya's services, and she likely spent other months at the palace of Mer-wer in the Fayum. The tomb of Huya records a visit that the queen mother made to Akhet-Aten, during which Akhenaten presented to her a Sunshade of Re. In depictions within Huya's tomb, at the entrance pylon the steward bows deeply, drawing our attention to the open court beyond, with a stepped altar in the center, its perimeter lined with columns and colossal statues: alternating pairs of Amunhotep III and Tiye and Akhenaten and Tiye. Beyond another pylon is the sanctuary of the Sunshade of Re, with offering tables, additional shrines, and over a dozen statues of the king and his mother, each statue holding a tray of offerings.

As depicted in the tomb of Huya, Tiye's Sunshade resembles a standard Aten temple. Its monumental royal statues allude to another important fact: anywhere except Akhet-Aten, a Sunshade of Re is part of a temple built by a king. One of the few extant structures labeled as a Sunshade of Re is the solar chapel in the temple of Ramesses III on the west bank of Waset. The decoration of this chamber depicts and describes the solar cycle, arcane knowledge into which a king is inducted. At Akhet-Aten, the Sunshade is exclusively and repeatedly a queenly structure.

Perhaps the existence of Sunshades of Re for royal females means that Nefertiti, Kiye, Meritaten, and Tiye, as presumably literate women, were also privy to religious texts that were otherwise known only to the king and high priests. Akhenaten is said to be "knowledgeable like Aten," and perhaps his mother, wives, and daughters commanded the same sacred wisdom.

A functioning temple required a vast amount of resources, especially the Estate of Aten with its thousands of offering tables. While we do not have texts describing the economic bases of Akhet-Aten's temples, each would have possessed royally decreed endowments of agricultural land, flocks of fowl, and herds of cattle. Temples also commanded fleets of ships and expeditions into the deserts that procured resources from further abroad, such as incense and ostrich feathers—the docks of Akhet-Aten would have teemed with crews unloading cargo both mundane and exotic.

A decree of the pharaoh Horemhab, promulgated about fifteen years after the death of Akhenaten, paints a bleak picture of Egypt during the reign of Akhenaten and his immediate successors: the army engaging in theft, tax collectors fraudulently making demands, and the courts handing down biased rulings. We cannot judge the accuracy of these alleged crimes, but a king focused so obsessively on a single city that required tremendous capital appears to have provided opportunity for unscrupulous behavior. Perhaps Akhenaten, his administrators, and his generals wanted those products by whatever means necessary and may have overridden the checks and balances of local officials. Maybe sating Aten's desires trumped all else.

Thus far, the nonroyal inhabitants of Akhet-Aten that we have met have been priests and policemen. Temples also required a host of other workers: brewers and bakers, metalworkers and potters, and crews to maintain the mud-brick walls and keep them covered with a fresh coat of whitewash. Scribes kept track of all these activities, from personnel absences to what sacred equipment needed repairs. But the evidence is silent about whether these people also worshipped in the temples, or whether the population of Akhet-Aten could even enter the sacred space if they were not performing a specific task. Did the massive open spaces in the Estate of Aten accommodate equally massive crowds?

No evidence from Akhet-Aten provides a direct answer, so we must turn to other temples for possible clues. Unlike the Aten temples, Luxor Temple, where Amunhotep III memorialized his divine birth, has survived virtually intact. The ritual offering scenes that make up most of its decoration include only the king and the gods. Yet an image at the bases of several columns indicates who might have been allowed to stand there. A lapwing—a bird species still common in Egypt and easily identifiable by a crest of long feathers that curls up from its head—perches on a basket; improbably, the bird also has human arms that are raised up, palms facing away from its body; a single star is placed below the arms and in front of the bird's body. These images write a sentence in ancient Egyptian: "All (basket) the people (lapwing) adore (star and praising arms)."

The object of the people's adoration is the king's cartouche. Even people who were not fully literate could probably recognize this image, which seems to have signaled an area of the sacred structure accessible to them. A gateway into the courtyard added by Ramesses II is similarly named: "All the People Adore, so That They Might Live"—through this portal, people may enter to praise the king. Those same people were not allowed to go deeper into the temple, and perhaps they were not even allowed through that gateway except during festivals.

The sheer size of the footprint of the Estate of Aten could have accommodated crowds, and temples before and after Akhenaten's reign certainly did so. The nearly two thousand offering tables in the Estate of Aten suggest another way in which the public interacted with the sacred space. Piled high with bread, vegetables, and choice cuts of meat, Aten took the spiritual sustenance of the food, which the Egyptians called ka. But Aten had no use for rotting meat and wilting lettuce, so people then consumed the actual calories after the sun disk had soaked up the metaphysical essence of the food.

Everyone most likely partook of the bounty. Certainly the highest-ranking officials received the largest portions. In the tombs of Akhet-Aten's elite, hieroglyphic texts state that one of the benefits of a high office was the claim to food from the temple. For the residents of Akhet-Aten, their continued existence in the afterlife was also made more luxurious if they could continue to feast from the temple offering tables.

Hieroglyphic texts within tomb chapels prior to Akhenaten's reign request that visitors recite offering formulas. These texts, literally "a going forth of the voice," called upon the largesse of the king and typically a funerary god, like Anubis or Osiris. If the visitor spoke the formula, the king and god would provide "a thousand of bread, a thousand of beer, a thousand of beef, a thousand of fowl."

But the residents of Akhet-Aten, especially the owners of the large rock-cut tombs, avoided depicting or mentioning the traditional funerary deities. The Underworld, *duat* in ancient Egyptian, a region defined as neither earth nor sky, is rare but not entirely absent from texts at Akhet-Aten. Even Akhenaten could not deny the existence of death and the place where the spirits of the dead were believed to dwell. Some beliefs about the afterlife remained unchanged, such as the necessity of the soul to unite daily with a mummified corpse in order to attain eternal life. But if Osiris, the divine ruler of the Underworld, is gone, and Anubis no longer oversees mummification, and the goddesses Isis and Nephthys are not present to embrace the deceased, what happens in the afterlife? Were the men and women of Akhet-Aten bereft of hope about their eternal existence?

The walls of tombs at Akhet-Aten are dominated by images of the king, queen, and princesses. Perhaps the courtiers' afterlives were equally dominated by the megalomaniacal Akhenaten. The tombs ignore the gods of the Underworld and instead insist that the dead dwell eternally at Akhet-Aten. But that may not have been such a bad prospect for some of Aten's worshippers. Tomb inscriptions at Akhet-Aten describe how the king commanded that the offering tables of Aten's temple continue to supply food, incense, and libations for the souls of his deceased officials. In these texts, the divine offerings assigned to benefit the soul came from the Estate of Aten, the Domain of the Benben, and the Staircase of the Living One, Aten. Fragmentary inscriptions from the Sunshade of Re for Nefertiti situate that temple within the "Staircase of the Living One, Aten." A deceased spirit could benefit from all of Akhet-Aten's temples, including those associated with royal women.

Earlier Eighteenth Dynasty tombs in Waset show the deceased taking part in festivals, especially the Beautiful Festival of the Valley in which the statue of the god Amun traveled from Karnak Temple to the west bank. In ancient Egyptian, "the West" was synonymous with the Underworld, and on the west bank families celebrated the festival in the tombs of their ancestors. Geographical realities in the Nile Valley meant that tombs could also be located on the east side of the Nile without losing their symbolic place in the West. For the residents of Akhet-Aten, their tombs' placement in the east acquired special meaning. They were buried in the land where Aten rose to illumine all of creation. They intended to spend eternity overlooking the chariot ride of the royal family, the bountiful offerings in the temples, and attaining immortality by remaining in the Horizon of Aten. At Akhet-Aten, daily celebrations serve both the living and the dead.

In traditional Egyptian funerary beliefs, the deceased wanted to join the sun god Re as he visited his corpse, Osiris, in the Underworld. Now, the dead desired to see Aten every day in Akhet-Aten. The tomb of General May expresses this wish eloquently: "Adoration when you rise in the horizon, o [living] Aten, Horakhty! You (the deceased) shall never cease seeing Re. May your two eyes be open to perceive him, so that your corpse might endure and your name might remain!"[3]

The yearning to see Aten eternally, as one's soul returns to earth each day, is not at odds with earlier funerary texts that express the desire to travel with the sun. What tombs in Akhet-Aten lack is the corresponding journey of the sun into the Underworld. Instead, the hours of darkness become a time of danger when animals lurk and thieves creep. No text explains Aten's experience of these hours, only that his absence makes the world bereft, all the more eager to rejoice at his emergence from the eastern horizon.

The elite buried in the elaborately decorated tombs at Akhet-Aten were the exceptions, the privileged in a society where the vast majority of people were farmers and laborers. Only in the early twenty-first century did excavations begin in a large cemetery where approximately six thousand citizens of Akhet-Aten were interred. While many of the burials had been robbed, even those that were relatively intact held few if any grave goods, and wooden coffins were rare. Some of the coffins were decorated with traditional imagery and texts, including a chapter from the *Book of Going Forth by Day* (often called by its modern title the *Book of the Dead*). Others included only images of men bearing offerings and women mourning, avoiding all mention of funerary gods like Osiris.

Among the most remarkable finds within the cemeteries were fragments of wax cones on the heads of the deceased. Wax cones were a way to place incense on the head so that the wax would presumably drip slowly down the wig and body of the wearer, maintaining the aroma of divinity during even the sweatiest and most raucous of festival events. These scented cones are ubiquitous in images of festival banquets from the Eighteenth Dynasty and beyond—yet for all of the thousands of representations of these objects, not a single physical specimen had been discovered previously. Wax head ornaments sometimes appear on the heads of mummies, including in tomb scenes from Akhet-Aten, in keeping with the idea of burial as both a time of mourning the passing from this existence and celebrating rebirth into another. Perhaps the inclusion of a cone in burials at Akhet-Aten further emphasized that a blessed afterlife lay in the temples of Akhet-Aten, as the deceased would spiritually attend the royal family's daily offerings.

No matter what social level to which a resident of ancient Akhet-Aten belonged, all people in the city likely desired to repeat the joys of existence on earth. For the wealthier, this might entail strolling in shade-filled groves, drinking from refreshing pools, wearing fine clothing, visiting Aten's temples, and hearing again the sweet voice of the king. For farmers, this might involve simpler wishes, such as sitting under the shade of a tree, enjoying the cool breeze from the north on a hot summer day. For those buried in the large rock-cut tombs in Akhet-Aten's eastern mountain, conformity to the king's political theology and sole reliance upon Aten seem to have been the prerequisites of eternal life. From hymns that the elite carved in their tombs to shrines they erected in their homes, we know that their only gods were the new trinity: Aten, Akhenaten, and Nefertiti.

IV

GODS ON EARTH

THE TRINITY

Ceiling painting from the palace of Amunhotep III at Malqata,
showing pigeons in flight.

Amunhotep III and his mother, Mutemwia.
(Facsimile of a painting from Theban Tomb 226 by Nina de Garis Davies)

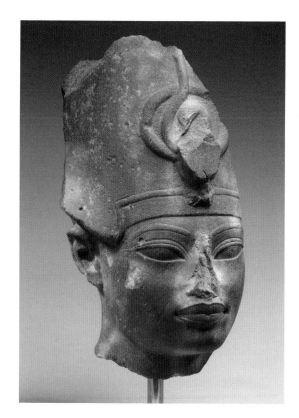

Head of a quartzite statue of Amunhotep III wearing a *khepresh* (blue crown) with uraeus.

Female dancers performing during the first jubilee of Amunhotep III, relief in the tomb of Kheruef.

View of East Karnak, between what was once the
Mansion of the Benben and the Gem-pa-Aten.

Egyptian alabaster goblet in the shape of a lotus,
inscribed with the cartouches of Aten,
Amunhotep IV, and Nefertiti.

Boundary Stela U at Akhet-Aten.

Akhenaten and Nefertiti driving their chariots south along the Royal Road.
(A relief in the tomb of the Greatest of Seers Meryre)

Talatat depicting dancers and musicians greeting the royal family as they arrive
at the Estate of Aten.

Akhenaten, Nefertiti, and princesses consecrating offerings before Aten;
the rays of the disk are decorated with a multicolored broad collar.
(A relief in the tomb of the Greatest of Seers Meryre)

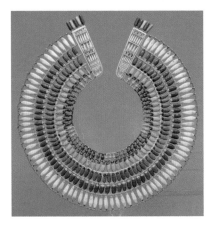

Faience broad collar from
Akhet-Aten.

Painting in the "Green Room" of the North Palace.
(Facsimile by Nina de Garis Davies)

Bust of Queen Nefertiti.
(Ägyptisches Museum und Papyrussammlung, Staatliche Museen, Berlin,
Inv. 21300, photograph by Margarete Büsing)

Artists working on a statue, painting from the tomb of Rekhmire (Theban Tomb 100).
(Facsimile by Nina de Garis Davies)

Stela of Akhenaten, Nefertiti, and daughters.
(From House Q 47.16 at Amarna, Egyptian Museum, Cairo JE 44865)

Painting from the small palace (King's House) showing two princesses in an intimate moment. (Facsimile by Nina de Garis Davies)

Relief showing two princesses.

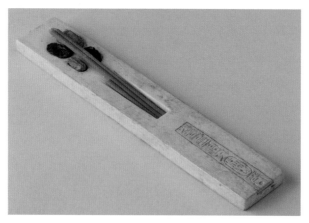

Scribal palette of
Princess Meketaten.

Stela of Nefertiti tying on Akhenaten's broad collar.
(Ägyptisches Museum und Papyrussammlung,
Staatliche Museen, Berlin, Inv. 14511,
photograph by Sandra Steiss)

Cuneiform letter from the Assyrian king
Assur-uballit to Amunhotep IV
(Amarna Letter EA 15).

A fishing and fowling scene from the tomb of Nakht; the damaged area at the prow of each papyrus skiff once held a depiction of a goose, later removed by iconoclasts during the reign of Akhenaten. (Facsimile by Norman de Garis Davies)

Painted stone statue of an elder princess, likely Meritaten. (Louvre, Paris, E 14715)

Stela of Pase, showing Akhenaten and his co-regent Neferneferuaten.
(Ägyptisches Museum und Papyrussammlung, Staatliche Museen, Berlin, Inv. 17813,
photograph by Jürgen Liepe)

Fragmentary faience shabti of Akhenaten,
holding two *ankh*-signs.

Canopic jar re-used in the burial of Akhenaten
in KV 55, originally part of the burial
equipment of Kiye.

Mutilated face of the coffin from KV 55. (Egyptian Museum, Cairo)

19

Secret Knowledge

Among the group of younger scribes and sculptors, the older man stands out not simply because of his graying hair. His kilt is of the less exuberantly flounced sort typical in the days before Akhenaten's ascendancy. The group has just returned from a visit to Men-nefer, officially in search of ancient imagery that Akhenaten might find useful. For the old man, it has also been a return to a scene of his early education.

One stop on their itinerary was the step pyramid of King Djoser, who had been buried beneath the great stone monument 1,300 years earlier. In the north chapel, the elder man had sought out a graffito that his friend Ahmose had written when they visited decades ago in the company of their old teacher, Sethemheb. Indeed, heaven had rained myrrh and dripped incense as Ahmose had prayed, and his friend had enjoyed a remarkable career before joining his ancestors long ago. Slipping away from his charges, the old man wrote another graffito in the south chapel, complementing the one his departed friend left on that earlier trip.

Now the older scribe and his pupils are back at Akhet-Aten, surveying the tomb of the god's father and chariot commander, Ay. First, they examine the entrance passage of the unfinished tomb, and the apprentices make notes. Most, even the two scribes from Waset, can barely remember visiting their ancestors' tombs in their hometowns. But several have attended family celebrations in the tombs of Akhet-Aten, in a sort of local reinterpretation of the old tradition of dining with the dead. The old man looks up at the ceiling of Ay's tomb, nodding his head in familiarity as he reads the request, "May the children of your house make offerings to you of bread, beer, and water, being the breath (of life) for your *ka*-spirit."[1]

The decoration within the entrance to Ay's tomb reminds the old man of something. He feels almost as if he were back in Waset, the mountain peak sacred to She Who Loves Silence towering in the distance. One of the young scribes suddenly appears next to him and asks what in the doorway interests his master. "Something seems familiar, but my thoughts are not as quick as they once were. Please, describe what you see," he requests, hoping the young scribe's words might summon forth the memory that is eluding him.

Facing in toward the tomb, the young man begins, "To our right is a text." He silently counts for a moment. "Thirteen columns in length, a hymn addressed to Aten and the royal couple, the longest hymn in all the tombs in the city. While on our left, we see the royal family consecrating a pile of food offerings to Aten. Beneath are Ay and his wife Tiy surrounded by a hieroglyphic text that praises Aten, Akhenaten, and Nefertiti." Quickly skimming the texts, the young man observes that whereas each of the two texts appears to be addressed to Aten and the royal couple, the long hymn on the right focuses on Aten, and the shorter on the left seems to emphasize the king.

"With your great experience, do you find this odd?" asks the young scribe.

"Only in part," the old man replies, then points to some phrases. "These constant claims of Aten's uniqueness are not so shocking. In my youth, many hymns to Amun-Re praised him as 'without his equal.' What is lacking are all the other gods who accompany Re in his journey through sunrise, noon, and sunset."

The young man scoffs slightly but remains respectful. "Why do we need all of these other gods—Aten, the god in heaven, and Akhenaten and Nefertiti, rulers on earth, are sufficient."

Then the old man remembers where he has seen this all before: the tomb of a man he had once served in Waset. The sights and sounds of the great jubilees flood his memories. How nervous he was to record all of steward Kheruef's orders for the massive ceremonies! Shortly before he moored in the West, Kheruef had given the scribe a tour of the tomb where the steward would spend eternity. They arrived just as the decoration of the entrance was being finished. On one side, the king, then still called Amunhotep, recited a remarkable crossword hymn—he couldn't imagine how long that had taken to compose!—and made offerings to his deceased father and his mother, Tiye. Below, Kheruef, the tomb owner, knelt and worshipped Re and Osiris.

Even then, Akhenaten's worship had literally overshadowed that of the tomb owner. The elderly scribe muses to himself how in the new city sprung from the desert this has all been taken to an extreme. Did the king and queen really believe themselves to be helping their subjects in the afterlife? Perhaps, but the old man wonders if they are not just getting in the way, making a fateful error in ignoring Osiris, Anubis, and all the gods who populated the Underworld.

Aten is unique, there is none except him. This is the central theme of hymns addressed to the sun god at Akhet-Aten. More such hymns may have been written on papyri stored in the libraries attached to one or more of the temples of Akhet-Aten. But what is available to us, over three thousand years later, is most often what was chosen for memorialization on a temple wall, or what was deemed useful for a deceased person.

As it is, we have a limited set of texts with which to evaluate other contemporary scholars' assertions, such as there is "little doubt that Akhenaten's encounter with Aten developed into a monotheistic faith";[2] or "Whatever pharaoh's own personal beliefs—and they remain elusive— Atenism itself was in practice little more than a pragmatic instrument of political control."[3] Modern presentations of Akhenaten—as teacher of Moses, as proto-messianic figure, as totalitarian dictator—frequently maintain only a tenuous connection with surviving records.

Here, we attempt to remain focused on the ancient sources as we explore the main chambers of the tombs in the eastern mountain of Akhet-Aten. In many of the tomb scenes, textual annotations are brief. But if we stand in the doorways of those same sepulchers, we see lengthy hieroglyphic texts and related images carved into the thicknesses of the tomb entrances. Usually, the side with a hymn to Aten receives much more attention in modern studies and translations, such as the southern side of the doorway into the tomb of Ay, with its unique attestation of the Great Hymn to Aten.

Context matters, however: no ancient Egyptian would have walked into a tomb and failed to see the texts on each side of the door as being essential to the overall meaning of *both* compositions. In the doorway of Ay's tomb, which the old man and young scribe were avidly discussing, the so-called Great Hymn is juxtaposed with two scenes: an image of the royal family praising Aten, and the tomb owners praising the trinity of Aten, Akhenaten, and Nefertiti.

Already at the beginning of his reign, as Amunhotep IV, the king claimed to be the high priest of Aten. This would not have seemed unusual to educated Egyptians, because such a role for the pharaoh was set out in a text now commonly called the *King as Solar Priest*. The treatise catalogs what the king knows about solar theology and describes, but does not reveal, the central mystery of ancient Egyptian religion. This information quite literally enabled the king, as well as properly inducted priests, to maintain *maat*. Without the appropriate rituals, the sun might fail to rise, and the world itself would collapse.

The king's knowledge includes the forms of the gods, their locations in the divine land, the words pronounced by the crew of the Night Bark and the Day Bark, the birth form of Re, and the mysterious portal that the great god enters. The king also understands the mysterious language of the baboons, creatures well known to the Egyptians and whose standing posture was interpreted as worship of the rising sun. Some of the treatises of solar knowledge survive within the tombs of New Kingdom pharaohs in the Valley of the Kings. In the corridors and on the ceilings of the royal tombs, the Egyptians did reveal the secret at the heart of their religion: in the bowels of the Underworld, Re united with his corpse, Osiris.

The first surviving attestations of the *King as Solar Priest* are from the reigns of Hatshepsut and Amunhotep III, who were among the greatest inspirations for Akhenaten. The final two sections of the composition provide a summary of the king's unique role in ancient Egypt:

> Re has set the king upon the earth for the living forever and ever,
>> judging men and pacifying the gods;
>> bringing about maat and destroying evil.
> He gives offerings to the deities and funeral offerings to the blessed dead.
> The name of the king is in heaven like Re; he lives in joy like Re-Horakhty.
> Through seeing him the nobles rejoice,
>> the people performing jubilation for him, in his visible form of the child.[4]

Here we read the first part of the name of Aten, Re-Horakhty, and about a population that worships the king as a form of the sun god. A priest or priestess who was well educated in solar religion from the years before the reign of Akhenaten thus would have found nothing shocking in the exclamation written in the tomb of Tutu at Akhet-Aten: "O living Aten who is born in heaven every day, so that he might give birth to his son, who comes forth from his body, in his form!"[5]

Yes, Akhenaten elevated himself and Nefertiti to a divine trinity with Aten. But as king of Egypt and chief solar priest, Akhenaten, just like Hatshepsut and Amunhotep III, possessed the god-given authority to identify himself as the solar child who deserves the adoration of all Egyptians. Akhenaten's unusual body, his elevation of Aten above all other deities, and his new city at Akhet-Aten have blinded many modern people to how Akhenaten's actions are within the purview of all pharaohs. It is only later in his reign, when Akhenaten updated Aten's didactic name to remove all mention of other deities and when he commanded that Amun's name and image be hacked out, that the king seems to have crossed a line firmly dividing an eccentric realization of earlier solar religion from something truly new and potentially threatening. While the hymns to Aten, Akhenaten, and Nefertiti that we find in the doorways of the tombs at Akhet-Aten do take the solar nature of rulership to a new level, those texts do not fully transgress well-established norms.

One Who Contains Millions

As AKHENATEN DISCUSSES THE GREAT HYMN, HIS FORMER TUTOR and now counselor, Ay, fidgets in his chair. Several times the older man begins to speak but stops himself. Finally, with a laugh, he interjects, "Should we not give Suty and Hor their due even in your Majesty's great hymn? Of course, you remember them?" Akhenaten feigns anger, but his twitching mouth soon spreads into a broad smile. After all, it was Ay who had introduced those famous twins to their future sovereign.

Years before, Ay and his royal pupil witnessed the exciting arrival and nerve-racking journey of the southern colossus of Amunhotep III's mortuary temple. They then visited the office of Meryptah, steward of the great complex. The colossus, roughed out but with much sculpting yet to go, was even then being finally moved into its final position, but Meryptah could spare a couple of hours for the prince's education. The steward picked up where he had left off the day before the statue's arrival, a survey of secondary Amun temples, and their relative importance as seen through how many *deben* of incense each required. With a mixture of surprise and approval, Ay noticed that the prince's eyes did not take on that glaze of faltering interest. Instead, the child began to ask about the inventories of temple holdings and supplies.

Two double knocks sounded on Meryptah's door, as though two people were knocking in unison. Meryptah rolled his eyes slightly—he knew well those responsible for the doubled knock, but they never tired of the joke. He said "Enter!" more out of habit than need, as the door was already opening. In stepped two men, identical not merely in dress but in all their appearance. They bowed to the prince, and Meryptah introduced them as Suty and Hor, twin overseers of royal constructions in Waset.

The father and son team of Bak and Men oversaw work at the quarries, the statue's transportation, and its final positioning. Then Suty and Hor took over, supervising the host of artists crawling spiderlike across the web of red grid lines. Meryptah could not resist clarifying the twins' method of sharing work: "Now as I understand it, when one of you is in charge on the west bank, the other has authority on the east, and vice versa."

Inspired by the work on the statues, the twin administrators wanted to discuss a text they were composing—a hymn to Amun as sole god, a manifestation of all gods. In a flood of excited imagery, the two explained how their plans for the finishing of the colossi suddenly caused them to think of the outer appearances and inner realities of the gods, particularly as they are manifest as statues. After reading portions of the hymn out loud, they proclaimed, "All statues are but specialized forms, ultimately, of the great creator Ptah, himself imagined as a great cult image."

Completing his recollection and returning to the present, Ay becomes more serious. "Your eyes, your Majesty, truly began to glow like the electrum the twins described when they read one particular passage extolling the sun god."

"I can quote it even now," replies the ruler—just as Ay expected—and with a slight pause, Akhenaten does just that:

Even electrum is not like your brilliance.
How Ptah-like are you, you gilding your flesh—
   fashioner unfashioned, unique traverser of eternity—
      one upon the ways, millions bearing his image.
Your brilliance is heaven's brilliance—more than its hue does your color
   scintillate.[1]

"A wonderful day it was," Ay says after a moment. "It gave birth to great things." Akhenaten does not reply, except to sigh contentedly, looking over at Nefertiti and his beloved daughters.

Ancient Egypt had a long tradition of solar hymns. The ancient Egyptians did not have a single book of scripture but rather a multiplicity of sources, often sharing similar imagery and phraseology. In the tombs at Akhet-Aten, we see two forms of Aten hymns, which overlap considerably in their vocabulary and conceptual framework. Written in thirteen columns of hieroglyphs on the right thickness of the tomb of Ay's entrance is the so-called Great Hymn, which shares many themes with another group of texts called the Short Hymn (our complete translation of the Great Hymn can be found in the Appendix).

In three examples, the shorter hymn to Aten is said to be spoken by Akhenaten. The tomb owners have carved the king's words, not their own, in the doorways of their tombs. Even before he was Akhenaten, Amunhotep IV explicitly claimed authorship of a festival song for his jubilee, and we should not doubt him capable of composing the text of the two Aten hymns. Besides the boundary stelae, the hymns to Aten and hymns to the king in the tombs of Akhet-Aten are the lengthiest texts from Akhenaten's entire seventeen-year reign.

These texts are among the most important and awe-inspiring works of ancient Egyptian literature. For these hymns, we need not make as many educated deductions, for the texts have few lacunae. Collecting parallels remains essential, or else we lose sight of what is innovative about the hymns to Aten and what is, in fact, a repetition of existing concepts. The first theme of the Aten hymns is the beauty and luminosity of the sun, whose light energy creates life. In the Great Hymn, Ay's adoration of Aten begins with the sun's rising:

> *May you appear beautifully in the horizon of heaven, o living Aten,*
> > *who initiates life,*
> > *you having arisen in the eastern horizon.*

That you have filled every land with your perfection,
  is with you being beautiful, great, dazzling, and high over every land.[2]

The word for "dazzling" is the same that qualifies Amunhotep III as the Dazzling Sun Disk, and the beauty and greatness of Aten are common attributes of the sun god throughout ancient Egyptian history. The light that Aten dispenses is not simply the bright rays of noon but the diverse shades of sunrise and sunset: "Your rays reach the eyes of all which you have created, your brilliant hues enlivening hearts."[3] Enough natural quartz existed in the Nile Valley that the ancient Egyptians were aware of a prismatic effect: light contains within itself a multitude of hues. The sum of these colors is perfection itself, Aten being "one scintillating of noble hues, o you who have inundated heaven and earth with your perfection."[4]

Just as the didactic name of Aten appeared with a slight variation already in the reign of Amunhotep III, so a remarkable pair of solar hymns on a stela of Suty and Hor, twins who "came forth from the womb on the same day," transform our understanding of solar beliefs around the time that Amunhotep IV came to the throne. Their hymns foreshadow both the language and the concepts of the Aten hymns. On the concept of brilliance and color, the stela of Suty and Hor praises Re as, "your brilliance is heaven's brilliance—more than its hue does your color dazzle."[5]

Aten's position in heaven makes him the ruler of all lands, not just Egypt, and for Akhenaten, the sun god vanquishes all foes, as the Great Hymn continues:

Your rays always encompass the lands,
  to the limit of all which you have created, you being as Re.
That you have attained their limits,
  is so that you might subdue them for the son whom you love.[6]

The deified southern colossus of Amunhotep III that still stands at the entrance to his temple on the west bank of Waset is named Re of the Rulers, the sun god who is the king of kings, master of all. In ancient Egypt, warfare was always presented as divinely sanctioned, and

Aten took up the mantle of the bellicose aspects of the god Amun. Aten created all Egyptians and all foreigners, and while he might provide for those outside of Egypt, he was quick to subdue any who might defy the authority of his true and beloved son.

In the next section of the Great Hymn, the text presents the paradox of Aten being remote yet everywhere:

> *You are far, while your rays are on earth.*
> *You are visible, but your movements are never seen.*[7]

Later in the Great Hymn, and in some versions of the Short Hymn, Aten created heaven explicitly to achieve that remoteness: "You have made heaven far, in order to shine within it, so that all that you have made might see."[8] All can see Aten's shining orb, but only the king knows his hidden movements.

What happens, then, when Aten goes to rest in the western horizon? The answer to this question is what sets Akhenaten's theology apart from everything that came before and all that would come afterward. Suty and Hor described how people lack fulfillment when the sun sets, but they still assumed a purpose for the solar journey through the night: "Just as you complete the hours of the night, so do you regulate it (the night)—there is no ceasing of your labors."[9] A few lines later they note that, when the sun sets, people, metaphorically called cattle, "sleep in the manner of death."

The Great Hymn to Aten expands upon this concept, describing night as a type of death, a time of fear and peril:

> *When you go to rest in the western horizon,*
> *   the land is in darkness in the manner of death,*
> *   the sleepers in the bedchamber, heads covered.*
> *No eye can see another,*
> *   so that all their possessions could be stolen—although they are beneath*
> *   their heads—without them knowing.*
> *Every lion has come forth from his den.*
> *All serpents bite.*
> *The shrine grows dark, the land is silent.*
> *The one who made them has gone to rest in his horizon.*[10]

The Short Hymns to Aten also describe night as a form of death: "When you set in the western horizon of heaven, they sleep in the manner of those who have died. Their heads are covered, nostrils obstructed."[11] The hymns provide no details about the dead in the Underworld, or even how Aten travels through the twelve hours of the night.

Night may be like death, but life resumes with full vigor when Aten rises again each day.

> *With you rising in the horizon does the day dawn,*
>   *you shining as the sun disk during the day.*
> *That you drive away darkness is so that you might give out your rays,*
>   *with the result that the two lands are in festival.*[12]

The sun god himself is perpetually in jubilee—nearly every caption to the multi-armed disk describes Aten as "one who is in jubilee (*heb sed*)." As people rouse themselves from slumber, they praise the eternally festive, light-giving sun disk. The Great Hymn elaborates on the effect of the sun's rays in the natural and manmade world.

> *The entire land carries out its work.*
>
> *All cattle are content with their fodder.*
> *The trees and plants flourish.*
> *Birds are flown from their nests,*
>   *their wings in praise of your ka-spirit.*
> *All small flocks leap on their feet.*
> *All which fly and alight live,*
>   *when you have arisen for them.*
>
> *Ships go north and south likewise.*
> *Every road is open because you appear in glory.*
> *The fish in the river leap up to your face.*
> *Your rays are in the sea.*[13]

The Nile Valley has sunshine in abundance, and the hymns to Aten link divine luminosity with the flourishing of life on earth. Some of the earliest extant solar temples in Egypt, from around 2430 BCE, include reliefs that showcase events from the seasons of the year, highlighting the annual cycle of procreation and birth in the natural world. Compositions as diverse as the Coffin Texts and hymns to Amun-Re praise a solar god in terms similar to the Aten hymn, with light creating life for all manner of creatures.

A version of the Short Hymn in the tomb of the chamberlain Tutu includes the most vivid description of the powerful physical effect that the sun disk has on his creation:

All flowering plants live continuously,
  growing on the ground,
  flourishing in your radiance,
  intoxicated at the sight of you.
All small flocks leap on their feet.
The birds in the nest fly up in joy,
  their folded wings now spread out in praise of living Aten.[14]

We learn from the Great Hymn not only that Aten was responsible for enlivening the entire cosmos but also that the solar orb was the specific force behind the process of conception in humans, their growth in the womb, and their birth at the proper time. This section finds no parallel in the shorter Aten hymns, and translating the text is challenging.

It is tempting to render a word like "water" as "semen" based on context, in the phrase "who transforms water into people"; since ancient Egyptian possessed a separate word for "semen," the choice of the typical noun for "water" must be intentional here, perhaps an allusion to the waters of Nun, out of which all creation arose. The description of a human fetus transitioning to a metaphor of a chick may strike a modern reader as odd. This would have been less surprising for an Egyptian reader who was accustomed to descriptions of a king already destined to rule "in the egg." Here is the embryology of the Great Hymn, how Aten's omniscience makes conception and birth possible.

O one who makes the fetus develop in women.
Who transforms water into people!

Who enlivens the son in the womb of his mother;
Who quiets him with that which will stop his tears.

Nurse in the womb, who gives breath in order to enliven all which he has
    made,
        so that he descends from the womb in order to breathe on his day of
        birth.

As for the one whose mouth you open completely,
        you take care of him,
            even the chick in the egg.
As for the one who speaks in the shell,
        you give him breath within it in order to enliven him.[15]

The visual nature of the determinatives, the classifying signs without phonetic value, create a parallel narrative to the verbal translation: the ejaculating phallus determinative for "fetus," a crying eye for "tears," and a female breast for "nurse." The physical universe of childbirth is drawn on the wall, even as the lines of the hymn describe the process.

The Great Hymn then transitions from the development of an individual fetus to creation on a cosmic scale, expounding on Aten's endless works:

How many are your deeds,
        although they are hidden from sight.
The sole god with no other besides him.
You created the earth according to your desire,
        you being alone.[16]

Aten creates alone, his actions hidden, just like his movements through heaven. In the shorter hymns, Aten is:

The august god;
    who built himself by himself;
    who made every land and fashioned all that is upon it:
        people, cattle, all small flocks, all trees, that which grows on the earth.

That they live is when you shine for them.
You are the mother and father of all which you have made.[17]

As the self-created solar god, Akhenaten contains in himself both male and female; he is both mother and father of the world. In the hymn of Suty and Hor, Re is praised as

One who fashioned himself,
    while modeling your own limbs;
who gives birth to himself,
    without one giving birth to him;
unique one, with no other except him.[18]

In ancient Egyptian cosmogonies, there is only one god at the beginning of time, and from him comes everything in the cosmos. Hymns may reference this primordial moment, but the creator god's solitude ends when he fashions additional divinities. What makes the Aten hymns unusual is that the created world does not include the expected generations of gods: Shu and Tefnut; Geb and Nut; Osiris and Isis, and their offspring.

Once the Great Hymn declares Aten's creation an act that the god performs in isolation, the hymn moves to a cosmopolitan perspective, in which Aten cares for all peoples of the world. Akhenaten reflected this on earth by choosing a bodyguard of diverse origins. People might speak different languages and have different skin tones, but they are all Aten's creatures.

The foreign lands of Syria, Kush, and the land[19] *of Egypt—*
You set every man at his (proper) place,
    and make their requirements,
        with the result that each one has his diet,
            his lifetime having been reckoned.
Tongues are distinguished in speech,
    their natures likewise.
Their skins are different,
    for you distinguish the foreigners.

As for all distant foreign lands,
  you make them live.
That it might descend for them have you placed an inundation in heaven.
That it makes waves upon the mountains like the sea
  is in order to water their fields with what pertains to them.[20]

Aten recognizes that not all people benefit from the regular inundation of the Nile that replenishes the soil of Egypt each year. Instead, Aten places an inundation in the skies, a poetic expression for rain (for which ancient Egyptian had a perfectly usable word). Wherever a person might live, Aten provides for them.

The Great Hymn then recapitulates Aten's omniscience and life-giving power. The god may be far away in heaven, but his heat-giving rays make his presence very real to all his creation.

That you have made heaven far
  is in order to rise within it, and to see all that you have made,
    you being alone and risen in your transformations as living Aten,
    you having appeared in glory,
    you shining, you being far (yet) near.
From yourself do you make millions of manifestations—sole one.[21]

The conclusion of the Short Hymn expresses the same themes: "You are unique, but millions of lives are within you in order to make them live."[22] Aten not only creates the world and everything within it but also fashions time itself. Light is the way that Aten communicates with his creation: "Their eyes: as soon as you rise, they see by means of you!"[23]

People can see the disk and feel its heat, but Aten is otherwise mute. Unlike other gods, Aten does not speak to anyone except the royal family. In earlier Eighteenth Dynasty private monuments, and especially stelae after the reign of Akhenaten, people addressed gods directly and expected to receive a verbal response. At Akhet-Aten, even the high priests of Aten only interacted directly with the king, who acted as the intermediary between the priests and the god that they served.

Among all the texts from Akhet-Aten, the only words Aten speaks are recorded on royal sarcophagi, granite monuments intended to hold the bodily remains of Akhenaten, Nefertiti, and the princess Meketaten. After Akhenaten's death, the sarcophagi were smashed into small pieces, the destruction so intense that only snippets of hieroglyphic text are preserved. On Akhenaten's sarcophagus, Aten says, "Come, my son, [that] you [may become] a luminous spirit by means of me."[24] To Meketaten, upon her tragically young death, Aten states, "My rays are upon her."[25] If only more of Aten's speech had survived!

In the concluding lines of the Great Hymn, Ay states that the king, referred to by his coronation name Neferkheperure-Waenre ("Beautiful are the Manifestations of Re, unique one of Re"), is the only person who knows Aten:

> There is no other one who knows you,
>   except for your son, Neferkheperure-Waenre,
>   whom you cause to become aware of your plans and your power:
> that the earth comes about is through your action, in as much as you make them;
> that you have arisen is so that they might live—as you set so they die.
>
> Lifetime is your very own—through you one lives.
>
> Everyone who hurries by foot, since you founded the land—
> you raise them up for your son, who comes forth from your flesh.
>
> Akhenaten, great in his lifetime;
> The king's great wife, his beloved, lady of the Two Lands,
>   Neferneferuaten Nefertiti, may she live and be youthful forever and ever.[26]

Akhenaten's theology attempted to halt the world in a primordial state, with Akhenaten and Nefertiti the only gods whom Aten has created. In art, the king and queen have nearly identical bodies as the first male-female pair, not yet fully differentiated but partaking in the androgyny of the creator god. When a hymn to Aten proclaims the god to be both "mother and father" of mankind, those same words could be applied to the unusual colossus at the Gem-pa-Aten, showing Akhenaten possessing both male and female attributes.

We need not see Akhenaten and the worship of Aten as the origin of the type of monotheism that is expressed in Judaism, Christianity, or Islam. Akhenaten's apparent monotheism is instead a question of time: the other gods do not exist because they do not yet exist, because the process of creation of further generations of divine beings has come to a halt after Aten fashions Akhenaten and Nefertiti. In the boundary stelae, Akhenaten describes his new city as "his place of the primeval event," and within Akhet-Aten, each day is repeated as a renewal of that first occurrence. For the population of the city, the king is the only god with whom they can speak.

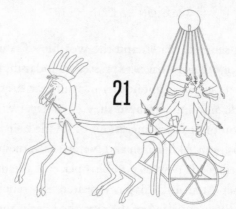

My God Who Fashioned Me

AY AND TIY HAVE ARRIVED EARLY AT THE KING'S HOUSE IN THE
Central City. Today they are to receive the gold of honor in recompense for their years of service. Soon the pair are joined by the royal
bodyguard and other attendants, standing before the Window of Appearances.

The window is more of an engaged kiosk, and indeed the young
king found inspiration in the festival pavilions of his royal predecessors.
He is as interested in architecture as he is in temple finances and solar
hymns. Emerging from the wall of the court is a rectangular box, elevated on a platform. In the middle of the structure is the actual window,
closed with door leaves and topped with the broken lintel typical of the
architecture of Akhet-Aten. The bottom half of the door is blocked by
a low wall with an elaborate version of the "uniting the Two Lands"
motif, showing bound foreign enemies tied to the intertwined plants of
Upper and Lower Egypt.

Ay and Tiy ascend the ramps to take up position just below the window. One of the palace butlers moves up and whispers to them that the
king suggested they stay back a bit—he has quite a bit to give them.
Just then, the two leaves of the doors swing inward, opened by bowing

courtiers. Stepping forward, Akhenaten and Nefertiti smile to Ay and Tiy. Three nurses appear behind the royal couple, leading to them three young daughters. Attendants bow, holding aloft platters filled with the rewards that will soon shower down from the window.

The ceremony takes somewhat longer than Ay and Tiy expected, with Akhenaten and Nefertiti pausing frequently to speak with their excited daughters. While little Ankhesenpaaten stands on the cushioned edge of the window, pointing and laughing, supported by her mother, the oldest, Meritaten, tries her best to copy her mother's gentle toss of a broad collar. But Meketaten gleefully pitches collars as hard as possible toward Ay and Tiy, who add them to the growing pile of baubles at their feet.

Behind them, ranks of courtiers and royal bodyguards bow, salute, and generally acclaim the proceedings, while a quartet of scribes busily record the event. The pile grows: gilded collars, signet rings, metal dishes, metal wine cups, and even fancy pairs of gloves.

While the ceremony is underway, Ay's attendants wait near the entrance to the hall. Some are already drinking wine directly from large painted and garlanded vessels. Several young members of the household run about near the door trailing freshly cut vines, the doorman alternately laughing at them and chiding them, brandishing his palm rib baton in a show of concern that his humor belies. Other young men of the court perform a high-stepping dance of joy.

At the end of the ceremony, Ay and his wife walk into the brilliant sunlight of the Royal Road, light bouncing off whitewashed walls and glittering on their awards. Several servants rush forward to support the arms of Ay's wife, intended as a show for onlookers to indicate the weight of gold with which she is weighed down. With seven broad collars tied in glittering disarray around his neck and shoulders, Ay is heavier by many *deben* of gold as well and holds out his hands, wearing the marvelous decorated gloves that he has just received. Two chariots await, each accompanied by a pair of runners holding staves and palm rib batons.

The attendants, many already approaching inebriation, have been joined by passersby who stop to learn about the event. Guards at palace checkpoints, not having seen Ay and Tiy when the couple arrived, ask a small boy who is running off his excitement: "For whom is acclamation made, my boy?"

"Shout praise for Ay, the god's father, and Tiy," says the boy. "They have been turned into people of gold."[1]

As they near their villa, Ay and Tiy pass between lines of musicians and welcoming household staff. A group of four women beat tambourines and sing praises of the couple, while two apprentices perform an ancient stomping dance. Even as additional people rush out to meet them, others are pushing past into the courtyard of the villa, laden with the last of the provisions for the enormous celebration that is already underway. The men seated on small folding stools and the women in their ethereal sheer finery lounging on cushions bask in the radiance of Ay and Tiy, who in their shining gold ornaments are literal mirrors of their royal patrons. Ay's house becomes a miniature of all of Akhet-Aten, its occupants spending the day and night in celebration in the glow of a radiant couple.

In tomb entrances, the great officials of Akhet-Aten recite a hymn to Aten on one side, while on the other they intone a brief praise of Aten followed by praise of their king. Panehesy, a high priest of Aten, speaks thus, his arms raised in adoration.

> *Praise to you, my god who fashioned me;*
> *the one who fated good events for me.*

> *I am giving praise to the height of heaven,*
>   *as I worship the lord of the Two Lands,*
>   *he who is effective (akh) for (n) Aten.*
>   *Fate who dispenses life,*
>   *lord of what is commanded.*[2]

Akhenaten is Panehesy's intercessor, a god in his own right. Above the scene where this hieroglyphic text is located, Akhenaten and Nefertiti consecrate offerings for Aten, while three princesses shake sistra.

The other high priest of Aten, Meryre, the Greatest of Seers, recites similar phrases in the right-hand thickness of the door that leads into the main, columned hall of his tomb:

Praise to you, o Waenre!
I give adoration to the height of heaven.
I pacify the one who lives on maat,
    the lord of glorious appearances, Akhenaten, great in his lifetime.
*O inundation (*hapi*), at whose command one prospers,*
    the food and provision of Egypt.
O beautiful ruler, my creator, who made me, who raised me,
    who placed me among officials.
*O, light (*shu*), at whose sight I live! My* ka-*spirit of every day!*[3]

One of the most common epithets that Akhenaten possessed through-out his reign is "one who lives on *maat*." Here, Akhenaten transgressed royal norms and usurped the role of a deity: he does not just "bring about" *maat*, as was the king's duty, but lives on *maat*. Kings offer *maat* to the gods, but only gods live on *maat*. His officials could not petition gods; instead, they praised Akhenaten, who controlled their fate, as he dictated the essence of the cosmos, justice and order.

For the officials who served Akhenaten, these precepts did not im-pact only their religious beliefs but also their very livelihoods, as Ay makes clear in a text from his tomb:

He (Akhenaten) doubled for me my rewards from gold and silver, since I
was first among the officials, at the forefront of the people. My character
and my nature were good, so he made my position commensurate. My
lord taught me, so that I might carry out his teaching.[4]

To achieve success in this life, as well as immortality in the afterlife, officials were required to follow the teachings of Akhenaten, the moral authority of *maat* redefined as unerring loyalty to the king's words. When Ay says that the king "doubled" rewards of precious metals, he is describing one of the most common scenes within tombs at Akhet-Aten: the Window of Appearances.

As officials left the palace following their reception of awards at the Window of Appearances, delightedly burdened with royal gifts, they returned to their villas in the main residential areas of the city. Spreading north and south from the central complex of palaces and temples, the suburbs of Akhet-Aten were home to tens of thousands of people. In the surviving remains of these houses we can still see much of the people's ordinary lives, from their pig pens to their bed stands. But when it was time to pray, especially among the elite families, the object of devotion was the royal family.

Beauty Incarnate

NEFERTITI'S CHARIOT DRAWS UP IN FRONT OF THE GREAT ART-ists' compound, which belongs to the chief sculptor Thutmose. Dismounting, the queen and her two attendants move through two lines of soldiers, who stamp the ground and present their spears. The doorman announces the queen.

Moments later she and the attendants are waiting in the cool entrance hall of the chief sculptor's house, its roof supported by two columns. Soon the chief sculptor enters, followed by apprentices—one so suddenly called from his work that he is still covered in specks of plaster and paint—carrying a large and gorgeously inlaid chair, and two folding stools no less elaborately embellished. Thutmose invites the queen to sit in the middle of the hall, her attendants on lower stools just behind her.

Thutmose and his pupils disappear into a small room on the other end of the hall and return with a tall, narrow stand, on which the sculptor places a cloth-covered object. Waiting a moment and building the suspense as though he were the old magician Djedi himself, the sculptor, with one swift motion, draws the cloth rapidly upward. As the covering falls to the ground, Thutmose spreads out his hands in a gesture of presentation. There on the table, looking into the eyes of the queen, at the same level as her own eyes—Thutmose had commissioned the stand precisely for this moment—is a sculpted bust of Nefertiti.

As she slowly rises and walks around the piece, Nefertiti expresses amazement and great pleasure. She pauses, looking at the bust, and begins to feel first her chin, then that of the sculpture, her cheeks and those of the sculpture. After a while she smiles and asks the sculptor if she might look briefly at the head of her husband, a piece she understands he had completed as a pendant to the marvel that stood before them.

The sculptor bows, and motions for Nefertiti to accompany him into the small side room. After a few minutes the queen and the sculptor return, the queen saying, "Yes, the resemblance. I see now what you did. Now, when shall I return for another modeling session?"

DECEMBER 6, 1912: AMARNA, HOUSE P47.2

Shortly after the midday break, a note summoned Ludwig Borchardt, architect, Egyptologist, and director of the German expedition excavating at Amarna, to House P47.2. Borchardt's colleague, Hermann Ranke, was supervising the clearance of a small room in a large residential and work compound and wanted the director to see what had emerged, and what might yet lie hidden beneath several feet of debris that still covered the ancient floor. The room was no more than a pantry or large walk-in closet in size and was connected to the unusually large entrance hall of a house. That house was part of a set of residences and workshops at the intersection of two major streets in central Akhet-Aten.

Between 1907 and the outbreak of the First World War, Borchardt's team from the Deutsche Orient-Gesellschaft carried out archaeological work at the site of ancient Akhet-Aten. This work began, like all modern excavations, with a general survey to set up a grid so that find spots could be easily located relative to each other. Today, in our work in the Egyptian deserts, we are aided by a total station, a digital and laser range-finding tool to measure distance, elevation, and angle, which enables us to lay out a grid of predetermined squares. In Borchardt's time—and still possible now, though cumbersome!—one could take a compass, a theodolite, a measuring line, and a set of stakes and establish a grid. An initial map grid for the site of Akhet-Aten began with marking a central point atop the German dig house—itself constructed upon the stumps of the walls of an ancient Egyptian house—using wooden stakes to mark out squares measuring two hundred meters along each side and oriented to magnetic north.

The resulting letter and number designations for squares at the site, with additional numbers for buildings within each square, is how we refer to portions of the site today. As we move along the grid from west to east, we proceed from A through the letters of the alphabet; as we move from north to south, the numbers of the grid grow larger. The structure on which Borchardt's team was focused on that day late in 1912—a day momentous for Egyptology, art history, and even modern popular culture—received the unprepossessing label of P47.2.

As workmen removed debris from the room in P47.2, stone sculptures—both whole and fragmentary—emerged from beneath the yellow sand and crumbling bits of dark mud brick. Lying where they had fallen thirty-two centuries before, over fifty art objects were unearthed, an unparalleled collection. Alongside the carved stone pieces were plaster images of human faces: men and women, young and old, apparently both royal and nonroyal. But no object from Borchardt's extraordinary 1912 season could compare—in terms of both quality of execution and an indefinable, almost magical, connection with viewers—with one of the limestone busts, its painted plaster exterior almost perfectly preserved.

When Borchardt arrived at P47.2, a fragmentary, life-size bust of Akhenaten, wearing the royal blue crown, had already been uncovered near the entrance to the small Room 19. The narrow room is near the front of the house and runs the length of the east wall of a broad entrance hall with two columns. As the excavators worked toward the north wall and further pieces of art emerged, they realized they had found a veritable treasury of sculpture. Borchardt decided that only he and Ranke, with the Egyptian foreman Mohammed Ahmed es-Senussi, would continue to clear debris from the room, with an assistant in charge of the field notes. Close to the east wall of the room, near the northeast corner, a sculpted neck appeared.

Soon the excavators realized they were uncovering a painted bust of Nefertiti, lying upside down at roughly knee level, face toward the wall. All tools were immediately set aside, and the men began carefully clearing away the encumbering debris by hand. Back at the dig house, after midnight following the momentous day of clearance, Borchardt described the day's finds. About the painted bust of Nefertiti, he wrote simply: "Pointless to describe, must be seen!"

From the base to the tip of the crown, the sculpture measures 19.25 inches high, the width at the shoulder a little more than 9.5 inches. The bust is carved from limestone, overlaid by a thin layer of plaster that allowed the sculptor to create the finest, most subtle details. The back of the crown is modeled from a thicker layer of plaster, which reduced the weight of the tall headdress and thus lessened the strain on the queen's slender neck. Plaster also added stability to the neck and shoulders. The only damage to the nearly perfectly preserved image of the queen is the missing cobra on her crown, some chipping to the ears, and a few scratches to the paint. Otherwise, the bust looks exactly as it did when an artist set it on the storeroom shelf.

The stone image translates into concrete form the ideal expressed within the queen's name: female beauty, ancient Egyptian *nefret*. Symmetry and proportion combine to create a face that—more than any other—has come to embody ancient Egypt for a modern viewer. For the sculptor who created this icon, Nefertiti's long neck, delicate nose and mouth, and high cheekbones embodied her epithet *Neferneferuaten,* "Beautiful is the Perfection of Aten." The queen is as perfect on earth as Aten is in heaven.

The bust captures the complex interplay between the face's underlying skeletal structure and its subtle musculature. The muscles at the rear of the neck are taut, as if supporting the actual weight of the tall, blue crown, which contrast with the queen's relaxed facial features that suggest an ethereal calm. The colors of the band that wraps around her blue crown are repeated in the broad collar she wears at her neck. Paint mimics the gold, lapis lazuli, turquoise, carnelian, and malachite of a piece of jewelry that the queen certainly wore in life.

Nefertiti's facial features are perfectly proportioned, yet faint wrinkles around her eyes and dimples at the edge of her mouth lend elements of verisimilitude. Her right eye is shockingly realistic, an effect created with a carefully carved rock crystal that fits perfectly into the eye socket. A simple method—black wax applied to the back of the rock crystal—creates the illusion of an actual pupil and iris; to either side of the pupil, the rock crystal allows us to see the white paint on the plaster of the eye socket, creating a simulacrum of the sclera. The left eye has no rock crystal inlay and may never have been fitted with one—this one omission in an otherwise perfect piece may reveal something of the bust's original function, as does its find spot in a sculptor's workshop.

The queen's makeup is understated, a far cry from the often-stylized cosmetics carved and painted on stone statues. Nefertiti's eyebrows are strongly delineated, but not by a solid line: instead, fine brushstrokes capture the individual hairs of the queen's brows. Her eyes are rimmed with kohl, and a thin line extends to the outer edge of her eye, ending at the crease of the eyelid. The queen's lips are tinted a wine red, while a faint blush is detectable at the cheeks.

The bust may preserve something of the appearance and character of the queen, but it does so within the system of proportions that the artist's grid dictated. All formal Egyptian art, both in two and three dimensions, was based on an established grid. The grids for Nefertiti's bust disappeared as the sculpture entered its final phases of carving, but we can overlay an imaginary grid on the completed sculpture. What we see is that the features of the bust scrupulously follow a grid of Egyptian "finger" divisions (0.75 inches).

Nearly every major feature of the queen's face falls on a full finger-measure unit of the reconstructed grid. In the bust of Nefertiti, art may indeed reflect physical beauty, but it does so at the service of artifice. Even if that is the queen's mouth, and that her long and sensual neck—the first part of her beauty that the excavators glimpsed—these features are subtly altered and subjected to the sizes and proportions determined by an artist's grid. Art treasure the bust of Nefertiti certainly is, but key to unlocking Nefertiti's secrets, even a mirror of her actual appearance, it is not.

Another set of sculptures found in Room 19, twenty-three portraits made from gypsum plaster, may be closer to the actual appearance of Akhet-Aten's elite. Originally thought to be "death masks," the plaster

Plaster cast from Thutmose's studio.
(Ägyptisches Museum und Papyrussammlung,
Staatliche Museen, Berlin, Inv. 21261; Photo by Jürgen Liepe)

images are actually casts taken from sculptures that had reached a certain state of completion, but not their final form. It is simply remarkable that objects that were seemingly disposable and probably intended to be used for a short period of time have survived.

Some of the faces are so realistically carved in plaster that we would not be shocked to meet them on the street today: an older woman with creases on her forehead, her lips curved in a slight smile; a girl with the smooth skin of youth, her mouth in a subtle pout; an older man, with crow's-feet at his eyes, a strong nose and mouth, and a distinctly asymmetrical set to his ears. Before these sculptures would be completed, they too would have been altered to conform, more or less, to the artist's grid. A final statue placed within a tomb chapel would be an idealized representation of a person's nature, carved with hieroglyphic texts to confirm their identity. The gypsum plaster casts in the artist's studio allow us to glimpse the portraits before that stylizing process had begun, one of the rare cases when we can truly look upon the faces of people who lived three thousand years ago.

The studio in which Nefertiti's bust was discovered was part of a series of workrooms along the side of House P47.2. In its final form, the sprawling villa appears to have been the communal compound of a master sculptor, with multiple artists living in a single enclosed area. A fragment of an artifact from the villa may bear the master artist's name. Partially preserved on a piece of an ivory horse blinker excavated from one of four tree pits in the complex is the name of "the overseer of works, sculptor Thutmose." The horse blinker indicates that Thutmose owned a chariot and at least two horses and could afford an expensive material for the tack of those already costly animals.

Borchardt realized that the blinker might have belonged to the owner of one of the major structures in the villa, but he was at first cautious in identifying the name with the master sculptor overseeing the complex. Nevertheless, over time the desire to know the name of the creator of a now universally acclaimed work of art has led to the routine designation of the large compound as the home and studio of the sculptor Thutmose, the artist who carved the bust of Nefertiti.

Ancient Egyptian artists rarely added their own names to their work, and no signed piece of royal sculpture from the reign of Akhenaten appears to be known. To imagine an ancient Egyptian workshop is to abandon the modern conception of the artist as a solitary hero. A scene in the tomb chapel of the vizier Rekhmire, who lived around 1400 BCE, provides a defining illustration of ancient Egyptian artistry. A group of five artists stand and sit as they work on a wooden scaffolding enclosing a standing statue; other workmen appear at the base of the statue itself. Egypt's artists created their sublimely massive works of stone and wonderfully intricate compositions in paint only by allowing personal artistry to be subsumed by the vision of a great communal work.

The artists' signatures that are known are primarily from the monuments of various officials, in which an important administrator takes visible pride in having secured the services of a famous artist. An artist's signature could thus glorify both the artist and the patron. Only a few minutes north of the expedition house where we spend our summer and winter field seasons is the ancient city of Nekheb and the necropolis where the highest-ranking men of the region were buried. We often visit these tombs, climbing the hillside and enjoying the view of the Nile and the ancient city. In the tomb of the late Ramesside governor Setau (ca. 1175 BCE), an artist named Merire left at least three surviving images and textual signatures. Merire is insistent that he is not merely an artist, but a learned scribe.

An artist named Irtysen, a man whose career unfolded four thousand years ago, has even more to tell us about what it meant to create art in ancient Egypt, and his words are the closest we may ever come to speaking with an ancient Egyptian artist. Irtysen explains how an artist could be someone trained in both visual style and scribal learning, a fact that Merire emphasizes as well. Part of an artist's education might also be religious in nature, even involving an application of magical practice to technical ability and artistic inspiration. The term *hemou,* "artist, craftsman," applies to those who create from knowledge and expertise, as distinct from the more basic *irou,* "maker" or "fabricator." With that background, we can better understand Irtysen's words in our translation of a notoriously difficult text:

> *I know: the secret of hieroglyphic script, the conduct of festival rituals.*
> *As for all (applicable) magic—*
> > *without anything escaping me have I acquired it.*
> *I am indeed a* hemou-*artist excellent in his craft,*
> > *successful because of what he knows.*[1]

We can confidently assume that the master sculptor at Akhet-Aten also read hieroglyphs, including Akhenaten's Great Hymn to Aten, and viewed the creation of Nefertiti's bust as an expression of his knowledge, not just his artistic skill.

Before we leave Thutmose's workshop, we must return to the most enigmatic feature of Nefertiti's face: her blank left eye. When Borchardt first uncovered the bust, he had the sand fill of Room 19 carefully sifted in an attempt to find the rock crystal inlay, but, alas, none was found. Careful examination of the eye socket suggests that no inlay was ever present, for there are no traces of adhesives. The most commonly accepted theory of the bust's function was that it was a master model and possibly a trial piece for artists to practice the challenging technique of fashioning inlaid eyes. Perhaps the most famous work of art from ancient Egypt was never intended to be seen outside the artist's studio.

Yet this is not the only explanation, and for an alternate theory we need to consider other sculptures found within the art-filled storeroom. In the debris above the painted head of Nefertiti was a much more damaged bust of Akhenaten. On the basis of its size and completed paint, the now fragmentary image of the king was a companion to the head of the queen. The band of the king's crown and the mandragora fruits of his broad collar appear to have been gilded, the gold leaf having been removed before the studio was abandoned. These features suggest that the bust of the king was in its final stages, if not finished.

A stand-alone bust was a rare object in ancient Egyptian art, and those of Akhenaten and Nefertiti are the only royal examples thus far identified. To study finished statues that only show the head and shoulders of an individual, we must travel to a village now called Deir el-Medina on the west bank of Luxor, home to the artisans who built the royal tombs in the Valley of the Kings (like Seta, whom we met earlier). Archaeologists uncovered sculptures known as "ancestor busts" in the houses there; some were placed in small shrines next to inscribed offering tables. Similar artifacts have been discovered at other settlement sites, including Akhet-Aten (one even from the complex belonging to the sculptor Thutmose).

The busts appear to represent powerful ancestors, and while the statues themselves are not labeled and are generic in appearance, they were probably placed atop plinths that included the names of the person represented. Small stelae, also from Deir el-Medina, sometimes include images of ancestors who are given the title "effective spirit of Re" followed by their name. The busts thus appear to be three-dimensional versions of these same spirits to whom one might make offerings in the hope that the powerful dead would in turn assist the living with problems on earth.

Residents of Deir el-Medina also manufactured stelae and statues (of the entire body, standing or seated) of their revered royal patrons, although no bust of a king or queen has been identified. Perhaps the busts of Akhenaten and Nefertiti were intended to be objects of veneration in a private shrine at Akhet-Aten, the king and queen being as powerful as effective spirits of the dead. Were the busts abandoned just before they were completed and ready to ship to their final destination? The most famous face from ancient Egypt may have been meant for display within the home of a single wealthy family.

Whether a sculptor's model or a sacred object, Nefertiti was almost certainly involved in approving her image and either visited Thutmose's studio to do so or summoned him to the palace. Other artists at Akhet-Aten, perhaps some of Thutmose's colleagues and apprentices, also created stelae whose function as private devotional objects is beyond doubt. We go next to the greatest repository of Egyptian art in the world to look upon one of those stelae, a small artifact that enables us to decode portraits of the royal family shown in their most intimate moments.

23

A Holy Family

Ramose reaches his hand across the bed in the moment between sleep and awakening. He dreads that time each day when he again becomes conscious that his beloved no longer slumbers beside him. She left this world just as their youngest child was born. Now, every night he says a prayer over her bust in the front room of their house. As he looks fondly at the wall paintings—the pregnant hippopotamus goddess Tawaret standing next to several images of the dwarf god Bes, banging drums and holding knives—he gives thanks to them for watching over the safety of his children. If only his beloved was not already with Osiris!

Ten years ago, Ramose and his wife had moved from their village nestled in the western hills of Waset, home to the servants of the Place of Truth. There he was one of the proud artisans responsible for hewing the pharaoh's tomb from the cliff, smoothing its walls, laying the plaster, and carving its hieroglyphs and elaborate scenes. His expertise is the final step in the process—painting the brilliant colors that breathe life into every image.

Now, Ramose does the same for a new king in a new city. His family was among the first to move to the new city of Akhet-Aten when Akhenaten declared it to be the place of the god who shines upon them.

Why the god who graces all of Egypt with his light needs so much attention at one rather inhospitable patch of ground has always eluded him. But who is he but a painter tasked with decorating the eternal resting place of the unique son of Aten?

Ramose steps out of his low-legged bed and goes downstairs to the delightful smell of breakfast awaiting him. He realizes that he slept longer than he intended—his daughter has already brought the food from the rear kitchen into the central room, where his three younger children are sitting on low mud-brick benches. As head of the household, Ramose sits in his fine ebony chair, a prized possession that he brought from Waset.

Ready for the day, he and his eldest son, who is also his apprentice, walk along the narrow street to the gate of the walled enclosure with its tightly packed houses, all very much like his own. He waves and shouts "Come in peace" as a formal greeting to a passing patrolman, who is completing his daily rounds of the tracks that crisscross the desert east of the main city.

Ramose and his son are on their way to the valley of the royal tomb, but, stirred by dreams of his deceased wife, he decides first to make an important stop. Skirting a pigpen and the village's rubbish heap, they make their way to the main village chapel, a mud-brick building. Here, and in smaller chapels for individual families, the living can communicate directly with the spirits of those buried farther to the east. In these uncertain times, there is so much to discuss! He walks past a shallow basin, a reminder to purify his thoughts as well as his hands and mouth. After dipping his hands in the water and seeing that his son does the same, Ramose reaches into his leather satchel and pulls out two small incense-infused balls of natron. In unison he and his son place the salt pellets in their mouths, cleansing the words they shall say. Now they can enter the shrine. Short on time, they go straight through the roofed halls and up the three stairs into the sanctuary.

Even though this chapel is for the entire village, it is a particularly special place for Ramose, since he personally painted the decoration of the chamber. Only a few years ago, he added the final strokes on the wings flanking the disk above the central chamber, the sharp talons of the vultures painted to either side, and the tall, vibrant bouquets. How long he had spent grinding the perfect shade of blue for the blossoms! Together, he and his son say a prayer in remembrance of the wife and mother that they lost.

Then, they turn to start a week of camping deep in the eastern wadi, where they will spend long days laboring on the reliefs in the king's tomb.

CAIRO, EGYPT

Having just completed our summer field season, filled with exciting discoveries of rock inscriptions, we are returning to Cairo to submit our report to the Ministry of Antiquities, which oversees all archaeological work in Egypt. Flying into Cairo International Airport, we pass over the Cairo district of Matariyyah (meaning "area of the airport") and touch down near where the temple of Re and Atum once rose, the complex that inspired so many of Aten's sacred spaces.

We collect our bags and hire a car for a drive to the Egyptian Museum in Tahrir Square, since 1901 the supreme repository of ancient Egyptian art and artifacts. Arriving at the museum, and after passing through the first of its metal detectors, we enter the garden with its papyrus-filled pool surrounded by monuments.

We go through another security checkpoint to the museum proper and see ahead of us the sunken floor and high ceiling of the main central atrium. At the far end is a restored colossal pair statue of Amunhotep III and Tiye, which originally stood at the southern gate to the king's west bank temple at Waset, just a few steps away from the jubilee city of Malqata. On the floor nearby is what remains of a painted pavement from the Great Palace at Akhet-Aten. The fragile paintings on the pavement are protected by a glass and wood cover, as though a low greenhouse is sheltering the plants and animals whom an artist froze in time over thirty-three centuries ago.

Our destination lies just beyond the atrium, a room devoted to objects from the time of Akhenaten. To the right are two of the colossi from the Gem-pa-Aten at Karnak, including the strange, androgynous statue.

To the left is an unfinished quartzite head of Nefertiti, the sculptor's ink guidelines—possibly those of Thutmose himself—still visible. Paintings from the palaces of Akhet-Aten hang on the walls, while a case is filled with the sorts of jars that would have been commonplace in the city's villas.

In this room are two stone objects—a miniature pylon and a stela—that decorated shrines in the residences of Akhet-Aten's elite, allowing Akhenaten's officials, even at home, to worship the royal family. The king does not seem to have required the construction of such shrines in every household, as many villas lack archaeological evidence for them. In more modest households, we see a greater diversity of religious objects that relate to the old Egyptian pantheon.

The extent to which the beliefs of Akhenaten and Nefertiti were shared by the population of Akhet-Aten is inscrutable, and we know even less about what the rest of Egypt may have thought of the religion of Aten and his beloved children. Perhaps the impact of Akhenaten's solar religion was relatively small, with most Egyptians worshipping the same gods as their ancestors, continuing cults with millennia-old traditions. We can be certain, however, that visible adherence to the cult of Akhenaten and Nefertiti as the children of Aten was a necessary aspect of high office at Akhet-Aten.

Shrines occur both inside villas and in their walled gardens. One of the most spectacular of the interior shrines is a miniature pylon, originally set up in a large room of the villa of the high priest Panehesy in the Central City and now housed in the Egyptian Museum. Panehesy's altar reproduces each element of an Aten temple pylon, complete with images of Akhenaten, Nefertiti, and Meritaten worshipping Aten. The temple entrance was originally fitted with doors, which could be opened to reveal an additional object of veneration, likely a statue or stela of the royal family. Still in situ at Amarna are several examples of garden chapels, such as that in the large house of the Overseer of Royal Works Hatiay (T34.1). The domestic garden shrines were scaled-down versions of a Sunshade of Re, places to praise the holy family among pools, trees, and flowering plants.

The Amarna gallery in the Egyptian Museum also contains the most important of a small group of stelae that were placed within niches in elite households. Scaled to befit their domestic contexts, typically just

Detail of Akhenaten, Nefertiti, and the princesses on a painted limestone stela in the Egyptian Museum, Cairo (JE 44865).

over a foot in height and width, these stelae are decorated with portraits of the royal family. They are not static images of ritual and offering but are filled with motion and emotion, a loving family of squirming princesses and languid royal parents. Whether Akhenaten actually went about his day-to-day life inseparable from Nefertiti and the princesses is unknowable. We can be certain, however, that the presence of so many royal women and children in the art of Akhenaten's reign says something essential about his rule and his religion.

The Cairo Stela—at the center rear of the gallery—is unique in its imagery and symbolism, still retaining much of its original paint. Recesses flanking the central image suggest that the stela once had two wooden panels that closed over the image, functioning like a medieval or Renaissance triptych, perhaps the earliest surviving example of a folding altar. In a dramatic series of events, this stela and the bust of Nefertiti were discovered only thirty-six days apart during the 1912/1913 field season of the German expedition at Amarna.

At the conclusion of the work, a division of finds was conducted, a formal process during which the French-directed antiquities service inspected the artifacts and decided which would remain in Egypt and which would be handed over to the institution that funded the excavations (in this case, a private individual, James Simon). The expedition director, Ludwig Borchardt, drew up a document with his suggestions: at the top of the list of objects that should, in his opinion, remain in Egypt is the stela we now stand before in the Egyptian Museum; at the top of the corresponding column of objects to go to Germany was the bust of Nefertiti.

Today, fortunately, the Egyptian Ministry of Antiquities, not foreign directors of expeditions or representatives of their sponsoring institutions, have authority over all ancient sites and ongoing excavations (many of them led by Egyptian archaeologists), and any newly discovered artifacts remain in the country. As Americans granted the privilege of conducting research in Egypt, we find that one of the most rewarding aspects of our work is collaborating with Egyptian colleagues and residents of towns near the sites where we record ancient rock inscriptions. Now, spectacular artifacts become the centerpieces of exhibitions in local and national museums in Egypt, where they are often displayed alongside the rich heritage of the Nile Valley that extends beyond antiquity to the artistic flowering of Islamic Egypt and modern art movements.

But in 1912, it was a Frenchman, Gustave Lefebvre, and not an Egyptian Egyptologist who was responsible for the approval of the lists. The division was made on site at Amarna, where Borchardt had already packed many of the objects. Borchardt apparently did not light the finds well when Lefebvre came to inspect them, and both inaccurately and misleadingly listed the queen's bust as a plaster portrait of a princess.

Lefebvre had an imperative to keep any unique or important objects in Egypt, yet Borchardt's deception led him to make the shocking decision to award the bust of Nefertiti to Simon, who would later donate it and other artifacts from Amarna to the Neues Museum in Berlin. In 1923, when the bust first went on display in Germany, after a delay that seems to acknowledge the questionable nature of the bust's arrival in Berlin, the French director of the Antiquities Service demanded its return to Cairo. When his request was rebuffed, he refused to allow German excavations in Egypt through the end of the decade.

The painted stela, which Borchardt's expedition had discovered outside of House Q47.16, went on to join other artifacts from Akhet-Aten in the Egyptian Museum in Cairo. The stela does not rival the bust of Nefertiti, and it is in no way an equal exchange for the loss of the marvelous image of the queen, but it is not without interest. Reigning supreme over the stela, top and center, is Aten, shining down on Akhenaten and Nefertiti. Aten's arms offer the signs of life to their nostrils, a visual manifestation of the concept of the breath of life. Akhenaten's skin and Aten's disk and arms are reddish-brown. This is the most commonly used color for the skin of Egyptian men in art from all periods of ancient Egypt. But for Akhenaten and his god, the similarity of tone was an artistic realization of a line from a royal hymn: "The beautiful hue of your members is like the rays of your father, when he rises, the living Aten."[1] The paint on Nefertiti's skin is mostly abraded, but according to the conventional representations of women in Egyptian art, and from a wealth of other depictions of the queen, we know that her images would have had a yellowish skin tone.

The royal parents sit on cushioned stools decorated with the "uniting the Two Lands" image: papyrus plants and lotus blossoms wound around the hieroglyph of a windpipe and lungs that phonetically writes the verb "unite." Akhenaten sits to the left, in a relaxed pose, his right hand resting against the back of the stool, while Nefertiti is positioned on the right. Together, they mirror the hieroglyph for *akhet,* "horizon," the bodies of the king and queen forming the twin hills between which the sun rises. Yet neither Akhenaten nor Nefertiti looks up at their god; instead, they appear to be absorbed by the antics of their three playful daughters.

Meritaten stands between her parents, facing her father and reaching her arms up, just about to grasp a large earring that the king dangles above her. Two small collars sit in Akhenaten's lap, ready to be given to the other princesses. Nefertiti's right hand extends to touch Meritaten lightly on the head. If we then follow the queen's arm, we see infant Ankhesenpaaten sitting in her lap, the child's head cradled in Nefertiti's other hand. Meketaten stands on her mother's knees, touching her mother's chin and handing a small earring to her younger sister.

The immediacy of the scene bridges more than three thousand years separating us from Akhenaten and his family. We should not be tempted to read such an image too literally as a scene of domestic bliss, however. The image on the Cairo Stela, an object placed in a domestic shrine, was sacred enough to be at times hidden by wooden doors. How do we see Akhenaten's family portrait for what it really is? To do so, we must compare the Cairo Stela with other known family portraits from domestic shrines. A girl and an earring—this is not the only time a historical art mystery has begun with such a juxtaposition.

Jewelry in Egypt, even what we might term "costume jewelry" made of faience, could be more than simply aesthetically pleasing. From small rings and amulets to elaborate collars and necklaces, such objects spoke a language of color and design, allowing the wearers to reveal inner aspects of themselves. On the Cairo Stela, the earring that Akhenaten hands to Meritaten, with its rosette shape and strings of beads hanging down, mimics the shape of Aten with his multiple rays. The princess's two hands, cupping the beads, not only mirror Aten's hands but also create another version of the horizon hieroglyph, the hands substituting for the hills.

If we go forward in time three hundred years and return to Waset, another set of images explains the power behind the combination of Akhenaten, his daughters, and jewelry. The Twentieth Dynasty king Ramesses III (ca. 1184–1153 BCE) constructed a large temple on the west bank of Waset, now called by the modern toponym Medinet Habu. The temple occupies the center of a great fortified compound, formerly accessed by twin towers in the middle of each end of the enclosure wall.

In the upper chambers of the eastern tower are reliefs of Ramesses III in the company of royal girls, their age suggested by their nudity, relatively diminutive stature, and hairstyles that include the sidelock of youth. A hieroglyphic annotation refers to them as "children of the king," although whether by blood or role we cannot definitively say. These royal children play the *senet* board game with the king and present him with broad collars made of precious stones and metals. In one scene, the children sing a hymn in which they liken portions of the body of the king to precious stones:

Receive the broad collars—
Your hair is lapis lazuli;
your eyebrows are black hematite(?);
your eyes are green malachite;
your mouth is red jasper.[2]

The translation is uncertain in some places, but upon receiving the broad collars, the body of Ramesses III becomes the very stones that an artist might use to create and embellish a royal statue. Each of the stones also possesses rich religious allusions, from the regenerative properties of lapis lazuli to the association of red jasper with the eye of Horus.

This process of transformation is further explained in texts from the last centuries of the living pharaonic religion, the time when Macedonian Greeks, the Ptolemies, and later still Roman emperors ruled Egypt and presented themselves as successors to the pharaohs of old. In temples of that date, the king frequently offers a broad collar composed of "gold and lapis lazuli, mixed with all precious stones" to the goddess Hathor. Hathor is already the "gold of the gods, silver of the goddesses, lapis lazuli within the nine gods (of Iunu)." In recompense for the collar, Hathor assigns to the ruler the mineral wealth over which she rules—to the pharaoh now belong the gold, silver, and all precious stones of her divine body.

As Akhenaten presents jewelry to his children, he transforms their flesh into that of a golden goddess, and they become daughters of Aten. For the ancient Egyptians, the very act of working with gold and precious stones was a process of translating messages from the world of the divine. Linking different rare materials together in objects, such as earrings and broad collars, is comparable to connecting words in a sen-

Aten wearing a broad collar, as Akhenaten pours incense on a massive pile of offerings,
attended by Nefertiti with Meritaten and Meketaten shaking sistra.
(Drawing of a relief in the tomb of the high priest Meryre, after N. de G. Davies,
The Rock Tombs of El Amarna, *vol. 1,* The Tomb of Meryra
[London: Egypt Exploration Fund, 1903], plate 22)

tence. Thus, a metalworker named Ankhy, who lived around 2200 BCE,
called himself "the interpreter of the eye of Horus."

At least once, even Aten himself wears jewelry, revealing the sun god
as creator of the precious metals and stones that manifest his power. In
the tomb of the high priest Meryre, in a scene of the royal family worshipping Aten, the rays of light as they emerge from the lower limb of

the solar orb are overlaid by three overlapping broad collars, represented with alternating bands of blue and red color. This unusual bedecking of Aten with jewelry finds a parallel on the opposite side of the same wall in the tomb of Meryre, with an enormous garland in the form of a broad collar hanging from the top of the low front of the Window of Appearances. In that scene, Akhenaten and Nefertiti, who wear jeweled collars, lean over the cushion above the great garland, dispensing smaller broad collars. Through the medium of the broad collar, the sun in the heavens is equated with his earthly incarnations.

Just as the princesses present Ramesses III with a broad collar of precious minerals that divinized the king, Nefertiti could bestow upon Akhenaten equally transformative jewelry. In one of the tenderest moments in the art of Akhet-Aten, a fragmentary stela, almost certainly from a household shrine, shows the royal couple face to face. Akhenaten and Nefertiti look as if they are about to kiss, and to achieve this intimate pose Nefertiti must be sitting in her husband's lap. Aten's rays caress their crowns as Nefertiti's long, elegant fingers tie on her husband's broad collar. Perhaps she did help Akhenaten don his daily regalia, but that this one moment was chosen to be memorialized on a devotional object proclaims the sacredness of Nefertiti's loving action.

24

Performing Princesses

THE DRIVERS ARRANGE THE CHARIOTS OF THE ROYAL ENTOURAGE—two to one side, two to the other of the royal chariot, which is distinguished by the great ostrich plumes of its span of stallions. While the horses neigh, the accompanying bodyguard, winded by their jog alongside the rattling royal conveyances, turn and bow toward the royal family and the front of the temple.

Followed by two men holding tall, semicircular ostrich-feather fans and six women holding thin, elegant single-feathered fans, the king and queen head toward the temple, the princesses in their wake. Greeted by the temple staff and passing by offering tables heaped with the food that first Aten and then his human worshippers will consume, the group makes its way to the sanctuary.

Today, Akhenaten and Nefertiti will elevate to Aten jeweled examples of the god's own name. Standing before an altar piled high with breads and all manner of cuts of beef, ringed by jars of wine, and topped with burning dishes of incense, the king raises an object with two miniature versions of himself adoring the twin cartouches of Aten. Each figure wears the sidelock of youth—the daughters had more than once that morning laughed at the depiction of their father as a child—and

Akhenaten and Nefertiti offering the name of Aten, accompanied by their daughters
shaking the sistra. (Drawing of a scene in the tomb of Apy, after N. de G. Davies,
The Rock Tombs of El Amarna, *vol. 4,* The Tombs of Penthu, Mahu, and Others
[London: Egypt Exploration Fund, 1906], plate 31)

bears multiple ostrich feathers atop his head, appropriate for the god Shu, son of the creator god.

Behind him, Nefertiti raises a slightly smaller version of the same. The object she offers has but one figure adoring the Aten cartouches, a squatting version of the queen in the pose of a child, her Tefnut to her husband's Shu. Behind them stand their own daughters Meritaten, Meketaten, and Ankhesenpaaten, in diminishing size and age.

Of course, Meketaten insists on taking up Ankhesenpaaten's small sistrum, as usual teasing her young sister, with the inevitable results, today bordering on a true tantrum. Nefertiti has to sort out the sistra, allotting each to its proper owner. Finally, each of the girls has her own instrument and shakes it, the rattling sound accompanying and giving rhythm to the proceedings. As small as the daughters are, and as much trouble as the young Ankhesenpaaten sometimes has in keeping time with her older sisters, their tinkling accompaniment is a key part of the ritual in the Estate of Aten. As a family, they ensure that the solar orb in heaven remains in a constant state of jubilee.

Akhenaten was unusual in showing his wife and daughters as his constant companions, but kings, including Amunhotep III, did include young men and women labeled "royal children" and "royal daughters" as actors in jubilee ceremonies, continuing a much older tradition. The classic work of Middle Kingdom literature, *The Story of Sinuhe*, describes how the daughters and the chief queen of Senwosret I—the women of the immediate royal family—entertain the king. This episode illuminates how an ancient Egyptian might have "read" the images of Nefertiti and her daughters continuously surrounding Akhenaten, especially those representations of the princesses wielding sistra. This story would have been familiar to the king, queen, and literate members of the royal court.

The modern title, *The Story of Sinuhe*, derives from the name of the tale's protagonist, Sinuhe, ancient Egyptian *Sa-Nehet*, "son of the sycamore," referencing a sacred tree of the goddess Hathor. Sinuhe somewhat mysteriously flees Egypt upon the death of king Amenemhat I, which took place around 1950 BCE. After adventures in the lands to the northeast of Egypt, he finally returns to his homeland. As Sinuhe enters the palace, the members of the royal family are shocked at the sight of the Egyptian Sinuhe, who is dressed and coiffed like a foreigner. After giving voice to their surprise, the royal children fetch beaded necklaces and sistra.

The queen and princesses then begin praising the king, Senwosret I, accompanied by their instruments.

> *Your hands be toward the beautiful thing—o established king—*
> *the adornment of the lady of heaven,*
> *with the result that the Gold gives life to your nose,*
> *that the lady of stars might unite with you.*[1]

Royal family on a limestone stela from a household shrine.
(Ägyptisches Museum und Papyrussammlung, Staatliche Museen, Berlin, ÄM 14145)

The queen and daughters of Senwosret I ritually transform the king and channel his royal passions, encouraging him to be gracious to the returning Sinuhe, who once fled in fear. Through song, the royal daughters elevate their parents into cosmic beings—the creator god Atum and his consort Hathor. The ubiquitous sistrum-playing princesses of Akhet-Aten delight the sun disk in heaven and heighten the divinity of their own parents.

Even when not participating in rituals, the very presence of the princesses transforms a time of domestic calm into an event of religious significance. On another of the devotional stelae from Akhet-Aten, now in the Neues Museum in Berlin, intimate gestures among the royal family become a signal of their divinity. The royal couple face each other beneath the rays of Aten, positioned as the hills of the horizon. Akhenaten cradles Meritaten in his arms and kisses her, as though bestowing on her the breath of life that he has received from his solar father. The king's blue crown has the typical central uraeus and adds a whole circlet of the serpents.

Ankhesenpaaten clings to Nefertiti's shoulder and caresses the uraeus hanging in front of her mother's cheek. The queen's crown also drips with cobras: she wears one on her brow as we might expect, and another uraeus wraps around the middle of the crown. The venom of the serpents symbolizes the power of the sun, and the cobras that Akhenaten and Nefertiti wear show that they shine with the same solar radiance as Aten in heaven. Meketaten, who sits on her mother's knee, looks back at her little sister while pointing forward to her big sister in the king's arms. While Meritaten receives life-giving breath, Ankhesenpaaten plays with one of the sun god's fiery serpents on Nefertiti's crown. Just as Meketaten points at Meritaten, the elder sister points back toward their mother. The eyes of the viewer are caught within a cyclical movement from one figure to the next, making the scene an eternal recurrence like Aten's motions through the sky.

Aten has a multitude of emanations: rays that end in hands. In ancient Egyptian, both the word "sunray" and the word "hand" are feminine nouns. The king surrounds himself with his own feminine elements, his wife and daughters—the constant presence of Nefertiti and the princesses transforms Akhenaten into an earthly version of his divine father. Thus, everywhere we see Akhenaten we also see women whose roles—mothers, wives, and daughters—are part of the eternal cycle of the sun.

25

Love Divine

"THE NOBLEWOMAN, GREAT OF PRAISE, LADY OF CHARM, UNITED with joy! That Aten rises is to give to her praise; that he sets is to double her love. The king's great wife, his beloved, mistress of Upper and Lower Egypt, lady of the Two Lands, Neferneferuaten Nefertiti, given life forever and ever."[1] Mahu announces the queen as she leaves the temple. Then he walks to the side to inspect the guards. Today the royal couple are visiting the watch posts of Akhet-Aten. For this longer ride, many of the policemen of Akhet-Aten, from Mahu's lieutenants to some recently trained recruits, run alongside the chariot. The chief of police is eager to showcase his force, and there's nothing like a long run across the plain of Akhet-Aten to allow his desert patrolmen to show off before the royal bodyguard.

Akhenaten has already been announced and waits in his chariot. Now, Mahu watches the queen pause and look around for her own vehicle. The policeman catches Akhenaten's eye, nods, and then runs up to the queen. Bowing, Mahu asks her to accompany him to the king's chariot, as Akhenaten would like to speak with her before departing. Nefertiti is clearly annoyed but follows without reply.

When he sees her, Akhenaten bursts out laughing and reaches out to help her into the chariot. The driver has already stepped down, and

Akhenaten takes up the reins. The grooms who held the stallions' harnesses step to either side, and with a flick of the whip, the horses start off, trotting away from the front of the temple. Akhenaten turns around to Nefertiti, says, "Stick out your lips and be careful of your teeth!" and then kisses her, a delicate procedure in even a slowly moving chariot. Looking forward again, he urges the horses on at a slow gallop. Mahu's policemen run alongside, singing the chants they knew from festivals, with the occasional shout of a common refrain, "Victory be to the ruler!"

Meanwhile, in the chariot Akhenaten recites to Nefertiti part of a poem he learned back in the classroom at his father's palace:

I shall kiss her in the presence of everyone,
that they might understand my love.
She is the one who has stolen my heart—
When she looks at me it is refreshment.[2]

"This is indeed rejoicing in the horizon, is it not?" With that, Akhenaten turns his full attention to the cleared track into the desert.

Mahu's tomb provides an important variant of the commuting scene: Akhenaten, Nefertiti, and Meritaten all ride in the same chariot. While the royal couple are shown just about to kiss, Meritaten reaches out from the front of the cab, mischievously tapping the horses' hindquarters with a stick. The three royals could occasionally have ridden in a single chariot, but the intimate gestures of Akhenaten and Nefertiti also possess a symbolic significance.

Hovering above the chariot of Akhenaten and Nefertiti is Aten, one of whose hands holds an *ankh* to their nearly touching noses. Here, as with all cartouches of Aten, the first name ring says that the sun god is one who "rejoices in the horizon." That verb "to rejoice" gives us the final clue to interpreting Akhenaten and Nefertiti about to kiss in the chariot: the king and queen too are rejoicing in their horizon. Did the king and queen actually kiss in the chariot, enacting their physical joy before priests

Akhenaten and Nefertiti kissing in the chariot. (Drawing from the tomb of Mahu,
after N. de G. Davies, The Rock Tombs of El Amarna, *vol. 4,*
The Tombs of Penthu, Mahu, and Others *[London: Egypt Exploration Fund, 1906], plate 22)*

and courtiers? Perhaps so, as we have suggested in our reconstruction, or perhaps these images were created to express religious concepts that tomb owners believed could aid them in their afterlives.

The blurring of distinctions between ritual and daily life through acts of tenderness is not always confined to royalty, as we learn from a genre of ancient Egyptian literature that has been rightly called "love poetry." Reading these poignant compositions makes the men and women of ancient Egypt come to life—we know that these poems were recited, and it is easy to imagine a lovestruck teenager courting their beloved with these very texts.

The predecessors to the love poetry, texts in which gods and temples may love and interact like humans, occur before the reign of Akhenaten, in the middle of the Eighteenth Dynasty. The poems spoken by human lovers are predominantly from the Nineteenth Dynasty, less than a century after Akhenaten's death. These poems have not been found at Akhet-Aten, and we cannot determine if Akhenaten and Nefertiti ever spoke them to one another. But they are the closest we can come to understanding the royal couple's relationship, especially how they exploited their amorous union for their religious goals.

The Eighteenth Dynasty tomb of a man named Amenemhat, who lived around 1450 BCE during the reign of Thutmose III, includes an image of a male singer named Bak and the lyrics of the unique hymn he intones. These words vividly imagine the temple of Amun-Re as a woman who is the object of the god's passions. The grammatically feminine gender of the word "temple" meant that these buildings could be personified as a goddess-consort. It is easy to forget that Bak's song is about a stone building once you read past the first line:

How well it goes for the temple of Amun-Re,
*   she who spends the day in festival,*
*   with the king of the gods within her, [spending the night(?) . . .]*
She is like a drunken woman,
*   seated outside the wall of the shrine,*
*   the braided locks [in which are . . .] upon her beautiful [breasts].*
She has linen and sheets.[3]

Bak describes the return of the god to the interior of his temple at the end of a festival procession, evoking the sexual unions of men and women during the celebrations. The reference to linen and sheets echoes the image on a *talatat* block from Karnak that shows Nefertiti leading the king to a nicely made bed.

Love between two humans is constant and shared throughout the later groups of love poetry. Some of the poems place the lovers within domestic settings: one partner, alone at home, suffers the pangs of lovesickness; a man stands outside observing or at least imagining his beloved within her home. More of the poems, however, set the pair of lovers and their interactions within a well-watered and pastoral landscape, where the amorous activities play out against the backdrop of a larger festival celebration, the New Year.

The return of the wandering goddess and the rising waters of the inundation were honored with the consumption of alcoholic beverages and the donning of one's most elaborate garments and jewelry. In the love poetry, we see both the drinking of wine and beer as well as the accoutrements and physical preparations of formal dress. Temporary structures could be set up in the marshes and become places of love and dalliance.

As herald and embodiment of the New Year, Hathor, Re's daughter-consort, hovers behind many of the festivities and personal interactions. In one poem, the beloved appears first as the star Sepdet (Sothis/Sirius), then as a beautiful woman who shines and glows as a celestial being:

One unique is the sister, without her equal, more beautiful than all women.
Behold her like the star,
> *having appeared in glory at the beginning of a good year.*

Shining of excellence, luminous of hue;
beautiful of eyes when glancing, sweet her lips when speaking—
for her, no word is excessive.

Long of neck, luminous of chest;
true lapis is her hair,
> *her arms putting on gold,*
> *her fingers like lotuses.*[4]

Love poetry can use the endearments "brother" and "sister," which here do not imply a familial relationship. The sister, the beloved, is like a star, the beacon of the New Year, the very time when these love poems might have received public performances. In the poem, the beloved's fingers become the languid stalks of the lotus plants cherished by festival attendees; she may wear actual gold adornments, which augment her natural charms. Her neck is long, a feature consistent with the canon of proportions for female figures during the time of the poem's composition in the Nineteenth Dynasty and already present in the bust of Nefertiti.

A love poem might even pretend as if a festival, with its musical performances, is celebrating a couple's love; here, a woman addresses her lover:

> *A holiday is my seeing you, brother; a great favor is the sight of you.*
> *May you cross over to me with beer, musicians equipped with instruments,*
>   *their mouths provided with (songs of) diversion, for joy and exultation.*[5]

The word "holiday" could apply to celebrations that ranged from funerary banquets to religious festivals. In the conclusion to the text, the pair attain divine adoration of each other:

> *Your excellent sister is in adoration before you,*
>   *kissing the ground at sight of you.*
> *May she be received by means of beer and incense,*
>   *like the appeasement of a deity.*[6]

The poems explain why Akhenaten interacts so intimately with Nefertiti in royal monuments (palace decorations and temple reliefs) as well as private contexts (tomb walls and domestic shrines). The royal couple are the cynosure of love: a god and goddess whose union maintains the world itself, and two people whose love catapults them into the heavenly realm.

V

TWILIGHT OF THE GOD

DEATH AND
TRANSFIGURATION

26

Rulers of the World

AKHENATEN AND NEFERTITI MAKE THEIR WAY RAPIDLY TO THE throne room to begin their day's work—the vizier has requested an immediate audience. Today they take particular notice of the cool plaster floor of the palace, their path marked by the painted images of bound enemies in a repeating pattern: a Nubian, three bows, a Syrian, and three more bows, the groups continuing from one end of their accustomed track to the other. With each step, the king and queen crush Egypt's foreign foes, now bringing a gorgeously sandaled foot down on the back of a northern enemy, now on the back of a southern opponent, and frequently trampling the painted bows that represent the ancient enemies of Egypt.

Beside these polychrome delineations of foreign perfidy are representations of the lush floral and ample faunal bounty of Aten's creation. Rectangular pools filled with fish and lily pads surrounded by lush marsh plants, in which calves frolic and upon which birds alight, edge the path of foreign conquest. The paintings that surround the king and queen manifest the words of the Great Hymn to Aten: cattle leaping, being content with their fodder, birds flapping their wings in praise of Aten's *ka*-spirit, fish of the river delighting in his rays; even the enemies, once brought to heel, are the foreigners whose speech Aten has differentiated.

The royal couple enters the throne room, and all in attendance bow deeply, stretching their arms out in praise of their sovereigns. Akhenaten and Nefertiti ascend the steps of their throne dais, its base painted with kneeling Nubians and Syrians, their arms forever raised in adoration. As Akhenaten settles into his gilded throne, he takes a moment to appreciate that he has been king for twelve years. Since moving to Akhet-Aten, he, Nefertiti, and their growing family have enjoyed a near idyllic existence.

Nefertiti leans over and whispers to her husband, "Today, I feel a tension here. Are we to receive bad news?" To which he replies with a smile, "With you at my side, there is nothing that we cannot solve."

The vizier, Nakhtpaaten, walks in a stooped posture toward the throne dais, bowing again deeply before greeting the king and queen with their full titulary. He then introduces the first item on the royal agenda, a report by a royal messenger who has traveled north to Akhet-Aten directly from the capital of the Egyptian administration in Nubia, the fortress city of Buhen. The messenger has brought alarming news from the south: "The foreign enemies of Akuyati have plotted rebellion against Egypt. They are descending from the desert to the land of the Nilotic Nubians, seizing grain from them."[1]

Akhenaten looks at Nefertiti, then at Nakhtpaaten, a wry smile on his face. "Well this is a scene for a royal inscription indeed. I suppose this is where I 'rage like a leopard,' correct? Actually, in this case, a lion would be more appropriate."

Akhenaten then issues his formal command: "My vizier, inform the King's Son of Kush, Djehutymose, that he will proceed at once to quash this rebellion. He may consider feigning a fighting retreat after a limited engagement, luring the wretched rebels into a trap prepared somewhere to the north of their northernmost wells." Akhenaten looks not at Nakhtpaaten but at Meritaten, who gives a sweet smile and nod of approval to her father. Nakhtpaaten has to admit he feels comfortable knowing this girl might one day control Egypt directly or exercise authority indirectly through some doting husband.

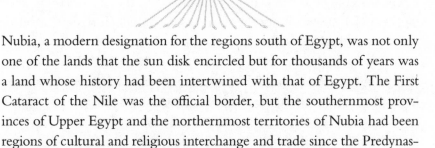

Nubia, a modern designation for the regions south of Egypt, was not only one of the lands that the sun disk encircled but for thousands of years was a land whose history had been intertwined with that of Egypt. The First Cataract of the Nile was the official border, but the southernmost provinces of Upper Egypt and the northernmost territories of Nubia had been regions of cultural and religious interchange and trade since the Predynastic Period. Nubia was the source of goods that the Egyptians coveted, the state needed, and the cult required: gold from the Eastern Desert, ostrich feathers that became elaborate fans for royal and divine ceremonies, the leopard skins of higher echelons of the priesthood, and the massive quantities of myrrh and incense that were burned daily on Aten's offering tables.

The Nilotic Nubians were part of a hybrid Nubian-Egyptian world, populated by Egyptian administrators, Nubian chiefs, and desert tribes who came to the Nile Valley to trade. The Akuyati who were raiding the predominantly settled populations of the Nubian Nile Valley were clearly not part of this world; they sought to disrupt Egyptian hegemony over Nubia. In the fifth year of his reign, Amunhotep III, who was probably only in his late teens, led his army against another rebellious Nubian group, and in Akhenaten's twelfth regnal year Egypt was confronted with a similar threat.

As Nubia was primarily a quiet region during his father's reign, so Akhenaten's rule over the southern territories was mostly peaceful, and the all-important gold shipments continued unabated. Djehutymose served both Amunhotep III and Akhenaten as the head of the Nubian administration, a position that the Egyptians called the "King's Son of Kush," an honorific title, as its occupant was not an actual son of the king. During the New Kingdom, the Egyptians transformed Nubia into a province whose administration, including the bipartite division of the region—northern Wawat and southern Kush—mirrored that of Egypt itself.

Akhenaten imprinted his, and Aten's, own stamp upon the cities and towns of Nubia. South of Egypt, the cultivable land was confined to a narrow band, with a corresponding lower overall population density. Egyptian-founded urban centers were placed at strategic locations: centers of trade, the terminuses of desert roads on which traders traveled, and areas of the Nile Valley linked with the Eastern Desert gold mines. Akhenaten founded or expanded several new cities in Nubia, complete with temples to Aten, thus following the precedent of his father, Amunhotep III, who endowed the temples at Soleb and Sedeinga.

We do not know whether Akhenaten and Nefertiti ever traveled to Nubia. The royal couple were at Akhet-Aten when they learned of the rebellion of the Akuyati, according to stelae found at two Nubian cities. Although both hieroglyphic texts are fragmentary, what remains is in equal parts informative and tantalizing. As with nearly all military encounters between ancient Egypt and ancient Nubia prior to the first millennium BCE, we hear only the Egyptian side: the Akuyati "plot rebellion against Egypt" according to Akhenaten's scribes. The Egyptians continuously strove to paint history with the brush of ritual. "Historical" texts describe events that likely occurred, but what exaggerations, distortions, or even inventions make their way into Akhenaten's stelae are difficult to identify.

Upon hearing the report, Akhenaten acted decisively: "Then his Majesty issued a directive to the King's Son of Kush." The rest of the sentence is missing, picking up again with "the enemies of the foreign land of Akuyati"; one can reasonably assume that Akhenaten commanded Djehutymose to muster an army to defeat said enemies. The text breaks off yet again, and the next preserved words are "of the river, to the north of the wells of the mining region." This phrase situates the conflict between Djehutymose's army and the Akuyati in the desert east of the Nile Valley, the location of Nubia's richest gold deposits and one of ancient Egypt's main sources for the precious metal.

Although the description of the battle is missing, we can assume that the Egyptian victory was recounted in the next lines. The hieroglyphic text then devotes three entire lines to the final tally of enemy captives and casualties. The numbers are only partially preserved: more than eighty-two Nubians are taken prisoner, including twelve children.

Two hundred and twenty-five Akuyati are slain, and among these some (the number is not preserved) are "placed upon the stake," the Egyptian idiom for impalement. This is one of only two known instances of impalement following a battle attested from three thousand years of Egyptian history.

The phrase "placed upon the stake" is determined by an image of an impaled body, the vertical element piercing the torso. Impalement is also a textually attested punishment for the robbing of a royal tomb, but we do not know whether the sentence served as a deterrence because of the pain it caused or because the thought of having one's corpse so publicly displayed was terrifying enough. Whatever the reality of the final moments of the Akuyati prisoners singled out for impalement, Akhenaten's Nubian stelae prove that Aten neither demanded peace nor eschewed violence when Egypt's interests were at stake.

If we mine the broken texts of the stelae for details, we can create a possible reconstruction of events. That the Akuyati were traveling with their children and robbing food suggests that hunger may have driven the desert-dwelling population into the Nile Valley. That the battle took place near the mining region explains why the Egyptians would see such a small group as a major threat. Perhaps the Akuyati were seeking more than just grain to feed their families. Or perhaps the Egyptians used extreme measures because even a minor disturbance in the precarious environment of the gold mines could set off an economic crisis, since the metal was essential to the functioning of the Egyptian state—both its domestic stability and its leverage in foreign exchange.

The stela ends with statements of global dominion addressed to Akhenaten (damaged passages indicated in brackets):

> There are none who rebel in your reign, for they have achieved non-existence. The chiefs [. . .] your power. Your war-cry is like a blasting flame in pursuit of all foreign lands. [. . .] all foreign lands assembled in one desire, that they might strip their lands daily [. . .] seeking breath for their noses.[2]

In the last line, the stela says that every country seeks "breath for their noses." Akhenaten would oblige this desire only a few months

Akhenaten and Nefertiti in the carrying chair during the Year 12 tribute ceremony.
(Drawing of relief from the tomb of Huya, after N. de G. Davies, The Rock Tombs
of El Amarna, *vol. 3,* The Tombs of Huya and Ahmes
[London: Egypt Exploration Fund, 1905], plate 13)

after the Nubian victory, during a celebration of his dominion over all lands. On the eighth day of the second month of Peret, corresponding to roughly December 23, 1341 BCE, Akhenaten and Nefertiti presided over a massive presentation of tribute, an event that brought together people from all over the known world.

We learn about this convergence of groups from throughout the Mediterranean, North Africa, and the Middle East from images on the walls of the tombs of two officials, Meryre and Huya. This is the only dated event within any of the tombs of Akhet-Aten and one of the few places where all six princesses appear together. Joining their elder sisters are

Neferneferuaten-tasherit (born perhaps in Regnal Year 9; her name means literally "Neferneferuaten junior"), Neferneferure (perhaps born the next year, Regnal Year 10), and Setepenre (perhaps born in Regnal Year 11).

Huya includes a scene of the royal couple on their way to the tribute presentation. The king and queen sit on a throne, decorated with a striding lion on each side; the faces of Akhenaten and Nefertiti have been hacked out, but we can see their bodies, which are almost entirely overlapping, as they will be depicted throughout the ceremonies. Soldiers, wearing the uniform of heart-shaped padding at the front of their kilts, carry the couple's sedan chair on two large poles, while ostrich feather standards and large fans are held in front of and behind the royal couple. A caption emphasizes the historic nature of that day:

> *Appearance in glory of the King of Upper and Lower Egypt Neferkheper-ure, the Unique One of Re, and the great wife of the king Neferneferu-aten Nefertiti, may she live forever and ever, upon the great sedan chair of electrum in order to receive the tribute of Syria and Kush, the West and the East, all foreign lands assembled on one occasion—even the islands in the midst of the sea—presenting tribute to the king on the great throne of Akhet-Aten for the receiving of the gifts of every foreign land, so that the breath of life might be given to them.*[3]

In the next scene, we see the tribute presentation and register after register of foreigners bearing the products of their respective regions. Libyans come from the west, bringing ostrich eggs and feathers; Nubians from the south, presenting cattle, ivory, shields, leopards and leopard skins, gold rings, and gold sculptures; people of the lands bordering the coast of the east Mediterranean offering chariots, horses, and their own princes to be raised in the Egyptian court; emissaries from the island of Crete, carrying large gold vessels; and bearded men from the region of Punt, to the far southeast, bearing the incense that was so plentiful in their lands and so necessary to the functioning of the divine cults of Egypt. In the tomb of Meryre, among the tribute and gifts brought from the four corners of the world, are a group of bound Nubians, most likely some of the men and women taken captive during the campaign of Djehutymose against the Akuyati.

Akhenaten, Nefertiti, and six princesses receiving foreigners during the Year 12 tribute ceremony. (Drawing of relief from the tomb of Meryre, after N. de G. Davies, The Rock Tombs of El Amarna, *vol. 2,* The Tomb of Meryra *[London: Egypt Exploration Fund, 1905], plate 38)*

Everyone in the scene is oriented toward the center of the image: the royal family within a stepped platform, slender columns supporting a roof decorated with uraei, symbols of the blinding light of the sun. Appropriately, this roof does not interrupt Aten's rays, which reach through the awning to caress the king and queen. In the center of the platform, Nefertiti sits enthroned next to her husband, but the artist contrived to show them so close together that they seem almost to be one person. The queen encircles her husband's waist with her arm, and the couple hold hands. The fruits of their union are assembled behind them, with the three eldest daughters also holding hands and embracing one another.

The elaborately carved scenes within the tombs of Meryre and Huya do not identify the celebration's physical setting. Given the number of people who participated in the event, one possible location is a flat stretch of desert east of the North City. There, a series of ruins called the "desert altars" occupies a cleared area, roughly 275 by 325 yards.

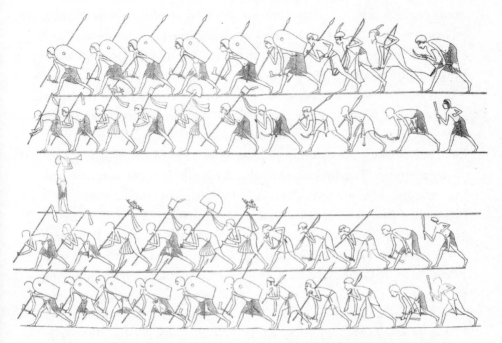

Akhenaten and Nefertiti's international bodyguard, drawing of relief from the tomb of Ahmes. (after N. de G. Davies, Rock Tombs of El Amarna, *vol. 3,* The Tombs of Huya and Ahmes *[London: Egypt Exploration Fund, 1905], plate 31)*

The proximate cause for the celebration may well have been the victory over the Akuyati, but Akhenaten and Nefertiti transformed the event into a pageant on a cosmic scale. Hundreds of foreigners attended, enacting the passage that we read in the Great Hymn to Aten: "Your rays always encompass the lands, to the limit of all which you have created, you being as Re. That you have attained their limits, is so that you might subdue them for the son whom you love." Even in December, the sun in Egypt can be quite strong, and while the heat was likely not overwhelming during the tribute celebrations, everyone would have felt Aten's presence, high and dazzling in the heavens.

In addition to the bound Nubians, a few people depicted as Syrians are also in manacles, being led into the royal presence. We do not have a record of a northern campaign at the time of the Nubian conflict with the Akuyati, so we can only assume that these captives were the result of a small-scale action executed by Egyptian forces stationed in the northeastern portion of Akhenaten's empire in the Levant. The remainder of the people presenting tribute are not shackled or physically restrained. These are the foreign populations for whom Aten provides, as the Great Hymn describes, "You set every man at his (proper) place and make their requirements, with the result that each one has his diet."

Were the paint fully preserved in the tombs of Meryre or Huya, we might see an illustration of another line from the hymn, "Their skins are different, for you distinguish the foreigners." Even lacking the original polychromy, the clothing and hairstyles serve to "distinguish" each foreign group. The Syrians wear flounced ankle-length garments and sport pointed beards and full, shoulder-length hair; the Libyans have a long braid that goes right in front of their ears, two ostrich feathers in their hair, and long cloaks, open at the front; the people of Punt have close-cropped hair, short beards, are bare-chested and wear long kilts; the people of Crete have long hair and full garments, with billowing sleeves and ankle-length skirts. The Nubians have hair styled close to the head—some adorn their heads with a single ostrich feather—and they often wear gold hoop earrings, while their garments combine linen kilts and colored leather sashes.

All of these representatives of foreign lands are depicted from an Egyptian perspective. Just as images of a human body in Egyptian art are a composite of hieroglyphic forms, the facial features, clothes, and accoutrements of foreigners in reliefs identify those people as residents of a certain territory. Just as obvious were the diverse ethnicities of the royal bodyguard. The Year 12 tribute showcases Akhenaten's world domination, just as the foreigners who ran along his chariot enhanced the ritual atmosphere of the royal family's daily actions. The king knew how to transform the mundane into the sacred—but he still needed to manage any real crises that might emerge in Egypt's empire.

27

Duplicity and Diplomacy

AKHENATEN AND NEFERTITI RELAX AGAINST THE CUSHION OF the balcony of the Window of Appearances, surveying the diversely attired people before them. The massive courtyard of the Great Palace, lined with colossal stone statues of Akhenaten and Nefertiti, dwarfs the delegation from Assyria below.

The Egyptian bodyguards stand to the sides of the court, but no one there can escape the heat of the noonday sun. Only the royal family is shaded within the Window of Appearances, the children chatting with one another while Akhenaten and Nefertiti confer with several scribes. Awaiting the attention of the royal couple, the Assyrian messengers begin to talk among themselves, forgetting that many of the Egyptian royal scribes are at least as well trained in "diplomatic" Akkadian as the delegates themselves. One of the scribes begins to translate in a whisper for the benefit of two members of Akhenaten's bodyguard, who lean close and with difficulty stifle their growing mirth.

The head of the delegation wipes sweat from his brow with a scarf, the perspiration replenished before he can return the scarf to one of the folds of his colorful woolen garment. "If this goes on much longer, we will all die out here!" The youngest member of the group locks his jaw in anger: "If we ever make it home, King Assur-uballit will hear of this!" To their dismay, they see that their torture is not yet over. The Egyptian king and queen have left the balcony, returning to the cool interior of the palace. To add to their discomfort, one of the Egyptian scribes allows himself to be overheard, telling a companion—in Akkadian—"Assur-uballit will indeed hear of this, but from whom?" The chief of the delegations makes a mental note to send the youngest member back to Assyria immediately and motions to his companions to say nothing more.

Akhenaten's eyes adjust to the darkness of the palace as he makes his way to his private office, and he sends for his vizier. "I need to review the last year of correspondence with the Assyrian king. His messengers are again whining about my lack of generosity. If I hear them say one more time 'Gold is like dirt in your country,' I might do more than just make them stand under Aten's relentless glare." Sensing the urgency—a foreign messenger's death would not help with future negotiations—Nakhtpaaten personally races to the office of royal scribes.

"Fetch the summary of the Assyrian file immediately!" A half dozen scribes stand to attention for a moment and then rush to crowd around a couple of shelves on the far wall, searching the hanging labels for the proper papyrus scroll. Finally, one retrieves it and quickly hands the document to Nakhtpaaten, who unrolls it to confirm that it has the most up-to-date information. "By Seth!"—he forgets in his frustration that the names of the old gods are not to be uttered in the palace—"At the very least the last two letters are not included!" He stares down the scribes, who shrink from his gaze. "Quickly, while I review this with Pharaoh, go straight to the Records Office and bring the most recent tablets from the Assyrian court—and remember, do not drop them. Aten forbid they break and crumble!"

Akhenaten did not neglect the practical aspects of governing Egypt or the foreign territories that he ruled. Evidence of this emerged from the debris beneath the collapsed walls of a building in the center of Akhet-Aten that is called the "Office of the Correspondence of Pharaoh, living, prosperous, healthy." Found there were almost four hundred clay tablets

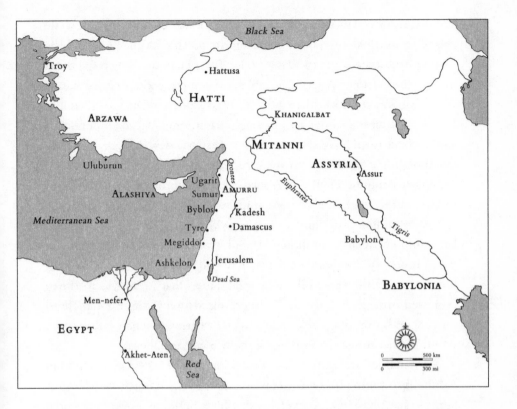

impressed with cuneiform writing, predominantly diplomatic correspondence but also some scribal exercises, reference lists, and literary texts, a uniquely rich archive. For a historian, reading the Amarna Letters, as these sources are most often called, is like entering Akhenaten's privy council, where secret missions are plotted and foreign allies are alternately rescued and sacrificed. The content of the letters appears to clear Akhenaten of modern historians' charge of dereliction of pharaonic duty.

The documents are written almost exclusively in Akkadian, the lingua franca of the western Mediterranean, inscribed as usual in the cuneiform script impressed on the mud tablets. A few tablets have Egyptian hieratic ink notations with year dates, suggesting an organized filing system. The cast of characters within these letters is considerable, and what was discovered at Akhet-Aten represents only a fraction of the foreign correspondence from the years covered by the surviving tablets. The Egyptian kings addressed in the letters are Amunhotep III and Amunhotep IV/Akhenaten, with one or two of the tablets possibly dating to the shadowy period between the death of Akhenaten and the final return of the court to Waset under Tutankhamun. When the court moved from Akhet-Aten, clay tablets that represented "closed cases" were abandoned within the Office of the Correspondence of Pharaoh. Letters that were still needed for reference in ongoing correspondence and disputes would have been transported to the new capital.

About forty tablets are missives from the kings of empires, men who addressed Amunhotep III or Akhenaten as a "brother." In the upper reaches of the Euphrates was Mitanni, whose king Tushratta wrote often to Amunhotep III, husband to two Mitannian princesses. The relationship between Amunhotep IV and Tushratta was initially fraught; Amunhotep IV had sent gold-plated wood statues to the Mitannian king, who instead wanted the solid gold statues that Amunhotep III had promised him. In one letter, Tushratta pleads with Amunhotep IV to speak with his mother, Tiye, assuming that her experience and wisdom will cause her to see the justness of the Mitannian request.

Personalities are equally on display in a letter to Akhenaten from Ashur-uballit, king of the rising power of Assyria in northern Mesopotamia. The Assyrian king explains that he is building a new palace and needs as much gold as possible but is receiving only a pittance in comparison to what his father and other kings have received. Ashur-uballit expresses surprise at Akhenaten's lack of generosity, for what would it cost Egypt? "Gold in your land is dirt," Ashur-uballit points out, a common refrain in the letters foreign kings send to Egypt. At the conclusion of Ashur-uballit's message, he expresses concern for the Assyrian envoys who make the long, dangerous journey to Egypt only to die of sun exposure, forced to stand outside before the king.

South of Assyria was the kingdom of Babylonia, centered in what is now Iraq. In one letter, the Babylonian king Kadashman-Enlil vents his anger toward Amunhotep III, referencing how the Egyptian king refused to send an Egyptian princess for him to marry, even though a Babylonian princess was already promised to Amunhotep III. What truly galled Kadashman-Enlil was Amunhotep III's subsequent rejection of another proposal: the Babylonian ruler had suggested, in desperation for an Egyptian wife of any background—why not dispatch *any* beautiful Egyptian woman to Babylon, for who would be able to say that she is not a princess? The Egyptian king denies this request as well. While pharaohs deemed it perfectly acceptable to marry foreign princesses, no Egyptian woman of any rank would be sent to wed a foreign ruler.

The letters involving Egyptian vassals in the Levant provide more insight into foreign policy decisions. Only a few of the letters in the archive originated in Egypt, while nearly three hundred tablets were sent by the leaders of city-states within Egypt's sphere of influence. The geographical location of the vassal states was primarily the coastal region of the Eastern Mediterranean, beginning with Ashkelon in the south and extending to Ugarit in the north, and territories under Egypt's control included both cities along the coast and those that lay along inland trade routes. In the letters, we read of men jockeying for greater power and influence or simply trying to survive the latest assault by a rival leader. The Egyptians did not rely on messages alone—administrators and small garrisons were assigned to key cities to secure trade and strategic roads.

The area of the Levant did not supply an overwhelming amount of essential goods—although the cedar of Lebanon was of great importance for shipbuilding. So the Egyptian aim in controlling the region was twofold: maintaining a geographic buffer against powerful states, originally Mitanni, and later Hatti (the kingdom of the Hittites), and ensuring the smooth functioning of east Mediterranean maritime trade routes, which supplied important metals—copper and tin—as well as luxury goods like olive oil and wine. This is why smaller, independent territories, such as Arzawa, along the southern coast of Asia Minor (modern Turkey), and Alashiya, the island of Cyprus, play a role in the Amarna Letters—they were key nodes of this trade network, with Alashiya a major supplier of copper.

The Amarna Letters teach us much about Akhenaten's approach to foreign policy. Among the dozens of events recorded within the letters, two incidents tested the king and his military advisors like no other. The first was a major Hittite offensive against Mitanni. Mitanni had once been Egypt's greatest military rival but was a close ally when Akhenaten came to the throne. When a powerful new king, Suppiluliuma, ascended to the throne of Hatti, he led an invasion of Mitanni, essentially destroying that empire, while taking no direct action against adjacent Egyptian vassal states.

Akhenaten did not send troops to support Mitanni as Suppiluliuma's armies swept through the kingdom. Many Egyptologists have seen Akhenaten's neglect of Mitanni as an expression of pacifism, disinterest, or even ineptitude. Instead, a careful reading of the Amarna Letters may indicate that Akhenaten was a clever strategist. Near the end of his reign, Amunhotep III received reports that Mitanni was encroaching on Egyptian territory. Perhaps Akhenaten made a careful calculation that Mitanni was an increasingly unreliable ally, and thus one undeserving of Egyptian aid. He may well have preferred to allow a far-off kingdom of uncertain loyalty to fall to the Hittites than commit Egyptian resources and soldiers.

The second event that posed a particular challenge to Akhenaten was the rise of a new power in Amurru. Centered on a region that is now southwestern Syria and northern Lebanon, Amurru, the kingdom of the Amorites, was a meeting point of north–south land routes. A constant stream of letters from Rib-Haddi, the ruler of Byblos, a key coastal trading city, reported on the consolidation of Amurru under the leadership of Aziru, a man whose strategic genius leaps from the cuneiform words impressed into the clay tablets.

During the reign of Amunhotep III, Rib-Haddi had already suffered depredations and constant harassment from Abdi-Ashirta, Aziru's father. Abdi-Ashirta treated Egyptian dependencies and allies aggressively; Rib-Haddi complained and begged Egypt for assistance; and Amunhotep III asserted Egyptian power late in his reign, but not fully and decisively enough to curb Amorite territorial ambition. Then, to the new king Akhenaten, Rib-Haddi sent increasingly panicked messages, often using metaphor-rich language—"like a bird in a trap am I in Byblos."[1]

According to Rib-Haddi's report, Aziru had taken over Sumur, one of Egypt's administrative capitals in the region, and killed its Egyptian governor. Aziru, in turn, protested that Rib-Haddi was misrepresenting his actions—the ruler of Amurru was only protecting Egypt's interests. Akhenaten likely knew that Aziru was distorting the truth, but perhaps

Akhenaten was willing to sacrifice Sumur because he had larger strategic goals. The rival kings of Mitanni and the Hittites and the hostility between Amurru and Byblos kept everyone busy, allowing time and resources for only limited attacks against Egyptian territory.

With the Hittites on the rise, what Egypt needed more than Sumur and vassal cities in northern Syria was a strong buffer state. Aziru's energetic leadership made him a dangerous ally, but also a useful one. Akhenaten invited Aziru to Egypt, and the Amorite leader spent a year there, likely feeling more of a hostage than a guest at Akhet-Aten. Threats to Amurru led Akhenaten to release Aziru, perhaps with the hope that the Amorite ruler would remain loyal to Egypt and ward off the growing threat of the Hittites.

Upon Aziru's return to his mountainous homeland, the Amorite ruler appears to have outmaneuvered Akhenaten and switched his allegiance to the Hittites. Akhenaten sent Aziru a threatening letter, one of the few documents in the Amarna Letters from the Egyptian king to a vassal ruler. Akhenaten angrily tells Aziru: "If because of riches, you prefer these deeds and if you harbor these treacherous things in your heart, then by the king's battle-axe you will die, with all your kin."[2]

Late in his reign, the Egyptian king assembled a fleet and an army that would proceed north against the Hittite-allied city of Kadesh. The Amarna Letters allow us to trace the intended path of the Egyptian forces, but Egyptian sources fail to preserve the outcome of the campaign. Hittite documents suggest that the Egyptian offensive failed and that Suppiluliuma counterattacked into Egyptian territory. But even then, Egyptian generals and administrators in the northeastern territories may not have been concerned. Based on the patterns of winds and currents in the eastern half of the Mediterranean, as long as Egypt controlled the ports from Beirut to the south, Egypt's fleet could well rule the waves needed to maintain the significant portions of their empire in the region. Akhenaten's strategy spared Egypt much expenditure in lives and wealth. Far from being an incompetent and distracted leader, he left the Two Lands well prepared to maintain the most important parts of its northeastern empire.

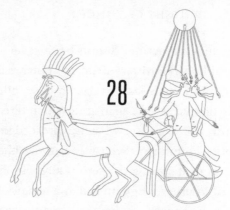

None Beside Him

THE OUTLINE ARTIST SETA COMES OUT OF THE FUNERARY CHAPEL and motions to his younger colleague, Nakht. Placing a hand on the back of each of the two dust-covered men holding chisels, Nakht propels the pair forward to meet Seta just outside the entrance to the chapel. "My eager assistants! You have done better than some of your kind, but let me instruct you in a few matters. What have you erased here?" Seta asks the men.

"Amun, o chief!" Baki and User cry in unison, with Baki adding, "And a few more things."

"Indeed, what other things?"

"See the small statue?" Baki, the more talkative of the two, says. He gestures to a small image of the tomb owner, depicted as kneeling and holding an inscribed stela before him. "We erased the name of Amun and the signs for 'gods.'"

Seta had already inspected the object. "So you did, very good. And what else?"

"Here we erased Amun, and just there"—the two chisel-wielding assistants point in unison—"we erased the name of the goddess Mut."

"No doubt you meant well, but what you erased was a vulture and a bread loaf, hieroglyphs in the writing of the word 'galena.' The man is presenting unguent and cosmetics to the tomb owner. You just infringed on his supply of black eye paint." Baki and User look down at their sandals. "But I see additional damage over here—tell me of that." Seta points to a scene of the tomb owner and his family fishing and fowling, wearing their finest clothing as though they were happily taking part in a great inundation festival. "Two things are removed here and here, in front of the prows of the two papyrus skiffs."

Baki draws himself up, proud of his discernment: "A cat was climbing a swamp plant, and in front of each vessel was a goose. Now my friend and I have worked in many tombs the past few days, and in one—which was that?" He turns to User, who whispers "Anen." "Yes, in the tomb of Anen, we saw a scene with a cat and goose, and that is how we knew."

"Well." Seta is impatient. "What did you see?"

"The king Amunhotep and his wife Tiye sat in their thrones in one scene, and beneath the queen's chair a cat hugged a goose, and over both a monkey leapt through the air. Now our friend said that not only were those animals pets but the goose is also an image of the god Amun."

Seta smiles and nods—the two are not quite so uninformed as he had thought. "As I was saying," Baki resumes, "the goddess may be the cat. Now she is angry in the winter, and we must eat and drink and sing for her return—I beg your pardon, I should say in the days before the rule of Aten and his children we did those things—we had to make her happy, and the god Thoth helped us do that. He was a monkey sometimes, so our friend said that the pets were acting out the return and marriage of the god and goddess."

Seta thanks them and sends them on their way to further destruction for the glory of Aten. Turning to Nakht, he complains, "The levels of literacy and the degrees of care these people are taking are entirely inconsistent. What then are we to do?"

Nakht pauses for a moment, and then replies, "Something makes me think we may be putting those hieroglyphs all back the way they were one of these days."

As Akhenaten was dealing with the geopolitical events shaking Egypt's empire, he was also making dramatic theological changes at Akhet-Aten. Despite the wealth of archaeological and artistic data from Akhenaten's capital city, only a handful of dated events are known. Otherwise, texts and images emphasize the overall timelessness and the ritual atmosphere of royal life at Akhet-Aten.

A day-to-day record of events at the palace was certainly kept, but those papyrus scrolls have long since vanished. Other year dates are not linked to events but appear on labels to jars, ceramic vessels that held everything from wine and beer to honey, fat, dried meat, and much more. From these broken jar fragments, like those that litter the surface of the jubilee city of Malqata, we can establish that Akhenaten's reign ended in his seventeenth year on the throne. But those hundreds of hieratic ink labels on jars do not allow us to establish a chronology of many events that occurred between the city's founding and the king's death.

One lingering mystery is the date on which Akhenaten commanded a change in the didactic name of Aten. The first name of Aten, originally written without cartouches and then, by the end of Regnal Year 4, enclosed within two royal name rings, was: "Re-Horakhty who rejoices in the horizon in his name of light who is in the sun disk." A short-lived intermediate name, again not precisely dateable, replaces the Horus falcon, writing the divine name *Hor* with the hieroglyph for just the first letter of the name, a twisted wick that writes an emphatic-*h* sound. Then, likely between Regnal Years 12 and 14, although we cannot be certain, Aten's name was more fully updated. Akhenaten now addressed his god as "Living one, Re, ruler of the two horizons, who rejoices in the horizon in his name of Re, the father, who has returned as the sun disk."

Aten's later didactic name removed all mention of deities other than the sun god Re: the falcon god Horus had been excised, as had the word *shu*, "light," since it is homophonous with the god Shu. Instead, the new name emphasized Aten's rule over the horizon and his identity as the solar father. The purification of Aten's didactic names appears to coincide with an increasingly hostile position toward the cult of Amun, with the names and images of Amun hacked out of temples, tombs, and private monuments from Nubia to the Delta. Since the center of the worship of Amun was Waset, that city was the epicenter of Akhenaten's iconoclasm.

Relief of Amunhotep III (right) offering flowers to Amun (left), from Karnak Temple; the image of the god was hacked out in the reign of Akhenaten and later recarved in shallower relief. The damage to the king is unrelated to Atenist activity.

The men dispatched to chisel out thousands of hieroglyphs and divine images did not leave their names or the dates on which they carried out their destructive duties. Many of them probably could not have written anything at all. Illiterate, they were apparently provided with lists of the words that needed to be effaced, as well as drawings of the gods that they were to target, but several mistakes indicate that at least some of them were looking more for patterns than for words.

The name Amun is written with three signs: a reed (for *i*, the same letter that begins the name Aten); a game board called *senet* (phonetically writing *mn*); and a water sign that repeats the *n* of *mn* (making the *n*-water a phonetic complement). The *mn*-game board and *n*-water are common in a number of ancient Egyptian words. Those tasked with hacking out the name of Amun could combine zeal with illiteracy and attack not just *imen* as the god's name, but also the words *men*, "to establish"; *meney*, "to moor"; and *menat*, "nurse," among others. Even though the word for nurse has an unmistakable determinative of a breast, and clearly—at least to one who can read the inscriptions—has nothing to do with the god Amun, it was chiseled away.

An exceptional case in the tomb of the steward Kheruef starkly contrasts the king's earlier theology with his later, uncompromising approach to the cult of Amun. Kheruef commissioned two scenes in his tomb's doorway early in Akhenaten's reign, when the king was still Amunhotep IV. In one, the king makes an offering to his parents, Amunhotep

III and Tiye; then, standing back-to-back with another representation of himself, the king is "consecrating a great offering to Re-Horakhty."[1] The object of the king's ministrations is not the expected image of a falcon-headed deity but a large rectangle, slightly taller than wide, and extensively damaged.

On close inspection, the rectangular area resolves into a grid, thirteen divisions high by fourteen wide. Most of the small rectangles reveal traces of hieroglyphs, and the whole resembles a great crossword puzzle. This is, in fact, an acrostic paean to two deities. Painstaking study by the scholars who published the tomb recovered sufficient traces of the original signs to reconstruct the words that once filled most of the rectangles. Read horizontally, the hieroglyphs within the grid are a hymn to Amun-Re. Read in vertical columns, the text presents a hymn to Re-Horus of the Horizon. In Waset, as Amunhotep IV, the king could inextricably intertwine his two heavenly fathers. Such was Akhenaten's zeal in his final years that the word-square hymn was not overlooked: Amun's destruction would proceed, even if it meant annihilating an early hymn to Aten in his form of Re-Horus of the Horizon.

Akhenaten's iconoclasm did not extend far beyond Amun, although a secondary target was the plural noun "gods." The vulture goddess Nekhbet suffered in many areas, including her chief cult center of Nekheb, probably because the signs writing her name resembled in general shape and arrangement the epithet of Amun as "king of the gods." Occasionally a ram-headed god like Khnum was hacked out, almost certainly because some of those unschooled agents confused the ram-headed divinity with a ram-headed form of Amun. As consort of Amun, Mut also suffered the wrath of the attackers; in the tombs of Akhet-Aten, the spelling of the word *mut,* "mother," normally written with the vulture, was altered to avoid the hieroglyph of a deity fallen out of favor, even though the vulture served only to write the sounds of the word.

But other gods worshipped throughout Egypt, including Osiris, Ptah, and Thoth, and most goddesses, were never physically censored. No evidence suggests that Akhenaten interfered with the operations of most temples in Egypt, besides siphoning off their revenues. Just before the move to Akhet-Aten, the king received a letter from a steward named Ipy reporting on the smooth functioning of all of the cults of

Men-nefer (Memphis), including the main temple to the creator god Ptah.

We can see some indication of the effect of Akhenaten's reign and its immediate aftermath through the eyes of one citizen of Waset, a priest named Pawah. About three years after Akhenaten's death, Pawah visited the tomb of Pairy, who had been high priest of Ptah at Karnak Temple during the reign of Amunhotep III. Pawah stood before a painting of a funerary banquet, a celebration that typically took place during one of the annual festivals, and took out his rush pen, water pot, and scribal palette to write a long text in hieratic on a door jamb next to the scene. As a priest, he may have also been in the sepulcher observing a nocturnal vigil.

Pawah extolls the god Amun, "who gives satiety without eating; drunkenness without drinking." Even the saying of Amun's name is sweet, the "taste of life" itself, but Pawah languishes in a darkness of Amun's making. The priest pleads with Amun to bestow light on him, so that he might see the god, for "Joyous is the person who sees you, o Amun! He is in festival every day."[2]

Waset was bereft in the final decade of Akhenaten's reign, but Akhet-Aten was bountiful. In the Akhet-Aten tomb of the royal scribe Ahmose, the tomb owner declaims a hymn to Aten. At the conclusion he states, "Joyous is one who follows the ruler! He is in festival every day."[3] The parallelism between Pawah's hieratic lament and Ahmose's confident statement is remarkable. What an Egyptian citizen believed a god dispensed, Akhenaten had usurped.

We lack a text that explains why Akhenaten took active measures against Amun's temples and embarked on his iconoclastic campaign, but we can propose a few possibilities. Since Amun was the god who engendered the new king, as the divine birth cycles of Hatshepsut and Amunhotep III make clear, when Akhenaten identified himself as the unique son of Aten, Amun's existence posed a theological conflict. Perhaps the king wanted to ensure that Aten retained his status as royal progenitor even after Akhenaten's death. Erasing Amun may have been a strategy for a longer-term maintenance of Aten's cult.

The earliest texts from Akhenaten's reign reveal that the young ruler developed his solar religion slowly. As the chief of works Parennefer says, one measures for Aten in heaps but still provides for the other gods in regular grain measurements. A decade or so into his reign, Akhenaten's attack on the wealthiest cult in Egypt—that of Amun-Re in Waset— deactivated the images of the god, making further offerings and rituals impossible. The proscription of Amun would have had the dual effect of removing a god whose universality could rival Aten and redirecting at the same time tax payments that had once flowed into Amun's coffers.

Akhenaten also ordered his henchmen to attack images of a particular type of religious official known as the *sem*-priest, the leopard skin that he typically wore making him easily recognizable. These priests officiated in the Opening of the Mouth ritual, which allowed a statue to be inhabited by a divine being or, when performed on a mummy, enabled the wrapped body to be a receptacle for the spirit of the deceased. Since Aten's form is unable to be rendered in statuary, removing *sem*-priests from temples—both in actuality and in imagery—would do no harm to the sun god, but prevented the consecration of sacred images of other deities.

One of the most repeated theories about Akhenaten's motivations is that he had an abiding hatred for the powerful priests of Amun. In this reconstruction of events, Amunhotep IV initially set out to replace Amun at Karnak with Aten, then abandoned Waset for Akhet-Aten to entirely separate himself from a city that Amun's priests controlled. However, the king had the ability to make appointments to the priesthood, such as Amunhotep III granting his brother-in-law Anen the office of second priest of Amun. By the time Amunhotep IV came to the throne, the administration of Karnak Temple was spread among many officeholders. The temples of Amun were among the wealthiest in the land, but no ancient sources suggest that Akhenaten was locked in a conflict with priests who could marshal resources against their sovereign.

Yet, on the Regnal Year 5 boundary stelae at Akhet-Aten, Akhenaten alludes to—although he does not detail—a series of long-standing horrible events with which he has had to contend:

> *Now as my father Aten lives, as for [. . .] in Akhet-Aten:*
> *It was worse than the things which I heard in Regnal Year 4;*
> *it was worse than the things which I heard in Regnal Year 3;*
> *it was worse than the things which I heard in Regnal Year 2;*
> *it was worse [than the things which I heard in Regnal Year 1].*

It was worse than the things which [Nebmaat]re (Amunhotep III)
heard . . .
It was worse than the things which Men[kheper]re (Thutmose III) heard.
[It was] worse [than the thing]s which any of the kings
who had ever assumed the White Crown (of Upper Egypt) heard.[4]

A fragmentary passage, which follows the statements of the increasingly negative "things" that were "heard," mentions "offensive" things that Egyptians and Nubians have spoken against Aten. Is Akhenaten referring to resistance to his new emphasis on the cult of Aten? Are the king's ethnically diverse bodyguards, perpetually in attendance at Akhet-Aten, and the patrols, whose routes were overseen by the chief of police Mahu, all somehow reactions to threats against the king's person? We cannot know.

Rather than an abhorrence of corrupt priests or a totalitarian plan to assume complete control of Egypt's temples and economy, Akhenaten's actions appear to be a logical extension of the reign of his father. Amunhotep III and Tiye became the sun god and Hathor, and their successors took their divine identity to a new level by stepping back in time.

Each major feature of Akhenaten and Nefertiti's worship of Aten can be explained by the process of creation. Throughout Egyptian religious history, the sun god Re is a creator god. It is Re's light that brings forth the world from the undifferentiated, dark, watery oneness that the Egyptians called *nun*. Humans cannot fully comprehend the act of creation, nor can they fully understand the sun god's return to *nun* each evening in the Underworld, for such events play out at a divine, cosmic scale. Yet that did not stop Egyptian theologians from composing a host of religious texts that described the fashioning of the world and Re's journey through sky and Underworld. Each center of sacred scholarship had its own creation account. To a modern reader, the apparently contradictory compositions can seem illogical, but the ancient Egyptians did not seek to align their multiplicity of approaches into a single narrative.

The creator god held within himself millions, the potentiality of everything: all gods, all people, all animals, all plants, the stars in heaven and the minerals of the earth. He, for the Egyptian conventionally called him such, was also androgynous, having male and female attributes. In the sexually charged creation myth of Iunu, Re-Atum masturbated, the male phallus brought to orgasm by the female hand, and from that act Shu and Tefnut were brought into existence. Even that account can vary: rather than masturbating, Atum sneezes out Shu (a pun on *ishesh*, "to sneeze") and spits out Tefnut (a pun of *tefen*, "to spit"). What unifies every ancient Egyptian creation account is that the *one* becomes *many*, until all of creation is complete.

For Akhenaten and Nefertiti, Aten is that creator: he fashioned the universe, and his light enlivens it. Aten is not only a cosmic architect but also a personal begetter, father and mother of mankind, who quickens the fetus and calms every child's tears. Akhenaten and Nefertiti are Aten's offspring, so close to the androgynous creator that their bodies are not fully differentiated. Borrowing from the theology of Iunu, the king and queen could take on the guises of Shu and Tefnut.

Akhenaten and Nefertiti signaled through art that their new world order is ultimately not new at all—it is a return to the moment of creation. Akhenaten may have located his capital city at Akhet-Aten for the same reason. According to the boundary stelae, Aten instructs the king to build his new horizon on "widowed" ground as his "place of the primeval event." The site of Akhet-Aten was indeed a blank slate, but the same cannot be said of the surrounding region. Only seven miles north of Akhenaten's capital was Khemenu (Hermopolis), the home of eight creator deities who appear as a quartet of frog-headed gods paired with a quartet of snake-headed goddesses. After the marsh-dwelling gods became the fathers and mothers of the world, all eight receded back into the primordial waters, but they still received offerings from their temple at Khemenu.

Did Akhenaten choose a place that was already charged with creative energy? Nowhere does Akhenaten claim such motivations, but of all the empty desert bays that Aten could have picked, the location to which he led the king was close to a place where the world was believed to have been born. Building their city in Akhet-Aten, Akhenaten and Nefertiti lived out their lives not only as a pair but also as a unit of creative power. The king and queen were slightly differentiated versions of a whole, in keeping with their position as the first male-female offspring of the creator god. And if they were the first, then no others could yet exist—and so Amun and Mut must be hacked out, for none could rival Aten and his children.

29

Tragedy Strikes

MERITATEN WALKS SOLEMNLY BEHIND HER PARENTS, TRYING TO maintain her composure. She still cannot believe that her sister Meketaten is dead, her soul flown to heaven to mingle with the sunrays of their creator. She remembers how less than a year ago she was holding Meketaten's hand at the tribute ceremony. Meritaten was so angry with her sister that day when hand holding devolved into violent squeezing. If only Meketaten had stopped tickling her in the ribs!

The keening cries of mourners interrupt Meritaten's reminiscing; she feels as if her heart is not even in her body. She looks out the corner of her eye at the women of the court, their dresses in shambles, their hands covering their faces or held up to heaven, other women kneeling and casting dirt over their bodies. Meritaten feels her knees buckle, and Ankhesenpaaten comes up behind her and wraps her arms around her faltering sister.

Standing next to her sisters, Neferneferuaten-tasherit begins to sob. She turns around, looking for comfort from Setepenre and Neferneferure, her rambunctious younger sisters, but they too are gone, their mummies resting in the tomb before which they now stand. Neferneferuaten-tasherit's sobs grow uncontrollable, and Meritaten pulls herself together enough to comfort her. The three sisters turn back to their parents and continue on toward the statue of Meketaten.

Akhenaten and Nefertiti are already in front of the elevated bower decorated with great papyrus blooms, winding vines, and draped fabric. Meketaten's statue stands in the middle of the bower, the same sort of structure where women go in the final days of pregnancy. Meritaten appears as she was in life, a beautiful girl dressed in the finest linen, gilded sandals on her feet, her head shaved but for the sidelock of youth. The king bends forward in grief and throws one arm before his face. "O, my beloved, my darling daughter!" He reaches back and grasps Nefertiti's wrist. She has buried three daughters in the span of a few months, and nothing can allay her grief. Her only comfort is that when Aten rises tomorrow morning, Meketaten's soul will continue to bask in his light.

It is time to proceed into the tomb to say their final prayers over Meketaten's mummy. Akhenaten and Nefertiti leave their daughters at the entrance to the royal tomb, descend a steep staircase, and then walk carefully down the sloping corridor before turning right into the suite of rooms where their three daughters now lie. Ahead of them is the chamber where eventually their own mummies will rest in their sarcophagi. The queen mother is still alive, but Nefertiti fears that hers may be the next funeral that the royal family celebrates. In the depths of Akhenaten's and Nefertiti's grief, their only comfort is their son, Tutankhaten, only a few months old, in the arms of a nurse just outside the tomb. In his presence the royal family manifests the unending cycle of their solar father: as we live in order to die, so we die in order to be born again.

After thirteen years on the throne, Akhenaten was probably in his midtwenties, his wife Nefertiti perhaps a bit younger. Despite their seeming youth, the king and queen ruled as gods on earth, and their union had produced six princesses and a prince. Their religious beliefs denied the progression of time, but even their daily offerings to Aten could not ward off tragedies.

Between Regnal Years 13 and 14, three of their daughters died: Meke-

Family mourning the death of Meketaten. (Drawing of scene in the Royal Tomb, after Geoffrey Martin, The Royal Tomb at El-'Amarna, *vol. 2 [London: Egypt Exploration Society, 1989], plate 68)*

taten and her two youngest sisters, Setepenre and Neferneferure. The princesses were buried in two chambers added to the main, descending corridor of the royal tomb, deep in a desert wadi east of Akhet-Aten. The first chamber served as the joint burial place of Setepenre and Neferneferure, who were not yet five years old when they died. In two registers of decoration in this chamber, we see the poignant scenes of Akhenaten and Nefertiti mourning the loss of their children.

In the second chamber, Akhenaten and Nefertiti again grieve, their emotions palpable in their anguished gestures as they bury Meketaten, who was probably no older than ten or eleven. We do not know what caused the death of the three princesses, but infant mortality was high in ancient Egypt: approximately one in five children died before the age of ten. Yet the most extreme modern portraits of Akhenaten accuse him of causing the death of Meketaten, the princess perishing as she gave birth to a baby sired by her own father.

But nowhere are the daughters buried in the royal tomb given the title "king's wife." Instead, the evidence most often cited for Akhenaten's sexual relations with his own daughters are reliefs that show Meritaten followed by a girl who is named Meritaten-tasherit, "Meritaten,

the little (junior)," with corresponding reliefs depicting Ankhesenpaaten and a child, "Ankhesenpaaten the little (junior)." The father of
these "junior" princesses, according to some scholars, could only be
Akhenaten.

The two princesses, in the company of their namesake progeny,
are surprising, but we must take note of where they appear. We see
Meritaten-tasherit and Ankhesenpaaten-tasherit with their mothers but
once, in reliefs from the Maru-Aten, the Sunshade of Re dedicated to
Queen Kiye.

After Regnal Year 12, and possibly as late as Regnal Year 16, Kiye's
images were erased. Without knowing her identity, it is impossible to
determine the reason for her disappearance. She may have fallen out
of favor with her husband, who then commanded her images removed
from every temple in Akhet-Aten. Or she may have returned to Mitanni
as relations between her homeland and Egypt took a turn for the worse.
An even more outlandish theory claims that Nefertiti took vengeance
on Kiye when the other queen gave birth to a male heir, Tutankhaten;
we may dismiss this last scenario, since texts suggest that the prince was
actually Nefertiti's son.

Whatever the cause, the images of Kiye and her daughter Baketaten
in the Maru-Aten were recut. Prior to Regnal Year 12, a handful of
reliefs show Akhenaten carrying out rituals and presenting offerings to
Aten with Kiye, the exceptions to the ubiquitous images of the king and
Nefertiti doing the same. After Kiye and Baketaten's removal, Akhenaten appeared to minister to the same cult in the company of two of his
daughters and granddaughters.

The sculptors who removed the name of Kiye replaced her name
with either that of Ankhesenpaaten or Meritaten. Instead of hacking out
Baketaten entirely, her name is replaced with the name of a nonexistent
daughter of the princess who usurped Kiye's image. Thus, Ankhesenpaaten replacing Kiye appears with a daughter labeled Ankhesenpaaten
tasherit, "the little," a small version of herself. The evidence of Akhenaten's sexual predations of his own daughters vanishes, as the "junior"
princesses are revealed to be artistic phantoms.

In the royal tomb, as Akhenaten and Nefertiti mourn for their deceased daughters, the reliefs suggest that the royal couple might at the

same time have been celebrating the birth of their first son. In both rooms, an image shows a woman holding a child and moving away from the funerary biers of the deceased princesses; one or two fan bearers follow the woman, signaling that the child is of royal birth. Some have seen these babies as the products of Akhenaten's incest, just like the "junior" daughters. But a late nineteenth-century photograph of a now much damaged inscription in the second chamber reveals that the baby is actually the son of Nefertiti. Although the reading is not certain, the likeliest translation of the hieroglyphs labeling the baby is "Son of the king of his own body, his beloved, Tutankhaten (Living Image of Aten) born of the king's great wife, his beloved Neferneferuaten Nefertiti, may she live forever and ever."[1]

A block from Khemenu, where it had been taken after the monuments of Akhet-Aten had been dismantled, identifies Tutankhaten as "the king's son of his body," supporting the restoration of the text labeling the baby in the royal tomb.[2] Little doubt remains that Akhenaten and Nefertiti were the parents of Tutankhaten. Just as Amunhotep IV did not appear as prince on his father's monuments, it is not surprising that Prince Tutankhaten does not appear elsewhere at Akhet-Aten. As a male child, Tutankhaten did not fit into the theology of his father's art, in which princesses enhance the divinity of Akhenaten and Nefertiti. Only when Tutankhaten ascends the throne and changes his name to Tutankhamun ("Living Image of Amun") do we have the opportunity to meet the person who would become the famous "boy king" buried with his golden treasures in the Valley of the Kings.

Following the deaths of three of the princesses and the birth of a son, likely all occurring around Regnal Years 13 and 14, the last dateable text from the reigns of Akhenaten and Nefertiti is an ink hieratic annotation within a quarry close to Akhet-Aten:

Regnal Year 16, first month of Akhet (Inundation Season), day 15. May (he) live, the king of Upper and Lower Egypt, who lives on maat, the Lord of the Two Lands Neferkheperure, unique one of Re—may he live, prosper, and be healthy—the son of Re, he who lives on maat, the lord of glorious appearances, Akhenaten—may he live, prosper, and be healthy—who is great in his lifetime, given life forever and ever;

and the king's great wife, his beloved, the mistress of the Two Lands, Neferneferuaten Nefertiti, given life forever and ever; (they who are) beloved of the Living one, Re, ruler of the two horizons, who rejoices in the horizon in his name of Re, the father, who returns as the sun disk: (re)opening the quarry; the work (for) the Mansion of Aten being under the control of the scribe Penthu, by the agency of the work overseer Nefer-renpet.[3]

On that day, approximately July 22, 1337 BCE, Nefer-renpet (or a subordinate delegated with the task) took a rush pen, dipped it in red ocher-based ink, and began to write those five lines of hieratic text. The scribe stood within a limestone quarry six miles north of Akhet-Aten, an area that had supplied many of the "bricks of stone" that formed the great temples to the sun god. The author of the hieratic text in the quarry followed the date with the cartouches of his two sovereigns, the king and queen who are beloved of Aten. The ink text in the quarry, a *dipinto*, was in part to ensure that the stones were directed to their proper destination.

The otherwise unremarkable quarry text proves that early in Akhenaten's sixteenth regnal year, Nefertiti was still alive and in the role of king's great wife. About a year later—we do not know the exact date— and at about thirty years of age, Akhenaten's soul left his body and became one with his heavenly father Aten. The cause of Akhenaten's death is unknown.

Nefertiti may have died around the same time as her husband or outlived him by a few years; she might even—according to some re- constructions of events—have succeeded Akhenaten as king. Textual records of that final, fateful year are sparse, pictorial evidence is incom- plete, and, at every turn, we find as many interpretations as there are artifacts and inscriptions.

30

Successors

MAANAKHTEF SURVEYS THE MUD-FILLED PIT. LABORERS, WEARING nothing but loincloths, tread in circles around the basin, while others pour baskets of chopped straw into the mud. Every few minutes the workers fill baskets of the mud-straw mixture, hoist them up to others at the edge of the basin, and return to repeat the process. On a flat stretch of ground, men with rectangular wooden forms start fashioning row after row of mud bricks. Maanakhtef calls to the scribe who sits within earshot but far enough away to keep his linen kilt unstained: "How many bricks are ready?"

The scribe ticks off a few totals on the papyrus on his lap. "Ten thousand, three hundred and fourteen, sir."

Good, Maanakhtef thinks, they are on schedule. He follows men carrying poles on their shoulders, piles of bricks slung from each side, to the building site itself. A new structure is being added to the southern end of the Great Palace of Pharaoh, may he be living, prosperous, and healthy! A few weeks ago, Maanakhtef had personally marked out the ground plan, a remarkable 260 cubits on each side. The walls are nearly complete, and the constant shipments of bricks are being stacked to form over five hundred rectangular pillars spaced close together.

Of all the structures—temples, palaces, and even guard posts—that

Maanakhtef has overseen, this forest of pillars is one of the most unusual—a pleasure garden of vineyards. He wanders over to where some of the bricks, brought over still moist, are being stamped with the name of the king to whom this vineyard is dedicated. Maanakhtef examines the cartouche, reading silently: *Ankh-kheperu-re*. No one has yet explained to him who exactly this new king is, and why Akhenaten has elevated him to co-regent.

Just the other day, visiting the house of the cupbearer Parennefer, he tried to steer the conversation subtly toward this new king. "Given Meritaten's prominence at court lately," Maanakhtef had mused, "why not make her king alongside her father? We may no longer speak her name, but some of us know how effective her ancestor Hatshepsut was as king."

"Hush," Parennefer had whispered, "and I will tell you a secret: this king is Meritaten!"

Akhenaten and Nefertiti appear in every boundary stela, in every tomb inscription, and as elements in the decoration of the temples and palaces in which the royal couple spent their days. Yet Akhenaten was not the only king who ruled from Akhet-Aten. From this city, two shadowy figures also reigned—one a man, the other a woman—but the dates of their rule, the order of their reigns, and their identities remain obscured by confusing and sparse evidence.

The male king used Semenkhkare as his birth name. Evidence of Semenkhkare's existence is so slight that we know neither the identity of his parents nor whether he had an independent reign as king, or if he was merely a short-lived co-regent with Akhenaten. Was he a younger brother of Akhenaten, an otherwise unattested son of Amunhotep III and Tiye? Or was he an otherwise unknown son of Akhenaten and Nefertiti, a brother of Tutankhaten?

The king's name means "He whom the *ka*-spirit of Re ennobles," and his cartouche can add the epithet "sacred are the manifestations (*kheperu*) of Re." The name Semenkhkare would be unique as an ancient Egyptian name given at birth, but it does conform to the expected

Painted outline of King Semenkhkare and his great royal wife Meritaten,
drawing of a scene in the tomb of Meryre II (inset: hieroglyphs copied by Lepsius).
(after N. de G. Davies, The Rock Tombs of El Amarna, *vol. 2,* The Tomb of Meryra
[London: Egypt Exploration Fund, 1905], plate 41)

pattern for a royal coronation name. The lack of a regular birth name has led some Egyptologists to suggest that Semenkhkare was not Egyptian but rather a prince of the Hittites sent to marry the eldest princess Meritaten.

The only time Semenkhkare is ever pictured is a scene of him with his great royal wife, Meritaten. In a now faded sketch in the tomb of the steward Meryre, we see the omnipresent Aten disk shining down upon Semenkhkare and Meritaten. Their names are given in cartouches, including the king's coronation name: "King of Upper and Lower Egypt, Ankhkheperure (Living One of the Manifestations of Re)."

Appearing more often in the ancient sources, both in the final years of the reign of Akhenaten and after his death, is yet another ruler, a woman. She used Neferneferuaten as her birth name, and her identity is nearly as mysterious as that of the even more ephemeral Semenkhkare. Yet, her coffin is on display in perhaps the busiest room in the Egyptian Museum in Tahrir Square, the chamber where the gold and jeweled possessions of Tutankhamun are located (in the future, these will be together with all the artifacts from Tutankhamun's tomb in the Grand Egyptian Museum).

Tutankhamun died only nine years into his reign, at the age of eighteen, of unknown causes, although malaria and an injury from a fall— perhaps from a chariot—are possibilities. After Tutankhamun's death, the seventy days of mummification rites began, culminating in the elaborate wrapping of the king's body, with its own treasure of amulets and jewelry placed among the linen strips that bound the corpse. The most magnificent of these adornments was the twenty-two-pound gold mask placed over the king's head.

In the Egyptian Museum, behind the case containing the mask, are three coffins of increasingly larger size, each now displayed separately, but in the king's burial, they had been nested within one another. The smallest, solid gold coffin held Tutankhamun's mummy and its golden mask; a second coffin of gilded wood, covered with semiprecious stones, held the solid gold coffin; and both of these were placed within a yet larger gilded wooden coffin, nearly seven and a half feet long.

Standing in the exhibit hall, we can easily compare each of the faces on the coffins and notice—like others before us—that one is not like the others. The visages on the outermost and innermost coffins share the features of the gold mask: an oval face with a full mouth, the upper and lower lips of similar width. The face of the second coffin has a squarer chin, discernible even though all three faces have long, braided beards. But the most noticeable difference is in the mouth. On the second coffin, the lower lip is fuller than the upper, and the corners of the mouth are set low, creating the overall impression of a pout.

Tutankhamun's name is the only one that appears on the coffins, and the facial features of the gold mask on the innermost and outermost coffins indicate that they were purpose-made for his burial. The second coffin, however, appears to have been prepared for someone else and reused for Tutankhamun. So how can we identify the person who was originally buried within the coffin that would later be used as the second in Tutankhamun's nested set of coffins? The answer leads us from one of the most important archaeological discoveries of the twentieth century to a careful analysis of artifacts from Akhet-Aten.

On November 1, 1922, Egyptian excavators working with British archaeologist Howard Carter began to trench beneath the remains of stone huts that had been occupied last around 1140 BCE by workmen decorating the tomb of Ramesses VI. Having spent years excavating in the Valley of the Kings, Carter knew that this small area was one of the last places to search for the lost tomb of Tutankhamun.

On November 4, the Egyptian excavators, whose names are sadly not recorded in the published accounts, revealed a step cut down into the hillside, the unmistakable sign of a tomb. After a feverish two days of clearance and anxious expectation, the upper portion of the stairway and the top of a sealed doorway were exposed by the time the sun set on November 5. The plaster covering the entrance bore the seal impressions of the ancient necropolis guards, meaning that it had remained undisturbed at least since the reign of Ramesses VI, when workmen inhabited the stone huts that accidentally, but more fortuitously, concealed any trace of the tomb below.

Despite his understandable desire to push forward and clear beyond the sealed door, Carter had the staircase refilled to await the arrival of his patron, the financier of his expedition, George Herbert, the Fifth Earl of Carnarvon. Lord Carnarvon and his daughter, Lady Evelyn Herbert, arrived in Luxor on November 23, and on the following day the debris covering the sixteen descending steps was fully removed, revealing the entire surface of the plastered doorway for the first time in three millennia. Carter could now read the name of the king whose tomb he had found: Tutankhamun. But the sealings on the plaster also showed that thieves had entered the tomb more than once. Those ancient robbers had apparently been caught in the act of their desecration, dropping some of their loot on the way out.

In the debris at the bottom of the staircase was the detritus of the thieves and those who cleaned up after their depredations. Among this debris was a perplexing box whose lid has five names written on it, none of which belong to Tutankhamun. The first two are the cartouches of

Akhenaten, followed by two cartouches of another king, Ankhkheper-ure Neferneferuaten; the final name is the cartouche of the king's great wife, Meritaten. The mention of this additional king Neferneferuaten gave Carter pause. Behind the blocked doorway, was he going to find a tumbled group of objects from several different plundered burials rather than the mostly intact burial of the long-sought Tutankhamun?

To Carter's relief and everlasting amazement, when he first peered through the opening in the sealed door, he saw what no living human had seen for over thirty-two hundred years—"gold, everywhere the glint of gold"—treasures nearly impossible to put into words. The sixty-second tomb discovered in the Valley of the Kings (hence its official designation, KV 62) was the only royal burial in the necropolis that survived mostly intact. The four chambers of the tomb contained thousands of artifacts, among them gilded chariots and shrines, jewelry of gold and semi-precious stones, the finest inlaid furniture, and humble objects, like ceramic vessels, loincloths, and a reed walking stick "cut by the king's own hand." Within the tomb's antechamber was another box with the name of King Neferneferuaten. The lid of this second box had an inscription that was usurped for Tutankhamun but originally bore three of the same cartouches as the box outside the entrance: King Ankhkheperure Neferneferuaten and the king's great wife Meritaten.

These boxes and other seemingly minor inscriptions from Tutankhamun's tomb provide important clues to Neferneferuaten's identity. She had the same coronation name as Semenkhkare; they are both "Living One (ankh) of the Manifestations (kheperu) of Re." As a woman, however, Neferneferuaten can at times—albeit not always—write her name as Ankhetkheperure, the-et added at the end of ankh indicating a female "Living One." This shared name leads to no end of confusion. Frequently, a monument or object is assigned to Semenkhkare when the cartouche is only that of Ankhkheperure. One prominent example is the so-called "Coronation Hall of Semenkhkare," a southern extension of the Great Palace at Akhet-Aten, which contains over five hundred mud-brick piers (about 4 feet × 4 feet) in a rectangular structure nearly 150 yards on each side (featured in our reconstruction above). Since the piers are, on average, about eight feet from one another, this building would not have been suitable for a grand public event like a coronation.

The building's architectural form, painted plaster fragments of grape vines found within it, and possible remains of root pits in the floor suggest an alternative interpretation: the piers supported trellises for a vineyard, a place for relaxation and enjoying Aten's bounty, just like the Sunshade temples. Bricks from the structure are stamped with the cartouche Ankhkheperure, so it is just as likely to belong to the female king Neferneferuaten as the male king Semenkhkare.

In both of her cartouches, the female king can be called one beloved of Akhenaten or one "effective for her husband (akh-en-hy-es)." These epithets confirm that Neferneferuaten was a woman who ruled as a king, whose name evoked that of her predecessor, taking us from Akhenaten to Akhenhyes. She is also the ruler whose face stares out from the gilded coffin that became part of Tutankhamun's nested set.

Who, then, is she? Compelling evidence exists for two candidates—Akhenaten's great royal wife Nefertiti, or their eldest daughter Meritaten—but no single object or text unambiguously identifies either woman as the female king Neferneferuaten. First, the case for Nefertiti. Between Akhenaten's fifth and sixteenth regnal years, Nefertiti's cartouche included the epithet or secondary name Neferneferuaten, and if she were King Neferneferuaten, she could certainly be called "one effective for her husband." The box lids from the tomb of Tutankhamun would mean that Nefertiti ruled as co-regent with her husband, while their daughter Meritaten assumed the then vacated title of king's great wife. We could interpret Meritaten's rank in two ways: either she retained the title that she had upon her marriage to Semenkhkare, who may have died before the box was carved, or Meritaten fulfilled the ritual role of "king's great wife" for her parents because Nefertiti was now a co-pharaoh.

Several pieces of evidence, however, speak against Nefertiti's elevation to king. In the royal tomb at Akhet-Aten, a funerary figurine and fragments of a granite sarcophagus belonging to Nefertiti give her only the title "king's great wife." These objects suggest that at her death, likely during Regnal Year 16, her most exalted position was as great queen of Akhenaten, not as a royal successor. The face of Tutankhamun's second coffin and the few other statues from KV 62 that appear to be images of King Neferneferuaten provide the strongest argument against Nefertiti as Akhenaten's successor. The coffin's most distinctive features are a slightly downturned mouth and seemingly sulky expression, which appear nearly identical to images of Princess Meritaten from Akhet-Aten, but does not resemble the many portraits of Nefertiti.

The case for Meritaten as King Neferneferuaten better fits the surviving artifacts, which capture her unique facial features, but that identification has its own complexities. It is odd that Meritaten abandoned her birth name and adopted her mother's epithet Neferneferuaten as her Son of Re name. Equally unusual is that the boxes in the tomb of Tutankhamun give the two names of King Neferneferuaten followed by the name of the great royal wife Meritaten. This would be one of the few examples of a king possessing three different cartouches within a single inscription.

Furthermore, the epithet "effective for her husband" would mean that Meritaten was wife to Akhenaten, just as two of Amunhotep III's daughters were royal wives of their father. Three Amarna Letters mention a woman named Mayati, which is the cuneiform writing of Meritaten, and one refers to her as the mistress of Akhenaten's house, a title in keeping with the eldest princess being elevated to a queenly rank. If Meritaten is King Neferneferuaten, then in her epithets she claims to be beloved of her father and possibly effective for him as his wife, if he is the husband to which the epithet refers. Maybe, just maybe, Akhenaten did take his identification with the sun god literally, finding sexual gratification in his daughter, as Re does of his divine offspring, the alluring Hathor. No evidence exists for such an incestuous relationship, but at the same time we cannot prove that it did not happen.

The tomb of Tutankhamun offers yet more evidence for the identity of King Neferneferuaten. In the antechamber was a poorly preserved linen garment onto which were sewn gold sequins, each decorated with two cartouches. No title appears before either name, understandable as the gold sequins are less than an inch in diameter. The cartouches are all written to be read right to left, as Ankhkheperure Meriaten. The name Meriaten is written in the masculine form but has a seated woman as a determinative, identifying the name as feminine. These sequins suggest that as King Neferneferuaten, Princess Meritaten could sometimes use her birth name in a royal context alongside her coronation name Ankh-

kheperure. In other cases, like on the boxes from the tomb of Tutankhamun, Meritaten as king Neferneferuaten juxtaposed her two cartouches
with her earlier "king's great wife" cartouche to represent her identity.

Additional evidence for Meritaten as Akhenaten's successor comes
from a handful of small stelae that depict two people wearing crowns
only worn by kings. The cartouches that would name them are either
blank or considerably damaged, but we can assume that one king is
Akhenaten. On one of these stelae, commissioned by the soldier Pase,
Aten shines down on a royal pair seated before a table of offerings. The
king on the left appears to be nude but for sandals and a blue crown,
while the king on the right sports the double crown of Upper and Lower
Egypt and a long and apparently diaphanous garment, as well as sandals.
The king with the blue crown has one arm around the forward king's
shoulders, while that double-crown-wearing ruler turns back and cups
a hand beneath the chin of the figure behind him.

Even without labels, the dress and posture of the kings allow us to
begin to identify them. Physically, they are essentially identical in appearance, but the nudity of the king in the blue crown would not be
appropriate for a member of the immediate royal family except for a
child. The gesture of the king with the double crown, placing a hand
underneath the chin of his companion, is another clue to the youthful
identity of the nude king.

In a painting of princesses from the King's House, the smaller palace
in the Central City of Akhet-Aten, one child tickles the other under
the chin. On the stela now in the Neues Museum in Berlin that shows
the royal family in intimate poses, Meritaten cups her hand beneath her
father's chin (see figure on page 217). In a number of scenes at Medinet
Habu near the image of the princesses presenting transformative broad
collars, Ramesses III caresses his nude daughters beneath their chins. In
ancient Egyptian imagery, tickling, particularly under the chin, appears
primarily to be by and for children. Might the one king's tickling pose
on Pase's stela prove that the nude king is indeed the daughter of the
king in the double crown? While a playful posture may seem an un-
likely clue, the specificity of the gesture, and the apparent nudity of
the second figure, tips the scales a bit more toward Meritaten being the
figure seated behind the equally unlabeled Akhenaten.

Pase's stela and similar monuments may have been carved after Akhenaten's death, but the depiction of two kings more likely indicates a brief period of joint rule between father and daughter. A label to a jar of honey from Akhet-Aten dates to this brief period; the hieratic text states that the honey was produced during Regnal Year 17 of Akhenaten and Regnal Year 1 of a ruler whose name is not preserved. When the ancient Egyptians provided such double dates, they were equating the regnal year of one sovereign with that of his co-ruler, thus Neferneferuaten appears to have ruled for at least part of a year while her father was still alive.

As Ankhetkheperure Neferneferuaten, Meritaten then ruled for another two years as sole king. Her short reign proves how the unusual prominence of royal women during Akhenaten's lifetime continued to change the course of Egyptian history even after his death. We can attribute to her no surviving major monuments, but Pawah's ink text in the tomb of Pairy, the lament about not seeing Amun in festival, is dated to Regnal Year 3 of her reign. His hieratic text provides one of the only clues we have to what Neferneferuaten accomplished as king. Pawah was not only a priest but also a scribe of divine offerings of Amun in the temple of Ankhkheperure (the coronation name of Neferneferuaten). The fact that Neferneferuaten had a temple where Amun was worshipped has profound implications. Along with her advisors, Neferneferuaten seems to have ended the religious upheavals that began with her father's move to Akhet-Aten, reopened the temples of Waset, and started Egypt back on a course of normalcy—all remarkable achievements for a young king.

From an archive of letters in the Hittite capital Hattusa, in roughly the central portion of modern-day Turkey, we learn of another unprecedented event that King Neferneferuaten may have initiated. According to the Hittite sources, an Egyptian queen wrote to Suppiluliuma, king of the Hittites, and describes how her husband has died and that she has no heir. The widowed queen then claims that she will not marry a commoner and makes a shocking proposal: she requests that one of Suppiluliuma's sons be sent to Egypt to become both her husband and the king of Egypt.

Neither the queen nor the Hittite prince is named; instead, they are referred to only by the cuneiform Hittite versions of their Egyptian titles: *dakhamunzu,* "king's wife," and *zananza,* "king's son." This allows for multiple interpretations of the documents, which is compounded by the ambiguity in the cuneiform writing of the name of the deceased Egyptian king, which might represent either the coronation name of Akhenaten or that of Tutankhamun. Scholars often identify the widow who requested the Hittite prince as the third daughter of Akhenaten and Nefertiti, Ankhesenpaaten. She renamed herself Ankhesenamun and married her brother Tutankhamun. At the death of Tutankhamun, his sister-queen had neither a son nor a male heir, which matches the claims of the Egyptian widow in the Hittite correspondence.

Another Hittite letter, heavily damaged, may suggest an alternate scenario: following the death of her first husband Semenkhkare and then her second husband Akhenaten, Meritaten sought a Hittite prince to marry. We do not have the Egyptian side of the correspondence, but the Hittite king Suppiluliuma quotes liberally from earlier letters from Egypt as he articulates his responses and concerns. In one clear and uniquely important line, Suppiluliuma says that the addressee is "as king of Egypt." Shortly thereafter the Hittite king explains that he was disposed to send his son after receiving a request from the Egyptian ruler: "I wanted to sen[d] him [to be ki]ng; but that you (already?) sat [upon the throne], that [I did] no[t know.]" In an equally fragmentary section, Suppiluliuma says: "[When the queen of E]gypt wrote [to] me, you(?) [. . .] not [. . .] you were (or "she was") [. . .]. But when you [sat yourself upon the throne] then you should have been able to send my son home."[1]

Might the queen who became king as Neferneferuaten be the pharaoh to whom Suppiluliuma writes here? Unless the queen herself had died, the suggestion seems to be that the queen was now seated upon the throne of Egypt. This scenario fits well with events immediately following the death of Akhenaten: the recently widowed Meritaten requests a Hittite prince, but by the time he has completed the journey to Egypt, Meritaten has become King Neferneferuaten. While Neferneferuaten was not lying about not having a son of her own, she was not being fully truthful with the Hittites about the existence of a male heir, Prince Tutankhaten. No matter who wrote to Suppiluliuma, the Hittite prince, the one called *zananza* in the letters, appears to have met a violent end—

according to later Hittite sources, he was murdered by the Egyptians. Some scholars have even sought to equate *zananza* with the ephemeral king Semenkhkare, as if two shadowy figures could be combined to create a more knowable individual.

The Hittite documents describe the marriage negotiations between the Egyptian and Hittite courts as taking place over several months. This delay also appears to rule out Ankhesenamun as the queen who requested a Hittite prince. The tomb of Tutankhamun shows the teenage king's mummified body being buried by his successor, Ay. The god's father Ay—likely the brother of Tiye and father of Nefertiti—had loyally served Akhenaten and his son as tutor, advisor, and counselor to the pharaoh.

Upon Tutankhamun's death, Ay, then in his sixties, became the sole king of Egypt. If we assume the typical seventy days for mummification and burial for Tutankhamun, that leaves no time for messengers traveling between Egypt and Turkey to deliver Ankhesenamun's missives about a Hittite prince. Yet such a timeline would fit perfectly with the uncertain months following the death of Akhenaten, when the widowed queen Meritaten bore the responsibility of sole pharaoh as Neferneferuaten.

We know nothing about the death of the female king Neferneferuaten. If she was Meritaten, then she died just before her brother took the throne, when she was approximately twenty years old. In this scenario, during her three years as king, Meritaten guided Egypt away from the extreme iconoclasm of the final part of her father's reign, and Tutankhamun, only about nine years old at his accession, expanded upon her policies.

As Tutankhamun's advisors eradicated the last vestiges of Akhenaten's religious reformations and directed Egypt's resources to restoring neglected temples, officials set about erasing the previous two decades of history. At Karnak Temple, Akhenaten's son erected a stela to proclaim the start of a new era; the preamble of the text summarizes the state of Egypt when Tutankhamun became king.

The temples of the gods and goddesses beginning in Elephantine and ending at the marshes of the Delta [. . .] had fallen into ruin. Their shrines had fallen into decay, turning into mounds, overgrown with weeds . . . The land was in distress, and the gods ignored this land. If an army was sent to Djahi (along the Levantine coast), in order to widen the boundaries of Egypt, they were unable to succeed. If one petitioned to a god in order to take counsel from him, he failed to come at all. If one prayed to a goddess likewise, she failed to come at all.[2]

This is a powerful indictment of Akhenaten's rule: just as he had turned against the gods, so had they ignored Egypt, dooming armies to failure and denying individuals divine succor. The stela's text then describes the day on which Tutankhamun was crowned pharaoh and how he began to rebuild the temple infrastructure, such that the new king could claim to have "surpassed what was done since the time of the ancestors." That phrase raised Tutankhamun's actions to cosmic significance, but it also reminds the modern reader that such hieroglyphic texts can exaggerate to achieve a grander purpose.

Did Tutankhamun's restorations actually surpass his grandfather's temple building projects? Had the temples of Egypt turned into mounds in the twenty years since Akhenaten was crowned pharaoh? Akhenaten's reign was probably devastating to some of the population, like the priesthood and dependents of Karnak Temple, but did most Egyptians believe that all the gods and goddesses had abandoned them? Even Akhenaten's tomb builders continued to worship other gods besides Aten, and objects from the workmen's homes indicate that Hathor and Horus still heard their petitions. Tutankhamun's stela takes historical facts—Akhenaten's focus entirely on Aten and rejection of Amun—and uses them to highlight the new king's accomplishments—restoring the cults of all the gods.

Akhenaten, who called himself "one who lived on *maat*," usurped the privilege of a god, and after his death, the king was cast as an enemy, a rebel against *maat*. Tainted by their association with Akhenaten, the reigns of Semenkhkare and Neferneferuaten were also condemned to oblivion. Denied the status of a legitimate king, some of Neferneferuaten's burial goods, including her royal coffin, were repurposed for Tutankhamun. It is possible that Meritaten was given a reburial as a princess, interred within a modest tomb in the Valley of the Kings, but the fate of her body remains unknown. Tutankhamun vehemently denounced his father, and from that point onward, Akhenaten's name would no longer be spoken; he would be referenced only through the circumlocution "the enemy (or rebel) of Akhet-Aten."

When Horemhab, a general who had served Tutankhamun, became king upon the death of Ay, the new king condemned Tutankhamun and Ay to the same fate as Akhenaten. Horemhab desired a complete break with any ruler tainted by the enemy who had ruled from Akhet-Aten. Even though Tutankhamun and Ay helped to rebuild the cult of Amun, they were the son and loyal courtier, respectively, of the "enemy of Akhet-Aten." So they too were erased from history.

The Nineteenth Dynasty, a long line of kings, most of whom were named Seti or Ramesses, revised the king lists so that Amunhotep III was followed immediately by Horemhab, omitting all kings with a direct connection to Akhenaten's family. The great constructions at Waset and Akhet-Aten built during the reign of the "enemy" were dismantled and reused as fill in new temples to the traditional pantheon. Aten was no longer the name of the unique solar god but the concept of divinity espoused by Suty and Hor and encapsulated in the Great Hymn to Aten survived in the theology of the Ramesside era.

The erasure of Akhenaten, Nefertiti, Semenkhkare, and Neferneferu-aten was so complete that they remained forgotten for three millennia. They were rediscovered in the nineteenth century from halting translations of hieroglyphic texts and remarkable objects emerging from the ruins of Akhet-Aten. As the twentieth century and a new age of archaeology dawned, the lives of Akhenaten and Nefertiti came into sharper focus. In 1907, among the jumbled remains of a small tomb nearby that of Tutankhamun, archaeologists discovered the mortal remains of Akhenaten.

31

Afterlife

THE YOUNG PRIEST WENNEFER, WEARING A FILTHY LINEN SHIRT and kilt soaked with sweat and covered in dust, bows to Amunmose, the overseer of workmen, and Panehesy, the senior priest, who are sitting comfortably beneath a square wood and cloth sunshade. As Wennefer speaks, he sees surprise and worry wash over the faces of both.

"This is indeed the tomb of the rebel of Akhet-Aten!" Wennefer whispers. "We have broken the intact sealings on the door as instructed—all date to the reign of the Son of Re Tutankhamun, justified. The names and images of the rebel of Akhet-Aten have been erased from the exterior surfaces of the shrine of the King's Great Wife Tiye, she who is justified in the Underworld." Without a word, Amunmose and Panehesy move together toward the entrance passage.

As they enter the tomb, debris tumbles around them, creating a cloud of dust, made more oppressive by the humidity within the chamber. Workmen were still clearing stones from the passageway to remove the gilded shrine that the officials were coming to inspect. All wait a while to allow the dust to settle, and those working in the tomb stand to attention.

"The moisture is appalling—one might recite that part of the Book of the Hidden Chamber that concerns the entry of the drowned into the Netherworld," says Panehesy. His forced levity is not well received. Then Amunmose, staring at a canopic jar, exclaims, "This was first prepared for someone whose name I cannot make out in this light, and then altered for use by the rebel of Akhet-Aten himself!"

Once they can examine the jars in the light, the overseer Amunmose pulls the senior priest Panehesy aside and speaks quietly. "These jars were prepared for the lesser wife of the rebel, Kiye, then reused when the Son of Re Tutankhamun moved the body of his father to Waset. The coffin we saw in the shrine must contain his mummy. I have some discretion here, but we must work quickly—Pharaoh desires that the burial become nameless but remain intact."

Workmen then take the jars with the names of the enemy of Akhet-Aten, erase the inscriptions, and remove the uraei from the brows of the heads that formed the lids to the vessels. The workmen set the jars back in the tomb, then extract the coffin and the funerary bier on which it sat; some workmen busy themselves with the coffin—names are to be removed from it and from the golden bands that bind the mummy within. Work on the wrapped corpse proves particularly grisly. The skin is rotting away, but the arms must be moved in the search for inscribed amulets around the chest. A gilded mask is removed from the head—Pharaoh would wish to see this, they reckon—but then, the head comes off with it.

To work on the body in the confined space, two of the workmen set the decapitated body on its feet. After a brief visit down in the tomb, the priest Panehesy remarks that he truly would never think of the decapitated damned in the Underworld in quite the same way. As the light begins to fail, the overseer Amunmose issues his final order. "The largest pieces of the shrine cannot be taken out without further removal of blocking debris. Therefore, we should close up the place and leave the shrine inside."

The overseer and senior priest take one last look inside the small and humid sepulcher, and Panehesy utters a final curse: "May his mouth remain open for eternity, not to eat from the offering formulae that will not be said, not to commune with the living who will not know him, but to bewail the fate of himself, whom even he will not know."

The last two workmen in the chamber bend over the coffin, admiring their handiwork. One notices a crack along the chin of the coffin's face. He inserts his fingernails and widens the gap, wrenching off the face, which tears unevenly at the top, leaving the right eye. "A souvenir for Pharaoh. The nameless one will not miss it." The violence of his motion causes part of the funerary bier, the rotten legs beneath the head of the coffin, to collapse. The lid of the coffin then slips to the side and exposes the head of the mummy.

The two workmen each wonder if the other senses a divine response to their disrespect of the dead, but neither is willing to admit it. Hastily they exit the chamber and help their coworkers refill the blocking debris. Darkness and damp, decay and oblivion settle over the final resting place of the rebel of Akhet-Aten, and all feel certain that his memory will surely die forevermore.

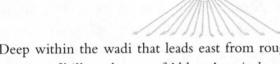

Deep within the wadi that leads east from roughly the middle of the crescent of hills to the east of Akhet-Aten is the royal tomb. Akhenaten's original plan for the city included provisions for the burial of the royal family in that as yet to be excavated sepulcher: "A tomb shall be made for me in the eastern mountain [of Akhet-Aten], in which I shall be buried for the duration of millions of jubilees that Aten, my father, decreed for me." He also stipulates, "If I shall die in any other town, either to the north, to the south, to the west, or to the east for millions of years, then one shall bring me back in order to bury me in Akhet-Aten."[1] The king makes the same commandment for Nefertiti and Meritaten, at the time their only daughter.

The king's plans were put into effect during his seventeenth year on the throne, approximately August 1336 BCE, when Akhenaten expelled his last breath. Shortly thereafter, priests began the preparations that would transform Akhenaten's corpse into a mummy. Did the traditional seventy-day process differ for the king who worshipped Aten and rejected Osiris, Foremost of the Westerners? In a typical royal burial, such as we know so spectacularly from the preserved mummy of Akhenaten's son Tutankhamun, gold amulets, plaques, collars, and jewelry were placed within the layers of wrappings. Did Akhenaten's priests commission similar pieces, or did they adhere to the aniconic strictures of the final years of their sovereign's reign?

One aspect of the mummification process definitely carried out for Akhenaten was the removal of the internal organs. In Akhenaten's tomb was a chest that held four canopic jars, stone vessels, which each contained one of the major internal organs: the lungs, the stomach, the liver, and the intestines. Another traditional item of burial equipment included within the king's tomb at Akhet-Aten were small statuettes that the ancient Egyptians called *shabtis*. The likeliest etymology for the term is the verb *wesheb*, "to answer," for the purpose of a *shabti* was to be on call for the soul of the deceased. While a pharaoh would normally wield a hoe or a measuring cord only during the foundation rituals of a temple, a royal tomb was well equipped with *shabti* figures who could perform any actual work required in the afterlife.

Only a handful of Akhenaten's *shabtis* survive, but his original interment may have been equipped with the same, full complement of figures as his son Tutankhamun: 413 individual *shabtis*, one for each day of the year; and 48 overseers, one for each ten-day week and another for each month. The *shabtis* of Akhenaten are mummiform and bear his name, with some adding the designation "true of voice." That epithet is an unusual concession to traditional conceptions of the afterlife. In the *Book of the Dead,* the heart of the deceased was weighed against *maat* to determine the moral weight of the life that person had lived. A soul that passed the test was granted the status "true of voice," justified before Osiris in the Judgment Hall.

Upon completion of the mummification process, Akhenaten's mummy was placed in a gilded coffin, perhaps even a nested set of them. Even if the mummification and closing of the coffins occurred in the desert east of Akhet-Aten, the funerary cortege had to travel an additional four miles east into the wadi to reach the entrance to the royal tomb. Once carefully maneuvered down the sloping passageway, Akhenaten's coffins were laid to rest in a granite sarcophagus in the large chamber at the rear of the tomb.

On other royal sarcophagi, winged goddesses guarded the corners of the stone container intended to hold the king's corpse. On Akhenaten's sarcophagus, those goddesses were replaced by the living goddess who accompanied him throughout his life: Nefertiti. The queen goddess wears the same diaphanous pleated dress that was her daily fashion, and her arms stretch out, placing her husband's body within her embrace. Aten, their divine father, spreads his rays over each side of the sarcophagus, illuminating the king in death as he did in life. Akhenaten intended to spend an eternity in the embrace of the god he worshipped and the woman he loved.

Most likely, Meritaten, as King Neferneferuaten, oversaw the burial of Akhenaten. In the royal tomb, Akhenaten joined his daughters Meketaten, Setepenre, and Neferneferure, as well as his mother Tiye and possibly his wife Nefertiti. When Neferneferuaten died and Tutankhaten was crowned king, he too needed to fulfill his duty to bury a royal predecessor. Whether he and his advisors accepted Neferneferuaten as king in life, they rejected her royal legitimacy in death. Instead, Tutankhamun organized the reburial of his father, the "rebel of Akhet-Aten."

Akhenaten's body was retrieved from the royal tomb in Akhet-Aten, and at the same time the stone sarcophagi of the king, Tiye, Nefertiti, and the princesses were smashed to pieces. We do not know what the newly crowned Tutankhamun thought of this desecration of his family's burials, or if he was even aware of its occurrence. While other items within the royal burials were also vandalized, Akhenaten's mummy was not damaged, and we can presume that the mummies of the queens and princesses also remained unviolated. Akhenaten's mortal remains were transported to Waset for interment in a small, roughly carved tomb, now designated KV 55 (being the fifty-fifth sepulcher found in the Valley of the Kings). Tutankhamun knew that Akhenaten had sinned against the gods, but it was still a duty of all pharaohs to bury their fathers.

In 1907, the objects within KV 55 were discovered in a tremendous state of disarray and composed of a mixture of burial goods from different members of the royal family of Akhenaten, including Tiye and Kiye. Some of the most spectacular items are panels from a gilded shrine showing Tiye and her son consecrating offerings before Aten, part of the queen mother's burial equipment at Akhet-Aten. The presence of that sadly damaged but still impressive object caused Theodore Davis, the man who funded the excavation of the tomb, to identify the mysterious assemblage in KV 55 as the tomb of Tiye.

Amunhotep III's queen appears, however, to have made her way to the tomb of her husband in the western branch of the Valley of the Kings. A hieratic inscription on a wall within Amunhotep III's burial indicates an entry of the tomb during Regnal Year 3 of some ruler. While that might have been Tutankhamun, one might also suggest Neferneferuaten. The date of the ink text in the tomb of Amunhotep III—Regnal Year 3, third month of Akhet, day 7—is only three days prior to the Year 3 date from the reign of Neferneferuaten given in the text of the priest Pawah. Perhaps Tiye's reburial and Pawah's outpouring of spiritual emotion were part of the restoration of Western Waset that King Neferneferuaten had initiated.

It was not until Tutankhamun's reign that Akhenaten's body too was relocated, an event that respected the father's corpse while signaling a complete break with the grand project at Akhet-Aten. In addition to Tiye's shrine, KV 55 included four canopic jars of Egyptian alabaster that had once been intended for Akhenaten's second wife Kiye. Her names and titles were erased from each, and Akhenaten's then added. The lid of each jar is an exquisite portrait of Kiye, so refined that every braid of her wig is delineated. Uraei were added to transform the jars into objects fit for a king's organs, but the heads were not otherwise altered.

Scattered in the tomb were remains of a mixed set of equipment used for the Opening of the Mouth, a ritual that allowed the deceased to eat, drink, and enjoy other bodily pleasures in the afterlife. Four magical bricks inscribed for the "Osiris King" Akhenaten, a title he would have almost surely rejected in life, were originally placed in a niche on each wall. The most truly enigmatic object among the strange assemblage of material in KV 55 is a mutilated coffin, originally intended to hold the body of Kiye but reworked for her husband.

The tomb was not left sealed for long. The original excavators of KV 55 noted two sealing events on the entrance. The positions of several items in the tomb, and the dismantled state of Tiye's old shrine, provide some evidence for the reopening of the tomb, as described in the re-created scene above. If this reopening occurred during the official looting of the royal tombs around 1050 BCE, a time when the government was weak and impoverished, then the goal was the stripping of valuable materials. Some portable treasures may well have been removed, and a golden burial mask does appear to have been taken; Akhenaten's names were hacked out of the mummy bands, his coffin, and the canopic jars. If not at the end of the New Kingdom, the decision to enter the tomb probably occurred sometime after the death of Tutankhamun and before the end of the reign of Ramesses II, the last ruler who appears directly to have concerned himself with the period of "the rebel of Akhet-Aten."

Whenever the workmen entered KV 55, when they resealed the entrance, they left the coffin of the long-since-damned Akhenaten, borrowed from the once beloved Kiye, alone in the darkness. For over three millennia, the single eye of a face without nose and mouth stared into the darkness. An inscription on the foot of the desecrated coffin is a fitting end to the story of a king who devoted his life to the worship of Aten and transformed Egypt in the process. The text was first spoken by Kiye to Akhenaten. By a sad irony, Akhenaten, condemned to eternal anonymity by his successors, was protected and loved through his long night of slumber in a borrowed tomb by the words of a wife he may himself have cast aside.

Those adapting the text on the foot end of Kiye's coffin appear to have felt no difficulty in making the hieroglyphic inscription one spoken by Akhenaten, and with careful decipherment we can read both the original text and its final version—the love poem of a queen to Akhenaten, transformed into the king's loving speech to his god. Restoring the name of Kiye, as the traces suggest, the text originally read:

Words spoken by [the greatly beloved royal wife, Kiye]:
May I breathe the sweet breath which comes from your mouth;
May I see your perfection daily!
My prayer is to hear your sweet voice of the north wind,
   that my limbs grow young in life through love of you.
May you give to me your hands, bearing your ka-spirit,
   that I might receive it and that I might live from it.
May you call out my name forever, without having to seek for it in your
   mouth,
   o my [lord Neferkheperure Unique One of Re].
You are [here(?)] forever and ever, living like Aten.

[The greatly beloved wife of] the King of Upper and Lower Egypt, who lives on maat, Lord of the Two Lands [Neferkheperure-Waenre], the perfect child of the living Aten who is here, the one who lives forever and ever, [Kiye, may she live forever and ever.][2]

The sweet voice that Kiye prays to hear is a voice of love, such a voice as was also possessed by Nefertiti, who is the one "who pacifies Aten with a sweet voice by means of her words." The "sweet breath" or "sweet wind" is how one may encounter a deity, coming in the north wind, bringing a pleasantly fragranced coolness.

The adaptation of the text on the foot of the coffin from KV 55 reveals that Akhenaten is to Kiye, and to Nefertiti, as Aten is to Akhenaten. For their family, for their courtiers, Akhenaten and Nefertiti had ruled as gods on earth, offspring of the unique solar god. We will never know how Akhenaten and Nefertiti truly felt about one another, and we cannot know the nature of the relationship between Akhenaten and Kiye, but the original text of Kiye's coffin provides us with an ideal of divine royal love. The king as the sun gives sweet breath to his beloved, and the two find eternal life in eternal love.

We shall allow an anonymous woman from ancient Egypt the final lines. As she addressed her lover, she acknowledges that the only victory of the grave is the lack of love:

I am calmly saying to my heart:
　　"You are my prayer.
　　[If] my great one [departs] in the night, I am like one who is in my tomb."[3]

Epilogue

IN MAY 2017, WE RETURNED TO THE ARCHAEOLOGICAL EXPEDI-
tion that John directs (and at the time was co-directed by the late Dr. Dirk
Huyge), the Elkab Desert Survey Project, a joint project of Yale University
and the Royal Museums of Art and History in Brussels that works alongside Egyptian archaeologists from the Ministry of Antiquities. The expedition's work concentrates on surveying and recording the ancient desert
hinterland of the city of Nekheb (now called Elkab), about fifty miles south
of Waset (modern Luxor), and continues John's previous two decades of
work in the Western Desert of Egypt. Within such desert areas are ancient
roads that literally lead from one site of ancient activity to another.

Among the rich finds of desert road archaeology, objects of gold are
all but entirely absent, but ancient art and inscriptions—from beautiful
images and clearly written hieroglyphic and hieratic texts to scratchy
figures and eroded writings—are fortunately plentiful. Rock art and
inscription sites have provided us with some remarkable material, and
none are more amazing than one we identified in May 2017. John was
looking out the window of one of the mission's old but trusty (if ever in
need of repair) Land Rovers, driven by the *reis* (foreman) of the expedition, Abdu Abdullah Hassan.

They were just a couple of miles north of a rock outcrop with impressive Predynastic rock art and an important First Dynasty inscription. Realizing that the light was striking the cliffs in just the sort of sharp rake that often makes art and inscriptions seem to pop off the rocky surface, John switched to the left side of the middle seat, and he and Abdu proceeded more slowly than usual. John knew that somewhere in the vicinity, another ancient track into the Eastern Desert may once have branched off from the north-south road paralleling the Nile. Staring intently at the desert cliffs above, John saw what looked too good to be true—two horned quadrupeds, perhaps bulls, seemed to decorate a large section of a vertical rock face. These bulls looked so deeply and crisply incised, so clear and impressive at such a distance as seen from a moving vehicle that, by application of the rule governing the relationship between graffiti-like appearance and distance, this was almost certainly an epigraphic mirage.

Nevertheless, John kept the location in mind, and shortly after Colleen's arrival, we both investigated the site, just east of the modern village of el-Khawy, along with Hanan Abdel Fatah, Ahmed Baghdadi Hassan, and Mahmoud Selim Ahmed, our colleagues from the Ministry of Antiquities. The bulls were indeed there, as large and impressive as they had appeared to be, and they were carved over the equally impressive earlier depiction of a boat. The site was more extensive than originally thought, with the bulls and their underlying boat occupying the left end of a long north-south face of the cliff. On the right end of the site, a large herd of elephants, carved sometime around 3800 BCE, trooped across the rock surface headed north, the largest measuring about three feet from the bottom of his front feet to the tips of his upraised tusks. The middle portion of the site contained Predynastic and Early Dynastic inscriptions, some carved one over another in a rather bewildering palimpsest.

What drew our most intense interest was a flat area toward the north end of the site, high up on the rock face—the perfect surface for an ancient inscription. Gazing up, we could make out the schematic depictions of two birds, quite large, back-to-back, and even at this distance the lines appeared to have been cut by the flat heads of chisels—this was something out of the ordinary! That this was an official ancient billboard was not in doubt—but whose, and for what purpose?

To answer these questions, we needed to construct scaffolding, and since ancient carvings are often located at points high on a rock face, we always have a collection of appropriate pieces of lumber at our expedition headquarters. Between the modern road, from which John first spotted the site, and the cliff with the carvings is a north-south railroad that connects Aswan with Cairo. Around 1898, the tracks were laid just below and in front of the inscribed rocks at el-Khawy, further contributing to the steep slope that now leads up to the site. The day after we confirmed the presence of the rock art and inscription site, we returned with the expedition's team and the elements of the wooden scaffolding.

Directed by *reis* Abdu, his three sons—Ahmed, Mohamed, and Mahmoud—assisted Ahmed Ali Ahmed in taking the planks down from the roof racks of the Rovers, handing the pieces down to the bed of the rail tracks, then bringing them across the tracks and up the scree slope. The clanging bells of the el-Khawy rail crossing would alert us to coming trains, the arrival of which often delayed the transport of another batch of wood. Ahmed Ali, the team's scaffolding expert, could also do a wonderful imitation of a train whistle, occasionally speeding a load of boards on its way across the tracks to the laughter of all involved.

First, we assisted digital archaeologist Alberto Urcia with the photography of the site. This needed to be done comprehensively. For the upper elements, we employed a camera pole with remote operator. Then the height of the scaffolding was increased, and we photographed the graffiti in detail and prepared initial epigraphic copies using our digital technique. Few activities can rival the joy of recording ancient carvings that were unknown to the world the previous week. We moved methodically, from south to north across the rock face, but we were impatient for the day we could turn our attention to the high, chiseled inscription.

Eventually, with the engineering talents of Ahmed Ali and the team, yet another set of scaffolding was erected, and we could stand face-to-face with the images—and they did in fact all have faces. Here was something different from anything we had ever seen at a rock inscription site. Before us were a total of five images, the largest nearly two feet in height, a remarkably large scale for rock art.

To the right was the depiction of a bull's head placed on a short pole, the bull's horns, eye, and ears all carved in detail. Then, to the left, placed as if in juxtaposition to the bull, a group of three birds: two saddlebill storks standing back-to-back—*addorsed,* to use the term from heraldry—with an ibis appearing to hover above the backs of the storks. In front of the right stork was the depiction of a small serpent, its head and neck reared above its otherwise horizontal body.

A bull's head, a snake, and three birds: with those five images the history of ancient Egyptian writing was about to be rewritten (or at least significantly augmented). As we studied the photographs that Alberto had taken on site—while he was processing the images into a 3D model that would become the basis for both our digital drawing and a full virtual reality reconstruction of the site—we realized that these were not just any images of animals. All five elements of the el-Khawy panel reminded us very much of artifacts from a tomb at Abydos (Tomb U-j) dating to just about 3250 BCE. Those artifacts were not just drawings from that tomb but *hieroglyphic* signs.

Buried in Tomb U-j was a ruler at the dawn of Dynasty 0, a king of Upper Egypt (who may possibly have been known by the name "Scorpion"). In the 1980s, a team with the German Archaeological Institute in Cairo re-excavated Tomb U-j, revealing an impressive array of artifacts, including hundreds of imported jars, an ivory crook (the same crook used to write "ruler" in hieroglyphs), and nearly two hundred small ivory tags. The director of the German mission, Günter Dreyer, realized that some of the labels, which had once been attached to other objects, bore inscriptions employing a limited set of signs. Many, but not all, of those signs were recognizable as hieroglyphs—they were the first attestations of an Egyptian writing system that would last for another 3,500 years, along the way and quite incidentally giving birth to the alphabet.

Since each label from Tomb U-j has but a few signs, and some only one, translating the inscriptions has proven difficult, with specific interpretations nearly impossible to corroborate. The ceramics within Tomb U-j make the date of these early hieroglyphs, roughly 3250 BCE, certain, but their messages prove more elusive. We both had taught classes discussing the birth of writing in Egypt, but never had we imagined finding anything like this at a desert site.

Yet, as we compared the five images from the large panel at el-Khawy with the ivory tags, we realized that John's initial assessment was correct—we indeed had found something not just comparable but paleographically identical, yet on an entirely new, more massive scale. The bull's head on a pole was probably not a hieroglyph per se but rather a royal image of Dynasty 0—one nearly identical to the image at el-Khawy was painted on a ceramic vessel in Tomb U-j. Those two-foot-high storks—they appeared numerous times on the inch-high ivory tags from Tomb U-j, all of which were clear ancestors of the saddlebill stork hieroglyph. For three millennia, the stork hieroglyph would be used to write the sound "ba": *ba* is a word for soul, but *bau* is also power. Could we have a statement of royal power, expressed with the bull's head and the two storks?

Perhaps it took only a minute or two—we cannot exactly remember anything but the feeling of happiness at the find, and the awe one always senses in working with rock art and inscriptions—but we quickly realized that something mute for five millennia was finally beginning to speak again, and speak first to us. We turned next to the ibis between the two storks, and again the labels in Tomb U-j provided near exact parallels. The storks and ibis as we know them from Tomb U-j are not drawings of birds, which potentially could vary greatly from one artist to another, but rather signs, like a letter, with a specific shape and number of strokes. A distance of one hundred miles along the Nile separates Abydos and el-Khawy (somewhat less, if you use a desert road shortcut), but the ivory labels and the rock inscription were both made by people trained to *write*. The signs are so similar that the scribes who carved the small tags and those responsible for the el-Khawy inscription probably lived within a decade or two of one another.

The shapes of the signs in the el-Khawy inscription are identical to those of the Tomb U-j labels—we had just found the earliest known monumental hieroglyphic inscription ever discovered. The el-Khawy inscription really was a billboard—a Dynasty 0 king's massive proclamation of power. A wonderful discovery that changes our understanding of the birth of writing in Egypt, but why end the story of Akhenaten and Nefertiti here, almost two thousand years before they came to the throne?

On one hand, the answer could be quite simplistic: the ibis between the two storks is an early example of a common hieroglyph that has the phonetic value *akh*, the same hieroglyph used to write *Akh* in the name Akhenaten. But if we look at that ibis within the context of the entire el-Khawy inscription, we see the origins of Akhenaten's kingship. Those five signs write nothing less than "royal power on earth (bull's head on pole) equals solar power in heaven (back-to-back storks and ibis)."

El-Khawy is not just the first monumental hieroglyphic inscription, but the signs included the first *written word* whose phonetic value and meaning could be corroborated with some confidence. The ibis in the el-Khawy inscription not only stands in the same place as the sun disk in common writings of the hieroglyphic depiction of the horizon, it actually writes the root *akh,* from which the word for horizon, *akhet,* derives. As the ibis takes the place of the sun disk, so the two storks substitute for the hills of the horizon in the sign for *akhet;* the storks between which the ibis "rises" transform *akh* into *akhet.* Later Egyptian art can similarly substitute lions, sphinxes, or even human heads for the hills of the horizon, so we were staying well within the bounds of visual interpretation. The storks were likely chosen because they simultaneously wrote the root *ba,* "power." The ibis and storks were literally the power of the sun as it rose and set in an infinite cycle. *Akhet,* "horizon," appears to be the first word that we can confidently read in the entire history of the ancient Egyptian language.

The bull's head on a pole does not survive as a hieroglyph, but the bull is a symbol of power, and certainly the bull's tail is a ubiquitous element of pharaonic regalia. Akhenaten's Horus name begins with the epithet "Victorious Bull," and he wears a bull's tail attached to his kilt, like all other rulers of Egypt. It might have taken Akhenaten and Nefertiti a moment to puzzle out the meaning of the el-Khawy inscription, but then again, Amunhotep III and Tiye had their images carved on the back of a palette that also dated to Dynasty 0. If Akhenaten had the opportunity to stand on that scaffolding beside us, he would almost certainly have recognized that here was his own credo: what Aten is in heaven, such is the king on earth. Royal power and the horizon— what more appropriate combination for Akhenaten, and here it is at el-Khawy, at the dawn of a tradition of solar kingship.

The reign of Akhenaten and Nefertiti indeed saw a remarkable equation of king, queen, and sun. Nevertheless, however innovatively Akhenaten may have interpreted and expressed this union, it was a concept that had already given rise to the first known monumental hieroglyphic inscription two millennia earlier.

Acknowledgments

WITHOUT OUR AGENT ROGER FREET AND THE AMAZING TEAM AT St. Martin's Press we would not have been able to embark on this project, which we hope will bring the fascinating lives of Akhenaten and Nefertiti to the widest possible audience. From our first meeting high above Manhattan, overlooking the city on a beautiful, sunny day, Elisabeth Dyssegaard encouraged us in our quest to tell the story of another great city that flourished three thousand years ago. Throughout many drafts, Elisabeth's invaluable insight helped us to make these ancient people come to life—from the parties they celebrated to the houses where they lived. Collaborating with her made this project less daunting—thank you, Elisabeth, for being such an amazing editor. At St. Martin's Press, we would also like to extend our appreciation to Alex Brown. We are indebted to Ginny Perrin, our production editor; Lizz Blaise, our managing editor; jacket designer Young Lim; Meryl Levavi for interior design; and Bill Warhop for his wonderful copyediting.

Our archaeological work in Egypt is carried out with the cooperation of the Ministry of Antiquities in Egypt, directed by His Excellency Dr. Khaled El-Enany. We would also like to thank the Secretary General Dr. Mostafa Waziri, the Director of Upper Egyptian Antiquities

Hani Abu el-Azm, and the General Supervisor of the Permanent Committee and Foreign Missions Dr. Nashwa Gaber. The Elkab Desert Survey Project, which John directs (co-directed with Wouter Claes and formerly with Dr. Dirk Huyge), is a joint expedition of Yale University and the Royal Museums of Art and History, Brussels, supported by funding from the Marilyn M. and William K. Simpson Egyptology Endowment. Our appreciation goes to Said Abd el-Menaim, the director of the Aswan inspectorate, and director Osama Ismaail in the Edfu antiquities office, who make our work possible.

We thank our colleague Osama Amer, whose dedication to cultural heritage continually inspires us. Our archaeological discoveries have been possible by working alongside the reis of the expedition, Abdu Abdullah Hassan, and the excavation team: Ahmed Ali Ahmed, Mohamed Abdu Abdullah, Ahmed Abdu Abdullah, and Mahmoud Abdu Abdullah. We thank Hesham A. Abdel-kader for sharing his expert knowledge of the site of Amarna with us.

We thank Candida Moss for her assistance with the earliest stages of this project. We are grateful to Christine Pendred who makes our travels possible. Charles and Cornelia Manassa were enthusiastic early readers of the manuscript—their support has meant so much to both of us.

Appendix:
Translation of the Great Hymn to Aten

May you appear beautifully in the horizon of heaven, o living Aten,
    who initiates life,
      you having arisen in the eastern horizon.
That you have filled every land with your perfection,
      is with you being beautiful, great, dazzling, and high over every land.

Your rays always encompass the lands,
      to the limit of all which you have created, you being as Re.
That you have attained their limits,
      is so that you might subdue them for the son whom you love.
You are far, while your rays are on earth.
You are visible, but your movements are never seen.

When you go to rest in the western horizon,
      the land is in darkness in the manner of death,
      the sleepers in the bedchamber, heads covered.
No eye can see another,
      so that all their possessions could be stolen—although they are beneath
      their heads—without them knowing.
Every lion has come forth from his den.
All serpents bite.
The shrine grows dark, the land is silent.
The one who made them has gone to rest in his horizon.

With you rising in the horizon does the day dawn,
      you shining as the sun disk during the day.
That you drive away darkness is so that you might give out your rays,
      with the result that the two lands are in festival,
         the sun-folk having awakened, standing upon their feet.
That you have lifted them up is so that their flesh might become pure,
      they putting on clothes,

their arms in adoration while you appear in glory.
The entire land carries out its work.

All cattle are content with their fodder.
The trees and plants flourish.
Birds are flown from their nests,
    their wings in praise of your ka-spirit.
All small flocks leap on their feet.
All which fly and alight live,
    when you have arisen for them.

Ships go north and south likewise.
Every road is open because you appear in glory.
The fish in the river leap up to your face.
Your rays are in the sea.

O one who makes the fetus develop in women.
Who transforms water into people!
Who enlivens the son in the womb of his mother.
Who quiets him with that which will stop his tears.

Nurse in the womb, who gives breath in order to enliven all which he has made,
    so that he descends from the womb in order to breathe on his day of birth.

As for the one whose mouth you open completely,
    you take care of him,
        even the chick in the egg.
As for the one who speaks in the shell,
    you give him breath within it in order to enliven him.
So that he might break out of his egg, you have made his appointed time,
    when he comes forth from the egg to speak at his appointed time.
When he comes forth from it, he can already walk on his two legs.

How many are your deeds,
    although they are hidden from sight.
The sole god with no other besides him.
You created the earth according to your desire,
    you being alone,

while all people, cattle, and small flocks,
everything on earth, go upon their feet,
all which is in heaven flying up with their wings.

The foreign lands of Syria, Kush, and the land of Egypt—
You set every man at his (proper) place,
    and make their requirements,
    with the result that each one has his diet,
       his lifetime having been reckoned.
Tongues are distinguished in speech, their natures likewise.
Their skins are different, for you distinguish the foreigners.

That you make the inundation in the Underworld,
    is with the result that you bring it as you desire
    in order to enliven people,
       in as much as you make them for yourself.
Their lord entirely,
    wearied by means of them.
The lord of every land, who shines for them.

The sun disk during the day, the one great of awe.
As for all distant foreign lands,
    you make them live.
That it might descend for them have you placed an inundation in heaven.
That it makes waves upon the mountains like the sea
    is in order to water their fields with what pertains to them.

How efficacious are they, your plans—
    O lord of eternity, inundation in heaven—
    with the result that you gain power
    for foreigners and for all small flocks, those who travel on their feet—
    O inundation, who comes forth from the Underworld to Egypt.

Your rays nurture all plants.
As you rise so they live;
As they grow for you so you make the seasons
    in order to nurture all that you make—
    the Growing Season to cool them;
    heat that they might experience you.

That you have made heaven far
> is in order to rise within it, and to see all that you have made,
> you being alone and risen in your transformations as living Aten,
> you having appeared in glory,
> you shining, you being far yet near.

From yourself do you make millions of manifestations—sole one.

Cities, towns, fields, the course of the river—
> every eye glimpses you on their level,
> for you are the solar disk during the day,
> chief of what you have traversed,
> and of what your eye has opened.

You create their faces, so that you need not see [yourself? . . .]
> . . . one . . . when you are in my heart.

There is no other one who knows you,
> except for your son, Neferkheperure, Unique One of Re,
>> whom you cause to become aware of your plans and your power:
>> that the earth comes about is through your action, in as much as you
>> make them;
>> that you have arisen is so that they might live—as you set so they die.

Lifetime is your very own—through you one lives.

That eyes are upon beauty,
> is until you set.

As one sets aside all work, so you go to rest upon the western side.

One who rises and makes flourish [. . .] for the king.

Everyone who hurries by foot, since you founded the land—
> you raise them up for your son, who comes forth from your flesh:
> the King of Upper and Lower Egypt, who lives on maat,
> Lord of the Two Lands Neferkheperure, Unique One of Re;
> Son of Re who lives on maat, lord of glorious appearances,
>> Akhenaten, great in his lifetime;
> The king's great wife, his beloved, lady of the Two Lands,
>> Neferneferuaten Nefertiti, may she live and be youthful forever and
>> ever.

Chronology of Ancient Egypt

Predynastic Period ca. 5000–3100 BCE
Early Dynastic Period: Dynasties 1–2, ca. 3100–2686 BCE
Old Kingdom: Dynasties 3–8, 2686–2160 BCE
First Intermediate Period: Dynasties 9–11, 2160–2055 BCE
Middle Kingdom: Dynasties 11–13, 2055–1650 BCE
Second Intermediate Period: Dynasties 14–17, 1650–1550 BCE

New Kingdom: Dynasties 18–20, 1550–1069 BCE

Eighteenth Dynasty
Ahmose 1550–1525 BCE
Amunhotep I 1525–1504 BCE
Thutmose I 1504–1492 BCE
Thutmose II 1492–1479 BCE
Thutmose III 1479–1425 BCE
Hatshepsut 1473–1458 BCE
Amunhotep II 1427–1400 BCE
Thutmose IV 1400–1390 BCE
Amunhotep III 1390–1352 BCE
Amunhotep IV/Akhenaten 1352–1336 BCE
Semenkhkare unknown
Neferneferuaten 1337–1334 BCE
Tutankhamun 1334–1325 BCE
Ay 1325–1321 BCE
Horemhab 1321–1302 BCE
Nineteenth Dynasty to Twentieth Dynasty 1302–1069 BCE

Third Intermediate Period: Dynasties 21–25, 1069–664 BCE
Late Period: Dynasties 26–30, 664–332 BCE
Ptolemaic Period 332–30 BCE
Roman and Byzantine Periods 30 BCE–641 CE

Bibliographic Essays

PROLOGUE

For reconstructions of the reign of Akhenaten, and how they relate to the times, opinions, and research interests of their authors, see Dominic Montserrat, *Akhenaten: History, Fantasy, and Ancient Egypt* (London: Routledge, 2000); Ronald T. Ridley, *Akhenaten, A Historian's View* (Cairo: American University in Cairo Press, 2019), 1–15; Dimitri Laboury, *Akhénaton* (Paris: Pygmalion, 2010), 9–41.

Our seemingly extreme portraits of Akhenaten adhere closely to those presented in previous biographies. The family-loving sovereign distrustful of the priests of Amun, seeking a one true god who transcends the polytheism of traditional Egyptian worship, is the protagonist of the two earliest "modern" treatments of the king: Arthur Weigall, *The Life and Times of Akhnaton*, 4th ed. (London: Thornton Butterworth, 1922); and James Henry Breasted, *The Dawn of Conscience* (New York: Charles Scribner's Sons, 1933). Over a half-century later, Egyptologists could present Akhenaten as a depraved pedophile and an authoritarian dictator, for which see Nicholas Reeves, *Akhenaten, Egypt's False Prophet* (New York: Thames & Hudson, 2001); and Donald Redford, *Akhenaten, the Heretic King* (Princeton, NJ: Princeton University Press, 1984).

The interpretation of Akhenaten's iconoclasm led to a rift between the two great figures of psychology. Freud had an abiding interest in antiquity and assembled a small collection of artifacts—Richard H. Armstrong, *A Compulsion for Antiquity: Freud and the Ancient World* (Ithaca, NY: Cornell University Press, 2005). Carl G. Jung, *Memories, Dreams, Reflections,* recorded and edited by Aniela Jaffé, trans. Richard Winston and Clara Winston (New York: Pantheon Books, 1961), 156–57, recounts Jung's version of Freud's fainting spell.

The number of articles and books about Akhenaten and Nefertiti is vast. Thirty years ago, Geoffrey Martin compiled *A Bibliography of the Amarna Period and Its Aftermath* (London: Kagan Paul International, 1991). Overviews of the reigns of Amunhotep III and Amunhotep IV/Akhenaten appear in broad surveys of Egyptian history, such as Claude Vandersleyen, *L'Egypte et la vallée du Nil,* vol. 2 (Paris: Presses universitaires de France, 1995), 363–465; Jacobus van Dijk, "The Amarna Period and the Later New Kingdom," in *The Oxford History of Ancient Egypt,* ed. Ian Shaw (Oxford: Oxford University Press, 2000), 272–313; Toby Wilkinson, *The Rise and Fall of Ancient Egypt* (New York: Random House, 2010), 257–78. Three of the most influential biographies are Redford, *Akhenaten, the Heretic King;* Cyril Aldred, *Akhenaten, King of Egypt* (New York: Thames & Hudson,

1988); and Laboury, *Akhénaton*. The chief contribution of Redford's volume is the description of the excavations at East Karnak and the study of the *talatat* blocks. The final sentence of the book epitomizes the underlying problem of Redford's presentation of Akhenaten as a man and a ruler (235): "I cannot conceive a more tiresome regime under which to be fated to live." Aldred's *Akhenaten, King of Egypt* is a more sympathetic presentation grounded in art history, but it suffers from the acceptance of a twelve-year co-regency between Amunhotep III and his son. Laboury, *Akhénaton*, incorporates new discoveries through 2010, presents an even-handed overview of Akhenaten's reign with careful attention to detail throughout, and is an essential source for all interested in the age of Akhenaten.

Catalogs of Amarna art are key sources for understanding the reigns of Akhenaten and Nefertiti; excellent examples are: Friederike Seyfried, ed., *Im Licht von Amarna, 100 Jahre Fund der Nofretete* (Berlin: Staatliche Museen zu Berlin, 2012); Jean-Luc Chappaz, ed., *Akhénaton et Néfertiti, Soleil et ombres des pharaons* (Milan: Silvana Editoriale, 2008); Dorothea Arnold, *The Royal Women of Amarna: Images of Beauty from Ancient Egypt* (New York: Metropolitan Museum of Art, 1996); Cyril Aldred, *Akhenaten and Nefertiti* (New York: Brooklyn Museum, 1973). William J. Murnane, *Texts from the Amarna Period in Egypt* (Atlanta: Scholars Press, 1995) presents translations of many key documents of this era.

1. A DIVINE CONCEPTION

The reconstruction of Mutemwia's bedchamber draws primarily from the excavations of the palace of Malqata and objects from Eighteenth Dynasty burials; the flying pigeons are discussed in W. Stevenson Smith, revised by William Kelly Simpson, *The Art and Architecture of Ancient Egypt*, 3rd ed. (New Haven, CT: Yale University Press, 1998), 166 (the painting is Metropolitan Museum of Art, 12.180.257). Ernesto Schiaparelli, *La tomba intatta dell'architetto Kha nella necropolis di Tebe* (Turin: Adarte, 2007), 102–4, provides the template for the queen's wig stand. The ceramic vessel with stylized floral, blue-painted designs is from the reign of Thutmose IV: Maria Cristina Guidotti and Flora Silvano, *La ceramica del tempio di Thutmosi IV a Gurna* (Pisa: Edizioni ETS, 2003), 82. A bed canopy from which to hang a textile, an ancient equivalent to modern mosquito netting, was buried with Queen Hetepheres—George A. Reisner, "The Bed Canopy of the Mother of Cheops," *Bulletin of the Museum of Fine Arts, Boston* 30, no. 180 (August, 1932): 56–60.

An archaeological project led by Dr. Mansour Boraik excavated over a mile of the processional route between Karnak and Luxor, lined by hundreds of sphinxes—he summarizes the work in "The Excavation of the Avenue of Sphinxes: Second Report," *Cahiers de Karnak* 14 (2013): 13–32. "Widowed obelisk" is the observation of Florence Nightingale: Florence Nightingale,

Letters from Egypt: A Journey on the Nile, 1849–1850, selected and introduced by Anthony Sattin (New York: Weidenfeld & Nicolson, 1987), 80. Egypt's obelisks, and their later history, are surveyed in Brian Curran, Anthony Grafton, Pamela O. Long, and Benjamin Weiss, *Obelisk: A History* (Cambridge, MA: Burndy Library, 2009). Important aspects of the theological significance of Luxor Temple are captured in an older, but still relevant, study: Lanny Bell, "Luxor Temple and the Cult of the Royal Ka," *Journal of Near Eastern Studies* 44, no. 4 (1985): 251–94; and his summary "The New Kingdom 'Divine' Temple: The Example of Luxor," in *Temple of Ancient Egypt,* ed. Byron E. Shafer (Ithaca, NY: Cornell University Press, 1997), 127–84.

The festival scenes in the Colonnade Hall are published in Epigraphic Survey, *Reliefs and Inscriptions at Luxor Temple,* vol. 1, *The Festival Procession of Opet in the Colonnade Hall* (Chicago: Oriental Institute of the University of Chicago, 1995). The divine birth scenes in the temple of Luxor are published alongside earlier and later examples of the texts and images in Hellmut Brunner, *Die Geburt des Gottkönigs, Studien zur Überlieferung eines altägyptischen Mythos* (Wiesbaden: Otto Harrassowitz, 1986). A statue of Mutemwia (British Museum EA 43) shows the queen enthroned on a ceremonial boat with a giant vulture behind her, a rebus of her name—Betsy M. Bryan, "Royal and Divine Statuary," in *Egypt's Dazzling Sun, Amenhotep III and His World,* ed. Arielle P. Kozloff, Betsy M. Bryan, and Lawrence M. Berman (Cleveland: Cleveland Museum of Art, 1992), 126.

A useful overview of queens' palaces, albeit employing the outdated term "harem," is the entry by Silke Roth, "Harem," in *UCLA Encyclopedia of Egyptology,* ed. Willeke Wendrich and Jacco Dieleman, 2012, https://escholarship .org/uc/item/1k3663r3 (accessed January 18, 2020). For a recent overview of the Ottoman harem, see Jane Hathaway, *The Chief Eunuch of the Ottoman Harem: From African Slave to Power-Broker* (Cambridge: Cambridge University Press, 2018). Mutemwia does not have the title "king's great wife" until after Amunhotep III ascends to the throne: Gay Robins, "Problems Concerning Queens and Queenship in Eighteenth Dynasty Egypt," *NIN: Journal of Gender Studies in Antiquity* 3, no. 1 (2002): 26–27.

For the *ka* of kingship, the work of Lanny Bell in "Luxor Temple and the Cult of the Royal Ka," 251–94, remains foundational; any discussion of New Kingdom divine birth scenes should acknowledge their existence in the early Middle Kingdom: Uroš Matić, "The Sap of Life: Materiality and Sex in the Divine Birth Legend of Hatshepsut and Amenhotep III," in *Perspectives on Materiality in Ancient Egypt—Agency, Cultural Reproduction and Change,* ed. Érika Maynart, Carolina Velloza, and Rennan Lemos (Oxford: Archaeopress Publishing, 2018), 37–38; see also Oleg Berlev, "The Eleventh Dynasty in the Dynastic History of Egypt," in *Studies Presented to Hans Jakob Polotsky,* ed. Dwight Young (East Gloucester, MA: Pirtle & Polson, 1981), 361–77. On Khnum's wheel we see the

Egyptian version of that influential concept of medieval political philosophy, the king's two bodies—see Ernst H. Kantorowicz, *The King's Two Bodies: A Study in Mediaeval Political Theology* (Princeton, NJ: Princeton University Press, 1966)—with the child as the body physical, and the *ka*-spirit as the body politic, as in the conclusion of Bell's 1985 article. A dissertation by Jonathan Winnermann, "Rethinking the Royal Ka" (unpublished PhD diss., University of Chicago, 2018), examines the concept of a distinct *ka* of kingship more broadly.

For the function and symbolism of birth-bricks, see Josef Wegner, "A Decorated Birth Brick from South Abydos: New Evidence on Childbirth and Birth Magic in the Middle Kingdom," in *Archaism and Innovation: Studies in the Culture of Middle Kingdom Egypt,* ed. David P. Silverman, William Kelly Simpson, and Josef Wegner (New Haven, CT: Department of Near Eastern Languages and Civilizations, 2009), 447–96.

Ronald Leprohon, *The Great Name: Ancient Egyptian Royal Titulary* (Atlanta: Society for Biblical Literature, 2013), lists royal titularies, with accessible translations.

2. AN ANGRY GODDESS

The hauling of the divine barks is based on the detailed reliefs in the Colonnade Hall of Luxor Temple, especially Epigraphic Survey, *Reliefs and Inscriptions at Luxor Temple,* vol. 1, *The Festival Procession of Opet in the Colonnade Hall* (Chicago: Oriental Institute of the University of Chicago, 1995), plates 17–34; the hymns sung in the re-creation are from hieroglyphic captions to those scenes, which are placed within the context of the festival and Egyptian theology in John Coleman Darnell, "Opet Festival," in *UCLA Encyclopedia of Egyptology,* ed. Willeke Wendrich and Jacco Dieleman, 2010, retrieved from https://escholarship.org/uc/item/4739r3fr (accessed September 3, 2019).

The most thorough examination of Tiye, with a focus on the artwork that depicts the queen, is Christian Bayer, *Teje: Die den Herrn Beider Länder mit ihrer Schönheit erfreut: Eine ikonographische Studie* (Wiesbaden: Verlag Harrassowitz, 2014). The "commemorative" scarabs are published in C. Blankenberg van Delden, *The Large Commemorative Scarabs of Amenhotep III* (Leiden: E.J. Brill, 1969); Lawrence M. Berman, "Large Commemorative Scarabs," in *Egypt's Dazzling Sun: Amenhotep III and His World,* ed. Arielle P. Kozloff, Betsy M. Bryan, and Lawrence M. Berman (Cleveland: Cleveland Museum of Art, 1992), 67–72.

The discovery of the tomb of Yuya and Tuya in the Valley of the Kings is discussed in John M. Adams, *The Millionaire and the Mummies: Theodore Davis's Gilded Age in the Valley of the Kings* (New York: St. Martin's Press, 2013); the original publication is Theodore M. Davis, *The Tomb of Iouiya and Touiyou* (London: Archibald Constable & Co., 1907). A historically informed interpretation of the DNA tests on royal mummies of the late Eighteenth Dynasty is Marc Gabolde, "L'ADN de la famille royale amarnienne et les sources égyptiennes—de la complémentarité des méthodes et des résultats," *Égypte Nilotique et Méditerranéenne (ENiM)* 6 (2013): 177–203 (accessible at http://www.enim-egyptologie .fr/index.php?page=enim-6&n=10). Details about Yuya and Tuya's mummies can be found in Zahi Hawass and Sahar N. Saleem, *Scanning the Pharaohs: CT Imaging of the New Kingdom Royal Mummies* (Cairo: American University in Cairo Press, 2018), 68–74. The social status and military significance of the "master of the horse" and "lieutenant general of the chariotry of his Majesty" are discussed in John Coleman Darnell and Colleen Manassa, *Tutankhamun's Armies: Battle and Conquest During Ancient Egypt's Late 18th Dynasty* (Hoboken, NJ: John Wiley, 2007), 63–64, noting the fundamental study of Andrea Maria Gnirs, *Militär und Gesellschaft: Ein Beitrag zur Sozialgeschichte des Neuen Reiches* (Heidelberg: Heidelberger Orientverlag, 1996), and her study, "Coping with the Army: the Military and the State in the New Kingdom," in *Ancient Egyptian Administration,* ed. Juan Carlos Moreno Garcia (Leiden and Boston: Brill, 2013), 639–717. The best summary of the textual evidence for the role of god's father as tutor remains Otto Schaden, "The God's Father Ay" (unpublished PhD diss., University of Minnesota, 1977), 75–78.

By the reign of Thutmose I, the Egyptian presence in Nubia extended to Karoy; for inscriptional evidence at the site, see W. V. Davies, "Nubia in the New Kingdom: The Egyptians at Kurgus," in *Nubia in the New Kingdom: Lived Experience, Pharaonic Control and Indigenous Traditions,* ed. Neal Spencer, Anna Stevens, and Michaela Binder (Leuven: Peeters, 2017), 67–75, 80–81. An overview of Nubian history in the reign of Amunhotep III is David O'Connor, "Amunhotep III and Nubia," in *Amenhotep III: Perspectives on His Reign,* ed. David O'Connor and Eric H. Cline (Ann Arbor: University of Michigan Press, 1998), 261–70. Sacred buildings are surveyed by Martina Ullmann, "Egyptian Temples in Nubia During the Middle and the New Kingdom," in *Handbook of Ancient Nubia,* vol. 1, ed. Dietrich Raue (Berlin: De Gruyter, 2019), 511–40.

The temples of Soleb and Sedeinga feature in many overviews of Amunhotep III's building program, and useful studies include: David O'Connor, "The City and the World: Worldview and Built Forms in the Reign of Amenhotep III," in O'Connor and Cline, *Amenhotep III,* 146–52; Susanne Bickel, "Le dieu Nebmaâtrê de Soleb," in *Soleb VI: Hommages à Michela Schiff Giorgini,* ed. Nathalie Beaux and Nicolas Grimal (Cairo: Institut français d'archéologie orientale, 2013), 59–82; Catherine Berger el-Naggar, "Contribution de Sedeinga à l'histoire de la Nubie," in *Between the Cataracts, Proceedings of the 11th Conference for Nubian Studies, Warsaw University 27 August–2 September 2006,* part 1, *Main Papers,* ed. Włodzimierz Godlewski and Adam Łatjar (Warsaw: Warsaw University Press, 2008), 179–94; Claude Rilly, "La mission archéologique française de Sedeinga de la reine Tiye aux dames de Nubie," in *50 ans section française de la direction des Antiquités du Soudan,* ed. Nicholas Grimal (Paris: Soleb, 2021), 27–49.

The scene of Amunhotep III worshipping his divine self is Michela Schiff Giorgini, with Clément Robichon and Jean Leclant, *Soleb V: Le temple, basreliefs et inscriptions* (Cairo: Institut français d'archéologie orientale, 1998), plate 193. The best edition of *The Book of the Heavenly Cow* is Erik Hornung, *Der ägyptische Mythos von der Himmelskuh, Eine Ätiologie des Unvollkommenen,* 3rd ed. (Freiburg: Universitätsverlag, 1982). The rich theology of the god Thoth, including his role in the Myth of the Eye of the Sun, appears in Martin A. Stadler, "Thoth," in *UCLA Encyclopedia of Egyptology,* ed. Willeke Wendrich and Jacco Dieleman, retrieved from https://escholarship.org/uc/item/2xj8c3qg (accessed June 10, 2020). A useful overview of the Egyptian civil calendar is Erik Hornung, Rolf Krauss, and David A. Warburton, "Methods of Dating and the Egyptian Calendar," in *Ancient Egyptian Chronology,* ed. Hornung, Krauss, and Warburton (Leiden: Brill, 2006), 45–51.

The scholarship on the myth of the goddess of the eye of the sun is extensive. A summary of New Kingdom and earlier sources is John C. Darnell, "A Midsummer Night's Succubus," in *Opening the Tablet Box: Near Eastern Studies in Honor of Benjamin R. Foster,* ed. Sarah C. Melville and Alice L. Slotsky (Leiden: Brill, 2010), 100–101; Barbara A. Richter, *The Theology of Hathor of Dendera, Aural and Visual Scribal Techniques in the Per-Wer Sanctuary* (Atlanta: Lockwood Press, 2016), 2–6; the later material in particular is examined in Danielle Inconnu-Bocquillon, *Le mythe de la déesse lointaine à Philae* (Cairo: Institut français d'archéologie orientale, 2001). For a thoughtful treatment of the genre of myth in ancient Egypt, see Katja Goebs, "A Functional Approach to Egyptian Myth and Mythemes," *Journal of Ancient Near Eastern Religions* 2 (2002): 27–59. For evidence bridging the New Kingdom and later periods, see Philippe Collombert, "Des animaux qui parlent néo-égyptien (relief Caire JE 58925)," in *Mélanges offerts à François Neveu,* ed. Chr. Gallois, Pierre Grandet, and Laure Pantalacci (Cairo: Institut français d'archéologie orientale, 2008), 63–72.

The relief of Tiye as a sphinx and the other images on the lunette of the false door are discussed in Bayer, *Teje,* 202–7; whether the carnelian sphinx from the Metropolitan Museum of Art (MMA 26.7.1342) depicts Tiye remains a topic of debate: compare Silke Roth, *Gebieterin aller Länder* (Freiburg: Universitätsverlag, 2002), 43–49, and Bayer, *Teje,* 378–79.

The martial imagery adopted by Tiye extends to unusually aggressive epithets, like "great of fearsomeness": Karl Richard Lepsius, *Denkmaeler aus Aegypten und Aethiopien* (Berlin: Nicolaische Buchhandlung, 1849), B1, plate 82g. Also note the statue, almost certainly of Tiye, with a similar epithet, in Betsy Bryan, "A Newly Discovered Statue of a Queen from the Reign of Amenhotep III," in *Servant of Mut: Studies in Honor of Richard A. Fazzini,* ed. Sue D'Auria

(Leiden: Brill, 2007), 32–43. Useful summaries of the bellicose iconography of Eighteenth Dynasty queens within the larger context of queenship are Robert Morkot, "Violent Images of Queenship and the Royal Cult," *Wepwawet* 2 (1986): 1–9; Friedhelm Hoffmann, "Warlike Women in Ancient Egypt," *Cahiers de Recherches de l'Institut de Papyrologie et d'Égyptologie de Lille* 27 (2008): 51–53.

3. ANCIENT RITES

Our re-creation of the first morning of the jubilee is based on the reliefs and hieroglyphic texts within the tomb of Kheruef: Epigraphic Survey, *The Tomb of Kheruef, Theban Tomb 192* (Chicago: Oriental Institute of the University of Chicago, 1980), plate 24. The jubilee scenes are also discussed by David Lorand, "Quand texte et image décrivent un même événement. Le cas du jubilé de l'an 30 d'Amenhotep III dans la tombe de Khérouef (TT 192)," in *Interprétation, mythes, croyances et images au risque de la réalité: Roland Tefnin (1945–2006) in memoriam,* ed. Michèle Bronze, Christian Cannuyer, and Florence Doyen (Brussels: Société Belge d'Études Orientales, 2008), 77–92.

The tomb of Kheruef includes detailed representations of the first and third *heb sed* festivals, which appear to share much in common with other depictions, especially those of Amunhotep IV and the much later Osorkon II (mid-tenth century BCE), while differing in important ways from the traditional "cycle" of jubilee scenes. Studies of the *heb sed* include Eva Lange-Athinodorou, *Sedfestritual und Königtum, Die Reliefdekoration am Torbau Osorkons II. im Tempel der Bastet von Bubastis* (Wiesbaden: Harrassowitz, 2019); Marc J. LeBlanc, "'In Accordance with the Documents of Ancient Times': The Origins, Development, and Significance of the Ancient Egyptian Sed Festival (Jubilee Festival)" (unpublished PhD diss., Yale University, 2011); Erik Hornung and Elisabeth Staehelin, *Neue Studien zum Sedfest* (Basel: Schwabe, 2006).

Many high officials who served Amunhotep III were involved in the planning of the jubilee, such as Amunhotep, son of Hapu: Arielle P. Kozloff, *Amenhotep III: Egypt's Radiant Pharaoh* (Cambridge: Cambridge University Press, 2012), 150–55, 182–88. Royal literacy is demonstrated in Filip Taterka, "Were Ancient Egyptian Kings Literate?" *Studien zur Altägyptischen Kultur* 46 (2017): 267–83. An overview of the "Turin Canon" and its main studies is Kim Ryholt, "The Turin King-List or So-Called Turin Canon (TC) as a Source for Chronology," in "Methods of Dating and the Egyptian Calendar," in *Ancient Egyptian Chronology,* ed. Erik Hornung, Rolf Krauss, and David A. Warburton (Leiden: Brill, 2006), 26–32.

The Predynastic palette recarved during the reign of Amunhotep III is studied by Melinda Hartwig, "Between Predynastic Palettes and Dynastic Relief: The Case of Cairo JE 46148 & BMA 66.175," in *Zeichen aus dem Sand: Streiflichter aus Ägyptens Geschichte zu Ehren von Günter Dreyer,* ed. Eva-Maria Engel, Vera Mueller, and Ulrich Hartung (Wiesbaden: Harrassowitz Verlag,

2008), 195–209. Useful studies of the comparative Predynastic material are Alejandro Jiménez Serrano, *Royal Festivals in the Late Predynastic Period and the First Dynasty,* BAR International Series 1076 (Oxford: Archaeopress, 2002); and LeBlanc, "In Accordance with the Documents of Ancient Times."

A convenient overview of Egyptian solar religion is Stephen Quirke, *The Cult of Ra: Sun-Worship in Ancient Egypt* (London: Thames & Hudson, 2001); and for the earliest periods of Egyptian history, Jochem Kahl, *"Ra Is My Lord": Searching for the Rise of the Sun God at the Dawn of Egyptian History* (Wiesbaden: Harrassowitz Verlag, 2007). The union of Re and Osiris is one of the central themes of Egyptian religion, as we summarized in our translation of the texts in the New Kingdom royal tombs: John Coleman Darnell and Colleen Manassa Darnell, *The Ancient Egyptian Netherworld Books* (Atlanta: Society for Biblical Literature, 2018), 6–7 (and references therein); the same volume discusses the union of the *ba*-soul and corpse as well as the Night Bark and the Day Bark.

The translation and derivation of the place name Malqata appears in William C. Hayes, *The Scepter of Egypt: A Background for the Study of the Egyptian Antiquities in the Metropolitan Museum of Art,* vol. 2, *The Hyksos Period and the New Kingdom (1675–1080 B.C.)* (New York: The Metropolitan Museum of Art, 1959), 245.

For Waset (Thebes) as the "ceremonial city" and the location of the Estate of Amun, see Barry Kemp, *Ancient Egypt: Anatomy of a Civilization,* 3rd ed. (London: Routledge, 2018), 262–68. The concept of the "mansion of millions of years" is treated in detail by Martina Ullmann, *König für die Ewigkeit—Die Häuser der Millionen von Jahren: Eine Untersuchung zu Königskult und Tempeltypologie in Ägypten* (Wiesbaden: Otto Harrassowitz, 2002). The economic aspects of the mortuary temples are examined in B. J. J. Haring, *Divine Households: Administrative and Economic Aspects of the New Kingdom Royal Memorial Temples in Western Thebes* (Leiden: Nederlands Instituut voor het Nabije Oosten, 1997).

Overviews of the site of Malqata include Peter Lacovara, *The New Kingdom Royal City* (London: Kegan Paul International, 1997), 24–28; Kemp, *Ancient Egypt,* 270–75 (with earlier bibliography); and for the Birket Habu, see Barry Kemp and David O'Connor, "An Ancient Nile Harbour: University Museum Excavations at the 'Birket Habu,'" *International Journal of Nautical Archaeology* 3, no. 1 (1974): 101–36; the Napoleonic map with the east bank lake is *Description de l'Égypte, Antiquités* (Paris: Impr. impériale, 1812), vol. 2, plate 1 (available at https://digitalcollections.nypl.org/items/510d47e0–0f8f-a3d9-e040 -e00a18064a99). A new portion of Malqata was excavated by a team led by Dr. Zahi Hawass in 2021—preliminary reports include Hawass, "Discovery of the Lost Golden City, 'The Dazzling Aten' of Amenhotep III," *Egyptian Archaeology* 59 (2021): 4–7; and Hawass, "Excavations in Western Thebes, 2021:

The Discovery of the Golden Lost City, A Preliminary Report," *Journal of the American Research Center in Egypt* 57 (2021): 83–110.

The location of Djarukha near Akhmim is established in Marc Gabolde, "La statue de Merymaât gouverneur de Djâroukha (Bologne K.S. 1813)," *Bulletin de l'Institut français d'archéologie orientale* 94 (1994): 27.

An enthroned image of Amunhotep III in a jubilee cloak in the tomb of Surer also displays the falcon tail feathers: Torgny Säve-Söderbergh, *Four Eighteenth Dynasty Tombs* (Oxford: Griffith Institute, 1957), plate 31; tail feathers can be part of jubilee attire since Predynastic times: Hornung and Staehelin, *Neue Studien zum Sedfest,* 56–59. The earlier Eighteenth Dynasty kings Hatshepsut and Thutmose III can appear with the bodies of falcons, expressing a similar equivalence between Horus and the king, as discussed in Tom Hardwick and Christina Riggs, "The King as a Falcon: A 'Lost' Statue of Thutmose III Rediscovered and Reunited," *Mitteilungen des Deutschen Archäologischen Instituts, Abteilung Kairo* 66 (2010): 107–19.

The joining of Amunhotep III, Tiye, and Hathor at the jubilee prior to rebirth was recognized by Edward F. Wente, "Hathor at the Jubilee," in *Studies in Honor of John A. Wilson,* ed. Gerald E. Kadish (Chicago: University of Chicago Press, 1969), 83–91; the queen's identification with Maat is stated explicitly in the tomb of Kheruef: "like Maat in the following of Re does she exist in the following of your Majesty" (Epigraphic Survey, *Tomb of Kheruef,* plate 26). For portraiture in ancient Egypt, see Jan Assmann, "Preservation and Presentation of Self in Ancient Egyptian Portraiture," in *Studies in Honor of William Kelly Simpson,* vol. 1, ed. Peter Der Manuelian (Boston: Museum of Fine Arts, 1996), 55–81. The rich nuance of the term *twt,* "image, likeness," is surveyed in Rune Nyord, *Seeing Perfection: Ancient Egyptian Images Beyond Representation* (Cambridge: Cambridge University Press, 2020), 9–12.

A foundational synthesis of the art styles and evolving ideology of the reign of Amunhotep III is W. Raymond Johnson, "Monuments and Monumental Art under Amenhotep III: Evolution and Meaning," in *Amenhotep III: Perspectives on His Reign,* ed. David O'Connor and Eric H. Cline (Ann Arbor: University of Michigan Press, 1998), 63–94 (he discusses the seal "Nebmaatre is the Dazzling Sun Disk" on 88). Additional ancient sources with the epithet "Nebmaatre is the Dazzling Sun Disk" are collected in William J. Murnane, *Texts from the Amarna Period in Egypt* (Atlanta: Scholars Press, 1995), 20–22. The youthful images of Amunhotep III and Tiye are collected in Betsy M. Bryan, "Royal and Divine Statuary," in *Egypt's Dazzling Sun, Amenhotep III and His World,* ed. Arielle P. Kozloff, Betsy M. Bryan, and Lawrence M. Berman (Cleveland: Cleveland Museum of Art, 1992), 159–61, 170–71, 175–77, and in her "Small-Scale Royal Representations," 198–99; Bayer, *Teje,* 102–5 is another important overview.

We adopt the ideological significance of the royal couple's youthful-looking art as presented in Johnson, "Monuments and Monumental Art," 63–94, while rejecting the existence of a co-regency of Amunhotep III with Amunhotep IV (especially a twelve-year-long one). Abundant textual and artistic evidence rebuts any such co-regency; surveys of the frequently discussed topic include Ronald T. Ridley, *Akhenaten, A Historian's View* (Cairo: American University in Cairo Press, 2019), 25–26; Dimitri Laboury, *Akhénaton* (Paris: Pygmalion, 2010), 87–92; James Romano, "A Second Look at 'Images of Amenhotep III in Thebes: Styles and Intentions' by W. Raymond Johnson," in *The Art of Amenhotep III: Art Historical Analysis,* ed. Lawrence M. Berman (Cleveland: Cleveland Museum of Art, 1990), 50–54.

Statistics that illuminate average life expectancy in ancient Egypt appear in Sonia Zakrzewski, "Life Expectancy," *UCLA Encyclopedia of Egyptology,* ed. Willeke Wendrich and Jacco Dieleman, published in 2015 (https://escholarship.org/uc/item/7zb2f62c, accessed June 3, 2020). References to an ideal lifespan of 110 years are collected in Rosalind M. Janssen and Jac J. Janssen, *Growing Up and Getting Old in Ancient Egypt* (London: Golden House Press, 2007), 201–3.

On the tremendous output of statuary during Amunhotep III's reign, see Betsy Bryan, "The Statue Program for the Mortuary Temple of Amenhotep III," in *The Temple in Ancient Egypt, New Discoveries and Recent Research,* ed. Stephen Quirke (London: British Museum Press, 1997), 57–81; Bryan, "Royal and Divine Statuary," in *Egypt's Dazzling Sun,* 105–84. The evidence for the second jubilee is sparse; in addition to jar stoppers from Malqata, two inscriptions from the now destroyed bark shrine on Elephantine also mention a second jubilee—see Daniele Salvoldi and Simon Delvaux, "The Lost Chapels of Elephantine. Preliminary Results of a Reconstruction Study Through Archival Documents," in *Proceedings of the XI International Congress of Egyptologists,* ed. Gloria Rosati and Maria Cristina Guidotti (Oxford: Archaeopress, 2017), 559.

4. A MYSTERIOUS PRINCE

We have drawn the details of the partygoers from the many images of Eighteenth Dynasty celebrations: Melinda K. Hartwig, *Tomb Painting and Identity in Ancient Thebes, 1419–1372 BCE* (Turnhout: Brepols, Fondation Égyptologique Reine Élisabeth, 2004), 98–103, citing scenes of vomiting on 101n425. The oasis amphorae are based on Colin Hope, "Oases Amphorae of the New Kingdom," in *Egypt and Nubia, Gifts of the Desert,* ed. Renée Friedman (London: British Museum Press, 2002), 95–131.

Much information is contained in the jar stoppers and hieratic labels on sherds from Malqata: Colin Hope, *Jar Sealings and Amphorae of the 18th Dynasty: A Technological Study; Excavations at Malkata and the Birket Habu 1971–1974* (Warminster: Aris & Phillips, 1978); M. A. Leahy, *The Inscriptions: Excavations at Malkata and the Birket Habu 1971–1974* (Warminster: Aris & Phillips, 1978). For Gebel Ghueita (*Per-wesekh*) in Kharga Oasis as the source of some jubilee wine, see John Coleman Darnell, David Klotz, and Colleen Manassa, "Gods on the Road: The Pantheon of Thebes at Qasr el-Gheuita," in *Documents de Théologies Thébaines Tardives,* ed. Christophe Thiers (Montpellier: Équipe Égypte Nilotique et Méditerranéennes, 2012), 6–7.

The jar stopper with the name of Prince Amunhotep is discussed in Dimitri Laboury, *Akhénaton* (Paris: Pygmalion, 2010), 43–44. In addition to appearing on colossal statues, Amunhotep IV's sisters are named in some depictions of their father's jubilee: Marc J. LeBlanc, "'In Accordance with the Documents of Ancient Times': The Origins, Development, and Significance of the Ancient Egyptian Sed Festival (Jubilee Festival)" (unpublished PhD diss., Yale University, 2011), 130–31. The monuments of the crown prince Djehutymose are cataloged in Aidan Dodson, "Crown Prince Djhutmose and the Royal Sons of the Eighteenth Dynasty," *Journal of Egyptian Archaeology* 76 (1990): 87–88; Laboury, *Akhénaton,* 58–61. The date of Amunhotep IV's accession is discussed in Marc Gabolde, *D'Akhenaton à Toutânkhamon* (Paris: Diffusion de Boccard, 1998), 14–16; we use the calculation of the date in Laboury, *Akhénaton,* 93. For the five-fold titulary of Amunhotep IV, see Ronald Leprohon, *The Great Name: Ancient Egyptian Royal Titulary* (Atlanta: Society for Biblical Literature, 2013), 104.

The age of Akhenaten at his accession is disputed; thoughtful remarks appear in Marc Gabolde, "Under a Deep Blue Starry Sky," in *Causing His Name to Live: Studies in Egyptian Epigraphy and History in Memory of William J. Murnane,* ed. Peter J. Brand and Louise Cooper (Leiden: Brill, 2009), 116. Cyril Aldred, *Akhenaten, King of Egypt* (London: Thames & Hudson, 1988), 193–94 proposed that Tiye's role in Amarna Letters EA 26 and EA 27 was possible evidence for the king's age at the beginning of his reign (note that Aldred dates the letter to Regnal Year 12 rather than the correct Regnal Year 2, arguing for the improbable theory of co-regency between Amunhotep III and Amunhotep IV). A useful overview of the difficulty of determining the age of death for mummified remains is Gabolde, "Under a Deep Blue Starry Sky," 115–16.

5. THE BEAUTIFUL ONE HAS COME

Sources about the experiences of ancient Egyptian schoolchildren are collected in Rosalind M. Janssen and Jac J. Janssen, *Growing Up and Getting Old in Ancient Egypt* (London: Golden House Press, 2007), 57–75. Nefertiti's diminutive scribal palette and reed pens are based on the surviving set belonging to the princess Meketaten (Metropolitan Museum of Art, 26.7.1295): William C. Hayes, *The Scepter of Egypt: A Background for the Study of the Egyptian Antiquities in the Metropolitan Museum of Art,* vol. 2, *The Hyksos Period and the New Kingdom (1675–1080 B.C.)* (New York: Metropolitan Museum of Art, 1959), 296–97, fig. 183. The text that the children are copying is *The Instruction of Amenemhat*: Faried Adrom, *Die Lehre des Amenemhet* (Turnhout: Brepols, 2006), 53; it is also the only Middle Egyptian literary text known from the admittedly scanty remains of papyri from Akhet-Aten—Richard B. Parkinson, "The Teaching of King Amenemhat I at el-Amarna: British Museum EA 57458 and 57459," in *Studies in Ancient Egypt in Honour of H. S. Smith,* ed. Anthony Leahy and John Tait (London: The Egypt Exploration Society, 1999), 221–26.

Although often differing in the interpretation of her origins and whether she is Akhenaten's successor Ankh(et)kheperure Neferneferuaten, the following sources serve as overviews of the queen's life: Aidan Dodson, *Nefertiti, Queen and Pharaoh of Egypt* (Cairo: American University in Cairo Press, 2020); Ronald T. Ridley, *Akhenaten, A Historian's View* (Cairo: American University in Cairo Press, 2019), 183–200; Dimitri Laboury, *Akhénaton* (Paris: Pygmalion, 2010), 223–36. Our discussion of the DNA evidence follows Marc Gabolde, "L'ADN de la famille royale amarnienne et les sources égyptiennes—de la complémentarité des méthodes et des résultats," *Égypte Nilotique et Méditerranéenne (ENiM)* 6 (2013): 177–203 (accessible at http://www.enim-egyptologie.fr/index.php?page=enim-6&n=10). For the role of Ay at the Amarna court and his later kingship, see Nozomu Kawai, "Ay versus Horemheb: The Political Situation in the Late Eighteenth Dynasty Revisited," *Journal of Egyptian History* 3, no. 2 (2010): 261–92; Marc Gabolde, *Toutankhamon* (Paris: Pygmalion, 2015), 401–81; Aidan Dodson, *Amarna Sunset: Nefertiti, Tutankhamun, Ay, Horemheb, and the Egyptian Counter-reformation* (Cairo: American University in Cairo Press, 2009).

6. TRANSFORMATION

The details of our reconstruction of the tomb of Ramose are based both on our observations within the tomb (Theban Tomb 55) and on the publication of Norman de Garis Davies, *The Tomb of the Vizier Ramose* (London: Egypt Exploration Society, 1941), plates 29, 33. The significance of grids is discussed in Gay Robins, *Proportion and Style in Ancient Egyptian Art* (Austin: University of Texas Press, 1994); additional useful studies include James Romano, "A Second Look at 'Images of Amenhotep III in Thebes: Styles and Intentions' by W. Raymond Johnson," in *The Art of Amenhotep III: Art Historical Analysis,* ed. Lawrence M. Berman (Cleveland: Cleveland Museum of Art, 1990), 50–54; Dimitri Laboury, *Akhénaton* (Paris: Pygmalion, 2010), 218–20; and Arlette David, *Renewing Royal Imagery, Akhenaten and Family in the Amarna Tombs* (Leiden: Brill, 2020), 86–90.

An artistic precedent for the multi-armed Aten appears on the Sphinx stelae of Amunhotep II: in the lunette, two arms come down from a winged sun disk, parallel to the two uraei that normally hang down from the sun—Andrea Klug, *Königliche Stelen in der Zeit von Ahmose bis Amenophis III* (Turnhout: Brepols, 2002), 235.

On the vizier Ramose's career, see William Murnane, "The Organization of Government under Amenhotep III," in *Amenhotep III: Perspectives on His Reign,* ed. David O'Connor and Eric H. Cline (Ann Arbor: University of Michigan Press, 1998), 203–6. Translations of the speeches that Ramose addresses to Amunhotep IV appear in Laboury, *Akhénaton,* 110–13; William J. Murnane, *Texts from the Amarna Period in Egypt* (Atlanta: Scholars Press, 1995), 62–63. The Window of Appearances in the tomb of Ramose might have been located in the monument called *Tjeny-menu,* "Elevated of monuments," at Karnak Temple, as outlined in Robert Vergnieux and Michel Gondran, *Aménophis IV et les pierres du soleil, Akhénaton retrouvé* (Paris: Les Editions Arthaud, 1997), 126–29.

The two main medical "diagnoses" of Akhenaten are Fröhlich's syndrome, as proposed by Cyril Aldred in his influential biography *Akhenaten, King of Egypt* (New York: Thames & Hudson, 1988), and Marfan syndrome, suggested in Alwyn L. Burridge, "Akhenaten: A New Perspective; Evidence of a Genetic Disorder in the Royal Family of 18th Dynasty Egypt," *Journal of the Society for the Study of Egyptian Antiquities* 23 (1993): 63–74. Marc Gabolde, *D'Akhenaton à Toutânkhamon* (Paris: Diffusion de Boccard, 1998), 9–11, suggests that proposals of Akhenaten suffering from Barraquer-Simons syndrome are worthy of consideration. The more severe medical diagnoses have primarily been dismissed in scholarly literature about the art of Akhenaten's reign.

The phases of Hatshepsut's art are described and illustrated in Dimitri Laboury, "How and Why Did Hatshepsut Invent the Image of Her Royal Power?" in *Creativity and Innovation in the Reign of Hatshepsut,* ed. José M. Galán, Betsy M. Bryan, and Peter F. Dorman (Chicago: Oriental Institute of the University of Chicago, 2014), 49–92; a useful catalog addressing many aspects of Hatshepsut's reign is Catherine H. Roehrig, ed., *Hatshepsut: From Queen to Pharaoh* (New York: Metropolitan Museum of Art, 2005). The statues of the Twelfth Dynasty female king Sobeknoferu may have served as an inspiration for Hatshepsut, and the Eighteenth Dynasty pharaoh is key to understanding later women rulers like Neferneferuaten and Tausret—see Richard H. Wilkinson, *Tausret: Forgotten Queen and Pharaoh of Egypt* (Oxford: Oxford University Press, 2012).

7. THE UNIQUE GOD

The servant in the Place of Truth Seta was buried in Deir le-Medina tomb 1352, and a *shabti* from his tomb mentions Aten, suggesting that he was a contemporary of Amunhotep IV—see Jaroslav Černý, *A Community of Workmen at Thebes in the Ramesside Period,* 3rd ed. (Cairo: Institut français d'archéologie orientale, 2004), 50–51. For the festival of Amunhotep I at Deir el-Medina, see Benedict G. Davies, *Life Within the Five Walls: A Handbook to Deir el-Medina* (Wallasey: Abercromby Press, 2018), 110–11; education at the village, including student ostraca, are discussed on 93–99.

For an overview of ancient Egyptian scripts and language, see Andréas Stauder, "Scripts," in *The Oxford Handbook of Egyptology,* ed. Ian Shaw and Elizabeth Bloxam (Oxford: Oxford University Press, 2020), 869–96; Antonio Loprieno, *Ancient Egyptian: A Linguistic Introduction* (Cambridge: Cambridge University Press, 1995); Henry George Fischer, *The Orientation of Hieroglyphs* (New York: Metropolitan Museum of Art, 1977), and his *L'écriture et l'art de l'Egypte ancienne: Quatre leçons sur la paléographie et l'épigraphie pharaoniques* (Paris: Presses universitaires de France, 1986) remain important studies on the intersection of art and writing.

Dynasty 0 and the invention of hieroglyphs, in the context of the development of the Egyptian script, with references to earlier sources, appear in Stauder, "Scripts," 873–74, while Dorian Vanhulle, "Boat Symbolism in Predynastic and Early Dynastic Egypt: An Ethno-Archaeological Approach," *Journal of Ancient Egyptian Interconnections* 17 (2018): 173–87, has effectively presented the role of boats in early Egyptian religious practice.

The pre-Akhenaten history of *aten* is discussed by Dimitri Laboury, *Akhénaton* (Paris: Pygmalion, 2010), 186–207; Cyril Aldred, *Akhenaten, King of Egypt* (New York: Thames & Hudson, 1988), 237–41; and Donald B. Redford, "The Sun-Disc in Akhenaten's Program: Its Worship and Antecedents, I," *Journal of the American Research Center in Egypt* 13 (1976): 47–61. An expansion of one point Redford makes about the Coffin Texts is Orly Goldwasser, "*Itn*-the 'Golden Egg': (CT IV 292b-c [B9Cª])," in *Essays on Ancient Egypt in Honour of Herman te Velde,* ed. Jacobus van Dijk (Groningen: Styx, 1997), 79–84. The epithet "lord of what the sun disk encircles" is ubiquitous in the tombs at Akhet-Aten in captions of Aten; the god in turn can grant dominion of what he encircles to the king—as in Maj Sandman, *Texts from the Time of Akhenaten* (Brussels: Édition de la Fondation égyptologique Reine Élisabeth, 1938), 21.

The magical wands are addressed in Joshua Roberson, "The Early History of 'New Kingdom' Netherworld Iconography: A Late Middle Kingdom Apotropaic Wand Reconsidered," in *Archaism and Innovation: Studies in the Culture of Middle Kingdom Egypt,* ed. David P. Silverman, William Kelly Simpson, and Josef Wegner (New Haven, CT: Department of Near Eastern Languages and Civilizations, 2009), 427–45; Fred Vink, "Boundaries of Protection: Function and Significance of the Framing (Lines) on Middle Kingdom *apotropaia,* in Particular Magic Wands," in *The World of Middle Kingdom Egypt (2000–1550 BC),* vol. 2, ed. Gianluca Miniaci and Wolfram Grajetzki (London: Golden House Publications, 2016), 257–84. Erik Hornung, *Conceptions of God in Ancient Egypt,* trans. John Baines (Ithaca, NY: Cornell University Press, 1982), 100–142, presents the flexibility of Egyptian iconography in embodying the divine. The composition known as the *Book of Adoring Re in the West* (or the *Litany of Re*) is translated and illustrated in John Coleman Darnell and Colleen Manassa Darnell, *The Ancient Egyptian Netherworld Books* (Atlanta: Society for

Biblical Literature, 2018), 61–126, with the seventy-five forms of the Great Litany on 76–102. The use of the shining sun disk (with hands) in the hieroglyphic script during the reign of Amunhotep IV/Akhenaten is examined by Orly Goldwasser, "The Aten is the 'Energy of Light': New Evidence from the Script," *Journal of the American Research Center in Egypt* 46 (2010): 159–65.

Different perspectives on the root *akh,* some emphasizing "luminosity," others "effectiveness," include Gertie Englund, *Akh: Une notion religieuse dans l'Égypte pharaonique* (Uppsala: Uppsala University, 1978); Florence Friedman, "ꜣḫ in the Amarna Period," *Journal of the American Research Center in Egypt* 23 (1986): 99–106; and Jiří Janák, "Akh," *UCLA Encyclopedia of Egyptology,* ed. Willeke Wendrich and Jacco Dieleman, published 2013 (retrieved from https://escholarship.org/uc/item/7255p86v).

The development of the didactic name of Aten is traced in Marc Gabolde, *D'Akhenaton à Toutânkhamon* (Paris: Diffusion de Boccard, 1998), 105–6, 110–18; Robert Vergnieux, *Recherches sur les monuments thébains d'Amenhotep IV à l'aide d'outils informatiques, Méthodes et résultats,* vol. 1, *Texte* (Geneva: Société d'Égyptologie, 1999), 17–18, 169–70; Laboury, *Akhénaton,* 125–35 (on 143 he dates the appearance of Nefertiti's epithet Neferneferuaten to after Regnal Year 5; see also Vergnieux, *Recherches sur les monuments thébains,* 179–84).

The recently discovered stela of Amunhotep III with the name of Re-Horakhty is published by Ali el-Asfar, Jürgen Osing, and Rainer Stadelmann, "A Stela of Amenhotep III with a Hymn to Re-Horakhty and Osiris," *Annales du Service des Antiquités de l'Égypte* 86 (2012–2013): 149–55. James Allen, *Genesis in Egypt: The Philosophy of Ancient Egyptian Creation Accounts* (New Haven, CT: Yale Egyptological Seminar, 1988), provides an introduction to Shu in the Heliopolitan creation myth.

8. A ROYAL WARRIOR

Based on analysis of his mummy, Amunhotep III had a large abscess in one of his teeth, and he was likely overweight. His grandson Tutankhamun was buried with 130 sticks and staves, which would have been useful to the young king who had a congenital disorder that affected his left foot—Zahi Hawass and Sahar N. Saleem, *Scanning the Pharaohs: CT Imaging of the New Kingdom Royal Mummies* (Cairo: American University in Cairo Press, 2018), 97–100. The training of ancient Egyptian horses is covered in Ulrich Hofmann, *Fuhrwesen und Pferdehaltung im alten Ägypten* (Bonn: Rheinische Friedrich-Wilhelms-Universität Bonn, 1989), 68–73; Ramesses III is shown personally training his horses at Medinet Habu—Epigraphic Survey, *Medinet Habu—Volume II, Later Historical Records of Ramses III* (Chicago: University of Chicago Press, 1932), plate 109; for royal horse training, see also John C. Darnell, "ϢⲰⲢⲘ, 'to train,' and *t͗my.t,* 'the bit,'" *Enchoria* 24 (1997–1998): 158–62. Chariots as mobile archery platforms are discussed in John Coleman Darnell and Colleen Manassa, *Tutankhamun's Armies: Battle and Conquest During Ancient Egypt's Late 18th Dynasty* (Hoboken, NJ: John Wiley, 2007), 63–65.

Karnak Temple's last centuries of active use are presented in detail in David Klotz, *Caesar in the City of Amun: Egyptian Temple Construction and Theology in Roman Thebes* (Turnhout: Brepols, 2012). Elaine Sullivan, "Visualising the Size and Movement of the Portable Festival Barks at Karnak Temple," *British Museum Studies in Ancient Egypt and Sudan* 19 (2012): 1–37, reconstructs the size of divine barks based on surviving architectural evidence. Amunhotep IV's construction of the vestibule of the Third Pylon with its smiting scene is published in Ramadan Sa'ad, "Les travaux d'Aménophis IV au IIIe pylône du temple d'Amon Re' à Karnak," *Kêmi* 20 (1970): 187–93; Dimitri Laboury, *Akhénaton* (Paris: Pygmalion, 2010), 95–99 (101–4 describes the Tutankhamun Opet scenes that depict this architectural feature).

For the imagery of Aten dispensing weapons to a martial king, see Claude Traunecker, "Données nouvelles sur le début au règne d'Amenéophis et son oeuvre à Karnak," *Journal of the Society for the Study of Egyptian Antiquities* 14 (1984): 60–69; Robert Vergnieux, "La période proto-amarnienne," in *Akhénaton et l'époque amarnienne* (Paris: Éditions Khéops et Centre d'Égyptologie, 2005), 35–50.

9. A BUSTLING QUARRY

Cargo ships of the New Kingdom—like those that would have been used to transport *talatat*—are discussed in Björn Landström, *Ships of the Pharaohs, 4000 Years of Egyptian Shipbuilding* (Garden City, NY: Doubleday & Company, 1970), 134–39; a graffito of a cargo ship near images of Akhenaten in the desert northwest of Waset serves as another basis for our reconstruction—John Coleman Darnell, *Theban Desert Road Survey II* (New Haven, CT: Yale Egyptological Seminar, 2013), 92–93, and plates 97–98. Details of the quarrying process are drawn from Robert Vergnieux and Michel Gondran, *Aménophis IV et les pierres du soleil, Akhénaton retrouvé* (Paris: Les Editions Arthaud, 1997), 96–101; Arris H. Kramer, "Talatat Shipping from Gebel el-Silsileh to Karnak: A Literature Survey," *Bibliotheca Orientalis* 66, nos. 1–2 (2009): 5–20.

The Gebel Silsila inscription of Amunhotep IV is published in Maj Sandman, *Texts from the Time of Akhenaten* (Brussels: Édition de la Fondation égyptologique Reine Élisabeth, 1938), 143–44, with additions given by William J. Murnane, *Texts from the Amarna Period in Egypt* (Atlanta: Scholars Press, 1995), 29–30, and important notes in Dimitri Laboury, *Akhénaton* (Paris: Pygmalion, 2010), 99–100. In our translation, we read *thm* as "pursue" with Coptic ⲦⲰⳢⲘ (W. E. Crum, *Coptic Dictionary* [Oxford: Oxford University Press, 1939], 459a). The term for compulsory labor occurs alongside a Semitic loanword *barti* for another sort of obligatory service in the Nauri Decree of Seti

I, for which see Arlette David, *Syntactic and Lexico-Semantic Aspects of the Legal Register in Ramesside Royal Decrees* (Wiesbaden: Harrassowitz Verlag, 2006), 49.

The inscriptions of the High Priest May in the Wadi Hammamat appear in Laboury, *Akhénaton,* 131, 134, and are placed in the context of the history of the Amun priesthood in Ben Haring, "The Rising Power of the House of Amun in the New Kingdom," in *Ancient Egyptian Administration,* ed. Juan Carlos Moreno García (Leiden: Brill, 2013), 622–24.

10. CITY OF THE SUN

The itinerary of Ay and Tutankhamun are the west bank pyramids of Saqqara and Abu Sir, with the Abu Gurob solar temples associated with the latter. Mark Lehner, *The Complete Pyramids* (London: Thames & Hudson, 1997), 84–93 and 142–53, summarizes what the two might have seen. For the early history of solar cults and Heliopolis, see the remarks of Massimiliano Nuzzolo, *The Fifth Dynasty Sun Temples, Kingship, Architecture and Religion in the Third Millennium* BC *Egypt* (Prague: Charles University, Faculty of Arts, 2018), 477–87.

A thorough presentation of archaeological evidence at Iunu and its sacred complexes is Dietrich Raue, with Aiman Ashmawy, *Reise zum Ursprung der Welt: Die Ausgrabungen im Tempel von Heliopolis* (Darmstadt: Philipp von Zabern, 2020). The relationship between the Benben and obelisks is further explained in Brian Curran, Anthony Grafton, Pamela O. Long, and Benjamin Weiss, *Obelisk: A History* (Cambridge, MA: Burndy Library, 2009), 13–34. The alignment of the Giza Pyramids is discussed in the still useful study by Georges Goyon, "Nouvelles observations relatives à l'orientation de la pyramide de Khéops," *Revue d'Égyptologie* 22 (1970): 85–98.

The Heliopolitan influence on Akhenaten's solar theology is explored in nearly every biography of the king; the Theban evidence is well summarized in Robert Vergnieux, *Recherches sur les monuments thébains d'Amenhotep IV à l'aide d'outils informatiques, Méthodes et résultats,* vol. 1, *Texte* (Geneva: Société d'Égyptologie, 1999), 153–67; see also Robert Vergnieux and Michel Gondran, *Aménophis IV et les pierres du soleil, Akhénaton retrouvé* (Paris: Les Editions Arthaud, 1997), 86, for the Great Benben being a reference to the unique obelisk, whose base was identified already by Paul Barguet, "L'Obélisque de Saint-Jean-de-Latran dans le temple de Ramsès á Karnak," *Annales du Service des Antiquités de l'Égypte* 50 (1950): 269–80. The Heliopolitan associations of Karnak are present from the reign of Senwosret I and are confirmed in the designation of the *Akh-menu* of Thutmose III as a *Hut-aat*—see Luc Gabolde, *Le "grand château d'Amon" de Sésostris 1er à Karnak: La décoration du temple d'Amon-Rê au Moyen empire* (Paris: Diff. de Boccard, 1998), 143–58; David Klotz, *Caesar in the City of Amun: Egyptian Temple Construction and Theology in Roman Thebes* (Turnhout: Brepols, 2012), 66–68, 149–54.

The etymology of *talatat* is examined in Dimitri Laboury, *Akhénaton* (Paris: Pygmalion, 2010), 145, and on 133–35 he notes that the brick-like blocks appear first in Regnal Year 4; Vergnieux and Gondran, *Aménophis IV,* 38, discuss the ancient Egyptian name for the small stones. Donald Redford, *Akhenaten, the Heretic King* (Princeton, NJ: Princeton University Press, 1984), remains a highly engaging history of the Akhenaten Temple Project. The artistic evolution of Amunhotep IV/Akhenaten during the Theban years is surveyed in Dimitri Laboury, "Amarna Art," in *UCLA Encyclopedia of Egyptology*, ed. Willeke Wendrich and Jacco Dieleman, published 2011 (retrieved from https://escholarship.org/uc/item/0n21d4bm). For an early block showing Amunhotep IV and the falcon-headed Horakhty (with the god's full name not in cartouches), now Berlin ÄM 2072, see also Friederike Seyfried, ed., *Im Licht von Amarna, 100 Jahre Fund der Nofretete* (Berlin: Staatliche Museen zu Berlin, 2012), 206. The Griffith Institute has made the archives of the Tutankhamun tomb excavation fully accessible and searchable: www.griffith.ox .ac.uk/discoveringTut/; the Regnal Year 3 and 4 linens are Carter handlist 281a and 291a, respectively; typeset copies are published in Horst Beinlich and Mohamed Saleh, *Corpus der hieroglyphischen Inschriften aus dem Grab des Tutanchamun* (Oxford: Griffith Institute, 1989), 131, 133 (the Regnal Year 4 date is incorrectly copied as Regnal Year 3). Images of the falcon-headed god, with the didactic name in cartouches, as well as computer-assisted reconstructions of the *talatat* appear in Vergnieux and Gondran, *Aménophis IV,* 56–71, 91–92.

11. AN ERUDITE KING

Amunhotep IV's dream about a giant griffin is based on the winged creatures that appear on the boundaries of the Egyptian world, such as those in the tomb of Khety at Beni Hasan—Naguib Kanawati and Linda Evans, *Beni Hassan,* vol. 6, *The Tomb of Khety* (Wallasey: Abercromby Press, 2020), plates 17B, 59A, 93. The cataclysm that accompanies a divine epiphany is based on texts such as the Cannibal Hymn in the Pyramid Texts—Christopher Eyre, *The Cannibal Hymn, A Cultural and Literary Study* (Liverpool: Liverpool University Press, 2002), 76–84. Texts and images of falling stars with human forms are discussed in John Coleman Darnell, *The Enigmatic Netherworld Books of the Solar-Osirian Unity: Cryptographic Compositions in the Tombs of Tutankhamun, Ramesses VI and Ramesses IX* (Fribourg: Academic Press, 2004), 426–48.

The description of the scriptorium is based on a depiction in the tomb of Tjay—Ludwig Borchardt, "Das Dienstgebäude des Auswärtigen Amtes unter den Ramessiden," *Zeitschrift für Ägyptische Sprache und Altertumskunde* 44 (1907): 59–61. The king addressing his counselors is drawn from the literary tradition of the "royal novel"—Andréas Stauder, "La *Königsnovelle*: Indices génériques, significations, écarts intertextuels," in *Questionner le sphinx: mélanges offerts à*

Christiane Zivie-Coche, vol. 1, ed. Philippe Collombert, Laurent Coulon, Ivan Guermeur, and Christophe Thiers (Cairo: Institut français d'archéologie orientale, 2021), 99–136.

The initial publication of the two blocks (given the designation X1/5 and 30/70 by the Akhenaten Temple Project) is Donald B. Redford, "A Royal Speech from the Blocks of the 10th Pylon," *Bulletin of the Egyptological Seminar* 3 (1981): 87–102; Redford published additional early Amunhotep IV blocks and repeats the "revelation" interpretation of the royal speech in "New Theories and Old Facts," *Bulletin of the American Schools of Oriental Research* 369 (2013): 9–34. A photograph of block X1/5 appears in Claude Traunecker, "Le dromos perdu d'Amenhotep IV et de Néfertiti à Karnak, Espaces cultuels et économiques au service de l'atonisme," in *Les édifices du règne d'Amenhotep IV-Akhenaton, Urbanisme et revolution,* ed. Marc Gabolde and Robert Vergnieux (Montpellier: Équipe Égypte Nilotique et Méditerranéenne, 2018), 188. The Tenth Pylon blocks are further discussed in Dimitri Laboury, *Akhénaton* (Paris: Pygmalion, 2010), 120–25; Robert Vergnieux, *Recherches sur les monuments thébains d'Amenhotep IV à l'aide d'outils informatiques, Méthodes et résultats,* vol. 1, *Texte* (Geneva: Société d'Égyptologie, 1999), 169–70. The history of the Franco-Egyptian Center for the Study of Karnak Temple and its current projects are available at www.cfeetk.cnrs.fr (accessed July 5, 2020).

The interpretation we present here of blocks X1/5 and 30/70 is based on John Coleman Darnell, "Epiphany or Erudition?—The Inception of Atonism," in *One Who Loves Knowledge: Studies in Honor of Richard Jasnow,* ed. Betsy Bryan et al. (Atlanta: Lockwood Press, 2022), with detailed references.

Parallels to the literary motif of buildings fallen into ruin, part of the "time of troubles topos," are collected in Colleen Manassa, *Imagining the Past: Historical Fiction in New Kingdom Egypt* (Oxford: Oxford University Press, 2013), 45, 64, and 169, and 222n109; the hieroglyphic text of Hatshepsut's description of inadequate knowledge on the part of the priests is James P. Allen, "The Speos Artemidos Inscription of Hatshepsut," *Bulletin of the Egyptological Seminar* 16 (2002): plate 2, lines 25–26 (translation is our own); the edition and copy in Alan H. Gardiner, "Davies's Copy of the Great Speos Artemidos Inscription," *Journal of Egyptian Archaeology* 32 (1946): 43–56, remains useful. For the Neferhotep I inscription, see the remarks and references in Maya Müller, "Die Königsplastik des Mittleren Reiches und ihre Schöpfer: Reden über Statuen-wenn Statuen reden," *Imago Aegypti* 1 (2005): 27–78.

The *talatat* with the taxation list were deposited in the lower fill courses of the west tower of the Ninth Pylon: see Claude Traunecker, "Amenhotep IV, percepteur royal du Disque," in *Akhénaton et l'époque amarnienne* (Paris: Éditions Khéops, 2005), 145–82; Laboury, *Akhénaton,* 175–78; Vergnieux, *Recherches sur les monuments thébains,* vol. 1, 132–34, and vol. 2, *Planches* (Geneva:

Société d'Égyptologie, 1999), plate 35. Inspection/inventory decrees are collected in Arlette David, *Syntactic and Lexico-Semantic Aspects of the Legal Register in Ramesside Royal Decrees* (Wiesbaden: Harrassowitz Verlag, 2006), 207–14.

A convenient overview of Egyptian phonology, including the complex issue of the *aleph,* is James P. Allen, *Ancient Egyptian Phonology* (Cambridge: Cambridge University Press, 2020). The verb *3b,* "to remain," in P. Mond is Eric T. Peet, "Two Letters from Akhetaten," *Annals of Archaeology and Anthropology* 17 (1930): pls. 19, pl. 25 (line 20); Edward Wente, *Letters from Ancient Egypt* (Atlanta: Society of Biblical Literature, 1990), 94–95 (no. 123), translates the entire letter.

Descriptions of gods who do something without ceasing are collected in Christian Leitz, ed., *Lexikon der ägyptischen Götter und Götterbezeichnungen,* vol. 3 (Leuven: Peeters, 2002), 8. In the same inscription of Ramesses II at Abydos that describes the cessation of offerings, line 36 of the text mentions statues that are cast aside, "on the ground," rendering them useless; hieroglyphic text copy published in Anthony J. Spalinger, *The Great Dedicatory Inscription of Ramesses II: A Solar-Osirian Tractate at Abydos* (Leiden: Brill, 2009), 129. Had Amunhotep IV/Akhenaten wanted to claim that divine statues had failed, he would have likely done so with similar phrases. The decoration of the tomb of Parennefer is discussed in Asunta F. Redford, "Theban Tomb No. 188 (The Tomb of Parennefer): A Case Study of Tomb Reuse in the Theban Necropolis" (PhD diss., Pennsylvania State University, 2006).

12. A TEMPLE OF HER OWN

The sphinx-lined alley of the Gem-pa-Aten is discussed in Claude Traunecker, "Le dromos perdu d'Amenhotep IV et de Néfertiti à Karnak, Espaces cultuels et économiques au service de l'atonisme," in *Les édifices du règne d'Amenhotep IV-Akhenaton, Urbanisme et revolution,* ed. Marc Gabolde and Robert Vergnieux (Montpellier: Équipe Égypte Nilotique et Méditerranéenne, 2018), 175–92. The decoration of the Mansion of the Benben was studied and reconstructed by the Akhenaten Temple Project—see Donald Redford, *Akhenaten, the Heretic King* (Princeton, NJ: Princeton University Press, 1984), 72–78; Dimitri Laboury, *Akhénaton* (Paris: Pygmalion, 2010), 154–57.

For the history of the office of God's Wife, see Mariam F. Ayad, *God's Wife, God's Servant, The God's Wife of Amun (c. 740–525 BC)* (New York: Routledge, 2009); Gay Robins, "The God's Wife of Amun in the 18th Dynasty in Egypt," in *Images of Women in Antiquity,* ed. Averil Cameron and Amélie Kuhrt (London: Routledge, 1983), 65–78; and the study of the Ahmose-Nefertari Donation Stela in Betsy Bryan, "Property and the God's Wives of Amun," in *Women and Property in Ancient Near Eastern and Mediterranean Societies,* ed. Deborah Lyons and Raymond Westbrook (Washington, DC: Center for Hellenic Studies, Harvard University, 2005), https://chs.harvard.edu/CHS/article

/display/1304 (accessed December 2, 2020). Anen's appointment to the office of second priest of Amun may be an echo of the queen's power over the office of God's Wife of Amun, even though Tiye does not appear to have held that title: William J. Murnane, "The Organization of Government under Amenhotep III," in *Amenhotep III: Perspectives on His Reign,* ed. David O'Connor and Eric H. Cline (Ann Arbor: University of Michigan Press, 1998), 209–10.

Atum's creation of Shu and Tefnut forms part of Coffin Text Spells 75 and 77; for the "Shu spells" and creation accounts in general, see Susanne Bickel, *La cosmogonie égyptienne avant le Nouvel Empire* (Freiburg: Universitätsverlag, 1994); James Allen, *Genesis in Egypt: The Philosophy of Ancient Egyptian Creation Accounts* (New Haven, CT: Yale Egyptological Seminar, 1988). Tiye's Hathoric crown is discussed in Christian Bayer, *Teje: Die den Herrn Beider Länder mit ihrer Schönheit erfreut; Eine ikonographische Studie* (Wiesbaden: Verlag Harrassowitz, 2014), 416–18; Nefertiti's uraei wear their own crowns—a particularly detailed example is Robert Vergnieux and Michel Gondran, *Aménophis IV et les pierres du soleil, Akhénaton retrouvé* (Paris: Les Editions Arthaud, 1997), 72–75; for this feature, see also René Preys, "L'uraeus "hathorique" de la reine," in *Proceedings of the Seventh International Congress of Egyptologists,* ed. Christopher Eyre (Leuven: Peeters, 1998), 911–19. For the significance of the crowns of Tiye and Nefertiti, see Katja Goebs, "'Receive the Henu—that you may shine forth in it like Akhty': Feathers, Horns, and the Cosmic Symbolism of Egyptian Composite Crowns," in *Royal versus Divine Authority, Acquisition, Legitimization and Renewal of Power,* ed. Filip Coppens, Jiří Janák, and Hana Vymazalová (Wiesbaden: Harrassowitz, 2015), 145–75. Examples of Nefertiti's epithet "high of plumes" include N. de G. Davies, *The Rock Tombs of El Amarna,* vol. 4, *The Tombs of Penthu, Mahu, and Others* (London: Egypt Exploration Society, 1906), plate 39; Maj Sandman, *Texts from the Time of Akhenaten* (Brussels: Édition de la Fondation égyptologique Reine Élisabeth, 1938), 59, lines 1–2; N. de G. Davies, *The Rock Tombs of El Amarna,* vol. 5, *Smaller Tombs and Boundary Stelae* (London: Egypt Exploration Society, 1908), plate 13; Sandman, *Texts,* 65, line 13.

The observations of Jacquelyn Williamson, "Alone Before the God: Gender, Status, and Nefertiti's Image," *Journal of the American Research Center in Egypt* 51 (2015): 179–92, miss the important parallels with Hatshepsut as God's Wife of Amun. For Hatshepsut performing rituals alone, note the reliefs in Luc Gabolde, *Monuments décorés en bas-reliefs aux noms de Thoutmosis II et Hatchepsout à Karnak* (Cairo: Institut français d'archéologie orientale, 2005). Sistra in the Amarna Period, with references to the instrument in general, appear in Lise Manniche, "The Cultic Significance of the Sistrum in the Amarna Period," in *Egyptian Culture and Society: Studies in Honour of Naguib Kanawati,* vol. 2, ed. Alexandra Woods, Ann McFarlane, and Susanne Binder (Cairo: Conseil Suprême des Antiquités d'Égypte, 2010), 13–26. A detailed examination of the ritual of shaking the papyrus is Peter Munro, *Der Unas-Friedhof Nord-West,* vol. 1, *Topographisch-historische Einleitung, das Doppelgrab der Königinnen Nebet und Khenut* (Mainz am Rhein: von Zabern, 1993), 95–118.

The scene of Nefertiti leading Akhenaten to a bed is published in Claude Traunecker, "Aménophis IV et Néfertiti: Le couple royal d'après les tala-tates du IXe pylône de Karnak," *Bulletin de la Société française d'Égyptologie* 107 (1986): 36 (*talatat* 31/216 and 31/206); with additional discussion in his article "Amenhotep IV, percepteur royal du Disque," in *Akhénaton et l'époque amar-nienne* (Paris: Éditions Khéops, 2005), 129–33. Forerunners to this scene are Old Kingdom reliefs of the preparation of the bed for the tomb owner, as an image of renewal and of continued sexual potency in the afterlife, for which see Hartwig Altenmüller, "Auferstehungsritual und Geburtsmythos," *Studien zur Altägyptischen Kultur* 24 (1997): 1–21.

Nefertiti's smiting scenes are often discussed, and references are collected in Uroš Matić, "'Her Striking but Cold Beauty': Gender and Violence in De-pictions of Queen Nefertiti Smiting the Enemies," in *Archaeologies of Gender and Violence,* ed. Uroš Matić and Bo Jensen (Oxford: Oxbow Books, 2017), 102–21; the practical implications of such scenes are treated in John Cole-man Darnell and Colleen Manassa, *Tutankhamun's Armies: Battle and Conquest During Ancient Egypt's Late 18th Dynasty* (Hoboken, NJ: John Wiley, 2007), 34; Silke Roth, *Gebieterin aller Länder* (Freiburg: Universitätsverlag, 2002), 26–29. Roth also discusses the role of Ahhotep, and a summary of Eighteenth Dynasty queens appears in Sylvia Schoske, "At the Center of Power: Tiye, Ahhotep, and Hatshepsut," in *Queens of Egypt: From Hetepheres to Cleopatra,* ed. Christiane Ziegler (Monaco: Grimaldi Forum, 2008), 188–98.

13. A PRECOCIOUS JUBILEE

We have given the anonymous artist of rock inscriptions of Amunhotep IV in the desert northwest of Thebes the same name as the military official and governor of the Western Desert of Waset, Dedi, buried in Theban Tomb 200. The inscription in the reconstruction is Gebel Akhenaton 7, published in John Coleman Darnell, *Theban Desert Road Survey II* (New Haven, CT: Yale Egyp-tological Seminar, 2013), 88–89. Our reconstruction of the jubilee events is based on the *talatat* blocks published in Jocelyn Gohary, *Akhenaten's Sed-Festival at Karnak* (London: Kegan Paul International, 1992), plate 1.

Standard jubilee events (like feet-washing) are described in Gohary, *Akhenaten's Sed-Festival,* 140–43, while those peculiar to Amunhotep IV in-clude offerings in kiosks (69–86), royal feasting (65–69, 111–12), chariots (43–44, 47–48, 60–61), and carrying chairs (89–92, 151–52). The hymn to Hathor is discussed in Claude Traunecker, "Le dromos perdu d'Amenhotep IV et de Néfertiti à Karnak, Espaces cultuels et économiques au service de l'atonisme," in *Les édifices du règne d'Amenhotep IV-Akhenaton, Urbanisme et revolution,* ed. Marc Gabolde and Robert Vergnieux (Montpellier: Équipe Égypte Nilotique et Méditerranéenne, 2018), 186–87; and Claude Traunecker, "Aménophis IV et Néfertiti: Le couple royal d'après les talatates du IXe pylône de Karnak," *Bulletin de la Société française d'Égyptologie* 107 (1986): 17–44.

Gohary, *Akhenaten's Sed-Festival,* 30–31, suggests that the jubilee might have taken place as early as Regnal Year 2; Dimitri Laboury, *Akhénaton* (Paris: Pygmalion, 2010), 178–85, provides compelling arguments for a Regnal Year 4 date. Sayed Tawfik, "Aten and the Names of His Temple(s) at Thebes," in *Akhenaten Temple Project,* vol. 1, ed. Ray W. Smith and Donald Redford (Warminster: Aris & Phillips, 1976), 59–60, notes that when Aten's cartouches are changed between Regnal Years 9 and 12, Aten's epithet is altered to "lord of jubilees." In another article in the same volume, Sayed Tawfik, "Religious Titles on Blocks from the Aten Temple(s) at Thebes," 95–99, discusses the priest of Neferkheperure.

The hymn of the royal children to Amunhotep IV is published in Anthony J. Spalinger, "A Hymn of Praise to Akhenaten," in *The Akhenaten Temple Project,* vol. 2, *Rwd-Mnw and Inscriptions,* ed. Donald B. Redford (Toronto: The Akhenaten Temple Project, 1988), 29–33; Marc J. LeBlanc, "'In Accordance with the Documents of Ancient Times': The Origins, Development, and Significance of the Ancient Egyptian Sed Festival (Jubilee Festival)" (unpublished PhD diss., Yale University, 2011), 131–34; smaller groups of "royal children," as they are labeled, also play a role in the jubilee—Gohary, *Akhenaten's Sed-Festival,* 95, 226n40. In the first jubilee of Amunhotep III as depicted in the tomb of Kheruef, royal daughters carrying sistra, *menat*-necklaces, and gazelle-head wands also sing a hymn when the king sails in the Night Bark (Epigraphic Survey, *The Tomb of Kheruef, Theban Tomb 192* [Chicago: Oriental Institute of the University of Chicago, 1980], plates 44–45).

14. STRANGE COLOSSI

The depictions of the obelisk ships of Hatshepsut in the temple of Deir el-Bahri are discussed by Björn Landström, *Ships of the Pharaohs, 4000 Years of Egyptian Shipbuilding* (Garden City, NY: Doubleday & Company, 1970), 128–33. The depth of the Birket Habu is based on Barry Kemp and David O'Connor, "An Ancient Nile Harbour: University Museum Excavations at the 'Birket Habu,'" *International Journal of Nautical Archaeology* 3, no. 1 (1974): 101–36. The method by which the colossus is hauled is taken from the colossus scene in the Twelfth Dynasty tomb of Djehutyhotep: P. E. Newberry, *El Bersheh,* vol. 1 (London: Egypt Exploration Fund, 1895), plates 12–15; Franck Monnier, "La scène de traction du colosse de Djéhoutyhotep: description, traduction et reconstitution," *Journal of Ancient Egyptian Architecture* 4 (2020): 55–72 (available at http://www.egyptian-architecture.com/JAEA4/JAEA4_Monnier2).

The inscriptions of Bak and Men are published in Alexandre Varille, "Un colosse d'Aménophis III dans les carriès d'Assouân," *Revue d'Égyptologie* 2 (1936): 173–76; Labib Habachi, "Varia from the Reign of King Akhenaten," *Mitteilungen des Deutschen Archäologischen Instituts, Abteilung Kairo* 20 (1965): 91–92, fig. 13. Pharaohs as ancient geologists are discussed in John C. Darnell, "Alchemical Landscapes of Temple and Desert," in *Ritual Landscape and Performance,* ed. Christina Geisen (New Haven, CT: Yale Egyptology, 2020), 121–40. In the tomb of the vizier Paser, an artist is shown seeking approval for a royal statue from the vizier (Theban Tomb 106)—Jan Assmann, "Ein Gespräch im Goldhaus über Kunst und andere Gegenstände," in *Festschrift für Emma Brunner-Traut,* ed. Ingrid Gamer-Wallert and Wolfgang Helck (Tübingen: Attempto, 1992), 43–60.

The excavations at East Karnak and the Gem-pa-Aten are summarized in Donald Redford, *Akhenaten, the Heretic King* (Princeton, NJ: Princeton University Press, 1984), 86–136; James K. Hoffmeier, *Akhenaten and the Origins of Monotheism* (Oxford: Oxford University Press, 2015), 98–101, 110–13; for Akhenaten's Theban constructions, see Dimitri Laboury, *Akhénaton* (Paris: Pygmalion, 2010), 137–85. The name of the temple appears in two variants: Gem-pa-Aten and Gemet-pa-Aten, which can refer to the king as "One Who Finds Aten," and the temple (a grammatically feminine object) being "She Who Finds Aten" (this would parallel the naming of west bank mortuary temples, Amun of Medinet Habu being "One Who Unites with Eternity," while the temple itself is "She Who Unites with Eternity"). The temple Gem-pa-Aten can be further qualified as "in the Estate of Aten in Southern Heliopolis" and *talatat* situate the Mansion of Aten and the Kiosk of Aten there—Sayed Tawfik, "Aten and the Names of His Temple(s) at Thebes," in *Akhenaten Temple Project,* vol. 1, ed. Ray W. Smith and Donald Redford (Warminster: Aris & Phillips, 1976), 61; the relief of the king stacking *talatat:* Robert Vergnieux and Michel Gondran, *Aménophis IV et les pierres du soleil, Akhénaton retrouvé* (Paris: Les Editions Arthaud, 1997), 137. The landscape of East Karnak prior to the reign of Amunhotep IV is reconstructed in Luc Gabolde, *Karnak, Amon-Rê: La genèse d'un temple, la naissance d'un dieu* (Cairo: Institut français d'archéologie orientale, 2018), 31 (fig. 11), 82–83.

A catalog of the Amunhotep IV colossi of the Gem-pa-Aten with an extensive bibliography is Lise Manniche, *The Akhenaten Colossi of Karnak* (Cairo: American University in Cairo Press, 2010); see also Hoffmeier, *Akhenaten and the Origins of Monotheism,* 94–97, 108–17. A recent overview of the "name blocks" on the colossi is Jacquelyn Williamson, "Evidence for Innovation and Experimentation on the Akhenaten Colossi," *Journal of Near Eastern Studies* 78, no. 1 (2019): 25–36, which suggests that the plaques are remnants of recarving. Magical papyri bound to the body for protection during the New Year are attested: Maarten Raven, *Egyptian Magic: The Quest for Thoth's Book of Secrets* (Cairo: American University in Cairo Press, 2012), 105.

The appearance of the colossi's faces when seen from a hypothetical ground level and the role of parallax in monumental New Kingdom sculpture is examined in Dimitri Laboury, "Colosses et perspective: De la prise en considération de la parallaxe dans la statuaire pharaonique de grandes dimensions au Nouvel Empire," *Revue d'Égyptologie* 59 (2008): 181–230. Smaller statues of Amunhotep III with a pronounced belly show the father's influence on the son's art: Betsy M. Bryan, "Royal and Divine Statuary," in *Egypt's Dazzling Sun, Amenhotep III and His World,* ed. Arielle P. Kozloff, Betsy M. Bryan, and Lawrence M. Berman (Cleveland: Cleveland Museum of Art, 1992), 204–5.

At Karnak, Nefertiti had monumental statuary: Jacobus van Dijk, "A Colossal Statue Base of Nefertiti and Other Early Atenist Monuments from the Precinct of the Goddess Mut in Karnak," in *Servant of Mut: Studies in Honor of Richard A. Fazzini,* ed. Sue H. D'Auria (Leiden: Brill, 2008), 246–61. At Akhet-Aten, Nefertiti can wear a garment so fine in a statue that she appears nude: Cyril Aldred, *Akhenaten and Nefertiti* (New York: Brooklyn Museum, 1973), 108 (Louvre E.25409).

JE 55938 does not show the nipples in relief, which has been used as further evidence of the statue as Nefertiti. Fan-shaped navels are examined in Marianne Eaton-Krauss, "Miscellanea Amarnensia," *Chronique d'Egypte* 56 (1981): 245–64. A quartzite statue of Seti I, Cairo CG 42139 (https://www.ifao.egnet.net/bases /cachette/ck63, accessed June 17, 2020) shows how a kilt in a separate material could be affixed (*contra* van Dijk, "A Colossal Statue Base of Nefertiti," 250n26, who uses the Seti I statue to suggest that JE 55938 originally had a separate kilt).

The Amunhotep IV colossi crowned with four ostrich feathers are collected in Manniche, *Akhenaten Colossi,* 36–40. A block from Amunhotep IV's earliest constructions at Karnak, copied in the mid-1800s and then lost, depicts Shu and Onuris-Shu next to the name of Re-Horakhty who rejoices in the horizon. For the implications of this block, see Hoffmeier, *Akhenaten and the Origins of Monotheism,* 75–76. For a contrasting perspective that rejects Amunhotep IV's association with Shu and Nefertiti's connection with Tefnut, see Marc Gabolde, "La tiare de Nefertiti et les origines de la Reine," in *Joyful in Thebes, Egyptological Studies in Honor of Betsy M. Bryan,* ed. Richard Jasnow and Kathlyn M. Cooney (Atlanta: Lockwood Press, 2015), 155–60. Colossi of Ramesses III in the first court of Medinet Habu also appear to show the king as Atum, with a prince and princess as Shu and Tefnut—see Uvo Hölscher, *The Mortuary Temple of Ramses III,* Part 1: *The Excavation of Medinet Habu,* vol. 3 (Chicago: Oriental Institute, 1941), plate 1 and 35–36.

Discussion of the colossal statues of Amunhotep IV and Hapi appears in Manniche, *Akhenaten Colossi,* 88–90 (with collected references). Several hymns at Akhet-Aten identify Akhenaten with Hapi, such as Ay's description of his king as "millions of inundations in flood daily" (N. de G. Davies, *The Rock*

Tombs of El Amarna, vol. 6, *Tombs of Parennefer, Tutu, and Ay* [London: Egypt Exploration Fund, 1908], plate 25, line 14; Maj Sandman, *Texts from the Time of Akhenaten* [Brussels: Édition de la Fondation égyptologique Reine Élisabeth, 1938], 92, line 4). References to Thebes as Akhet-ni-aten are collected in William J. Murnane, "Observations on Pre-Amarna Theology during the Earliest Reign of Amenhotep IV," in *Gold of Praise, Studies on Ancient Egypt in Honor of Edward F. Wente,* ed. Emily Teeter and John A. Larson (Chicago: Oriental Institute of the University of Chicago, 1999), 304–7.

15. "THIS IS IT!"

Akhenaten and Nefertiti's tent is called "Aten is pleased" in the later proclamation—William J. Murnane and Charles C. Van Siclen, *The Boundary Stelae of Akhenaten* (London: Kegan Paul International, 1993), 86 (hieroglyphic text); for *pšš.t,* "matting," see also Roland Enmarch, *A World Upturned: Commentary on and Analysis of the Dialogue of Ipuwer and the Lord of All* (Oxford: Oxford University Press, 2008), 164. We based our description of the royal tent on the depiction of an elaborate campaign tent in the tomb of Horemhab at Saqqara, as discussed in John Coleman Darnell and Colleen Manassa, *Tutankhamun's Armies: Battle and Conquest During Ancient Egypt's Late 18th Dynasty* (Hoboken, NJ: John Wiley, 2007), 87–89.

Men carrying trays of offerings appear in *talatat* from Karnak (Robert Vergnieux and Michel Gondran, *Aménophis IV et les pierres du soleil, Akhénaton retrouvé* [Paris: Les Editions Arthaud, 1997], 76–77); the folding stool, bull's tail, and broad collar describe objects found in the tomb of Tutankhamun: Nicholas Reeves, *The Complete Tutankhamun* (London: Thames & Hudson, 1990), 187 (Carter no. 140), 150–54 (jewelry and regalia). The royal chariots, attendants, and multiethnic soldiers are based on the scenes of the chariot ride in multiple tombs at Akhet-Aten, especially that of Meryre (N. de G. Davies, *The Rock Tombs of El Amarna,* vol. 1, *The Tomb of Meryra* [London: Egypt Exploration Fund, 1903], plates 15–17). Details of the royal offering on the founding day derive directly from the hieroglyphic text of the first proclamation—Murnane and Van Siclen, *Boundary Stelae of Akhenaten,* 20.

Scribes often attend the king and record the dispensing of rewards at the Window of Appearances (N. de G. Davies, *The Rock Tombs of El Amarna,* vol. 2, *The Tombs of Panehesy and Meryra II* [London: Egypt Exploration Fund, 1905], plates 10, 35). Akhenaten's new titulary is collected in Ronald Leprohon, *The Great Name: Ancient Egyptian Royal Titulary* (Atlanta: Society for Biblical Literature, 2013), 104–5. The date of the founding of the city follows Luc Gabolde, "'L'horizon d'Aton', exactement?" in *Verba manent, Recueil d'études dédiées à Dimitri Meeks,* ed. Isabelle Régen and Frédéric Servajean (Montpellier: Université Paul Valéry, 2009), 145–57. Gabolde does not choose a specific date among the competing chronologies, so we have chosen one likely possibility; Gabolde's article refines the important earlier studies: R. A. Wells, "The Amarna M, X, K Boundary Stelae Date: A Modern Calendar Equivalent," *Studien zur Altägyptischen Kultur* 14 (1987): 313–33; and William J. Murnane, "The 'First Occasion of the Discovery' of Akhet-Aten," *Studien zur altägyptischen Kultur* 14 (1987): 239–46. Alternatively, for a date in early March, compare Dimitri Laboury, *Akhénaton* (Paris: Pygmalion, 2010), 237.

The boundary stelae at Amarna are divided into those containing the "Earlier Proclamation" of Regnal Year 5 and the "Later Proclamation" on the one-year anniversary of the founding of the city; the hieroglyphic texts of the stelae were first published in N. de G. Davies, *The Rock Tombs of El Amarna*, vol. 5, *Smaller Tombs and Boundary Stelae* (London: Egypt Exploration Society, 1908), which remains useful for its drawings and photographs; updated parallel text copies appear in Murnane and Van Siclen, *Boundary Stelae of Akhenaten*. Each stela was assigned a letter, with X being the northernmost and M being the southernmost (later replaced by K due to the poor quality of the limestone where M was carved). Jen Thum, "When Pharaoh Turned the Landscape into a Stela: Royal Living-Rock Monuments at the Edges of the Egyptian World," *Near Eastern Archaeology* 79, no. 2 (2016): 68–77, surveys royal stelae carved in natural landscapes.

The Late Egyptian grammar of the boundary stelae is addressed in Essam Hammam, "Echnaton, seine Leute und die Sprache: Ein politisch induzierter Sprachwandel in der Amarnazeit," in *Sprachen, Völker und Phantome: Sprach- und kulturwissenschaftliche Studien zur Ethnizität*, ed. Peter-Arnold Mumm (Berlin: De Gruyter, 2018), 147–200. The Nauri decree of Seti I says repeatedly "not to allow" such and such a thing, suggesting that we should understand Akhenaten's language in legalistic terms as well; on the Nauri decree, see Arlette David, *Syntactic and Lexico-Semantic Aspects of the Legal Register in Ramesside Royal Decrees* (Wiesbaden: Harrassowitz Verlag, 2006), 17–107.

The latitude and longitude are those of the Great Altar, the first construction at the small temple; for the stratigraphy of the Mansion of Aten see Michael Mallinson, "Report on the 1987 Excavations Investigation of the Small Aten Temple," in *Amarna Reports*, vol. 5, ed. Barry Kemp (London, 1989), 117–19.

16. HORIZON OF ATEN

The life of Mahu is represented in his tomb at Amarna, published by N. de G. Davies, *The Rock Tombs of El Amarna*, vol. 4, *The Tombs of Penthu, Mahu, and Others* (London: Egypt Exploration Society, 1906); plate 26 shows Mahu speaking with policemen before a brazier and then presenting the three captives to the vizier and other high officials. The map of Akhet-Aten that Mahu consults is based on the Ramesside Period map of the Wadi Hammamat: Julien Cooper, *Toponymy on the Periphery, Placenames of the Eastern Desert, Red Sea, and South Sinai in Egyptian Documents from the Early Dynastic Until the End of the New Kingdom* (Leiden: Brill, 2020), 363–86. For policing at Akhet-Aten, see John Coleman Darnell and Colleen Manassa, *Tutankhamun's Armies: Battle and Conquest During Ancient Egypt's Late 18th Dynasty* (Hoboken, NJ: John Wiley, 2007), 191–96; Barry Kemp, *The City of Akhenaten and Nefertiti: Amarna and Its People* (London: Thames & Hudson, 2012), 160, identifies the men whom Mahu apprehends as tomb robbers. The theft of the silver is an extrapolation from an actual horde found near house T36.74, not far from the house of Hatiay—details of the silver objects in the clay jar are given in Kemp, *City of Akhenaten and Nefertiti*, 214–17. Similarly, the moving of a boundary marker is based on small stones that labeled the corners of buildings during the construction process—Kemp, *City of Akhenaten and Nefertiti*, 125–28.

Overviews of the city of Akhet-Aten, with references to original excavation volumes and reports, include Anna Stevens, "The Archaeology of Amarna," *Oxford Handbooks Online,* DOI: 10.1093/oxfordhb/9780199935413.013.31; Kemp, *City of Akhenaten and Nefertiti*; Kom el-Nana as the sunshade of Nefertiti is published in Jacquelyn Williamson, *Nefertiti's Sun Temple: A New Cult Complex at Tell el-Amarna,* vol. 1 (Leiden: Brill, 2016), 150–75 (and 9–11 on the original trajectory of the Royal Road). An accessible overview of the city and how to visit each part of the site is Anna Stevens, ed., *Amarna: A Guide to the Ancient City of Akhetaten* (Cairo: American University in Cairo Press, 2020). The distribution of palaces at Akhet-Aten is discussed in Kemp, *City of Akhenaten and Nefertiti*, 123–53; Barry J. Kemp, "The Window of Appearance at El-Amarna, and the Basic Structure of This City," *Journal of Egyptian Archaeology* 62 (1976): 81–99 (which includes the thesis that the king and queen lived in the North Riverside Palace); Fran Weatherhead, *Amarna Palace Paintings* (London: Egypt Exploration Society, 2007), publishes the palaces' decoration; an overview of palace layout, especially a comparison of axial versus nonaxial palaces, can be found in Kate Spence, "The Palaces of el-Amarna: Towards an Architectural Analysis," in *Egyptian Royal Residences,* ed. Rolf Gundlach and John H. Taylor (Wiesbaden: Harrassowitz Verlag, 2009), 165–87.

On the planning of the city, Kemp, *City of Akhenaten and Nefertiti*, 161, goes so far as to say, "Amarna appears to be the antithesis of geometric planning." For the temples of the city, see 79–121; and 131–35 for the function of the King's House. A survey of the tombs of Akhet-Aten is Janne Arp-Neumann, "Amarna: Private and Royal Tombs," *UCLA Encyclopedia of Egyptology*, published 2020 (retrieved from https://escholarship.org/uc/item/0227n3wp); with detailed analysis of images of the royal family in the tombs in Arlette David, *Renewing Royal Imagery, Akhenaten and Family in the Amarna Tombs* (Leiden: Brill, 2020); Erika Meyer-Dietrich, *Auditive Räume des alten Ägypten: Die Umge-*

staltung einer Hörkultur in der Amarnazeit (Leiden: Brill, 2018), reconstructs the soundscapes of ancient Thebes and Amarna.

An overview of ancient Egyptian desert roads is John C. Darnell, *Egypt and the Desert* (Cambridge: Cambridge University Press, 2021), with extensive references to earlier literature; the patrol tracks and other footpaths in the desert bay at Akhet-Aten, east of the city, are surveyed in Kemp, *City of Akhenaten and Nefertiti,* 155–61. The palace with *malqaf* detail in the royal bedroom appears in several tombs including Meryre (N. de G. Davies, *Rock Tombs of El Amarna,* vol. 1, *The Tomb of Meryra* [London: Egypt Exploration Society, 1903], plate 10, 18) and Ahmose (N. de G. Davies, *The Rock Tombs of El Amarna,* vol. 3, *The Tombs of Huya and Ahmes* [London: Egypt Exploration Fund, 1905], plate 33).

17. CHARIOT OF SOLAR FIRE

Details of Tiye and the royal family dining are based on scenes in the tomb of Huya—N. de G. Davies, *The Rock Tombs of El Amarna,* vol. 3, *The Tombs of Huya and Ahmes* (London: Egypt Exploration Fund, 1905), plates 4 and 6. The international bodyguard is present in most of the tombs at Akhet-Aten, and the scene with the trumpeter is inspired by Davies, *Rock Tombs,* vol. 3, plate 31. The paintings in the North Palace are published in Fran Weatherhead, *Amarna Palace Paintings* (London: Egypt Exploration Society, 2007), 157–68. The papyrus with paintings of Libyans engaged in combat with Egyptians and Sherden is British Museum EA 74100, discussed in John Coleman Darnell and Colleen Manassa, *Tutankhamun's Armies: Battle and Conquest During Ancient Egypt's Late 18th Dynasty* (Hoboken, NJ: John Wiley, 2007), 198–99 (and references therein).

The tomb of the Greatest of Seers Meryre is N. de G. Davies, *The Rock Tombs of El Amarna,* vol. 1, *The Tomb of Meryra* (London: Egypt Exploration Society, 1903), and the chariot scene upon the Royal Road is plates 10 and 15–20. A thorough, formal analysis of the chariot scenes in the tombs at Akhet-Aten appears in Arlette David, *Renewing Royal Imagery, Akhenaten and Family in the Amarna Tombs* (Leiden: Brill, 2020), chapter 2. The hieroglyphic text of the autobiography of Ahmose, son of Ibana, describing the king's chariot in battle is Kurt Sethe, *Urkunden der 18. Dynastie,* vol. 1 (Leipzig: J. C. Hinrichs'sche Buchhandlung, 1906), 3, lines 5–6. For the solar significance of chariots in the New Kingdom, see Amy M. Calvert, "Vehicle of the Sun: The Royal Chariot in the New Kingdom," in *Chasing Chariots: Proceedings of the First International Chariot Conference (Cairo 2012),* ed. André J. Veldmeijer and Salima Ikram (Sidestone: Leiden, 2013), 45–71. Tutankhamun's chariots are published in Mary A. Littauer and Joost H. Crouwel, *Chariots and Related Equipment from the Tomb of Tut'ankhamūn* (Oxford: Griffith Institute, 1985). Nefertiti's use of a chariot as queen is discussed in Heidi Köpp-Junk, "Nofretete auf dem Streitwagen,"

Kemet 3 (2010): 34–35; and chariots for Tutankhamun and Ankhesenamun are present at the Opet Festival as shown in Luxor Temple, although the royal couple are not depicted riding in the chariot: Epigraphic Survey, *Reliefs and Inscriptions at Luxor Temple,* vol. 1, *The Festival Procession of Opet in the Colonnade Hall* (Chicago: Oriental Institute of the University of Chicago, 1995), 7–8, commentary to plate 18 (the same plate has the hymn that soldiers sing for Tutankhamun, which is similar to the hymn for Akhenaten sung by police, as recorded in the tomb of Mahu).

The scene with ships docked in front of the palace is N. de G. Davies, *The Rock Tombs of El Amarna,* vol. 5, *Smaller Tombs and Boundary Stelae* (London: Egypt Exploration Society, 1908), plate 5. The waterfront of the Great Palace is discussed in Barry Kemp, *The City of Akhenaten and Nefertiti: Amarna and Its People* (London: Thames & Hudson, 2012), 48–49. On the falcon ships, see Edward K. Werner, "Montu and the 'Falcon Ships' of the Eighteenth Dynasty," *Journal of the American Research Center in Egypt* 23 (1986): 120–21. Royal barges help tow the barges of Amun and Mut in the festival of Opet, as recorded in the Colonnade Hall of Luxor Temple; in those scenes, four towboats accompany the queen's barge, like the four next to the barge of Nefertiti in the tomb of May; perhaps the barge of the king there was originally attended by ten towboats, like the ten that assist the royal barge in the Opet scenes.

18. A HOLY PLACE IN THE SUN

We reconstruct the musicians greeting the royal family from tomb depictions: N. de G. Davies, *The Rock Tombs of El Amarna,* vol. 1, *The Tomb of Meryra* (London: Egypt Exploration Fund, 1903), plates 10A, 13. The Short Hymn to Aten perfectly summarizes what takes place in the temple (N. de G. Davies, *The Rock Tombs of El Amarna,* vol. 4, *The Tombs of Penthu, Mahu, and Others* [London: Egypt Exploration Society, 1906], plate 33; Maj Sandman, *Texts from the Time of Akhenaten* [Brussels: Édition de la Fondation égyptologique Reine Élisabeth, 1938], 13): "The singers and the musicians shout with joy in the open court of the Mansion of the Benben and every temple in Akhet-Aten. The place of truth in which you delight—food and provisions are offered there!" Cattle brands are discussed in Ben Haring, *From Single Sign to Pseudo-Script* (Leiden: Brill, 2018), 39–41; for sacred cattle at Akhet-Aten, see Barry Kemp, *The City of Akhenaten and Nefertiti: Amarna and Its People* (London: Thames & Hudson, 2012), 110–12.

The detail of the knots on the flagpoles is taken from the Opet scenes of Tutankhamun: Epigraphic Survey, *Reliefs and Inscriptions at Luxor Temple,* vol. 1, *The Festival Procession of Opet in the Colonnade Hall* (Chicago: Oriental Institute of the University of Chicago, 1995), plate 100; Kemp, *City of Akhenaten and Nefertiti,* 89, mentions the small ramp between the pylons. The reconstruction of Akhenaten and Nefertiti atop a platform offering to Aten is based on an image in the tomb of Panehesy (N. de G. Davies, *The Rock Tombs of El Amarna,* vol. 2, *The Tombs of Panehesy and Meryra II* [London: Egypt Exploration Society, 1905], plate 18). For metal vessels excavated at Akhet-Aten, compare Kemp, *City of Akhenaten and Nefertiti,* 106–7. References to plates filled with myrrh being poured at once over large piles of offerings are collected in Epigraphic Survey, *Reliefs and Inscriptions at Luxor Temple,* 18; and the rituals that took place within the Estate of Aten are discussed in Petra Vomberg, *Untersuchungen zum Kultgeschehen im Grossen Aton-Tempel von Amarna* (Göttingen: Hubert & Co., 2014).

The process of constructing the temple, with the ground plan drawn out on gypsum, is explained in Kemp, *City of Akhenaten and Nefertiti,* 64–71. A *talatat* from Luxor shows the king stretching the cord, a ritual he may have performed in the laying out of the Aten temples (Ray W. Smith and Donald Redford, ed., *The Akhenaten Temple Project,* vol. 1 [Warminster: Aris & Phillips, 1976), plate 18 no. 6). In addition to Gebel Silsila, smaller, local quarries may also have been exploited—Kemp, *City of Akhenaten and Nefertiti,* 59–63. Kemp, *City of Akhenaten and Nefertiti,* 89–93, discusses the front of the Estate of Aten and its arrangement of flagpoles, noting that the depiction in the tomb of Meryre shows a portico in front of the pylon, while that in the tomb of Panehesy does not. As informative as the reliefs in the tombs of Meryre and Panehesy are, representations of buildings in tombs differ from working architectural drawings—Corinna Rossi, *Architecture and Mathematics in Ancient Egypt* (Cambridge: Cambridge University Press, 2003), 96–147.

For the meaning of daily life scenes on *talatat,* we follow Dimitri Laboury, "Amarna Art," in *UCLA Encyclopedia of Egyptology,* published 2011 (retrieved from https://escholarship.org/uc/item/0n21d4bm), 4. The location and shape of a monument at Akhet-Aten based on the Benben is discussed in Kemp, *City of Akhenaten and Nefertiti,* 83; James K. Hoffmeier, *Akhenaten and the Origins of Monotheism* (Oxford: Oxford University Press, 2015), 214–16, suggests that the obelisk did not fit the "post–year 9 era when Atensim had attained its final form." What can be reconstructed of Heliopolitan architecture appears in Stephen Quirke, *The Cult of Ra: Sun-Worship in Ancient Egypt* (London: Thames & Hudson, 2001), 102–5; Herbert Ricke, "Ein Inventartafel aus Heliopolis im Turiner Museum," *Zeitschrift für Ägyptische Sprache und Altertumskunde* 71 (1935): 111–33; the broken lintel is covered extensively in Diana Larkin, "The Broken-Lintel Doorway of Ancient Egypt and Its Decoration" (unpublished PhD diss., New York University, 1994); and examples of parapets/balustrades in the architecture of Akhet-Aten are collected in Ian Shaw, "Balustrades, Stairs and Altars in the Cult of the Aten at el-Amarna," *Journal of Egyptian Archaeology* 80 (1994): 109–27.

An introduction to Akhenaten's constructions at Heliopolis is Aiman

Ashmawy and Dietrich Raue, "The Temple of Heliopolis: Excavations 2012–14," *Egyptian Archaeology* 46 (2015): 8–11; for the identification of a sunshade temple of Meritaten in Heliopolis (with references to other Heliopolitan constructions), see Josef Wegner, *The Sunshade Chapel of Meritaten from the House-of-Waenre of Akhenaten* (Philadelphia: University of Pennsylvania Museum of Archaeology and Anthropology, 2017). A summary of standard temple architecture of the New Kingdom is Lanny Bell, "The New Kingdom 'Divine' Temple: The Example of Luxor," in *Temples of Ancient Egypt,* ed. Byron E. Shafer (Ithaca, NY: Cornell University Press, 1997), 127–80.

The Sunshades of Re are discussed by Jacquelyn Williamson, "Death and the Sun Temple: New Evidence for Private Mortuary Cults at Amarna," *Journal of Egyptian Archaeology* 103 (2017): 117–23; Jacquelyn Williamson, *Nefertiti's Sun Temple: A New Cult Complex at Tell el-Amarna,* vol. 1 (Leiden: Brill, 2016); Fran Weatherhead, *Amarna Palace Paintings* (London: Egypt Exploration Society, 2007), 273–343. The Sunshade of Tiye is depicted in the tomb of Huya: N. de G. Davies, *The Rock Tombs of El Amarna,* vol. 3, *The Tombs of Huya and Ahmes* (London: Egypt Exploration Fund, 1905), plates 8–11; archaeologically the Sunshade of Re of Tiye may be the now destroyed "Lepsius Building," but that remains uncertain: Barry J. Kemp, "Outlying Temples at Amarna," in *Amarna Reports,* vol. 6, ed. Barry J. Kemp (London: Egypt Exploration Society, 1995), 459.

Kiye as Akhenaten's second queen was first recognized in William C. Hayes, *The Scepter of Egypt: A Background for the Study of the Egyptian Antiquities in the Metropolitan Museum of Art,* vol. 2, *The Hyksos Period and the New Kingdom (1675–1080 B.C.)* (New York: The Metropolitan Museum of Art, 1959), 294; an overview of the early history of scholarship on Kiye appears in Nicholas Reeves, "New Light on Kiya from Texts in the British Museum," *Journal of Egyptian Archaeology* 74 (1988): 91–101; for Kiye's identity, see Marc Gabolde, *D'Akhenaton à Toutânkhamon* (Paris: Diffusion de Boccard, 1998), 166–70. If Kiye is Tadukhepa, then she may have returned to Mitanni during a period of renewed hostilities with Egypt—Dan'el Kahn, "One Step Forward, Two Steps Backwards: The Relations Between Amenhotep III, King of Egypt and Tushratta, King of Mitanni," in *Egypt, Canaan and Israel: History, Imperialism, Ideology and Literature,* ed. Shay Bar, Dan'el Kahn, and Judith J. Shirley (Leiden: Brill, 2011), 136–54. A reconstructed scene of Akhenaten and Kiye is published in W. Raymond Johnson, "The Duck-Throttling Scene from Amarna: A New Metropolitan Museum of Art/Copenhagen Ny Carlsberg Glyptotek Amarna Talatat Join," in *Joyful in Thebes, Egyptological Studies in Honor of Betsy M. Bryan,* ed. Richard Jasnow and Kathlyn M. Cooney (Atlanta: Lockwood Press, 2015), 293–99; note also the overlapping portraits of Akhenaten and Kiye in the Ny Carlsberg Glyptotek, Copenhagen (Dorothea Arnold, *The Royal Women of Amarna: Images of Beauty from Ancient Egypt* [New York: Metropolitan Museum of Art, 1996], 88, fig. 79), and a block in the Roemer- and Pelizaeus-Museum, Hildesheim, in which the royal couple make offerings at the Estate of Aten: Petra Vomberg, *Untersuchungen zum Kultgeschehen im Grossen Aton-Tempel von Amarna* (Göttingen: Hubert & Co., 2014), 59–65.

References to Sunshades of Re are collected in Janusz Karkowski, *The Temple of Hatshepsut: The Solar Complex* (Varsovie: Éditions Neriton, 2003); the Amunhotep III example is Andrea Klug, *Königliche Stelen in der Zeit von Ahmose bis Amenophis III* (Turnhout: Brepols, 2002), 379; and Ramesses III is Epigraphic Survey, *Medinet Habu,* vol. 6 (Chicago: University of Chicago Press, 1963), plate 427.

Akhet-Aten's resources are summarized in Kemp, *City of Akhenaten and Nefertiti,* 44–77; temple economies and their intersection with royal theology during the New Kingdom are addressed in Bary Kemp, *Ancient Egypt: Anatomy of a Civilization,* 3rd ed. (London: Routledge, 2018), 247–93. Horemhab's decree is discussed in John Coleman Darnell and Colleen Manassa, *Tutankhamun's Armies: Battle and Conquest During Ancient Egypt's Late 18th Dynasty* (Hoboken, NJ: John Wiley, 2007), 187–88 (with additional references); the text is published in Jean-Marie Kruchten, *Le Décret d'Horemheb* (Brussels: Université Libre de Bruxelles, 1981).

Our presentations of the symbolic group "all the people adore" follows the interpretation of Bell, "The New Kingdom 'Divine' Temple," 164–73; with more recent discussion in Kenneth Griffin, *All the Rhyt-People Adore: The Role of the Rekhyt-People in Egyptian Religion* (London: Golden House Publications, 2018). For interesting thoughts on "How Did It All Work?" see Kemp, *City of Akhenaten and Nefertiti,* 114–17. The deceased receiving offerings from Aten temples and a possible depiction of the reversion of offerings in the tomb of Ahmose are discussed in Ronald J. Leprohon, "Cultic Activities in the Temples at Amarna," in *The Akhenaten Temple Project,* vol. 2, *Rwd-Mnw and Inscriptions,* ed. Donald B. Redford (Toronto: Akhenaten Temple Project, 1988), 49. Relevant texts include Davies, *Rock Tombs,* vol. 2, plate 9; Sandman, *Texts,* 26, lines 17–18; and Davies, *Rock Tombs,* vol. 2, plate 33, middle text; Sandman, *Texts,* 101, line 19—the translation of *rwd,* "staircase," in William J. Murnane, *Texts from the Amarna Period in Egypt* (Atlanta: Scholars Press, 1995), 120, accords well with the platform accessed by staircases that is attested archaeologically at Kom el-Nana—see the architectural discussion in Williamson, *Nefertiti's Sun Temple,* 166–72.

Conceptions of the afterlife during the reign of Akhenaten are surveyed in Boyo Ockinga, "The Non-Royal Concept of the Afterlife in Amarna," in *Studies in Honour of Margaret Parker, Ancient History: Resources for Teachers* 38:1, ed. J. Lea Beness (Sydney: Macquarie Ancient History Association, 2008), 16–37; Williamson, *Journal of Egyptian Archaeology* 103 (2017): 1–7, and again in *Nefertiti's Sun Temple,* 158–61. Any role that the "desert altars" may have played in the funerary cult of the owners of the North Tombs remains unproven—see Barry J. Kemp, "Outlying Temples at Amarna," in *Amarna Reports,* vol. 6, ed. Barry J. Kemp (London: Egypt Exploration Society, 1995), 448–52.

At Akhet-Aten, the *ba*-soul of the deceased comes forth from the tomb to "see your rays and take sustenance from his offerings" (Sandman, *Texts,* 34, lines 3–5), combining eternal viewing of Aten and the bounty of the temple altars (the pronoun "his" either being a confusion or assigning the altars to the king). Excavations of the non-elite cemeteries are presented in Anna Stevens, "Death and the City: The Cemeteries of Amarna in their Urban Context," *Cambridge Archaeological Journal* 28, no. 1 (2018): 103–26; and for the coffins: Anders Bettum, "The Amarna Coffins Project: Coffins from the South Tombs Cemetery. Decorative Scheme," in Barry Kemp, "Tell el-Amarna, 2014–15," *Journal of Egyptian Archaeology* 101 (2015): 29–32. The unusual survivals of the wax cones are published in Anna Stevens, Corina E. Rogge, Jolanda E. M. F. Bos, and Gretchen R. Dabbs, "From Representation to Reality: Ancient Egyptian Wax Head Cones from Amarna," *Antiquity* 93 (2019): 1515–33.

For an elite person desiring to return to his home, note an inscription in the tomb of Penthu, in which the tomb owner requests that his soul be allowed to visit earth and his own house, including spending time in the shade of his own trees and drinking from his own pool (Davies, *Rock Tombs,* vol. 4, plate 4; note the restoration and translation in William J. Murnane, *Texts from the Amarna Period in Egypt* [Atlanta: Scholars Press, 1995], 181). Artifacts relating to the traditional Egyptian pantheon found in Amarna households are collected in Anna Stevens, *Private Religion at Amarna: The Material Evidence* (Oxford: Archaeopress, 2006), 291–93; Kemp, *City of Akhenaten and Nefertiti,* 235–45.

19. SECRET KNOWLEDGE

The graffiti from Saqqara left by Sethemheb and the apprentice scribe Ahmose are in Hana Navratilova, *Visitors' Graffiti Abusir and Northern Saqqara, with a Survey of the Graffiti at Giza, Southern Saqqara, Dashur and Maidum,* 2nd ed. (Wallasey: Abercromby Press, 2015), 119–22; a scribe from the fourteenth year of the reign of Akhenaten, whose name is sadly not preserved, is on 153–54. The conversation between that unnamed elder scribe and his younger associate takes place in the entrance of the tomb of Ay—N. de G. Davies, *The Rock Tombs of El Amarna,* vol. 6, *Tombs of Parennefer, Tutu, and Ay* (London: Egypt Exploration Fund, 1908), plates 25–27, 39–41. Citations of texts describing Amun as a unique god are collected in Jan Assmann, *Egyptian Solar Religion in the New Kingdom: Re, Amun and the Crisis of Polytheism* (London: Kagan Paul International, 1995), 105, 111. The reliefs in the tomb of Kheruef are Epigraphic Survey, *The Tomb of Kheruef, Theban Tomb 192* (Chicago: Oriental Institute of the University of Chicago, 1980), plates 11–22.

The crossword puzzle in the tomb of Kheruef, wherein Amunhotep IV simultaneously praises Amun-Re and Re-Horakhty, is published in Epigraphic Survey, *Tomb of Kheruef,* plates 11–13, with a discussion in William J. Murnane, "Observations on Pre-Amarna Theology During the Earliest Reign of Amenhotep IV," in *Gold of Praise, Studies on Ancient Egypt in Honor of Edward F. Wente,* ed. Emily Teeter and John A. Larson (Chicago: Oriental Institute of the University of Chicago, 1999), 308–11.

The text "King as Solar Priest" is discussed in Assmann, *Egyptian Solar Religion in the New Kingdom,* 17–30, with citations of earlier publications; and John Coleman Darnell and Colleen Manassa Darnell, *The Ancient Egyptian Netherworld Books* (Atlanta: Society for Biblical Literature, 2018), 37–41 for the relationship between the text and the Netherworld Books.

20. ONE WHO CONTAINS MILLIONS

The career of Meryptah is discussed in William J. Murnane, "The Organization of Government under Amenhotep III," in *Amenhotep III: Perspectives on His Reign,* ed. David O'Connor and Eric H. Cline (Ann Arbor: University of Michigan Press, 1998), 215. The hieroglyphic text of the stela of the twins Suty and Hor (British Museum EA 826) is Wolfgang Helck, *Urkunden der 18. Dynastie, Heft 20, Historische Inschriften Amenophis' III* (Berlin: Akademie-Verlag, 1957), 1943–47. For the architects' relationship to Luxor Temple, see András Gulyás, "The Solar Hymn of Suty and Hor and the Temple of Luxor: A Comparison of God-Concepts," in *7. Ägyptologische Tempeltagung: Structuring Religion,* ed. René Preys (Wiesbaden: Harrassowitz Verlag, 2009), 113–31. Other possibilities for the two men's relationship have been proposed—Steven Blake Shubert, "Double Entendre in the Stela of Suty and Hor," in *Egypt, Israel, and the Ancient Mediterranean World: Studies in Honor of Donald B. Redford,* ed. Gary N. Knoppers and Antoine Hirsch (Leiden: Brill, 2004), 143–65. For the passage of Suty and Hor's hymn quoted by Akhenaten in our reconstruction, the term *sšm* is most often translated as "command," although the determinative makes clear this is *sšm,* "image" (as demonstrated by the parallel in P. Berlin 3049, XIV—Svenja A. Gülden, *Die hieratischen Texte des P. Berlin 3049* [Wiesbaden: Harrassowitz, 2001], 67, and plate 12, lines 4–8).

The literature on the Aten hymns is extensive, and nearly every book about Akhenaten presents a partial or complete translation. Many of the foundational studies of the hymns have been authored by Jan Assmann, who situates the texts in the larger context of New Kingdom solar religion in (among others) "Akhanyati's Theology of Light and Time," *Proceedings of the Israel Academy of Sciences and Humanities* 7, no. 4 (1992): 143–76; *Egyptian Solar Religion in the New Kingdom: Re, Amun and the Crisis of Polytheism* (London: Kagan Paul International, 1995); and "Theological Responses to Amarna," in Knoppers and Hirsch, *Egypt, Israel, and the Ancient Mediterranean World,* 179–91. More recently, James K. Hoffmeier, *Akhenaten and the Origins of Monotheism* (Oxford: Oxford University Press, 2015), as the title suggests, has returned to an interpretation of Atenism as monotheism. The hieroglyphic text in the tomb of Ay is in N. de G. Davies, *The Rock Tombs of El Amarna,* vol. 6, *Tombs of Parennefer, Tutu, and Ay* (London: Egypt Exploration Fund, 1908), plate 27; the short hymns are presented in parallel copies in Maj Sandman, *Texts from the Time of Akhenaten* (Brussels: Édition de la Fondation égyptologique Reine Élisabeth, 1938), 10–16.

Solar hymns of the Nineteenth Dynasty claim that even the gods around Re do not truly understand him and other gods do not approach him (Assmann, *Egyptian Solar Religion in the New Kingdom,* 70–72), maintaining the earlier, Atenist emphasis on the remoteness of the solar deity. The passage about night in the Great Hymn that we translate as "the shrine grows dark" interprets *kk* as a verb and *ḥꜣ* as a noun for a part of a temple, as it is especially in the Greco-Roman period: Penelope Wilson, *A Ptolemaic Lexikon: A Lexicographical Study of the Texts in the Temple of Edfu* (Leuven: Peeters, 1997), 612–13. The standard translation "darkness is a tomb" postulates an A–B nominal sentence and sees the word *ḥꜣ* as a conflation of the common word *ḥꜣ.t* for "tomb" (*Wb.* III 12.19–21) with the word *ḥꜣi,* "to illuminate" (*Wb.* III 14.9ff), which would use a visual pun to diminish the importance of the Underworldly journey of the sun. A conceptual parallel might be a passage in line 16 of the much later (reign of Cleopatra VII) funerary inscription of Taiemhotep, describing the west as the land of the dead: "Heavy darkness is the dwelling place for those who are there" (see Maxim Panov, "Die Stele der Taimhotep," *Lingua Aegyptia* 18 [2010]: 182, and 190 line 16).

The natural world rejoices when Aten rises in the eastern horizon, and such passages have led some to equate Atenism to natural philosophy; see James Allen, "The Natural Philosophy of Akhenaten," in *Religion and Philosophy in Ancient Egypt,* ed. William Kelly Simpson (New Haven, CT: Yale Egyptological Seminar, 1989), 89–101. Jan Assmann, *Search for God in Ancient Egypt* (Ithaca, NY: Cornell University Press, 2001), 55–61 suggests Old Kingdom solar temples as a precedent for the Aten hymn; for a different interpretation, see Massimiliano Nuzzolo, *The Fifth Dynasty Sun Temples, Kingship, Architecture and Religion in the Third Millennium BC Egypt* (Prague: Charles University, Faculty of Arts, 2018), 195–200. The light of the sun enlivening creation is treated in Hoffmeier, *Akhenaten and the Origins of Monotheism,* 234–35. Animals from the royal tomb that serve to illustrate the hymn are published in Geoffrey T. Martin, *The Royal Tomb at el-'Amarna,* vol. 2, *The Reliefs, Inscriptions, and Architecture* (London: Egypt Exploration Society, 1989), plate 34; these scenes are discussed in Lise Manniche, "Amarna Deserts," in *Another Mouthful of Dust: Egyptological Studies in Honour of Geoffrey Thorndike Martin,* ed. Jacobus van Dijk (Leuven: Peeters, 2016), 383–93.

Ontological treatises are best known from the Roman period hieroglyphic text in Esna temple—Christian Leitz and Florian Löffler, *Chnum, der Herr der Töpferscheibe: altägyptische Embryologie nach Ausweis der Esnatexte; das Ritual "Darbringen der Töpferscheibe"* (Wiesbaden: Harrassowitz, 2019). The term *m3y* as a fetus is also used as a description of Ramesses II's assumption of his crowns, even as a fetus, in the womb of Isis: Herbert Ricke, George R. Hughes, and Edward F. Wente, *The Beit el-Wali Temple of Ramesses II* (Chicago: University of Chicago Press, 1967), 17 note g.

A unique god who makes himself into millions appears often in Ramesside hymns: Assmann, *Egyptian Solar Religion in the New Kingdom,* 150–55. For the re-creation of time, see John Coleman Darnell and Colleen Manassa Darnell, *The Ancient Egyptian Netherworld Books* (Atlanta: Society for Biblical Literature, 2018), 42–43, 460–61, and 5–6 for light as speech. Texts both before and after the reign of Akhenaten include deities' responses to a person's praise and worship; a private rock shrine of a man named Pahu, from the reign of Thutmose IV, even records an informal speech of Taweret who calls the man "her very own" (John Coleman Darnell, *Theban Desert Road Survey II* [New Haven, CT: Yale Egyptological Seminar, 2013], 22–25).

21. MY GOD WHO FASHIONED ME

The scene at the Window of Appearances is based on N. de G. Davies, *The Rock Tombs of El Amarna,* vol. 6, *Tombs of Parennefer, Tutu, and Ay* (London: Egypt Exploration Fund, 1908), plates 29–31; Susanne Binder, *The Gold of Honour in New Kingdom Egypt* (Oxford: Aris and Phillips, 2008), 112–13 (in note 467 she observes that Thomas Mann almost certainly based a scene in *Joseph und seine Brüder* on the depiction of the ceremonial rewarding of Ay). Much additional material, especially regarding the return home and activities at the villa of Ay and Tiy, is taken from the scenes of royal rewarding of Neferhotep and his wife in Norman de G. Davies, *The Tomb of Nefer-Hotep at Thebes,* vol. 1 (New York: Metropolitan Museum of Art, 1933), plates 9–18. For the window, see Petra Vomberg, *Das Erscheinungsfenster innerhalb der amarnazeitlichen Palastarchitektur: Herkunft—Entwicklung—Fortleben* (Wiesbaden: Harrassowitz Verlag, 2004), particularly the reconstruction plate 4b; and Barry J. Kemp, "The Window of Appearance at El-Amarna, and the Basic Structure of This City," *Journal of Egyptian Archaeology* 62 (1976): 91–92.

Dimitri Laboury, *Akhénaton* (Paris: Pygmalion, 2010), 184, summarizes the king's special relationship to *maat,* while Jan Assmann, "Die 'loyalistische Lehre' Echnaton," *Studien zur Altägyptischen Kultur* 8 (1980): 1–32, describes the expectation of personal loyalty. The king's monopoly on *maat* stands in contrast to the state of "true (*maa*) of voice (*kheru*)" that is achieved in traditional funerary belief following the weighing of the heart; only the king achieves this state of "true of voice," presumably because Aten himself judges Akhenaten, whereas the king performs that same process for all other Egyptians, as noted in Boyo Ockinga, "The Non-Royal Concept of the Afterlife in Amarna," in *Studies in Honour of Margaret Parker, Ancient History: Resources for Teachers* 38:1, ed. J. Lea Beness (Sydney: Macquarie Ancient History Association, 2008), 30–31.

22. BEAUTY INCARNATE

For the discovery of the bust of Nefertiti, with discussions of the original documentary material, see Friederike Seyfried, ed., *Im Licht von Amarna, 100 Jahre Fund der Nofretete* (Berlin: Staatliche Museen zu Berlin, 2012); this volume contains a detailed description of the studio of Thutmose, its layout, and the objects found within the villa (such as the ivory horse blinker), including the other plaster sculptures. The magician Djedi is one of the protagonists in the story known as "Khufu and the Magicians"—William Kelly Simpson, ed., *The Literature of Ancient Egypt*, 3rd ed. (New Haven, CT: Yale University Press, 2003), 13–24.

A popular account of the bust and its reception is Joyce Tyldsley, *Nefertiti's Face: The Creation of an Icon* (Cambridge, MA: Harvard University Press, 2018). For the mapping of Akhet-Aten, and the legacy thereof, see Barry J. Kemp and Salvatore Garfi, *A Survey of the Ancient City of El-'Amarna* (London: Egypt Exploration Society, 1993). Marc Gabolde, "La tiare de Nefertiti et les origines de la Reine," in *Joyful in Thebes, Egyptological Studies in Honor of Betsy M. Bryan,* ed. Richard Jasnow and Kathlyn M. Cooney (Atlanta: Lockwood Press, 2015), 155–70, discusses the origin of Nefertiti's blue crown. The use of a grid in the creation of the bust is demonstrated in Rolf Krauss, "Les représentations de Néfertiti et Akhénaton sont-elles realists?" in *Akhénaton et l'époque amarnienne,* ed. T.-L. Bergerot (Paris: Kheops, 2005), 135–44 (he also proposes that the faces of Akhenaten and Nefertiti are nearly identical from the top of the head through the tip of the nose); see also Dimitri Laboury, *Akhénaton* (Paris: Pygmalion, 2010), 220–21.

The artisans at work in the tomb of Rekhmire appear in Norman de Garis Davies, *The Tomb of Rekh-mi-Rē at Thebes,* vol. 2 (New York: Metropolitan Museum of Art, 1943), plate 60; the tomb of Ipuy also shows a group of artists at work on a single large work, a shrine with intricate carved detail: Charles Wilkinson and Marsha Hill, *Egyptian Wall Paintings: The Metropolitan Museum of Art's Collection of Facsimiles* (New York: The Metropolitan Museum of Art, 1983), no. 45. A collection of artist's signatures and discussion of their significance is Dimitri Laboury, "Le scribe et le peintre: À propos d'un scribe qui ne voulait pas être pris pour un peintre," in *Aere perennius: Mélanges égyptologiques en l'honneur de Pascal Vernus,* ed. Philippe Collombert et al. (Leuven: Peeters, 2016), 371–96. On artists in ancient Egypt, see Gianluca Miniaci et al., ed. *The Arts of Making in Ancient Egypt: Voices, Images, and Objects of Material Producers 2000–1550 BC* (Leiden: Sidestone Press, 2018), especially Andreas Stauder, "Staging Restricted Knowledge: The Sculptor Irtysen's Self-Presentation (ca. 2000 BC)," 239–71.

The Deir el-Medina busts were first excavated and their function as "ancestor" images described in Bernard Bruyère, *Les Fouilles de Deir el Médineh: 1934–35* (Cairo: Institut français d'archéologie orientale, 1939); a comprehensive summary of the busts, their functions, and find spots appears in Nicola Harrington, *Living with the Dead: Ancestor Worship and Mortuary Ritual in Ancient Egypt* (Oxford: Oxbow Books, 2013), 49–59; for the corresponding royal ancestor worship, with comparison to the veneration of private ancestors, see Yasmin el-Shazly, *Royal Ancestor Worship in Deir el-Medina During the New Kingdom* (Wallasey: Abercromby, 2015). The ancestor bust from the villa of Thutmose is published in Anna Stevens, *Private Religion at Amarna: The Material Evidence* (Oxford: Archaeopress, 2006), 128–29.

23. A HOLY FAMILY

Djehutymose is a name we have assigned to a hypothetical resident of Deir el-Medina who was transplanted to the workmen's village at Akhet-Aten; an upstairs sleeping chamber and rear kitchen are as described in Barry Kemp, *The City of Akhenaten and Nefertiti: Amarna and Its People* (London: Thames & Hudson, 2012), 190–94. A similar ebony chair of Reniseneb is Metropolitan Museum of Art 68.58—Catherine H. Roehrig, ed., *Hatshepsut: From Queen to Pharaoh* (New York: Metropolitan Museum of Art, 2005), 259. The painting of Taweret and the Bes figures is Kemp, *City of Akhenaten and Nefertiti*, 240, fig. 7.11; and Barry J. Kemp, "Wall Paintings from the Workmen's Village at El-'Amarna," *Journal of Egyptian Archaeology* 65 (1979): 47–53. Details of the chapel are taken from Fran Weatherhead and Barry J. Kemp, *The Main Chapel at the Amarna Workmen's Village and Its Wall Paintings* (London: Egypt Exploration Society, 2007).

The history of the Egyptian Museum appears as one element of late nineteenth- and early twentieth-century Egyptology in Jason Thompson, *Wonderful Things: A History of Egyptology*, vol. 2 (Cairo: American University in Cairo Press, 2016), 128–29. The "family portrait stelae" often appear in museum catalogs of Akhenaten-and-Nefertiti-themed exhibits: Jean-Luc Chappaz, ed., *Akhénaton et Néfertiti, Soleil et ombres des pharaons* (Milan: Silvana Editoriale, 2008) 186, 246–47; Dorothea Arnold, *The Royal Women of Amarna: Images of Beauty from Ancient Egypt* (New York: Metropolitan Museum of Art, 1996). Arnold's work and Dimitri Laboury, *Akhénaton* (Paris: Pygmalion, 2010), 223–36, survey the role of royal women at Akhet-Aten. The shrine resembling a small temple from Panehesy's official residence is discussed (in the context of other domestic shrines), in Kemp, *City of Akhenaten and Nefertiti*, 230–34. Hatiay's lintel is reconstructed in color in Kemp, *City of Akhenaten and Nefertiti*, plate 30, and a translation appears in William J. Murnane, *Texts from the Amarna Period in Egypt* (Atlanta: Scholars Press, 1995), 130. Salima Ikram, "Domestic Shrines and the Cult of the Royal Family at el-Amarna," *Journal of Egyptian Archaeology* 75 (1989): 89–101, remains a useful overview; Anna Stevens, *Private Religion at Amarna: The Material Evidence* (Oxford: Archaeopress, 2006), presents the stelae within the context of other expressions of personal spiritual practices at Akhet-Aten.

The Cairo Stela (Journal d'entrée 44865) was published alongside the bust of Nefertiti in Ludwig Borchardt, *Porträts der Königin Nofret-ete aus den Grabungen 1912/13 in Tell el-Amarna* (Leipzig: J.C. Hinrichs'sche Buchhandlung, 1923), 2–24. Amarna tomb art depicts an unusual frequency of intimate gestures between Akhenaten and Nefertiti and their daughters, as discussed by Arlette David, *Renewing Royal Imagery, Akhenaten and Family in the Amarna Tombs* (Leiden: Brill, 2020), 215–18; note also tender touching in palace scenes (Fran Weatherhead, *Amarna Palace Paintings* [London: Egypt Exploration Society, 2007], 243–49).

Some elements of this chapter are based on John C. Darnell, "The Rituals of Love in Ancient Egypt: Festival Songs of the Eighteenth Dynasty and the Ramesside Love Poetry," *Welt des Orient* 46 (2016): 22–61; and his "A Midsummer Night's Succubus," in *Opening the Tablet Box: Near Eastern Studies in Honor of Benjamin R. Foster,* ed. Sarah C. Melville and Alice L. Slotsky (Leiden: Brill, 2010), 99–140 (both of which have references to other sources).

The princesses in the Medinet Habu high gate have been often misunderstood. Although David O'Connor, "The Eastern High Gate: Sexualized Architecture at Medinet Habu," in *Structure and Significance: Thoughts on Ancient Egyptian Architecture,* ed. Peter Jánosi (Vienna: Verlag der Österreichischen Akademie der Wissenschaften, 2005), 439–54, acknowledges the label of "royal daughters," he nevertheless prefers to follow an unfounded declaration that the girls are *nfr.wt*— "beauties"—who are further interpreted as concubines. Rosalind M. Janssen and Jac J. Janssen, *Growing Up and Getting Old in Ancient Egypt* (London: Golden House Press, 2007), 119–20, note that at least some of the girls are clearly labeled as daughters of the king but suggest that some may be "royal ornaments."

For the significance of minerals in the broad collars, see Sydney Aufrère, *L'Univers minéral dans la pensée égyptienne* (Cairo: Institut français d'archéologie orientale, 1991); John Coleman Darnell, "Ancient Egyptian Cryptography: Graphic Hermeneutics," in *Enigmatic Writing in the Egyptian New Kingdom*, vol. 1, *Revealing, Transforming, and Display in Egyptian Hieroglyphs,* ed. David Klotz and Andréas Stauder (Berlin: De Gruyter, 2020), 7–48 (also citing the passage about Hathor and the text of Ankhy).

Ankhesenpaaten reaches up to a round earring with six golden tassels (a very clear evocation of Aten itself) in UPMAA E325; photo published in David P. Silverman, Josef W. Wegner, and Jennifer Houser Wegner, *Akhenaten & Tutankhamun, Revolution & Restoration* (Philadelphia: University of Pennsylvania Museum of Archaeology and Anthropology, 2006), 140–41, fig. 128; see also Arnold, *Royal Women,* 98 and 102.

For the scene of Aten wearing broad collars, see N. de G. Davies, *The Rock*

Tombs of El Amarna, vol. 1, *The Tomb of Meryra* (London: Egypt Exploration Fund, 1903), plate 22 (with 30–32) and plate 6 for the Window of Appearances with great broad collar wreath (see also Petra Vomberg, *Das Erscheinungsfenster innerhalb der amarnazeitlichen Palastarchitektur: Herkunft—Entwicklung—Fortleben* [Wiesbaden: Harrassowitz Verlag, 2004], 207–8, 215–16, 298–99, 334, and 338). Aten wearing the broad-collar is discussed in Katja Goebs, "King as God and God as King: Colour, Light, and Transformation in Egyptian Ritual," in *Palace and Temple: Architecture-Decoration-Ritual,* ed. Rolf Gunlach (Wiesbaden: Otto Harrassowitz, 2011), 71–72; David, *Renewing Royal Imagery,* 174–75.

Berlin ÄM 14511 is published in Chappaz, ed., *Akhénaton et Nefertiti,* 186, cat. no. 31; Louvre E 11624 also shows the queen seated in the king's lap— see Arlette David, "A Throne for Two: Image of the Divine Couple During Akhenaton's Reign," *Journal of Ancient Egyptian Interconnections* 14 (2017): 1–10 (although disagreeing with her belief that the imagery shows Mesopotamian influence). Already at Karnak, Akhenaten is shown affixing his own broad collar—*talatat* no. 27–536, in Robert Vergnieux and Michel Gondran, *Aménophis IV et les pierres du soleil, Akhénaton retrouvé* (Paris: Les Editions Arthaud, 1997), 190–91; Robert Vergnieux, *Recherches sur les monuments thébains d'Amenhotep IV à l'aide d'outils informatiques, Méthodes et résultats* vol. 1, *Texte* (Geneva: Société d'Égyptologie, 1999), 134–35 and plates 40–41.

24. PERFORMING PRINCESSES

The scene of Akhenaten and Nefertiti offering the names of Aten appears in the tomb of Apy—N. de G. Davies, *The Rock Tombs of El Amarna,* vol. 4, *The Tombs of Penthu, Mahu, and Others* (London: Egypt Exploration Society, 1906), plate 31.

The literature on the Story of Sinuhe is vast; Richard Parkinson, *Poetry and Culture in Middle Kingdom Egypt: A Dark Side to Perfection* (London: Continuum, 2002), summarizes the tale and collects relevant sources. On the reception of Sinuhe and the performance of the queen and the royal daughters, older studies remain important: Philippe Derchain, "La réception de Sinouhé à le cour de Sésostris Ier," *Revue d'Égyptologie* 22 (1970): 79–83; Wolfhart Westendorf, "Noch Einmal: Die 'Wiedergeburt' des heimgekehrten Sinuhe," *Studien zur altägyptischen Kultur* 5 (1977): 293–304. For *menat*-necklaces and nonroyal tomb scenes of ritual activity, compare the tomb of Senebi, conveniently reproduced in Richard Parkinson, *Voices from Ancient Egypt: An Anthology of Middle Kingdom Writings* (London: British Museum Press, 1991), 78–81.

25. LOVE DIVINE

Akhenaten and Nefertiti kissing in the chariot in the tomb of Mahu is N. de G. Davies, *The Rock Tombs of El Amarna,* vol. 4, *The Tombs of Penthu, Mahu, and Others* (London: Egypt Exploration Society, 1906), plates 20, 22. The tomb of

Ahmose has a similar (albeit now fragmentary) scene: N. de G. Davies, *The Rock Tombs of El Amarna,* vol. 3, *The Tombs of Huya and Ahmes* (London: Egypt Exploration Fund, 1905), plate 32 (restored version on plate 32a).

Arlette David, *Renewing Royal Imagery, Akhenaten and Family in the Amarna Tombs* (Leiden: Brill, 2020), 274–79, identifies (unpersuasively) the intimate action as breathing and smelling but not kissing. In the tomb of Mahu, the guard posts mounted on pillars have also been interpreted as schematic representations of the boundary stelae—David O'Connor, "Demarcating the Boundaries: An Interpretation of a Scene in the Tomb of Mahu at El-Amarna," *Bulletin of Egyptological Studies* 9 (1987–88): 41–52. For the debate about the identification of the crenellated building in the tomb of Mahu as the North Riverside Palace, see David, *Renewing Royal Imagery,* 253 (and references therein).

For the kissing in the royal chariot and the concept of "rejoicing in the horizon," see John C. Darnell, "Two Notes on Marginal Inscriptions at Medinet Habu," in *Essays in Egyptology in Honor of Hans Goedicke,* ed. Betsy Bryan and David Lorton (San Antonio: Halgo Press, 1994), 41–42; Jan Assmann, *Liturgische Lieder an den Sonnengott* (Berlin: B. Hessling, 1969), 325–26.

In addition to the articles cited for chapter 23, the main studies of the love poetry are Michael Fox, *The Song of Songs and the Ancient Egyptian Love Songs* (Madison: University of Wisconsin Press, 1985); Bernard Mathieu, *La poéise amoureuse de l'Égypte ancienne: Recherches sur un genre littéraire au Nouvel Empire* (Cairo: Institut français d'archéologie orientale, 1996); Renata Landgráfová and Hana Navrátilová, *Sex and the Golden Goddess,* vol. 1, *Ancient Egyptian Love Songs in Context* (Prague: Czech Institute of Egyptology, 2009); and the volume they edited, *Sex and the Golden Goddess,* vol. 2, *World of the Love Songs* (Prague: Faculty of Arts, Charles University, 2015).

26. RULERS OF THE WORLD

The date that we provide for the announcement of Nubian unrest is one possibility, since the dates themselves differ between the two hieroglyphic stelae that record the events (Dimitri Laboury, *Akhénaton* [Paris: Pygmalion, 2010], 292–93). The palace paintings that we describe are published in Fran Weatherhead, *Amarna Palace Paintings* (London: Egypt Exploration Society, 2007), 10–22; the equation between the palace paintings and the Great Hymn was made in David O'Connor, "Mirror of the Cosmos: The Palace of Merneptah," in *Fragments of a Shattered Visage,* ed. Edward Bleiberg and Rita Freed (Memphis, TN: Memphis State University, 1991), 167–98. The description of the throne dais that Akhenaten and Nefertiti ascend is based on the one in the King's House—Weatherhead, *Amarna Palace Paintings,* 78–84—while the thrones themselves imitate those found in the tomb of Tutankhamun.

Monuments of the vizier Nakhtpaaten are collected in William J. Murnane,

Texts from the Amarna Period in Egypt (Atlanta: Scholars Press, 1995), 166–67. The description of the Nubian war and associated quotations are taken from the stelae of Buhen and Amada: Harry S. Smith, *The Fortress of Buhen, the Inscriptions* (London: Egypt Exploration Society, 1976), 124–29 (no. 1595), plates 29 and 75; Wolfgang Helck, "Ein 'Feldzug' unter Amenophis IV. gegen Nubien," *Studien zur altägyptischen Kultur* 8 (1980): 117–26; Murnane, *Texts from the Amarna Period,* 101–3; see also John Coleman Darnell and Colleen Manassa, *Tutankhamun's Armies: Battle and Conquest During Ancient Egypt's Late 18th Dynasty* (Hoboken, NJ: John Wiley, 2007), 117–19. Judging by jar-sealings and dockets on wine amphorae, the rebuilt administrative center at Buhen flourished during the reigns of Amunhotep III and Akhenaten, although the Nubian war report might have originated in another city (Smith, *Fortress of Buhen,* 188).

For the career of Djehutymose, see David Klotz and Marina W. Brown, "The Enigmatic Statuette of Djehutymose (MFA 24.743): Deputy of Wawat and Viceroy of Kush," *Journal of the American Research Center in Egypt* 52 (2016): 269–302. Impalement in ancient Egypt is discussed in Uroš Matić, *Body and Frames of War in New Kingdom Egypt: Violent Treatment of Enemies and Prisoners* (Wiesbaden: Harrassowitz, 2019), 91–100. Amunhotep IV/Akhenaten's building activity in Nubia is summarized in Timothy Kendall and El-Hassan Ahmed Mohamed, "Jebel Barkal in the New Kingdom: An Emerging Picture," in *Nubia in the New Kingdom: Lived Experience, Pharaonic Control and Indigenous Traditions,* ed. Neal Spencer, Anna Stevens, and Michaela Binder (Leuven: Peeters, 2017), 169–74 (with references therein).

Our date for the presentation of tribute follows Marc Gabolde, *Toutankhamon* (Paris: Pygmalion, 2015), 57. The tribute scenes are published in N. de G. Davies, *The Rock Tombs at El Amarna,* vol. 2, *The Tombs of Panehesy and Meryra II* (London: Egypt Exploration Fund, 1905), plate 37, 38–40 (Meryre); and N. de G. Davies, *The Rock Tombs of El Amarna,* vol. 3, *The Tombs of Huya and Ahmes* (London: Egypt Exploration Fund, 1905), plate 13 (Huya). That Akhenaten's and Nefertiti's reception of tribute may be tied to the Nubian war, as well as other New Kingdom celebrations of the "durbar," see Darnell and Manassa, *Tutankhamun's Armies,* 125–28. The desert altars as the location for the tribute presentation is suggested in Barry Kemp, *Ancient Egypt: Anatomy of a Civilization,* 1st ed. (London: Routledge, 1991), 286–87. The intersection of artistic representations of foreigners and the complex topic of ethnicity is nicely summarized in Juan Carlos Moreno García, "Ethnicity in Ancient Egypt: An Introduction to Key Issues," *Journal of Egyptian History* 11 (2018): 1–17.

27. DUPLICITY AND DIPLOMACY

We locate the reception of Assyrian emissaries in the large courtyard of the Great Palace—Barry Kemp, *The City of Akhenaten and Nefertiti: Amarna and*

Its People (London: Thames & Hudson, 2012), 138–40. A letter from Ashur-uballit complains of the death of his messengers through sun exposure in EA 16—Anson F. Rainey, *The El-Amarna Correspondence: A New Edition of the Cuneiform Letters from the Site of El-Amarna Based on Collations of All Extant Tablets*, 2 vols., ed. W. M. Schniedewind and Z. Cochavi-Rainey, (Leiden: Brill, 2015), 131–33; the idiom of gold being as plentiful as dirt appears on 16.

The Amarna Letters are of unparalleled significance in understanding the Mediterranean and Near Eastern worlds of the late second millennium. In addition to Rainey's edition, the main translation is William L. Moran, *The Amarna Letters* (Baltimore: Johns Hopkins University Press, 1992); Raymond Cohen and Raymond Westbrook, eds., *Amarna Diplomacy: The Beginnings of International Relations* (Baltimore: Johns Hopkins University Press, 2000) remains a useful introduction to the corpus. Rainey, *El-Amarna Correspondence,* 1, suggests that the oft-repeated story about a woman in 1887 digging through the decomposing mud brick for fertilizer was a cover story for illicit digging. We follow Rainey on 5 in his description of the Amarna Letters representing "closed cases." The letter from Kadashman-Enlil about marrying an Egyptian woman is EA 4: Rainey, *El-Amarna Correspondence,* 74. Sun exposure as a possible punishment is discussed in Uroš Matić, *Body and Frames of War in New Kingdom Egypt: Violent Treatment of Enemies and Prisoners* (Wiesbaden: Harrassowitz, 2019), 20–23 (concluding that the harm was likely unintentional).

The interpretation of Akhenaten's foreign policy presented here follows our earlier work John Coleman Darnell and Colleen Manassa, *Tutankhamun's Armies: Battle and Conquest During Ancient Egypt's Late 18th Dynasty* (Hoboken, NJ: John Wiley, 2007), 137–78 (with references therein); Trevor Bryce, *Kingdom of the Hittites* (Oxford: Oxford University Press, 2005), 154–83; Dimitri Laboury, *Akhénaton* (Paris: Pygmalion, 2010), 297–312. An interesting reappraisal of the Amorite kingdom is Ellen Morris, "Opportunism in Contested Lands, B.C. and A.D.: Or How Abdi-Ashirta, Aziru, and Padsha Khan Zadran Got Away with Murder," in *Millions of Jubilees: Studies in Honor of David P. Silverman,* ed. Zahi Hawass and Jennifer Houser Wegner (Cairo: Conseil Suprême des Antiquités d'Égypte, 2010), 413–38.

28. NONE BESIDE HIM

We situate the discussion between the draughtsman and his associates in the tomb of Nakht—Norman de Garis Davies, *The Tomb of Nakht at Thebes* (New York: Metropolitan Museum of Art, 1917). The painting of the cat hugging a goose beneath the throne of Queen Tiye from the tomb of Anen is William C. Hayes, *The Scepter of Egypt: A Background for the Study of the Egyptian Antiquities in the Metropolitan Museum of Art,* vol. 2, *The Hyksos Period and the New Kingdom*

(1675–1080 B.C.) (New York: Metropolitan Museum of Art, 1959), 237, and is available online, https://www.metmuseum.org/art/collection/search/548566.

The names of Aten are categorized in Marc Gabolde, *D'Akhenaton à Toutânkhamon* (Paris: Diffusion de Boccard, 1998), 105–7, 110–18; Dimitri Laboury, *Akhénaton* (Paris: Pygmalion, 2010), 206, 314–21. The proscription of Amun is difficult to date, and among the many discussions of the Amarna "iconoclasm," see Gabolde, *D'Akhenaton à Toutânkhamon*, 32–34; Orly Goldwasser, "The Essence of Amarna Monotheism," in *jn.t ḏr.w: Festschrift für Friedrich Junge*, vol. 1, ed. Gerald Moers et al. (Göttingen: Lingua Aegyptia, 2006), 267–79; Laboury, *Akhénaton*, 199–203; Betsy Bryan, "Episodes of Iconoclasm in the Egyptian New Kingdom," in *Iconoclasm and Text Destruction in the Ancient Near East and Beyond*, ed. Natalie Naomi May (Chicago: Oriental Institute, 2012), 375–76; Joachim Friedrich Quack, "'Lösche seinen Namen aus!': Zur Vernichtung von personenreferenzierter Schrift und Bild im Alten Ägypten," in *Zerstörung von Geschriebenem: Historische und transkulturelle Perspektiven*, ed. Carina Kühne-Wespi, Klaus Peter Oschema, and Joachim Friedrich Quack (Berlin: De Gruyter, 2019), 56–57; Rune Nyord, *Seeing Perfection: Ancient Egyptian Images Beyond Representation* (Cambridge: Cambridge University Press, 2020), 71–75. How the hacking of names worked in a practical sense is effectively conveyed in Peter der Manuelian, "Semi-Literacy in Egypt: Some Erasures from the Amarna Period," in *Gold of Praise: Studies on Ancient Egypt in Honor of Edward F. Wente*, ed. Emily Teeter and John A. Larson (Chicago: Oriental Institute of the University of Chicago, 1999), with 288–89 listing words that were mistaken for the name Amun.

The meaning of the Pawah graffito and its intersection with festival performance is discussed in Jan Assmann, "Ocular Desire in a Time of Darkness: Urban Festival and Divine Visibility in Ancient Egypt," in *Ocular Desire = Sehnsucht des Auges*, ed. Aharon R. E. Agus and Jan Assmann (Berlin: Akademie, 1994), 13–29; Dieter Kessler, "Dissidentenliteratur oder kultischer Hintergrund? Teil I: Überlegungen zum Tura-Hymnus und zum Hymnus in TT 139," *Studien zur Altägyptischen Kultur* 25 (1997): 161–88, and "Dissidentenliteratur oder kultischer Hintergrund? (Teil 2)," *Studien zur Altägyptischen Kultur* 27 (1999): 173–221; Gabolde, *d'Akhenaton à Toutânkhamon*, 161–62.

The possible economic significance of the removal of Amun's name is discussed in Dieter Kessler, "Die juristische Relevanz der Tilgung des Amunnamens durch Echnaton," in *Auf den Spuren des Sobek: Festschrift für Horst Beinlich*, ed. Jochen Hallof (Dettelbach: Röll, 2012), 163–72. One passage from the tomb of Tutu suggests that the king really did prosecute people who resisted some of his economic and religious decisions (Maj Sandman, *Texts from the Time of Akhenaten* [Brussels: Édition de la Fondation égyptologique Reine Élisabeth, 1938], 86, lines 15–16): "When he (the king) rises, he musters his power against the one who does not know his teachings; his favors are for the one who knows him." For the decentralization of the Amun priesthood during the reign of Amunhotep III, see Ben Haring, "The Rising Power of the House of Amun in the New Kingdom," in *Ancient Egyptian Administration,* ed. Juan Carlos Moreno García (Leiden: Brill, 2013), 621–23, and references therein. We suggested a link between Hermopolis and Amarna and the creation theology of the Ogdoad in John Coleman Darnell and Colleen Manassa, *Tutankhamun's Armies: Battle and Conquest During Ancient Egypt's Late 18th Dynasty* (Hoboken, NJ: John Wiley, 2007), 42–43.

29. TRAGEDY STRIKES

The funeral of Meketaten is based on the publication of rooms *alpha* and *gamma* in Geoffrey Martin, *The Royal Tomb at El-'Amarna,* vol. 2, *The Reliefs, Inscriptions, and Architecture* (London: Egypt Exploration Society, 1974), with analysis in Dimitri Laboury, *Akhénaton* (Paris: Pygmalion, 2010), 314–21; the body language in the mourning scenes is discussed in Arlette David, *Renewing Royal Imagery, Akhenaten and Family in the Amarna Tombs* (Leiden: Brill, 2020), 439–51.

Marc Gabolde, *D'Akhenaton à Toutânkhamon* (Paris: Diffusion de Boccard, 1998) assembles compelling evidence—including an analysis of the hieroglyphic annotation accompanying the image of the infant—that the baby in the mourning scenes is Tutankhaten. A very different perspective—that the baby is Meketaten herself reborn—is offered in Geoffrey Martin, "The Dormition of Princess Meketaten," in *Under the Potter's Tree: Studies on Ancient Egypt Presented to Janine Bourriau on the Occasion of Her 70th Birthday,* ed. David Aston et al. (Leuven: Peeters, 2011), 633–44. That Ankhesenpaaten-tasherit and Meritaten-tasherit are phantom daughters, see Laboury, *Akhénaton,* 314–22. The recut inscriptions in the Maru-Aten are also discussed in Christine Meyer, "Zum Titel 'Ḥmt njswt' bei den Töchtern Amenophis' III. und IV. und Ramses' II," *Studien zur Altägyptischen Kultur* 11 (1984): 259–63; Angela P. Thomas, "Some Palimpsest Fragments from the Maru-Aten at Amarna," *Chronique d'Égypte* 57 (1982): 5–13.

The Year 16 text is published in Athena Van der Perre, "The Year 16 Graffito of Akhenaten in Day Abū Hinnis: A Contribution to the Study of the Later Years of Nefertiti," *Journal of Egyptian History* 7 (2014): 67–108; our translation follows the corrections to her hieroglyphic transcription in Marc Gabolde, *Toutankhamon* (Paris: Pygmalion, 2015), 59. For the word "(re)open" of the quarry, we read the traces following the vertically drawn *mr*-sign with two reed leaves, *w*-coil, and man-with-hand-to-mouth as the right horn of *wp* over a more hieroglyphic *p* (compare *r* in this text), the expected X-shaped determinative lost to damage. This has not been recognized in earlier publications, but the date appears to indicate the start of quarry activity.

30. SUCCESSORS

A door frame from the house Maanakhtef provides his title "overseer of successful building projects," and the brickmaking he witnesses is based on paintings in the tomb of Rekhmire (Theban Tomb 100). We have imagined Maanakhtef as the man responsible for constructing what is most often called the "Coronation Hall of Semenkhkare" in modern descriptions of Amarna. A reexamination of the structure and its association with a vineyard, the interpretation we follow here, is Claude Traunecker and Françoise Traunecker, "Sur la salle dite 'du couronnement' à Tell-el-Amarna," *Bulletin de la Société d'Égyptologie de Genève* 9–10 (1984–1985): 285–307. A painting from the tomb of Neferhotep (from the reign of Ay) shows a similar juxtaposition of palace and vineyard: Norman de Garis Davies, *The Tomb of Nefer-Hotep at Thebes,* vol. 1 (New York: Metropolitan Museum of Art, 1933), plate 14.

The painted image of King Semenkhkare and Queen Meritaten in the tomb of the palace steward Meryre is N. de. G. Davies, *The Rock Tombs of El Amarna,* vol. 2, *The Tombs of Panehesy and Meryra II* (London: Egypt Exploration Fund, 1905), plate 41. Debate has raged since the 1970s about Akhenaten's immediate successors; our discussion benefits from the careful work and argumentation of two scholars who suggest that Ankhetkheperure Neferneferuaten is Meritaten: Marc Gabolde, *D'Akhenaton à Toutânkhamon* (Paris: Diffusion de Boccard, 1998) and his *Toutankhamon* (Paris: Pygmalion, 2015); and Dimitri Laboury, *Akhénaton* (Paris: Pygmalion, 2010), 329–54 (both with extensive references to earlier sources).

Summaries of different theories appear in Ronald T. Ridley, *Akhenaten, A Historian's View* (Cairo: American University in Cairo Press, 2019), chapter 7; and the case for Nefertiti as the female ruler is made recently by Aidan Dodson, *Nefertiti, Queen and Pharaoh of Egypt* (Cairo: American University in Cairo Press, 2020). Other surveys of the state of the debate include James P. Allen, "The Amarna Succession," in *Causing His Name to Live: Studies in Egyptian Epigraphy and History in Memory of William J. Murnane,* ed. Peter J. Brand and Louise Cooper (Leiden: Brill, 2009), 9–20; Aidan Dodson, "Amarna Sunset: The Late-Amarna Succession Revisited," in *Beyond the Horizon: Studies in Egyptian Art, Archaeology and History in Honour of Barry J. Kemp,* vol. 1, ed. Salima Ikram and Aidan Dodson (Cairo: American University in Cairo Press, 2009), 29–43. Nicholas Reeves, graphics and animation by Peter Gremse, *The Tomb of Tutankhamun (KV 62): Supplementary Notes (The Burial of Nefertiti? III)* (Amarna Royal Tombs Project, Valley of the Kings, *Occasional Paper No. 5,* 2020) maintains that Nefertiti is also Semenkhkare.

Pawah's mention of a temple of Ankhetkheperure, using Neferneferuaten's coronation name, may in fact reveal the intended adoption of the unfinished temple of Amunhotep IV at Thebes as her mortuary temple. That renovation appears never to have occurred, and Amunhotep IV's temple may have stood relatively unaltered until it was incorporated into the great mortuary temple of Ramesses II—on the earlier temple, see Christian Leblanc, "À propos du Ramesseum et de l'existence d'un monument plus ancient à son emplacement," *Memnonia* 21 (2010): 61–108.

As Carter recollected shortly after the events of first seeing the sealed door into the tomb of Tutankhamun, which included the discovery of the box in the debris with the names of Akhenaten, Neferneferuaten, and Meritaten: "The balance of evidence so far would seem to indicate a cache rather than a tomb, and at this stage in the proceedings we inclined more and more to the opinion that we were about to find a miscellaneous collection of objects of the Eighteenth Dynasty kings, brought from Tell el Amarna by Tut-ankh-Amen and deposited here for safety" (Howard Carter and A. C. Mace, *The Tomb of Tut-ankh-Amen,* vol. 1 [New York: Cooper Square Publishers, 1963], 93). The reed that Tutankhamun cut with his own hand was banded with gold and inscribed with hieroglyphs describing the king's action (Carter handlist 229; Horst Beinlich and Mohamed Saleh, *Corpus der hieroglyphischen Inschriften aus dem Grab des Tutanchamun* [Oxford: Griffith Institute, 1989], 67).

A reappraisal of the objects from the tomb of Tutankhamun that bear on the identity of Akhenaten's immediate successors is Tarek Tawfik, Susanna Thomas, and Ina Hegenbarth-Reichardt, "New Evidence for Tutankhamun's Parents: Revelations from the Grand Egyptian Museum," *Mitteilungen des Deutschen Archäologischen Instituts, Abteilung Kairo* 74 (2018): 177–92.

Additional sequins, perhaps also deriving from the tomb of Tutankhamun, offer further insights. One sequin, in Edinburgh, has two cartouches, with no titles, written right to left and reading "Ankhkheper(u)re-Meri(t)ate(n), (Nefer) neferuaten-Ruler." The size of the small object has led both to the omission of the titles and even the elimination of a few more integral signs within the cartouches. The texts on the other two sequins, in Kansas City, also without titles and also written right to left, read "Ankh(et)kheperure-Meri(t)aten, Neferneferuaten-Ruler." Taken together, the sequins known to be from the tomb of Tutankhamun and those in the Edinburgh and Kansas City museums appear to represent variations of the name of a ruler Ankh(et)kheperure, whose birth name is either Meri(t)aten or Neferneferuaten. In the Edinburgh and Kansas City examples, the nomen is indeed Neferneferuaten, but there we may see the name of Meritaten retained as the epithet Meriaten within the prenomen. These sequins support the conclusion that the ruler Ankhk(et)kheperure is Meritaten. In Nefertiti's epithet Neferneferuaten, the word *Aten* faces the opposite direction as the rest of the signs. King Neferneferuaten's name does not always have a similar reversal.

On box 1k the name of Akhenaten is followed by the epithet "great in his lifetime"; the name of Ankhkheperure Neferneferuaten, with epithets, is followed by no wish, but the name of the Great Royal Wife Meritaten is indeed followed by "may she live forever [and ever]," suggesting a final epithet for all three names. On the lid of box 79+574, we find the same thing, with Ankhkheperure Neferneferuaten with epithets having no wish, but the third name, that of the Great Royal Wife Meritaten, receiving the concluding wish "may she live forever," as though all three names belong to one and the same person. The elements that follow the names on box 1k and on the lid of box 79+574 support the understanding that we have here to do with two people—Akhenaten and Ankh(et)kheperure Neferneferuaten Meritaten, a great royal wife who later became a king.

The "co-regency" stelae (including Berlin 17813) are published in a number of places, and assembled in Friederike Seyfried, ed., *Im Licht von Amarna, 100 Jahre Fund der Nofretete* (Berlin: Staatliche Museen zu Berlin, 2012); note also Geoffrey Martin, "The Co-regency Stela University College London 410," in *Sitting Beside Lepsius: Studies in Honour of Jaromir Malek at the Griffith Institute,* ed. Diana Magee, Janine Bourriau, and Stephen Quirke (Leuven: Peeters, 2009), 343–59. Tickling scenes at Medinet Habu are Epigraphic Survey, *Medinet Habu,* vol. 8 (Chicago: University of Chicago Press, 1970), plates 639, 646, 651, and 654.

The cuneiform evidence for the "Dakhamunzu affair" is collected in Gabolde, *D'Akhenaton à Toutânkhamon,* with summaries in Gabolde, *Toutankhamon.* The translation of KUB XIX, 20 + KBo XII, 23 follows T. J. P. van den Hout, "Der Falke und das Kücken: Der neue Pharao und der hethitische Prinz?" *Zeitschrift für Assyriologie und vorderasiatische Archäologie* 84 (1994): 60–88. Among the many reviews of the complex state of affairs is Christoffer Theis, "Der Brief der Königin Daḥamunzu an den hetitischen König Šuppiluliuma I. im Lichte von Reisegeschwindigkeit und Zeitabläufen," in *Identities and Societies in the Ancient East-Mediterranean Regions: Comparative Approaches; Henning Graf Reventlow Memorial Volume,* ed. Thomas R. Kämmerer (Münster: Ugarit-Verlag, 2011), 301–31; Juan Antonio Belmonte, "DNA, Wine & Eclipses: The Dakhamunzu Affaire," Supplement, *Anthropological Notebooks* 19 (2013): 419–41. Mursili II claims in one of his plague prayers that Suppiluliuma is told that the Egyptians murdered Zananza—translation in Itamar Singer, *Hittite Prayers* (Atlanta: Society of Biblical Literature, 2002), 58.

31. AFTERLIFE

Our scene of the desecration of the burial in tomb King's Valley 55 relies on photographs in the original publication Theodore M. Davis, *The Tomb of Siphtah with the Tomb of Queen Tiyi* (1910; repr., London: Duckworth Egyptology,

2001), plates 24–30; Arthur Weigall, "The Mummy of Akhenaton," *Journal of Egyptian Archaeology* 8 (1922): 193–200; and the reconstruction in Marc Gabolde, *D'Akhenaton à Toutânkhamon* (Paris: Diffusion de Boccard, 1998), 227–76. The poorly recorded cache of objects in KV 55 has fascinated many Egyptologists; for a fair appraisal see Marc Gabolde, "Under a Deep Blue Starry Sky," in *Causing His Name to Live: Studies in Egyptian Epigraphy and History in Memory of William J. Murnane,* ed. Peter J. Brand and Louise Cooper (Leiden: Brill, 2009), 109–20, 185–88: the tomb is that of Akhenaten with burial goods adopted from Tiye and Kiye, with some (like the "magical bricks") created specifically for the king's interment.

The honey label is J. D. S. Pendlebury, *The City of Akhenaten,* part 3 (London: Egypt Exploration Society, 1936), plate 95 no. 279. Amulets in the wrappings of Tutankhamun are described in Nicholas Reeves, *The Complete Tutankhamun* (London: Thames & Hudson, 1990), 112–13. Akhenaten's *shabtis* are discussed in Geoffrey Thorndike Martin, *The Royal Tomb at El-'Amarna,* vol. 1, *The Objects* (London: Egypt Exploration Society, 1974), 40–41 (with the *shabti* of Nefertiti on 72); and Kai Widmaier, "Totenfiguren ohne Totenreich: Überlegungen zu den königlichen Uschebti aus Armana," in *Miscellanea in honorem Wolfhart Westendorf,* ed. Carsten Peust (Göttingen: Seminar für Ägyptologie und Koptologie, 2008), 153–60.

For the images of Nefertiti on Akhenaten's sarcophagus and her possible role in private mortuary cult, see Anna Stevens, "The Amarna Women as Images of Fertility: Perspectives on a Royal Cult," *Journal of Ancient Near Eastern Religions* 4 (2004): 107–27. The text on the foot end of the coffin is discussed in Gabolde, *D'Akhenaton à Toutânkhamon,* 247–49 and plate 36; a comparison to love poetry was made already in Dorothea Arnold, *The Royal Women of Amarna: Images of Beauty from Ancient Egypt* (New York: Metropolitan Museum of Art, 1996), 38. The "sweet breath" as a means of encountering a deity: Bernard Mathieu, *La poéise amoureuse de l'Égypte ancienne: Recherches sur un genre littéraire au Nouvel Empire* (Cairo: Institut français d'archéologie orientale, 1996), 49n129.

EPILOGUE

The discovery of the earliest monumental hieroglyphic inscription is published by John C. Darnell, "The Early Hieroglyphic Inscription at el-Khawy," *Archéo-Nil* 27 (2017): 49–64. The publication of tomb U-j and the early labels is Gunter Dreyer, *Umm el-Qaab I, Das prädynastische Königsgrab U-j und seine frühen Schriftzeugnisse* (Mainz am Rhein: P. von Zabern, 1998); Andreas Stauder, "The Earliest Egyptian Writing," in *Visible Speech: Inventions of Writing in the Ancient Middle East and Beyond,* ed. Chris Woods (Chicago: Oriental Institute, 2010), 137–47. Our analysis benefited from the extensive paleography in Ilona Regulski, *A Palaeographic Study of Early Writing in Egypt* (Leuven: Peeters, 2010).

Notes

EPIGRAPH

1. N. de G. Davies, *The Rock Tombs of El Amarna*, vol. 3, *The Tombs of Huya and Ahmes* (London: Egypt Exploration Fund, 1905), plate 29 (with restorations from earlier copies). Neither of the words for a type of bird appears elsewhere. For the bird that becomes black, "swan" seems to fit the context best, and these birds do appear rarely in ancient Egyptian art—Patrick F. Houlihan, *The Birds of Ancient Egypt* (Cairo: University of Cairo Press, 1986), 50–53; the "black bird" may be a crow, although this would be an otherwise unattested ancient name for the species.

1. A DIVINE CONCEPTION

1. Hellmut Brunner, *Die Geburt des Gottkönigs, Studien zur Überlieferung eines altägyptischen Mythos,* Ägyptologische Abhandlungen 10 (Wiesbaden: Otto Harrassowitz, 1986), plate 4.
2. Brunner, *Die Geburt des Gottkönigs,* plate 4.
3. Brunner, *Die Geburt des Gottkönigs,* plate 6.
4. Brunner, *Die Geburt des Gottkönigs,* plate 14.
5. Brunner, *Die Geburt des Gottkönigs,* plate 15.

2. AN ANGRY GODDESS

1. John Coleman Darnell, "The Rituals of Love in Ancient Egypt: Festival Songs of the Eighteenth Dynasty and the Ramesside Love Poetry," *Die Welt des Orients* 46 (2016): 38.
2. Darnell, *Die Welt des Orients,* 39.
3. Karl Richard Lepsius, *Denkmaeler aus Aegypten und Aethiopien* (Berlin: Nicolaische Buchhandlung, 1849), Band III, B1, plate 82g.

3. ANCIENT RITES

1. Epigraphic Survey, *The Tomb of Kheruef, Theban Tomb 192* (Chicago: Oriental Institute of the University of Chicago, 1980), plate 32.
2. Epigraphic Survey, *Tomb of Kheruef,* plate 34–40.
3. Epigraphic Survey, *Tomb of Kheruef,* plate 28, line 9.
4. Epigraphic Survey, *Tomb of Kheruef,* plate 28, lines 10–11.
5. Epigraphic Survey, *Tomb of Kheruef,* plate 28, line 8.
6. William C. Hayes, "Inscriptions from the Palace of Amenhotep III," *Journal of Near Eastern Studies* 10, no. 3 (1951): 163–64, and fig. 30.
7. Wolfgang Helck, *Urkunden der 18. Dynastie, Heft 20, Historische Inschriften Amenophis' III* (Berlin: Akademie-Verlag, 1957), 1737.

4. A MYSTERIOUS PRINCE

1. Dimitri Laboury, *Akhénaton* (Paris: Pygmalion, 2010), 43–44.

5. THE BEAUTIFUL ONE HAS COME

1. From the introductory section of the first proclamation on the boundary stelae at Akhet-Aten; for the hieroglyphic text, see William J. Murnane and Charles C. Van Siclen, *The Boundary Stelae of Akhenaten* (London: Routledge, 1993), 19.

6. TRANSFORMATION

1. Donald Redford, *Akhenaten: The Heretic King* (Princeton, NJ: Princeton University Press, 1984), 57–58.

7. THE UNIQUE GOD

1. This passage from the Book of Kemyt is published in Georges Posener, *Catalogue des ostraca hiératiques littéraires de Deîr el Médînéh,* vol. 2, fascicle 1 (Cairo: Institut français d'archéologie orientale, 1951), plates 2–3.

2. Kurt Sethe, *Urkunden der 18. Dynastie,* vol. 2 (Leipzig: J.C. Hinrichs'sche Buchhandlung, 1906), 332, line 11.

3. Pierre Lacau and Henri Chevrier, *Une chapelle d'Hatshepsout à Karnak,* vol. 1 (Paris: Publications de l'Institut français d'archéologie orientale, 1977), 150.

8. A ROYAL WARRIOR

1. Arthur Weigall, *The Life and Times of Akhnaton, Pharaoh of Egypt* (London: Thornton Butterworth, 1922), 201.

2. Weigall, *Life and Times of Akhnaton,* 202.

3. W. C. Hayes, *The Scepter of Egypt* 2 (New York: Metropolitan Museum of Art, 1959), 280.

9. A BUSTLING QUARRY

1. Following the copy in Maj Sandman, *Texts from the Time of Akhenaten* (Brussels: Édition de la Fondation Égyptologique Reine Élisabeth, 1938), 144.

10. CITY OF THE SUN

1. Herodotus, *Histories,* Book 2, Chapter 3.

2. Alan Gardiner, "Thutmosis III Returns Thanks to Amun," *Journal of Egyptian Archaeology* 38 (1952): plate 5, line 45.

11. AN ERUDITE KING

1. Translation of A. H. Gardiner, "The Coronation of King Haremhab," *Journal of Egyptian Archaeology* 39 (1953): plate 2, line 23.

2. Wolfgang Helck, *Historisch-biographische Texte der 2. Zwischenzeit und neue Texte der 18. Dynastie* (Wiesbaden: Harrassowitz, 2002), 21.

3. Anthony J. Spalinger, *The Great Dedicatory Inscription of Ramesses II: A Solar-Osirian Tractate at Abydos* (Leiden: Brill, 2009), 129, line 37.

4. Sandman, *Texts from the Time of Akhenaten,* 143, lines 1–7.

12. A TEMPLE OF HER OWN

1. Kurt Sethe, *Urkunden der 18. Dynastie,* vol. 1, *Historisch-biographische Urkunden* (Leipzig: J. C. Hinrichs'sche Buchhandlung, 1906), 60, lines 1–2.
2. N. de G. Davies, *The Rock Tombs of El Amarna,* vol. 6, *Tombs of Parennefer, Tutu, and Ay* (London: Egypt Exploration Fund, 1908), plate 25, lines 21–23.

13. A PRECOCIOUS JUBILEE

1. Donald B. Redford, *The Akhenaten Temple Project 2: Rwd-Mnw and Inscriptions* (Toronto: The Akhenaten Temple Project, 1988), figure 16.

15. "THIS IS IT!"

1. William J. Murnane and Charles C. Van Siclen, *The Boundary Stelae of Akhenaten* (London: Routledge, 1993), 23–24.
2. Murnane and Van Siclen, *Boundary Stelae,* 20.
3. Murnane and Van Siclen, *Boundary Stelae,* 20–21.
4. Murnane and Van Siclen, *Boundary Stelae,* 24.
5. Murnane and Van Siclen, *Boundary Stelae,* 21.

16. HORIZON OF ATEN

1. N. de G. Davies, *The Rock Tombs of El Amarna,* vol. 4, *The Tombs of Penthu, Mahu, and Others* (London: Egypt Exploration Society, 1906), plate 26.
2. Davies, *Rock Tombs,* vol. 4, plate 26.
3. Murnane and Van Siclen, *Boundary Stelae,* 90–91.
4. Murnane and Van Siclen, *Boundary Stelae,* 93–94.
5. Murnane and Van Siclen, *Boundary Stelae,* 96.
6. Murnane and Van Siclen, *Boundary Stelae,* 24–25.
7. Murnane and Van Siclen, *Boundary Stelae,* 25.

17. CHARIOT OF SOLAR FIRE

1. Murnane and Van Siclen, *Boundary Stelae,* 86.
2. Mary A. Littauer and Joost H. Crouwel, *Chariots and Related Equipment from the Tomb of Tut'ankhamun* (Oxford: Griffith Institute, 1985), plates 49 and 65A (whip-stock I2, obj. no. 50ss).
3. Murnane and Van Siclen, *Boundary Stelae,* 23.
4. Davies, *Rock Tombs,* vol. 4, plates 18–19.
5. N. de G. Davies, *The Rock Tombs of El Amarna,* vol. 5, *Smaller Tombs and Boundary Stelae* (London: Egypt Exploration Society, 1908), plate 4.

18. A HOLY PLACE IN THE SUN

1. Nicholas Reeves, "New Light on Kiya from Texts in the British Museum," *Journal of Egyptian Archaeology* 74 (1988): 91.
2. Kenneth A. Kitchen, *Ramesside Inscriptions, Historical and Biographical,* vol. 4 (Oxford: B. H. Blackwell, 1982), 30, lines 5–8.
3. Davies, *Rock Tombs,* vol. 5, plate 4; Sandman, *Texts from the Time of Akhenaten,* 60, line 15.

19. SECRET KNOWLEDGE

1. Davies, *Rock Tombs,* vol. 6, plate 33, middle line; Sandman, *Texts from the Time of Akhenaten,* 101, line 16.

2. James K. Hoffmeier, *Akhenaten and the Origins of Monotheism* (Oxford: Oxford University Press, 2015), 237.

3. Nicholas Reeves, *Akhenaten, Egypt's False Prophet* (New York: Thames & Hudson, 2001), 146.

4. John Coleman Darnell and Colleen Manassa Darnell, *The Ancient Egyptian Netherworld Books* (Atlanta: Society for Biblical Literature, 2018), 38.

5. Short hymn from the tomb of Tutu: Sandman, *Texts from the Time of Akhenaten,* 14, line 12.

20. ONE WHO CONTAINS MILLIONS

1. Helck, *Urkunden der 18. Dynastie,* 1944, lines 5–6.

2. Davies, *Rock Tombs,* vol. 6, plate 27, line 2.

3. Sandman, *Texts from the Time of Akhenaten,* 10, lines 11–15.

4. Davies, *Rock Tombs,* vol. 4, plate 15, line 2.

5. Helck, *Urkunden der 18. Dynastie,* 1944, lines 5–6.

6. Davies, *Rock Tombs,* vol. 4, plate 27, lines 2–3.

7. Davies, *Rock Tombs,* vol. 4, plate 27, line 3.

8. Sandman, *Texts from the Time of Akhenaten,* 15, lines 1–6.

9. Helck, *Urkunden der 18. Dynastie,* 1944, lines 15–16.

10. Davies, *Rock Tombs,* vol. 4, plate 27, lines 3–4.

11. Sandman, *Texts from the Time of Akhenaten,* 12, line 13; 13, line 4.

12. Davies, *Rock Tombs,* vol. 4, plate 27, lines 4–5.

13. Davies, *Rock Tombs,* vol. 4, plate 27, lines 5–6.

14. Sandman, *Texts from the Time of Akhenaten,* 15, lines 7–14.

15. Davies, *Rock Tombs,* vol. 4, plate 27, lines 6–7.

16. Davies, *Rock Tombs,* vol. 4, plate 27, lines 7–8.

17. Sandman, *Texts from the Time of Akhenaten,* 11, line 16; 12, line 12 (all five attestations, with only slight variations on vocabulary that do not affect the overall meaning of the passage).

18. Helck, *Urkunden der 18. Dynastie,* 1944, lines 1–3.

19. Reading the *z*-door bolt as a mistake for the *t3*-land sign.

20. Davies, *Rock Tombs,* vol. 4, plate 27, lines 8–10.

21. Davies, *Rock Tombs,* vol. 4, plate 27, lines 10–12.

22. Sandman, *Texts from the Time of Akhenaten,* 15, lines 4–9.

23. Sandman, *Texts from the Time of Akhenaten,* 12, lines 8–12.

24. Geoffrey T. Martin, *The Royal Tomb at El-'Amarna,* vol. 1, *The Objects* (London: Egypt Exploration Society, 1974), plate 7.

25. Martin, *Royal Tomb at El-'Amarna,* plate 13, no. 308.

26. Davies, *Rock Tombs,* vol. 4, plate 27, lines 12–13.

21. MY GOD WHO FASHIONED ME

1. Davies, *Rock Tombs,* vol. 6, plate 30 provides the snippets of conversation.
2. N. de G. Davies, *The Rock Tombs of El Amarna,* vol. 2, *The Tombs of Panehesy and Meryra II* (London: Egypt Exploration Society, 1905), plate 7.
3. N. de G. Davies, *The Rock Tombs of El Amarna,* vol. 1, *The Tomb of Meryra I* (London: Egypt Exploration Society, 1903), plate 38; Sandman, *Texts from the Time of Akhenaten,* 16.
4. Davies, *Rock Tombs,* vol. 6, plate 25, lines 13–14; Sandman, *Texts from the Time of Akhenaten,* 92, lines 1–3.

22. BEAUTY INCARNATE

1. Andreas Stauder, "Staging Restricted Knowledge: The Sculptor Irtysen's Self-Presentation (ca. 2000 BC)," in *The Arts of Making in Ancient Egypt: Voices, Images, and Objects of Material Producers 2000–1550 BC,* ed. Gianluca Miniaci et al. (Leiden: Sidestone Press, 2018), 245, fig. 2, lines 6–8.

23. A HOLY FAMILY

1. Davies, *Rock Tombs,* vol. 6, plate 21, line 31; Sandman, *Texts from the Time of Akhenaten,* 84, lines 9–10.
2. Epigraphic Survey, *Medinet Habu 8: The Eastern High Gate* (Chicago: Oriental Institute of the University of Chicago, 1970), plate 648.

24. PERFORMING PRINCESSES

1. Roland Koch, *Die Erzählung des Sinuhe* (Brussels: Éditions de la Fondation Égyptologique Reine Élisabeth, 1990), 77.

25. LOVE DIVINE

1. Davies, *Rock Tombs,* vol. 4, plate 31; Sandman, *Texts from the Time of Akhenaten,* 55, lines 2–3.
2. Jaroslav Černy and Alan Gardiner, *Hieratic Ostraca* (Oxford: Griffith Institute, 1957), plate 38, 2 (O. Gardiner 304).
3. Nina de Garis Davies and Alan H. Gardiner, *The Tomb of Amenemhet (No. 82)* (London: Egypt Exploration Society, 1915), plate 15.
4. Alan Gardiner, *The Library of A. Chester Beatty. The Chester Beatty Papyrus no. 1* (London: E. Walker, 1931), plate 22.
5. O. Borchardt 1: Bernard Mathieu, *La poéise amoureuse de l'Égypte ancienne, recherches sur un genre littéraire au Nouvel Empire* (Cairo: Institut français d'archéologie orientale, 1996), plates 22–24, recto lines 1–4 (O. Borchardt 1).
6. Mathieu, *La poéise amoureuse,* plates 22–24, verso lines 1–4

26. RULERS OF THE WORLD

1. Harry S. Smith, *The Fortress of Buhen, the Inscriptions* (London: Egypt Exploration Society, 1976), plate 29.
2. Smith, *Fortress of Buhen,* plate 29.
3. Davies, *Rock Tombs,* vol. 3, plate 13.

27. DUPLICITY AND DIPLOMACY

1. William Moran, *The Amarna Letters* (Baltimore: Johns Hopkins University Press, 1992), 143.
2. Anson F. Rainey, *The El-Amarna Correspondence: A New Edition of the Cuneiform Letters from the Site of El-Amarna based on Collations of all Extant Tablets*, ed. W. M. Schniedewind and Z. Cochavi-Rainey, vol. 1 (Leiden: Brill, 2015), 805.

28. NONE BESIDE HIM

1. Epigraphic Survey, *Tomb of Kheruef*, plate 12.
2. Alan Gardiner, "The Graffito from the Tomb of Pere," *Journal of Egyptian Archaeology* 14 (1928): plate VI, lines 27–28.
3. Davies, *Rock Tombs*, vol. 3, plate 28.
4. Murnane and Van Siclen, *Boundary Stelae of Akhenaten*, 26.

29. TRAGEDY STRIKES

1. Our translation follows the restoration of the hieroglyphs in Marc Gabolde, *D'Akhenaton à Toutânkhamon* (Paris: Diffusion de Boccard, 1998), 119.
2. A drawing of the block is published in Marc Gabolde, *Toutankhamon* (Paris: Pygmalion, 2015), 87.
3. Gabolde, *Toutankhamon*, 59.

30. SUCCESSORS

1. Our English rendering of the German translation in T. J. P. van den Hout, "Der Falke und das Kücken: der neue Pharao und der hethitische Prinz?" *Zeitschrift für Assyriologie und vorderasiatische Archäologie* 84 (1994).
2. Helck, *Urkunden der 18. Dynastie*, 2027, lines 1–18.

31. AFTERLIFE

1. Murnane and Van Siclen, *Boundary Stelae*, 25.
2. Text published in Marc Gabolde, *D'Akhenaton à Toutânkhamon* (Paris: Diffusion de Boccard, 1998), pl. 36.
3. Papyrus Harris 500 5,4–5,5: Michael Fox, *The Song of Songs and the Ancient Egyptian Love Songs* (Madison: University of Wisconsin Press, 1985), 377, lines 1–3.

Credits/Permissions

Public Domain, Metropolitan Museum of Art, 30.4.90
Insert 15
Scala/Art Resource, NY (ART123911)
Insert 16
Public Domain, Metropolitan Museum of Art, 30.4.135
Insert 17
Public Domain, Metropolitan Museum of Art, 1985.328.6
Insert 18
Public Domain, Metropolitan Museum of Art, 26.7.1295
Insert 19
Art Resource, NY (ART547753)
Insert 20
Public Domain, Metropolitan Museum of Art 24.2.11
Insert 21
Public Domain, Metropolitan Museum of Art 15.5.19e
Insert 22
Erich Lessing / Art Resource, NY (ART62948)
Insert 23
Art Resource, NY (ART178300)
Insert 24
Public Domain, Metropolitan Museum of Art, 66.99.37
Insert 25
Public Domain, Metropolitan Museum of Art, 07.226.1 (jar) and 30.8.54 (lid)

All other images in this work are Courtesy of the Authors.

Index

NOTE: Page numbers in *italics* indicate illustrations